Six Sigma

Basic Tools and Techniques

Donna C. S. Summers
University of Dayton

PEARSON
Prentice
Hall

Upper Saddle River, New Jersey
Columbus, Ohio

Library of Congress Cataloging in Publication Data

Summers, Donna C. S.
   Six sigma: basic tools and techniques / Donna C. S. Summers.
      p.cm.
   Includes bibliographical references and index.
   ISBN 0-13-171680-8 (paper)
    1. Total quality management.   2. Six sigma (Quality control standard) I. Title.

  HD62.15.S845 2007
  658.4'013–dc22   2006040646

Editor in Chief: Vernon R. Anthony
Acquisitions Editor: Jill Jones-Renger
Editorial Assistant: Yvette Schlarman
Production Editor: Louise N. Sette
Design Coordinator: Diane Ernsberger
Cover Designer: Thomas Mack
Production Manager: Deidra M. Schwartz
Marketing Manager: Jimmy Stephens

Pearson Prentice Hall™ is a trademark of Pearson Education, Inc.
Pearson® is a registered trademark of Pearson plc
Prentice Hall® is a registered trademark of Pearson Education, Inc.

Pearson Education Ltd.   Pearson Education Australia Pty. Limited
Pearson Education Singapore Pte. Ltd.   Pearson Education North Asia Ltd.
Pearson Education Canada, Ltd.   Pearson Educación de Mexico, S.A. de C.V.
Pearson Education—Japan   Pearson Education Malaysia Pte. Ltd.

ISBN: 0-13-171680-8

To Karl

What would I be without you?

Preface

The term Six Sigma has come to stand for business excellence, the achievement of virtually defect-free production and performance. Based on the application of a wide variety of tools and techniques, the Six Sigma methodology improves business performance by targeting improvement efforts on critical customer issues. This text is about those tools and techniques, what they are, how to use them, and where to apply them. As each chapter unfolds, concepts, ideas, methods, and formulas are described and taught. Examples from industry provided throughout the chapters show you how Six Sigma tools have been used to improve processes for businesses seeking to improve their results.

ABOUT THE TEXT

As Dr. W. Edwards Deming once said, "No one comes to work to do a bad job." People want to work to the best of their abilities. The tools, techniques, and information provided in this text enable users to find ways to improve the value their customers receive, which generates success for their companies. The focus of the Six Sigma methodology is broad, ranging from leadership and teamwork skills, to project and process management, to statistical methods, quality control, process capability, and design of experiments, to failure modes and effects analysis, and lean manufacturing. This text provides an introduction to these and other areas related to Six Sigma.

The first five chapters, "Six Sigma Origins," "Quality Masters," "Leadership and Strategic Planning," "Creating a Customer Focus," and "Teams," provide a foundation for Six Sigma basics. Following these, the focus of the next three chapters turns to key Six Sigma tools and techniques: "Project Management," "Measures and Metrics," and "Problem-Solving Using Design, Measure, Analyze, Improve, Control." Statistical process control tools and techniques play an important role in the Six Sigma methodology. Training for these is provided in Chapters 9–13: "Statistics," "Variable Control Charts," "Process Capability," "Probability," and "Attribute Control Charts." More advanced tools and techniques are provided in Chapters 14–17: "Reliability," "Failure Modes and Effects Analysis," "Design of Experiments," and "Lean Enterprises."

Six Sigma is a way of managing. Companies whose managements are committed to providing customers with what they need, when they need it, rely on Six Sigma tools and techniques to solve problems and optimize critical processes. Money spent on training for and implementation of Six Sigma tools and techniques is an investment in an organization's future. The tools and techniques in this text provide a road map for process-focused change resulting in bottom-line financial benefits. Regardless of whether the organization is involved in manufacturing, health care, financial services, entertainment, information technology, logistics, or any of a host of other functions, the application of Six Sigma tools and techniques leads to improved business and financial performance.

ONLINE INSTRUCTOR'S MANUAL

To access supplementary materials online, instructors need to request an instructor access code. Go to **www.prenhall.com**, click the **Instructor Resource Center** link, and then click **Register Today** for an instructor access code. Within 48 hours after registering you will receive a confirming e-mail including an instructor access code. Once you have received your code, go to the site and log on for full instructions on downloading the materials you wish to use.

ACKNOWLEDGMENTS

I would like to express my deep appreciation to those who helped create this text—my colleagues and my students. A special heartfelt thanks goes to the following people for their contributions and advice: Karl Summers, Holly Fabry, Amy Brown, and Paul Cushwa. I would also like to thank my very special editor Jill Jones-Renger. I would like to thank my reviewers for their valuable input: Holly Fabry, Chris Honious, and Jeff Hobbs.

Contents

Six Sigma Origins

In the 1970s, Motorola learned about quality the hard way—by being consistently beaten in the market. When a Japanese firm took over a Motorola factory that manufactured television sets in the United States, it promptly set about making drastic operational changes. Under Japanese management, the factory was soon producing TV sets with one-twentieth the number of defects they had produced under previous management. Bob Galvin, then CEO of Motorola, started the company on the quality path and became a business icon largely as a result of what he accomplished in quality at Motorola. In accepting the first ever Malcolm Baldrige National Quality Award at the White House in 1988, Bob Galvin briefly described the company's turnaround. He said it involved something called Six Sigma.

Paraphrased from "Six Sigma is Primarily a Management Program" Quality Digest, June 1999

Objectives:

1. To introduce the concept of Six Sigma
2. To familiarize the reader with the benefits of implementing Six Sigma
3. To introduce the concept of variation as it relates to Six Sigma
4. To introduce the concept of Six Sigma projects

SIX SIGMA ORIGINS

Six Sigma is a methodology that blends together many of the key elements of past quality initiatives while adding its own special approach to business management. Essentially, Six Sigma is about results, enhancing profitability through improved quality and efficiency. Six Sigma emphasizes the reduction of variation, a focus on doing the right things right, combining of customer knowledge with core process improvement efforts, and a subsequent improvement in company sales and revenue growth. The Six Sigma methodology encourages companies to take a customer focus in order to improve their business processes.

The Six Sigma concept was conceived by Bill Smith, a reliability engineer for Motorola Corporation. His research lead him to believe that the increasing complexity of systems and products used by consumers created higher than desired system failure rates. His reliability studies showed that to increase system reliability and reduce failure rates, the components utilized in complex systems and products have to have individual failure rates approaching zero. With this in mind, Smith took a holistic view of reliability and quality and developed a strategy for improving both. Smith worked with others to develop the Six Sigma Breakthrough Strategy which is essentially a highly focused system of problem-solving. Six Sigma's goal is to reach 3.4 defects per million opportunities over the long term.

The Six Sigma methodology is based on knowledge. Practitioners need to know statistical process control techniques, data analysis methods, and project management techniques. Systematic training within Six Sigma organizations must take place. Motorola Corporation utilizes terminology from the martial art of karate to designate the experience and ability levels of Six Sigma project participants. Green Belts are individuals who have completed a designated number of hours of training in the Six Sigma methodology (Figure 1.1). To achieve Green Belt status, they must also complete a cost-savings project of a specified size, often $10,000, within a stipulated amount of time. Black Belts are individuals with extensive training in the Six Sigma methodology (Figure 1.2). To become a Black Belt, the individual must have completed a specified number of successful projects under the guidance and direction of Master Black Belts. Often companies expect the improvement projects overseen by

Quality Philosophies	Statistics
Performance Measures/Metrics	Data Collection: Data types and sampling
Problem Solving	techniques
Process Mapping	$\overline{X}$ and R charts
Check Sheets	Process Capability Analysis
Pareto Analysis	P, u, c charts
Cause and Effect Diagram Analysis	Root Cause Analysis
Scatter Diagrams	Variation Reduction
Frequency Diagrams	Six Sigma philosophy
Histograms	Green Belt Project

Figure 1.1   Training Typically Required for Green Belt Certification

Green Belt Requirements plus:	
Variables Control Charts	Reliability
Attribute Control Charts	ISO 9000, MBNQA
Process Capability Analysis	Voice of the Customer: Quality Function Deployment
Hypothesis Testing	Regression Analysis
Design of Experiments	Black Belt Project
Gage R&R	

Figure 1.2   Training Typically Required for Black Belt Certification

a Black Belt to result in savings of $100,000 or more. Certification as a Black Belt is offered by the American Society for Quality. Master Black Belts are individuals with extensive training who have completed a large scale improvement project, usually saving $1,000,000 or more for the company. Often before designating someone a Master Black Belt, a company will require a Master's Degree from an accredited university. Master Black Belts provide training and guide trainees during their projects. Figure 1.3 shows the responsibilities of project participants.

SIX SIGMA BENEFITS

Companies using the Six Sigma methodology see an enhanced ability to provide value for their customers. Internally, they have a better understanding of their key business processes and these processes have undergone process flow improvements. Improved process flow means reduced cycle times, elimination of defects, and increased capacity and productivity rates. Accelerated improvement efforts reduce costs and waste while increasing product and service reliability. All of these changes result in improved value for the customer as well as improved financial performance for the company.

SIX SIGMA PROJECTS

The Six Sigma methodology focuses on customer knowledge. By translating customer needs, wants, and expectations into areas for improvement, the Six Sigma methodology concentrates effort on improving critical business activities. Six Sigma focuses

Responsibility	Phase
Management	Recognize
Management/Master Black Belts	Define
Black Belts/Green Belts	Measure
Black Belts/Green Belts	Analyze
Black Belts/Green Belts	Improve
Black Belts/Green Belts	Control
Management	Standardize
Management	Integrate

Figure 1.3   Six Sigma Responsibility Matrix

attention on these processes to make sure that they deliver value directly to the customer.

The backbone of Six Sigma efforts are improvement projects, chosen based on their ability to contribute to the bottom line on a company's income statement by being connected to the strategic objectives and goals of the organization. Since the Six Sigma methodology seeks to reduce the variability present in processes, Six Sigma projects are easy to identify. Project teams seek out sources of waste, such as overtime and warranty claims, investigate production backlogs or areas in need of more capacity, and focus on customer and environmental issues. Six Sigma projects have eight essential phases:

recognize,
define,
measure,
analyze,
improve,
control,
standardize, and
integrate.

This cycle is often expressed as DMAIC (define, measure, analyze, improve, and control). As Figure 1.4 shows, the generic steps for Six Sigma project implementation are similar to the Plan-Do-Study-Act problem-solving cycle espoused by Dr. W. Edwards Deming and Dr. Walter Shewhart, early pioneers of the quality field. Using DMAIC as a guideline, organizations seek opportunities to enhance their ability to do business. Process improvement of any kind leads to benefits for the company, including the

Define, Measure, Analyze (Plan)
1. Select appropriate metrics: key process output variables (KPOV).
2. Determine how these metrics will be tracked over time.
3. Determine current baseline performance of project/process.
4. Determine the key process input variables (KPIV) that drive the key process output variables (KPOV).
5. Determine what changes need to be made to the key process input variables in order to positively affect the key process output variables.

Improve (Do)
6. Make the changes.

Control (Study, Act)
7. Determine if the changes have positively affected the KPOVs.
8. If the changes made result in performance improvements, establish control of the KPIVs at the new levels. If the changes have not resulted in performance improvement, return to step 5 and make the appropriate changes.

Figure 1.4 Six Sigma Problem-Solving Steps

APQP	Advanced product quality planning
CTQ	Critical to quality
DFSS	Design for Six Sigma
DMAIC	Define, measure, analyze, improve, control
DPMO	Defects per million opportunities
DPU	Defect per unit
EVOP	Evolution operation
FMEA	Failure modes and effects analysis
KPIV	Key process input variable
KPOV	Key process output variable
Process Owners	The individuals ultimately responsible for the process and what it produces
Master Black Belts	Individuals with extensive training qualified to teach black belt training classes, who have completed a large scale improvement project, often a master's degree is required
Black Belts	Individuals with extensive training in the Six Sigma methodology who have completed a number of improvement projects of significant size
Green Belts	Individuals trained in the Six Sigma methodology who have completed an improvement project of a specified size
Reliability	Measured as mean-time-to-failure
Quality	Measured as process variability and defect rates

Figure 1.5   Six Sigma Acronyms and Definitions

reduction of waste, costs, and lost opportunities. Ultimately, it is the customer who enjoys enhanced quality and reduced costs.

The tools utilized during a project include statistical process control techniques, customer input through Quality Function Deployment, Failure Modes and Effects Analysis, Design of Experiments, reliability, teamwork, and project management. Six Sigma also places a heavy reliance on metrics and graphical methods for analysis. Statistical and probabilistic methods, control charts, process capability analysis, process mapping, and cause and effect diagrams are key components of Six Sigma. As with any methodology, a variety of Six Sigma acronyms exist (Figure 1.5).

SIX SIGMA AND REDUCTION OF VARIATION

The term Six Sigma describes a methodology, while the mathematical designation, 6σ (also referred to with lowercase letters as six sigma), is the value used to calculate process capability. Providers of products and services are very interested in whether or not their processes can meet the specifications as identified by the customer. The spread of a distribution of average process measurements, that is, what the process produces, can only be compared with the specifications set by the customer by using C_p, where

$$C_p = \frac{USL - LSL}{6\sigma}$$

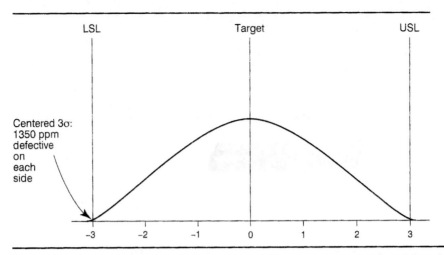

Figure 1.6   Three Sigma Occurs When 6σ = USL − LSL, Process Capability, C_p = 1

When 6σ = USL − LSL, process capability C_p = 1. When this happens, the process is considered to be operating at three sigma (3σ). This means that three standard deviations added to the average value will equal the upper specification limit and three standard deviations subtracted from the average value will equal the lower specification limit (Figure 1.6). When C_p = 1, the process is capable of producing products that conform to specifications provided that the variation present in the process does not increase and that the average value equals the target value. In other words, the average cannot shift. That is a lot to ask from a process, so those operating processes often reduce the amount of variation present in the process so that 6σ < USL − LSL.

Some companies choose adding a design margin of 25% to allow for process shifts, requiring that the parts produced vary 25% less than the specifications allow. A 25% margin results in a C_p = 1.33. When C_p = 1.33, the process is considered to be

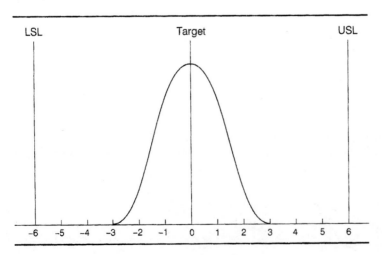

Figure 1.7   Six Sigma Occurs When 6σ < USL − LSL, Process Capability, C_p = 2

Sigma	Defects per Million Opportunities	Yield (%)
1	690,000	30.90
2	308,000	69.20
3	66,807	93.30
4	6,210	99.40
5	320	99.98
6	3.4	99.9997

Figure 1.8   Six Sigma Performance

operating at four sigma. Four standard deviations added to the average value will equal the upper specification limit and four standard deviations subtracted from the average value will equal the lower specification limit. This concept can be repeated for five sigma and $C_p = 1.66$.

When $C_p = 2.00$, six sigma has been achieved. Six standard deviations added to the average value will equal the upper specification limit and six standard deviations subtracted from the average value will equal the lower specification limit (Figure 1.7). Those who developed the Six Sigma methodology felt that a value of $C_p = 2.00$ provides adequate protection against the possibilities of a process mean shift or an increase in variation.

Operating at a Six Sigma level also enables a company's production to have virtually zero defects. Long term expectations for the number of defects per million opportunities is 3.4. Compare this to a process that is operating at three sigma and centered. Such a process will have a number of defectives per million opportunities of 1350 out on each side of the specification limits for a total of 2,700. If the process center were to shift 1.5 sigma, the total number of defects per million opportunities at the three sigma level would be 66,807. A process operating at four sigma will have 6,210 defects per million opportunities over the long term, while a process operating at the five sigma level will have 320 defects per million opportunities long term. Even if the cost to correct the defect is only $100, operating at the three sigma level while experiencing a process shift will cost a company $6,680,700 per million parts. Improving performance to four sigma reduces that amount to $621,000 per million parts produced. Six sigma performance costs just $340 per million parts with a yield rate of 99.9997% (Figure 1.8).

 SIX SIGMA TOOLS AT WORK

Organizational Evolution

PLC Inc., a job shop specialized in machining forgings into finished products, utilizes three separate inspections as their primary method of ensuring the quality of their products. The first inspection occurs following the initial machining operations, (grinding, milling, and boring) and before the part is sent to a subcontractor for heat-treating. After the part returns from heat treatment, key dimensions are checked at the second inspection. A final inspection is conducted before the finished part leaves the plant.

With these three inspections, discrepancies between actual part dimensions and the specifications are found only after the part had completed several machining operations. This approach results in significant scrap and rework costs. If the forgings pass incoming inspection and begin to progress through the machining operations, for a typical part, four to six operations will have been completed before any errors are caught during the in-process inspection that occurs before the part is shipped out for heat treatment. The work done after the operation where the error occurred is wasted because each subsequent machining operation is performed on a faulty part.

A project team studied the inspection method and determined that process improvements could be made to improve incoming forging consistency. Operators at each step in the process are now responsible for checking actual part dimensions against specifications. The team also initiated a corrective action plan that required a root cause analysis and corrective action for each nonconformance to standards. Corrective actions plans prevent future errors.

As a result of their efforts, PLC, Inc. has seen an improvement of one sigma which translates to a ten-fold reduction in the number of defects. At three sigma, they could expect 66,807 defects per million. At an average cost of $10/piece to fix, the costs incurred were $668,007. Now that they are operating at four sigma, they expect 6,210 defects per million. At $10/piece to fix, their costs are $62,100. Further improvement activities are planned to improve performance to five sigma.

SIX SIGMA AND OTHER QUALITY METHODOLOGIES

As with any process improvement methodology, there are issues that need to be examined carefully. One criticism is that Six Sigma methodology does not offer anything new. Comparisons have been made between the qualifications for a Black Belt and those for a Certified Quality Engineer (CQE). The similarities are striking (Table 1.1). Certifications are available through the American Society for Quality (www.asq.org). Comparisons have also been made between ISO 9000 and Six Sigma, the Baldrige Award and Six Sigma, and continuous improvement strategies and Six Sigma strategies; and significant similarities exist (Table 1.2).

The Six Sigma methodology is often adopted by large corporations with the financial resources to focus on training and projects. Because the methodology requires training and team participation, it is perceived to be costly to implement. Six Sigma should not be limited to large firms. Its ideas and concepts are viable regardless of the size or type of industry with costs being scaled accordingly.

Table 1.1 Body of Knowledge Comparison of CQE and Black Belt Certification

Category	ASQ Certified Quality Engineer (CQE) Certification Requirements	Black Belt Requirements
Leadership	Management and Leadership in Quality Engineering	Enterprise-Wide Deployment
Business Processes	Not covered	Business Process Management
Quality Systems	Quality Systems Development, Implementation, and Verification	Not covered
Quality Assurance	Planning, Controlling, and Assuring Product and Process Quality	Not covered
Reliability	Reliability and Risk Management	Not covered
Problem-Solving	Problem-Solving and Quality Improvement	Define-Measure-Analyze-Improve-Control
Quality Tools	Problem-Solving and Quality Improvement	DMAIC
Project Management	Not covered	Project Management
Team Concepts	Not covered	Team Leadership
Statistical Methods	Probability and Statistics Collecting and Summarizing Data	Probability and Statistics Collecting and Summarizing Data
Design of Experiments	Designing Experiments	Design of Experiments
Process Capability	Analyzing Process Capability	Analyzing Process Capability
Statistical Process Control	Statistical Process Control	Statistical Process Control
Measurement Systems (metrology/ calibration)	Measurement Systems Metrology	Measurement Systems Metrology
Lean Manufacturing	Not covered	Lean Enterprise
Other Techniques	FMEA, FMECA, FTA	FMEA, QFD Multi-Variate Studies

Another criticism is the focus on defectives per million. Can an organization really call them defectives? The term itself brings to mind product liability issues. How does a customer view a company that is focused on counting defectives? Should defect counts be seen as the focus or are companies really trying to focus on process improvement? Six Sigma organizations must be prepared to face these issues.

SUMMARY

Six Sigma is a data driven and profit focused improvement methodology for business. Organizations interested in increasing their customer satisfaction and overall organization success can use the Six Sigma methodology and its attendant tools and techniques to study their processes and become more proactive when dealing with issues that prevent excellent performance. The Six Sigma methodology not only reduces process defects, it also provides a framework for overall organizational culture change.

Table 1.2 Comparison of ISO 9000, the Malcolm Baldrige Award Criteria, and Continuous Improvement/Quality Management

	ISO 9000	Baldrige Award	CI/QM	Six Sigma
Scope	Quality management system Continuous improvement	Quality of management	Quality management and corporate citizenship Continuous improvement	Systematic reduction of process variability
Basis for defining quality	Features and characteristics of product or service	Customer-driven	Customer-driven	Defects per million opportunities
Purpose	Clear quality management system requirements for international cooperation Improved record keeping	Results-driven competitiveness through total quality management	Continuous improvement of customer service	Improve profitability by reducing process variation
Assessment	Requirements-based	Performance-based	Based on total organizational commitment to quality	Defects per million opportunities
Focus	International trade Quality links between suppliers and purchasers Record keeping	Customer satisfaction Competitive comparisons	Processes needed to satisfy internal and external customers	Locating and eliminating sources of process error

σ ■ *Take Away Tips*

Six Sigma is data driven and profit focused.

Six Sigma enhances an organization's ability to provide value for their customers.

Six Sigma enhances an organization's understanding of their key business processes.

Six Sigma improves profit performance.

Six Sigma requires training in statistical process control techniques, data analysis methods, project management techniques, and other areas shown in Table 1.1. ■

Chapter Questions

1. Describe the Six Sigma methodology to someone who has not heard of it.

2. What do Six Sigma projects focus on? Why?

3. Describe the changes that occur to the spread of the process when the amount of variation in the process decreases.

4. What are the benefits of implementing the Six Sigma methodology?

5. Why would a company want to follow the Six Sigma methodology?

6. Describe what it takes to become a green belt.

7. What does a person need to do to become a black belt?

8. Describe the difference between a black belt and a master black belt.

9. How do green belts, black belts, and master black belts interact when working on a project?

10. How does the six sigma methodology compare with the continuous improvement methodology?

2

Quality Masters

Marshall Field, who, in 1880, created of one of the United States' first department stores, was an involved manager. Each day during his 40 year reign as owner, he would walk through his flagship store on State Street in Chicago, Illinois, and observe his customers and their interactions with his employees. The author of Give the Lady What She Wants, *describes the situation that created the store's famous philosophy.*

One day while making his rounds, Marshall Field came upon an assistant retail manager involved in a heated argument with a female customer. He pulled the employee aside and asked him what he was doing. The employee responded that he was resolving a customer complaint concerning returning merchandise. Marshall Field retorted, "No you're not! Give the lady what she wants!" Marshall Field had established a policy of accepting merchandise returns from customers, a procedure not followed by any other department store at the time.

Paraphrased from *Give the Lady What She Wants*,
Lloyd Wendt and Herman Kogan,
and books, 1952

■ Objectives:

1. To introduce the reader to key individuals in the quality field
2. To help the reader understand how the teachings of these individuals relate to the Six Sigma methodology ■

QUALITY MASTERS

The fundamental philosophical foundation for the Six Sigma methodology is based on the work and philosophies of the individuals in this chapter. Their work challenges organizations to improve their products, services, and processes.

Dr. Armand Feigenbaum

Armand Feigenbaum (1920–) is considered to be the originator of the total quality movement. Dr. Feigenbaum defined quality based on a customer's actual experience with the product or service. His landmark text, *Total Quality Control*, first published in 1951 and updated regularly since then, has significantly influenced industrial practices. In his original text, he predicted that quality would become a significant customer-satisfaction issue, even to the point of surpassing price in importance in the decision-making process. As Six Sigma organizations know, consumers have come to expect quality as an essential dimension of the product or service they are purchasing.

In his text, Dr. Feigenbaum defines quality as:

> A customer determination which is based on the customer's actual experience with the product or service, measured against his or her requirements—stated or unstated, conscious or merely sensed, technically operational or entirely subjective—always representing a moving target in a competitive market.

Dr. Feigenbaum's definition of quality is broad-reaching. It stresses that quality is customer determination, meaning that only a customer can decide if and how well a product or service meets his or her needs, requirements, and expectations. These needs, requirements, and expectations may be stated or unstated, conscious or merely sensed, technically operational or entirely subjective. Quality is also based on the customer's actual experience with the product or service throughout its life, from purchase to disposal. Dr. Feigenbaum's definition recognizes that quality and therefore customer satisfaction is a moving target in a competitive market.

To Dr. Feigenbaum, quality is more than a technical subject; it is an approach to doing business that makes an organization more effective. Throughout his life, he has consistently encouraged treating quality as a fundamental element of a business strategy. In his article "Changing Concepts and Management of Quality Worldwide," from the December 1997 issue of *Quality Progress*, he asserts that quality is not a factor to be managed but a method of "managing, operating, and integrating the marketing, technology, production, information, and finance areas throughout a company's quality value chain with the subsequent favorable impact on manufacturing and service effectiveness." The Six Sigma methodology is a method of managing, enabling an organization to achieve higher customer satisfaction, lower overall costs, higher profits, and greater employee effectiveness and satisfaction.

Dr. Walter Shewhart

During his lifetime, Dr. Walter Shewhart (1891–1967) worked to create the statistical methods that enable Six Sigma organizations to control and improve the quality of their processes. While working at Bell Laboratories in the 1920s and 1930s,

Dr. Shewhart was the first to encourage the use of statistics to identify, monitor, and eventually remove sources of variation found in repetitive processes.

Dr. Shewhart identified two sources of variation in a process. **Controlled variation, *also termed common causes, is variation present in a process due to the very nature of the process.*** This type of variation can be removed from the process only by changing the process. For example, consider a person who has driven the same route to work dozens of times and determined that it takes about 20 minutes to get from home to work regardless of minor changes in weather or traffic conditions. If this is the case, then the only way the person can improve upon this time is to change the process by finding a new route. **Uncontrolled variation, *also known as special or assignable causes, comes from sources external to the process.*** This type of variation is not normally part of the process. It can be identified and isolated as the cause of the change in the behavior of the process. For instance, the commuter described above would experience uncontrolled variation if a major traffic accident stopped traffic or a blizzard made traveling difficult. Uncontrolled variation prevents the process from performing to the best of its ability. Six Sigma organizations strive to remove excess variation from their processes.

It was Dr. Shewhart who put forth the fundamental principle of quality that once a process is under control, exhibiting only controlled variation, future process performance can be predicted, within limits, on the basis of past performance. In his text, *Economic Control of Quality of Manufactured Product* (Van Nostrand Reinhold, 1931, p. 6), he wrote:

> A phenomenon will be said to be controlled when, through the use of past experience, we can predict, at least within limits, how the phenomenon may be expected to vary in the future. Here it is understood that prediction within limits means that we can state, at least approximately, the probability that the observed phenomenon will fall within the given limits.

Based on this principle, Dr. Shewhart developed the formulas and a table of constants used to create the most widely utilized statistical control charts in quality: the $\bar{X}$ and R charts. These charts (Figure 2.1) first appeared in a May 16, 1924, memo of Dr. Shewhart's and later in his 1931 text, *Economic Control of Quality of Manufactured Product*. Six Sigma organizations use control charts for three purposes: to define standards for the process, to aid in problem-solving efforts to attain the standards, and to serve to judge if the standards have been met.

Dr. W. Edwards Deming

Dr. W. Edwards Deming (1900–1993) made it his mission to teach optimal management strategies and practices to effective organizations. Dr. Deming encouraged top-level management to get involved in the process of creating an environment that supports continuous improvement. A statistician by training, Dr. Deming graduated from Yale University in 1928. Following his work with the census bureau, he first began spreading his quality message shortly after World War II. In the face of American prosperity following the war, his message was not heeded in the United States. His work with the Census Bureau and other government agencies led to his eventual contacts with Japan

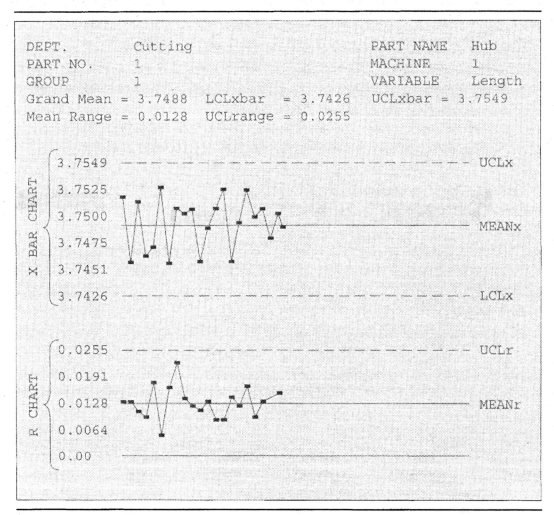

```
DEPT.          Cutting                          PART NAME    Hub
PART NO.       1                                MACHINE      1
GROUP          1                                VARIABLE     Length
Grand Mean  =  3.7488    LCLxbar  =  3.7426     UCLxbar  =  3.7549
Mean Range  =  0.0128    UCLrange =  0.0255
```

Figure 2.1 Typical X̄ and R Charts

as that nation began to rebuild. There he helped turn Japan into an industrial force to be reckoned with. It was only after his early 1980s appearance on the TV program "If Japan Can, Why Can't We?" that Dr. Deming found an audience in the United States. Over time, he became one of the most influential experts on quality assurance.

Six Sigma organizations understand Dr. Deming's economic chain reaction (Figure 2.2). They know that quality and process improvement activities act as the catalyst necessary to start an economic chain reaction. Improving quality leads to decreased costs, fewer mistakes, fewer delays, and better use of resources, which in turn leads to improved productivity, which enables a company to capture more of the market, which enables the company to stay in business, which results in providing more jobs.

Dr. Deming's philosophies focus heavily on management involvement, continuous improvement, statistical analysis, goal setting, and communication. His message, in

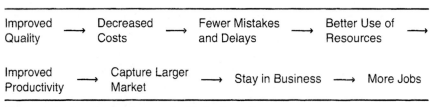

Figure 2.2 Deming's Economic Chain Reaction

the form of 14 points, is aimed primarily at management (Figure 2.3). Dr. Deming's philosophy encourages company leaders to dedicate themselves and their companies to the long-term improvement of their products or services. Dr. Deming's first point—*Create a constancy of purpose toward improvement of product and service, with the aim to become competitive and to stay in business and to provide jobs*—encourages leadership to accept the obligation to constantly improve the product or service through innovation, research, education, and continual improvement in all facets of the organization. A company is like an Olympic athlete who must constantly train, practice, learn, and improve in order to attain a gold medal. Without dedication, the performance of any task cannot reach its best. Dr. Deming's second point—*Adopt a new philosophy*—that rejects "acceptable" quality levels and poor service as a way of life, supports continuous improvement in all that we do. The 12 other points ask management to rethink past practices, such as awarding business on the basis of price tag alone, using mass inspection, setting arbitrary numerical goals and quotas, enforcing arbitrary work time standards, allowing incomplete training or education, and using outdated methods of supervision. Mass inspection has limited value because quality cannot be inspected

1. Create a constancy of purpose toward improvement of product and service, with the aim to become competitive and to stay in business and to provide jobs.
2. Adopt the new philosophy.
3. Cease dependence on inspection to achieve quality.
4. End the practice of awarding business on the basis of price tag alone. Instead minimize total cost.
5. Constantly and forever improve the system of production and service.
6. Institute training on the job.
7. Institute leadership.
8. Drive out fear.
9. Break down barriers between departments.
10. Eliminate slogans, exhortations, and targets for the workforce.
11. Eliminate arbitrary work standards and numerical quotas. Substitute leadership.
12. Remove barriers that rob people of their right to pride to workmanship.
13. Institute a vigorous program of education and self-improvement.
14. Put everybody in the company to work to accomplish the transformation.

Figure 2.3 Deming's 14 Points
SOURCE: Reprinted from *Out of the Crisis* by W. Edwards Deming by permission of MIT and The W. Edwards Deming Institute. Published by MIT, Center for Advanced Educational Services, Cambridge, MA 02139. Copyright © 1986 by The W. Edwards Deming Institute.

into a product. Quality can be *designed* into a product and manufacturing processes can *produce* it correctly. However, after it has been made, quality cannot be *inspected* into it. Similarly, awarding business on the basis of price tag alone is shortsighted and fails to establish mutual confidence between the supplier and the purchaser. Low-cost choices may lead to losses in productivity elsewhere.

Six Sigma organizations understand that leadership, along with the concepts of authority and responsibility, plays a significant role in business success. Throughout his life, Dr. Deming encouraged leadership to create and manage systems that enable people to find joy in their work. Dr. Deming's point about driving out fear stresses the importance of communication between leadership and management. Effective leaders in Six Sigma organizations welcome the opportunity to listen to their employees and act on valid suggestions and resolve key issues. Dr. Deming also points out the need to remove barriers that rob individuals of the right of pride in workmanship. Barriers are any aspect of a job that prevents employees from doing their jobs well. By removing them, leadership creates an environment supportive of their employees and the continuous improvement of their day-to-day activities. Improved management-employee interaction, as well as increased communication between departments, will lead to more effective solutions to the challenges of creating a product or providing a service. Six Sigma organizations focus on education and training, an integral part in Dr. Deming's plan. Continual education creates an atmosphere that encourages the discovery of new ideas and methods. This translates to innovative solutions to problems. Training ensures that products and services are provided that meet standards established by customer requirements.

Dr. Deming defined quality as *"non-faulty systems."* At first glance this seems to be an incomplete definition, especially when compared to that of Dr. Feigenbaum. Consider, however, what is meant by a system. Systems enable organizations to provide their customers with products and services. Faulty systems cannot help but create faulty products and services, resulting in unhappy customers. By focusing attention on the systems that create products and services, Dr. Deming is getting at the heart of the matter.

Dr. Deming used the red bead experiment to help leaders understand how a process with problems can inhibit an individual's ability to perform at his or her best. Dr. Deming used this experiment to create an understanding of his point—*Remove barriers that rob people of their right to pride of workmanship.* To conduct his experiment, Dr. Deming filled a box with 1000 beads, 800 white and 200 red. Participants randomly scooped 100 beads from the box. The participants have no control over which beads the scoop picked up or the percentage of red beads in the box. Given these constraints, 20% of the beads selected were red. Since only white beads are acceptable, Dr. Deming chastised those who scooped red beads from the box even though they had no control over their performance. Similarly, employees in an organization may often be blamed for faulty performance when in actuality it is the system that is faulty. The red beads represent problems in the system or process that can be changed only through leadership involvement. Six Sigma organizations strive to remove red beads from their organization's processes.

Define, Measure, Analyze (Plan)

1. Select appropriate metrics: key process output variables (KPOV).
2. Determine how these metrics will be tracked over time.
3. Determine current baseline performance of project/process.
4. Determine the key process input variables (KPIV) that drive the key process output variables (KPOV).
5. Determine what changes need to be made to the key process input variables in order to positively affect the key process output variables.

Improve (Do)

6. Make the changes.

Control (Study, Act)

7. Determine if the changes have positively affected the KPOVs.
8. If the changes made result in performance improvements, establish control of the KPIVs at the new levels. If the changes have not resulted in performance improvement, return to step 5 and make the appropriate changes.

Figure 2.4   Six Sigma Problem-Solving Steps

Dr. Deming encouraged the use of Dr. Shewhart's Plan-Do-Study-Act (PDSA) cycle for isolating and removing the root causes of process variation. Six Sigma organizations use a modified version of the PDSA cycle, Design, Measure, Analyze, Improve, Control (DMAIC), covered in detail in Chapter 8 (Figure 2.4).

σ   SIX SIGMA TOOLS AT WORK

Organizational Changes

KH Manufacturing makes components for the automotive industry. Unfortunately, several of the parts, due to design complexities, experienced numerous rejections from the customer. As a stopgap measure, KH instituted 100% inspection to minimize the chance of the customer receiving components that didn't meet specifications. Scrap rates were high. Due to the complexities of the components, rework, typically, was not an option.

When products don't live up to a customer's expectations, customers shop elsewhere. The automotive customer, recognizing that they faced a high probability of receiving defective parts because 100% inspection is rarely 100% effective, began to "shop the work."

At KH Manufacturing, costs associated with 100% inspection and manufacturing replacement components mounted. The thought of losing a customer disturbed them. KH recognized that Dr. Deming's philosophy of "creating a constancy of purpose toward improvement of product and service" would enable them to keep the component job, become more competitive, stay in business, and provide jobs. Since 100% inspection is expensive and ineffective, KH wanted to enact process changes that would allow them to follow Dr. Deming's third point and "cease dependence on inspection to achieve quality."

Following Dr. Deming's fifth point, "constantly and forever improve the system of production and service," KH formed product improvement teams composed of engineers and machine operators most closely associated with each component. Dr. Shewhart's $\overline{X}$ and R charts, recording process performance, formed the center of the improvement efforts.

The benefits of this approach to doing business were numerous. By "putting everyone in the company to work to accomplish the transformation," a change came over the production line. As operators learned to use and understand the $\overline{X}$ and R charts, they learned about their manufacturing processes. Process improvements, based on the knowledge gained from these charts, significantly improved component quality. Employee morale increased as they started to take an interest in their jobs. This was a big change for the union shop.

Changes happened on an individual level too. As management followed Dr. Deming's seventh, sixth, and eighth points "institute leadership" by "instituting training on the job," they were able to "drive out fear." One operator, who originally was very vocal about not wanting to be on a team, eventually ended up as a team leader.

Unbeknownst to his coworkers, this operator faced a significant barrier that "robbed him of his right to pride of workmanship" (Dr. Deming's 12th point). He had dropped out of school after sixth grade and had a very difficult time with math and reading. His understanding of math was so limited, he couldn't understand or calculate an average or a range. To hide his lack of math skills, he memorized which keys to use on the calculator. As he attended classes offered by the company, he learned how to plot and interpret data in order to make process adjustments based on trends and out of control points. The more involved he became in the improvement efforts, the more he realized how interesting his work had become. His involvement with the team inspired him to go back to school and get his High School Graduate Equivalency Degree at the age of 55. He followed Dr. Deming's 13th point, "institute a vigorous program of education and self-improvement."

Rather than rely on "slogans, exhortations, and targets for the workforce," KH Manufacturing followed Dr. Deming's advice and eliminated "arbitrary work standards and numerical quotas." KH was able to "cease dependence on inspection to achieve quality." They "substituted leadership," earning awards for being the most improved supplier. With their ability to manufacture complex components to customer specifications with nearly zero scrap, the plant has become the most profitable of the entire corporation.

Dr. Genichi Taguchi

Dr. Genichi Taguchi (1924–) developed methods that seek to improve consistency of performance and significantly reduced variation through the identification of key product and process characteristics before production. Dr. Taguchi introduced the concept that quality, or the lack of it, is a loss to society. Six Sigma practitioners understand the concept that the total loss to society generated by a product is an important dimension of the quality of a product. Any deviation from target specifications causes loss, even if the variation is within specifications. In his "loss function" concept, Dr. Taguchi expresses

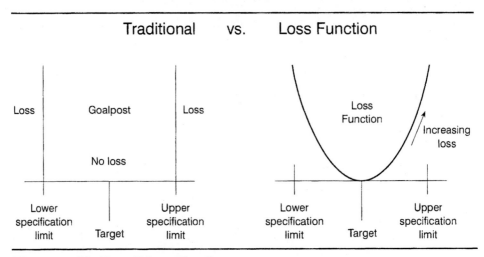

Figure 2.5   The Taguchi Loss Function

the costs of performance variation (Figure 2.5). When the variation is within specifications, the loss may be in the form of poor fit, poor finish, undersize, oversize, or alignment problems. Scrap, rework, warranty claims, and loss of goodwill are examples of losses when the variation extends beyond the specifications. Understanding the loss function helps Six Sigma practitioners to set product and manufacturing tolerances. Capital expenditures are more easily justified by relating the cost of deviations from target value to quality costs. Losses are minimized by improving the consistency of performance.

Dr. Taguchi is also known for his work in experiment design. Statistically planned experiments help identify the settings of product and process parameters that reduce performance variation. Dr. Taguchi's methods design the experiment to systematically weed out a product's or process's insignificant elements. The focus of experiment efforts is then placed on the significant elements. There are four basic steps:

1. Select the process/product to be studied.
2. Identify the important variables.
3. Reduce variation on the important variables through redesign and process improvement.
4. Open up tolerances on unimportant variables.

SUMMARY

Six Sigma, like most improvement strategies, methodologies, and standards, has its foundation in the teachings of the men discussed in this chapter.

σ ■ *Take Away Tips*

Dr. Shewhart introduced the concepts of controlled and uncontrolled variation.
Dr. Shewhart developed statistical process control charts for process management.

Dr. Deming encouraged companies to manage for quality by defining quality in terms of customer satisfaction.

Dr. Deming created his 14 points as a guide to management.

Dr. Taguchi's loss function shows that quality, or a lack of it, is a loss to society.

Dr. Taguchi's experiment designs focus on reducing performance variation. ▓

Chapter Questions

1. Why is an organizational philosophy focusing on delighting customers key to organizational success?

2. Use Dr. Feigenbaum's definition of quality as a guide and describe an experience you have had with a product or service.

3. Describe in your own words the two types of variation that Shewhart identified.

4. Which of Dr. Deming's 14 points do you find the most interesting? Why?

5. Describe an example from industry related to one of Dr. Deming's 14 points.

6. How do Dr. Deming's 14 points interact with each other?

7. How are the teachings of each of the people in this chapter similar? Where do they agree?

8. How are the teachings of each of the people in this chapter different? Where do they disagree?

9. Describe Taguchi's Loss Function. What was he trying to get company leaders to think about?

10. How do the teachings of the people in this chapter relate to Six Sigma?

Leadership and Strategic Planning

The aim of leadership should be to improve the performance of man and machine, to improve quality, to increase output and simultaneously to bring pride of workmanship to people. Put in a negative way, the aim of leadership is not merely to find and record failures of men, but to remove the causes of failure: to help people to do a better job with less effort.

W. Edwards Deming,
Out of the Crisis, 1986

"Cheshire-Puss," she began, rather timidly, as she did not at all know whether it would like the name: however, it only grinned a little wider. "Come, it's pleased so far," thought Alice, and she went on.
"Would you tell me, please, which way I ought to go from here?"
"That depends a good deal on where you want to get to," said the Cat.
"I don't much care where—" said Alice.
"Then it doesn't matter which way you go," said the Cat.
"—so long as I get somewhere," Alice added as an explanation.
"Oh, you're sure to do that," said the Cat, "if you only walk long enough."

Lewis Carroll,
Alice's Adventures in Wonderland, Chapter 6

■ Objectives:

1. To discuss the role of leadership in a Six Sigma organization
2. To discuss the role of strategic planning in a Six Sigma organization ■

A CUSTOMER FOCUSED CULTURE

Leaders at Six Sigma organizations create a culture focused on customer and organizational success. A culture is defined as "a pattern of shared beliefs and values that provides the members of an organization with rules of behavior or accepted norms for conducting operations." It is the philosophies, ideologies, values, assumptions, beliefs, expectations, attitudes, and norms that knit an organization together. In a Six Sigma organization, the philosophies, ideologies, values, assumptions, beliefs, expectations, attitudes, and norms are focused on providing value for their customers. Six Sigma leaders apply a missionary zeal to the job of creating an organizational culture focused on creating value for their customers. By visibly practicing and supporting the desired culture daily, leadership aligns this expectation at three levels: the overall organizational goals and objectives, the organization's processes, and the performance of individuals during their day-to-day activities. Six Sigma leaders define systems and standards that support the overall organizational goals and objectives. Leaders get people to do what they have not done before thus leading to the organization being more successful. Under their guidance, employees work within the system to create value for the organization's customers.

LEADERSHIP STYLES

Four primary styles of leading exist: directing, consultative, participative, and delegating (Figure 3.1). Different situations call for different leadership styles. Leaders are skilled at recognizing when to use each style.

The *directing* style of leadership is normally used when the leader must make a unilateral decision that must be followed without comment or question from the rank and file. The need to use the directing style of leadership may come about because the

Participative	**Consultative**
Provides guidance	Seeks input, advice, and suggestions
Gets involved only when necessary	Makes final decision based on employee input
Accepts work and decisions of employees	Recognizes employees for their contributions
Helps others analyze and solve problems	
Recognizes employees for seeking support	

Delegating	**Directing**
Assigns responsibility	Engages in unilateral decision making
Assigns authority	Expects employees to follow orders
Provides minimal input	Gives information about what to do
Provides recognition	Gives information about how to do it
Verifies work	Gives information about why it should be done
Recognizes employees for accepting responsibility	Recognizes employees for following directions

Figure 3.1   Leadership Styles

leader has more knowledge of the situation or the decision affects the common good of the organization. This style of leadership style may be something as simple as a "no horseplay will be tolerated on the job" rule or as complex as "here are the customers the organization will focus on." Leaders using this style expect to be obeyed. Those that work for them have very little, if any, input.

The *consultative* style of leadership is utilized when a situation exists that the leader is seeking input from those working under them. They may be facing a customer issue that requires the input of a specialist or from all employees. When using this style of leadership, the leader seeks the advice, suggestions, and input of those around them, but still remains the final decision-maker.

When using the *participative* style of leadership, a leader assigns work to the employees, provides guidance during the work process, and makes decisions based on the conclusions reached by the employees working on the task. Unlike the consultative style of leadership, in this situation, the leader is more likely to take the conclusions of the employee(s) as the final decision in the matter.

With the *delegating* style of leadership, the leader essentially tells the employee or team what needs to be done, assigns the responsibility, and provides the individual or team with the authority to get the job done. The individual or team, having been given both the responsibility and the authority, completes the work, with minimal input from the leader. In this style of leadership, the leader checks to verify the successful completion of the assignment and participates only if necessary.

Care must be taken to wisely match the leadership style to the situation. Using a directing style when a participative style is called for may leave an employee feeling stifled and asking the question, "Why was I even asked to participate?" The directing style of leadership is the most heavy-handed. Applied incorrectly, it could stifle employee creativity and motivation. Conversely, employing a delegating style instead of a consultative style of leadership when more guidance is needed will leave the employee feeling stranded. The delegating style allows the employee the most freedom. However, if the needs of the project have not been clearly communicated, or if the employee is inadequately prepared to do the work, both the leader and the employee will be dissatisfied with the result. Leaders who try to apply the participative or consultative styles in all situations may discover that employees make decisions contrary to key policies and procedures. Effective leaders feel comfortable affecting each leadership style in appropriate situations.

MANAGING BY FACT AND WITH A KNOWLEDGE OF VARIATION

Effective leaders know that people must be included in the organization's decision-making processes. They also know that sharing information is critical to making good decisions. Management by fact involves understanding the how's and why's of a situation before taking action. Management by fact requires an appreciation for and understanding of the key systems of an organization. Effective leaders realize that management of systems requires knowledge of the interrelationships between all the components within the system and the people that work in it. When leaders manage by fact, they use objective evidence to support their decisions. Objective evidence is not biased and is expressed as simply and clearly as possible. More importantly, it is traceable back to its origin, whether that be a customer, an order number, a product code, a machine, or an employee. Effective leaders are the ones who remember to ask Dr. Deming's favorite question: "How do we know?" Knowing the answer to this question verifies where the information has come from, its importance, and its relationship with the issue at hand. Having this knowledge means having the facts available to support a plan of action.

 SIX SIGMA TOOLS AT WORK

Managing by Fact and with a Knowledge of Variation

A sales manager has three salespeople, each covering different areas of the country. The performance of each salesperson is reviewed monthly. These reviews are often followed by praise for the highest achiever and a "pep talk" for the underachievers.

In response to upper management's request, the sales manager has graphed the performance of each salesperson versus the sales goal for the past 15 months. When the resulting graphs have been prepared (Figure 3.2), the sales manager's suspicions concerning performance have only been justified.

It is only when he combines these graphs with factual information and an understanding of variation that the true patterns of performance begin to emerge. Figure 3.3 shows how control limits can be calculated based on the variation present in each individual's process. These limits show what each process is actually capable of versus the previous graph which showed performance versus specifications (goals set). For more information on how these limits were calculated, please see the discussion on control charts in Chapter 10.

Note the cycle present in the Great Lakes Region sales. When the variation present in the process is studied, it appears that this salesperson expends efforts to get sales at first, and then relaxes efforts until approaching the established goal. Another fact to add to this analysis is that this is a firm specializing in automotive components and the sales territory encompasses the lucrative territories of Michigan, Ohio, and Indiana. Making sales in this region is relatively easy.

Note the Mid-Region (Kentucky, Tennessee, North Carolina, and South Carolina) performance. There is a large amount of variation present in the process. This region has been experiencing a lot of growth in the automotive field. The large amount of variation present could signify a lackadaisical attitude on the part of this salesperson or a need for more training.

Note the performance of the Southern Region salesperson. The first graph, Figure 3.2, shows his performance is consistently below the goal. Yet, if he were managed by facts with a knowledge of variation, it becomes apparent that something good is going on here. Based on this graph, this salesperson has achieved high performance on several occasions. Further investigation reveals that though his region encompasses Florida, Georgia, and Alabama, areas not prime for

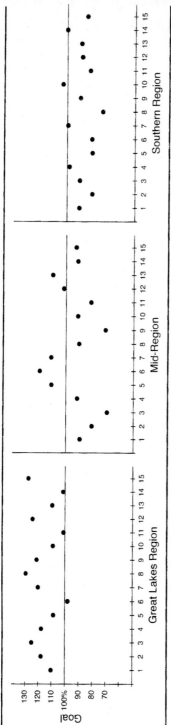

Figure 3.2 Performance Graphs of Each Salesperson for the Past 15 Months

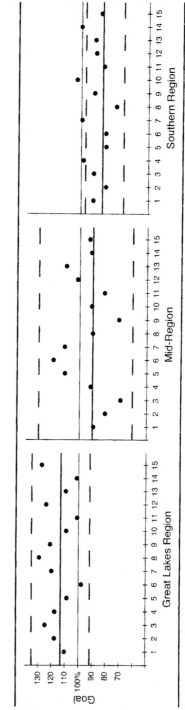

Figure 3.3 Graphs with Control Limits

> automotive work, he has been able to generate significant sales. These sales, in the area of medical and computer devices, are helping the manufacturing firm diversify away from its dependence on automotive business. This salesperson should be congratulated for his efforts.
>
> Using control charts and managing with a knowledge of variation provides a whole different outlook for the performance of these individuals.

Effective leaders have a very powerful tool that helps to link the activities of individuals within an organization with the customers served by the organization: the strategic plan. Strategic plans allow leadership to put down in writing the direction the organization is heading and how it plans to get there. In a competitive business environment, Six Sigma organizations utilize carefully designed strategic plans in order to create and sustain their competitive advantages and profit position.

CREATING STRATEGIC PLANS

Strategic plans enable an organization's leadership to translate the organization's vision and mission into actionable and measurable activities. Developing a strategic plan requires taking a systematic look at the organization to see how each part of it interrelates with the whole (Figure 3.4). Strategic plans enable an organization to advance from wishful thinking: the customer is #1; to taking action: changing corporate behavior and the actions of employees in order to support a focus on the customer.

A strategic plan defines the business the organization intends to be in, the kind of organization it wants to be, and the kind of economic and noneconomic contribution it will make to its stakeholders, employees, customers, and community. The plan spells out the organization's goals and objectives and how the organization will achieve these goals and objectives. The strategic plan concentrates on the critical success factors (CSFs) for the organization, providing plans for closing the gaps between what the organization is currently capable of doing versus what it needs to be able to do. Using indicators or performance measures, the organization will monitor its progress toward meeting the short-term, mid-term, and ultimately long-term goals. These indicators of performance are critical because they enable an organization to determine whether or not they are on target toward reaching their goals. Six Sigma organizations analyze the gap between what the current performance is and what was originally planned for in the strategic plan. In the case of a negative gap showing lower than expected performance, the organization must take corrective action to eliminate the root cause, improve performance toward the goal, and narrow the gap. In the case of a positive gap, showing better than expected performance, the organization may choose to take action to further enhance the gap. A good strategic plan also includes contingency plans in case some of the basic assumptions are in error or significant changes in the market occur.

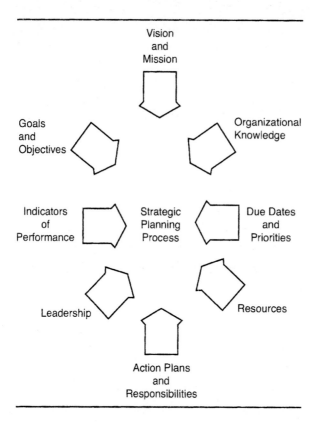

Figure 3.4   Elements Needed for an Effective Strategic Planning Process

In preparation for creating a strategic plan, the organization's leaders should determine:

1. The organization's business (The business they are really in?)
2. The principal findings from the internal and external assessments
   a. Strengths and weaknesses
   b. Customer information
   c. Economic environment information
   d. Competition information
   e. Government requirements
   f. Technological environment

Once these issues have been addressed, the creation of a strategic plan can begin. The strategic plan is essentially a framework that assists the organization in achieving its vision while allowing flexibility to deal with unforeseen changes in the business environment (Figures 3.5 and 3.6). The components of a strategic plan are:

1. *Vision:* the organization's strategic direction for the foreseeable future
2. *Mission:* the translation of the organization's vision into strategic actions

Critical Success Factors			→ Goal A	→	Objective A1, A2, . . .	→	Measures A1, A2, . . .	→	Action (Project) A1, A2, . . .
as Identified by Customers	→ Vision →	Mission →	Goal B	→	Objective B1, B2, . . .	→	Measures B1, B2, . . .	→	Action (Project) B1, B2, . . .
			→ Goal C	→	Objective C1, C2, . . .	→	Measures C1, C2, . . .	→	Action (Project) C1, C2, . . .
			→ Goal D	→	Objective D1, D2, . . .	→	Measures D1, D2, . . .	→	Action (Project) D1, D2, . . .

Figure 3.5   Strategic Planning

3. *Critical success factors*: the three to ten things, as identified by customers, that absolutely must be done well if the company is going to thrive
4. *Goals*: what must be achieved in order to support the critical success factors
5. *Objectives*: the specific and quantitative actions that must be taken in order to support the accomplishment of the goals and ultimately the mission and vision

---

Preparation
1. The organization's business (what business are they really in?)
2. The principal findings from the internal and external assessments
    A. Strengths and weaknesses
    B. Customer information
    C. Economic environment information
    D. Competition information
    E. Government requirements
    F. Technological environment

Planning
1. *Vision:* the organization's strategic direction for the foreseeable future
2. *Mission:* the translation of the organization's vision into strategic actions
3. *Critical success factors as identified by customers:* the three to ten things that a company absolutely must do well if the company is going to thrive
4. *Goals, objectives, and indicators of performance:*
    A. Goal 1
        Objective 1.1
            Indicator
        Objective 1.2
            Indicator
    B. Goal 2
        Objective 2.1
            Indicator
    C. Goal 3
        :
5. Contingency plans

Figure 3.6   Generic Strategic Plan

6. *Indicators:* the performance measures that indicate whether or not the organization is moving toward meeting their objectives, goals, mission, and vision

7. *Contingency plans:* the plans in place that enable an organization to remain flexible in a complex, competitive environment

 SIX SIGMA TOOLS AT WORK

Strategic Planning

PREPARATION

Leaders of PM Printing and Design recently met to clarify portions of their strategic plan. Using the plan they hope to communicate to their employees the importance of creating and maintaining a customer-focused process orientation as they improve the way they do business.

Based on their meeting, the leaders have determined that their best market niche, or the business that they are really in, is concept to delivery. This includes designing, reproducing, and mailing customer brochures and literature. Market research has shown that no other full service printing and design company exists in their market area and customers are seeking an organization that can take their ideas and turn them into a finished product in their customers' mailboxes. This research has identified their strengths and weaknesses, provided customer information, defined their economic, technological, and competitive environments, as well as specified appropriate government requirements.

PLANNING

PM Printing and Design Vision

- PM Printing and Design will be recognized as the best source for printed and duplicated material through the recognition and implementation of customer-driven-change in a service focused environment.

PM Printing and Design Mission

- PM Printing and Design is a full service design, reprographic, and mailing facility committed to serving the local community, producing the highest quality product in the most cost effective manner.

Critical Success Factors

- Provide a full service reprographic facility.
- Provide a full service design process.
- Provide a full service mailing facility including mailer creation and mailing processes.
- Employing talented designers and skilled technicians.
- Providing quality printed material at cost effective services.

Goals, Objectives, and Indicators of Performance

- Goal 1: Improve customers' knowledge of our services.

  Objective 1.1: Advertise services community wide.
  Indicator: Number of customers
  Indicator: Number of repeat sales

  Objective 1.2: Increase market share.
  Indicator: Number of customers
  Indicator: Number of repeat sales
  Indicator: Number of referrals

- Goal 2: Improve customers' perceptions of our services.

  Objective 2.1: Reduce the number of customer complaints.
  Indicator: Number of complaints per month
  Indicator: Average time to resolve complaints

- Goal 3: Design and process orders rapidly while maintaining high quality.

  Objective 3.1: Reduce order time to completion.
  Indicator: Average order turnaround time

- Goal 4: Increase customer value.

  Objective 4.1: Improve quality and lower cost.
  Indicator: Cost per printed unit (impression)
  Indicator: Cost avoidance (work performed in-house versus contracting work)

  Objective 4.2: Remove non–value-added activities.
  Indicator: Cost per printed unit (impression)

  Objective 4.3: Improve first time through quality.
  Indicator: Reduction in rework/scrap

- Goal 5: Provide a desirable work environment for PM employees.

  Objective 5.1: Expand employee opportunities for growth.
  Indicator: Progress toward cross-training goals for critical processes as identified by customers

  Objective 5.2: Improve employee retention.
  Indicator: Length of employee service
  Indicator: Number of employees with 1+ years of service

Contingency Plan

- Maintain good relationships with other area printers in order to have a source of extra production capability if needed for a rush job or in the event of an equipment malfunction.

Though this strategic plan is still in a state of development, it does provide a concrete example of how a strategic plan is aligned throughout. This alignment can be seen by goals, supported by objectives, and monitored by performance indicators. Leaders of PM Printing and Design used the strategic plan deployment tree

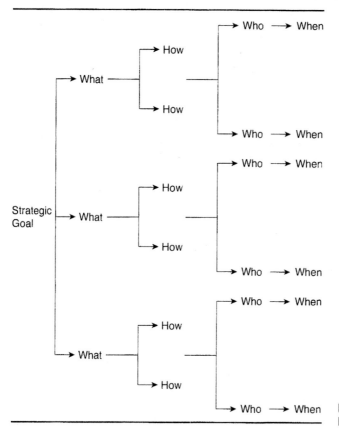

Figure 3.7   Strategic Plan Deployment Tree

(Figure 3.7) as an example and created a responsibilities matrix (Figure 3.8). The matrix assigns activities and responsibilities to specific individuals, shows the time frame for accomplishment, and establishes priorities for the objectives.

Beyond a lack of understanding, commitment, and participation by leadership, a variety of pitfalls in strategic planning and its deployment exist. It is not unusual for an unbelievable vision to be proposed, only to be followed up by an inadequate definition of operating expectations. A strategic plan that lists objective after objective suffers from a lack of prioritizing. A strategic plan that fails to clearly assign responsibility for results is weak as is one that fails to identify and utilize performance measures. The performance measures themselves may be a problem. Organizations do not benefit from strategic plans containing performance measures that are not connected with the activities proposed by the plan or that are vague or unclear. Strategic plans are also hampered when *what* the organization wants to accomplish is not supported by a corresponding *how* the *what* is going to be accomplished.

To be effective, a strategic plan must be deployed. As living documents, strategic plans are not meant to sit on a shelf, only to be touched when it is time for an annual

Goal 1: Improve customers' knowledge of our services

Objective 1.1: Advertise services community wide
  Action: Contract with local radio, TV, and newspapers for advertisements
  Responsibility: QS, MF
  Due: September 15
  Priority: 1
    Indicator: Number of customers
    Indicator: Number of repeat sales
    Indicator: Number of referrals

Goal 4: Increase customer value

Objective 4.1: Improve quality and reduce cost
  Action: Compare and contrast reproducing machines available
  Action: Select improved machine if available
  Responsibility: RP
  Due: October 15
  Priority: 2
    Indicator: Cost per printed unit (impression)
    Indicator: Cost avoidance (work performed in-house versus
        contracting work)

Objective 4.2: Remove non–value-added activities
  Action: Create process maps for all critical processes
  Action: Set up one team per process to identify and remove non–value-added
      activities
  Responsibility: DS
  Due: December 1
  Priority: 1
    Indicator: Cost per printed unit (impression)

Figure 3.8   PM Printing and Design Responsibilities Matrix

revision. Essentially, creating alignment is policy deployment. *Alignment means that if you push on one end, the other end will move in the direction you want.* Effective leaders enable members of the organization to make the transition between the strategic plan and daily business activities by translating *what* needs to be accomplished into *how* it will be accomplished. Effective leaders make sure that the day-to-day activities and the goals of the strategic plans of the organization are in harmony and are focused on what is critical to the success of the organization. The leaders want to ensure that if they push on the strategic plan, the actions of their employees will go in the desired direction. For this reason the strategy must be clearly communicated throughout the organization. Effective leaders make sure that the strategic plan contains clear objectives, provides and utilizes measures of performance, assigns responsibilities to specific individuals, and denotes timing (see the sample Design Responsibilities Matrix, Figure 3.8). For effective strategic plan deployment, the organization's reward and recognition system must support plan deployment.

SUMMARY

Six Sigma organizations recognize that good leadership combined with strategic planning and deployment maximize long-term organizational health. If good strategic planning is not practiced:

> Goals are not known throughout the company
> Goals change too often
> Goals are not achieved
> Goals are achieved without real improvement
> Progress is not sustained
> Organizational frustration exists

σ ■ *Take Away Tips*

1. Leaders create a customer-focused culture that works to create value for their customers each and every day in all of a company's activities.
2. Leaders match leadership styles with specific situations in order to motivate employees.
3. Leaders manage by fact with a knowledge of variation when making decisions.
4. Strategic plans align the needs, wants, and expectations of the customer with the processes and day-to-day activities of its employees.
5. Strategy deployment is as crucial as strategy development. ■

Chapter Questions

1. What is an organizational culture? What cultural aspects would you expect to see in a Six Sigma organization?
2. Describe each type of leadership style. Include a description of where you have seen each of these styles used.
3. What role does leadership play in strategic planning?
4. What does it mean to manage by fact and with a knowledge of variation?
5. Why does an effective organization need a strategic plan?
6. What are the benefits of a strategic plan?
7. Describe each of the elements needed for the strategic planning process.
8. Describe the steps necessary to create a strategic plan.
9. Why is strategy deployment as important as strategic planning?
10. For the company you work for or have worked for, ask to see the strategic plan. How does it compare with what you've learned about the strategic planning process?

4

Creating a Customer Focus

From a customer's standpoint, neither quality, cost nor schedule always comes first. When customers evaluate the products and services they receive, they make trade-offs between all three key factors in order to maximize value. The challenge that suppliers face is to provide their customers with the maximum value, which often is a balancing act between quality, cost and schedule.

The First Among Equals,
Quality Digest, June 1999

▨ Objectives:

1. To explain the difference between satisfaction and perceived value
2. To discuss how customers define value
3. To acquaint the reader with the tool of Quality Function Deployment
4. To introduce the concept of benchmarking ▨

CUSTOMER VALUE PERCEPTIONS

The current global business environment is extremely competitive. Today's consumers are more than willing to switch from supplier to supplier in search of better service or availability or courtesy or features or for any variety of reasons. To attract and retain customers, Six Sigma organizations focus on determining and providing what their customers want and value. Advertising, market positioning, product/service imaging, discounting, crisis handling, and other methods of attracting the customer's attention are not enough. Organizations utilizing the Six Sigma methodology do well because they talk to customers, translate what their customers said into appropriate actions, and align their key business processes and projects to support what their customers want.

Six Sigma organizations recognize that customers base their decisions about the quality of a product or service on the perceived value they receive. *Value, a product's or service's attributed or relative worth or usefulness,* is judged by a consumer each time they trade something of worth (usually money) in order to acquire the product or service. More simply, value can be defined as a solution to a customer's problem or an activity that a customer is willing to pay for. Customer value judgments, because they involve actual experience, requirements, wants, needs, and expectations, are complex. Six Sigma organizations realize that they are offering product or service features to their customers, but what the customers are really buying is the benefits those products or services offer. Perceived value is the customer's viewpoint of those benefits. Customer satisfaction, on the other hand, centers around how they felt the last time they bought a product or service from a company. It is a comparison between customer expectations and customer experience. Perceived value goes beyond customer satisfaction and concentrates on future transactions. Consumers' perception of the value they have received in the recent transaction will affect their future decision to purchase the same thing again. If they perceive their overall experience with the product or service as valuable, they will most likely purchase in the future; if they do not, they won't. Six Sigma organizations realize that how the customer perceives the value of that transaction will determine whether or not they will buy from the same organization the next time.

Six Sigma organizations seek to understand every aspect of their customers' interaction with their company. They understand that this process begins when the customer first contacts the company and continues until the product has been consumed or the service completed. Six Sigma organizations study their processes from their customers' point of view, selecting improvement projects that focus on designing, developing, and improving key customer processes, making them seamless, flawless, and easy to negotiate. Having hassle-free processes adds considerable value from the customer's viewpoint. These types of processes save money and time. Customers willingly participate in processes they can understand, which is essential in the service industries where customer input is vital to the success of the process. Information, whether about customer perceived value or customer satisfaction, is more meaningful if it is obtained on the customers' terms and from their perspective.

Organizations practicing the Six Sigma methodology need an accurate understanding of the gap between their current performance and what the customer requires. Companies use information related to how their customers define quality and value to help select and refine improvements to their processes. To guide project selection and focus, Six Sigma organizations talk with their customers.

QUALITY FUNCTION DEPLOYMENT

Quality Function Deployment (QFD) is a technique that seeks to bring the voice of the customer into the process of designing and developing a product or service. Using this information, effective organizations align their processes to meet their customers' needs the first time and every time. Six Sigma companies use the voice of the customer information obtained by a QFD to drive changes to the way they do business. Information taken directly from the customer is used to modify processes, products, and services to better conform to the needs identified by the customer.

Developed in Japan in the 1970s by Dr. Akao, QFD was first used in the United States in the 1980s. Essentially, QFD is a planning process for guiding the design or redesign of a product or service. The principal objective of a QFD is to enable a company to organize and analyze pertinent information associated with its product or service. A QFD can point out areas of strengths as well as weaknesses in both existing or new products.

Utilizing a matrix, information from the customer is organized and integrated into the product or process specifications. QFD allows for preventive action rather than a reactive action to customer demands. When a company uses the QFD format when designing a product or service, they stop developing products and services based solely on their own interpretation of what the customer wants. Instead, they utilize actual customer information in the design and development process. Two of the main benefits of QFD are the reduced number of engineering changes and fewer production problems. QFD provides key action items for improving customer satisfaction and perceived value. A QFD can enable the launch of a new product or service to go more smoothly because customer issues and expectations have been dealt with in advance. Gathering and utilizing the voice of the customer is critical to the success of world class companies.

A QFD has two principal parts. The horizontal component records information related to the customer. The vertical component records the organization's technical response to these customer inputs. Essentially, a QFD matrix clearly shows what the customer wants and how the organization is going to achieve those wants. The essential steps to a QFD are shown in Figures 4.1 and 4.2.

QFD begins with the customer. Surveys and focus groups are used to gather information from the customers about their wants, needs, and expectations. Several key areas that should be investigated include performance, features, reliability, conformance, durability, serviceability, aesthetics, and perceived quality. Often, customer information, specifically, the way they say it, must be translated into actionable wording for the organization. When a customer says "I can never find parking" this needs to be interpreted as "close, convenient parking readily available." In the first statement,

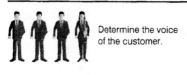
Determine the voice of the customer.

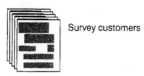
Survey customers

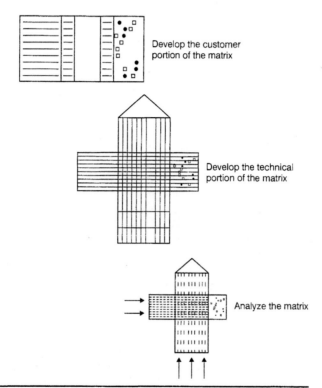

Develop the customer portion of the matrix

Develop the technical portion of the matrix

Analyze the matrix

Figure 4.1   The QFD Process

the customer is expressing a need. The second statement turns that need into something the organization can act on.

Once this information is organized into a matrix, the customers are contacted to rate the importance of each of the identified wants and needs. Information is also gathered about how customers rate the company's product or service against the competition. Following this input from the customers, technical requirements are developed. These technical aspects define how the customer needs, wants, and expectations will be met. Once the matrix is constructed, the areas that need to be emphasized in the design of the product or service will be apparent. The following Six Sigma Tools at Work feature shows the steps associated with building a QFD matrix.

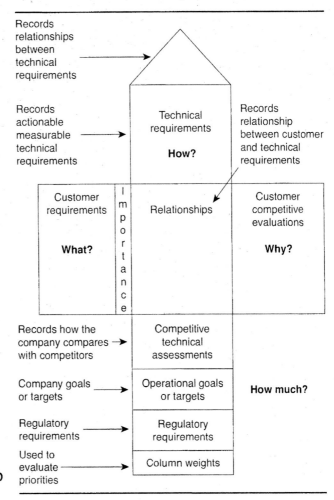

Figure 4.2   Summary of a QFD Matrix

Creating a QFD

AM Corporation sells sports drinks to the general public. They have always been very in tune to the health and nutritional needs of their customers. Recently their focus has turned to another aspect of their business, the containers their drinks are provided in. They have decided to utilize a QFD when redesigning their sports drink bottles.

Customer Requirements

Container	Lids	Doesn't Leak	1	
		Interchangable Lids	2	
		Freshness	3	
		Open/Close Easily	4	
		Sealed When Purchased	5	
		Resealable Lid	6	
	Shape	Doesn't Slip Out of Hands	7	
		Fits In Cupholder	8	
		Doesn't Tip Over	9	
		Attractive	10	
		Fits In Mini-Cooler	11	
		Doesn't Spill When You Drink	12	
Material	Characteristics	No Dents	13	
		Doesn't Change Shape	14	
		Is Not Heavy (Light)	15	
		Does Not Break When Dropped	16	
		Clear	17	
		Reusable	18	
		Recyclable	19	
		Stays Cool	20	
		No Sharp Edges	21	
MISC	Cost	Inexpensive	22	

Figure 4.3   Customer Requirements

   1. *Determine the voice of the customer: What does the customer want?* The first
step in creating the QFD involves a survey of their customer expectations, needs,
and requirements associated with their sports drink bottles. AM Corp. met with several focus groups of their customers to capture the information. Following these
meetings, they organized and recorded the wants of the customers in the column
located on the left side of the matrix (Figure 4.3).

Customer Requirements / Ranking

Container	Lids	Doesn't Leak	1	2	
		Interchangable Lids	2	6	
		Freshness	3	6	
		Open/Close Easily	4	3	
		Sealed When Purchased	5	6	
		Resealable Lid	6	8	
	Shape	Doesn't Slip Out of Hands	7	4	
		Fits In Cupholder	8	1	
		Doesn't Tip Over	9	8	
		Attractive	10	10	
		Fits In Mini-Cooler	11	11	
		Doesn't Spill When You Drink	12	9	
Material	Characteristics	No Dents	13	11	
		Doesn't Change Shape	14	8	
		Is Not Heavy (Light)	15	7	
		Does Not Break When Dropped	16	6	
		Clear	17	10	
		Reusable	18	6	
		Recyclable	19	11	
		Stays Cool	20	5	
		No Sharp Edges	21	10	
MISC	Cost	Inexpensive	22	5	

Figure 4.4   Rankings

2. *Have the customer rank the relative importance of their wants.* After AM Corp. organized the data, they reconvened the focus groups. At that time, they gave each of the participants an imaginary $100 to spend on the recorded wants. The participants were instructed to allocate more dollars to their more important wants. They recorded their values on the matrix next to the list of recorded wants. Following the meetings, AM Corp. created the final matrix (Figure 4.4) by combining the values assigned by all the customers. The wants with higher dollar values are those the customers consider more desirable.

3. *Have the customer evaluate your company against competitors.* At the same meeting, the customers also evaluated AM Corp.'s competitors. In this step, the participants used $100 to divide among AM Corp. and its competitors. The customers awarded money to the company that they felt provided the best product or service for their recorded want. Following the meetings, AM Corp. created the final matrix by combining the values assigned by all the customers. Looking at the right side of the chart (Figure 4.5), customers ranked AM Corp. against their competitors. Higher values represented where AM Corp. needed to focus their efforts.

4. *Determine how the wants will be met: How will the company provide the wants?* At this point, AM Corporation's efforts focused on determining how they were going to provide the wants identified by the customers. They spent many hours in meetings discussing the technical requirements necessary for satisfying the customers' recorded wants. These were recorded at the tops of the columns in the matrix. AM Corp. made sure that the technical requirements or hows were phrased in terms that are measurable and actionable. Several of the wants needed two or more technical requirements to make them happen (Figure 4.6).

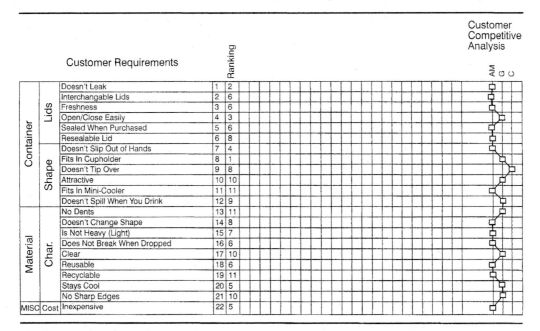

		Customer Requirements	Ranking		Customer Competitive Analysis (AM, G, C)
Container	Lids	Doesn't Leak	1	2	
		Interchangable Lids	2	6	
		Freshness	3	6	
		Open/Close Easily	4	3	
		Sealed When Purchased	5	6	
		Resealable Lid	6	8	
	Shape	Doesn't Slip Out of Hands	7	4	
		Fits In Cupholder	8	1	
		Doesn't Tip Over	9	8	
		Attractive	10	10	
		Fits In Mini-Cooler	11	11	
		Doesn't Spill When You Drink	12	9	
Material	Char.	No Dents	13	11	
		Doesn't Change Shape	14	8	
		Is Not Heavy (Light)	15	7	
		Does Not Break When Dropped	16	6	
		Clear	17	10	
		Reusable	18	6	
		Recyclable	19	11	
		Stays Cool	20	5	
		No Sharp Edges	21	10	
MISC	Cost	Inexpensive	22	5	

Figure 4.5   Customer Competitive Analysis

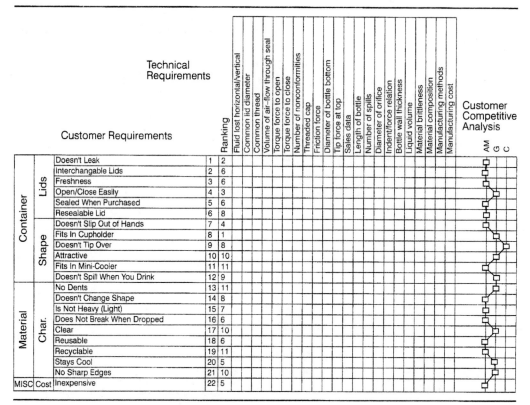

Figure 4.6 Technical Requirements

5. *Determine the direction of improvement for the technical requirements.* During the meetings discussing technical requirements, those involved also discussed the appropriate specifications for the technical requirements. They were able to identify how those technical requirements could be improved. For instance, for the comment "Fluid lost horizontal/vertical," the appropriate direction of improvement for this is "less," denoted by the downward arrow (Figure 4.7).

6. *Determine the operational goals for the technical requirements.* AM Corp. identified the operational goals that will enable them to meet the technical requirements (Figure 4.8).

7. *Determine the relationship between each of the customer wants and the technical requirements: How does action (change) on a technical requirement affect customer satisfaction with the recorded want?* The team members at AM Corp. studied the relationship between the customer wants and the technical requirements (Figure 4.9). They used the following notations:

A strong positive correlation is denoted by the value 9 or a filled-in circle.
A positive correlation is denoted by the value 3 or an open circle.
A weak correlation is denoted by the value 1 or a triangle.

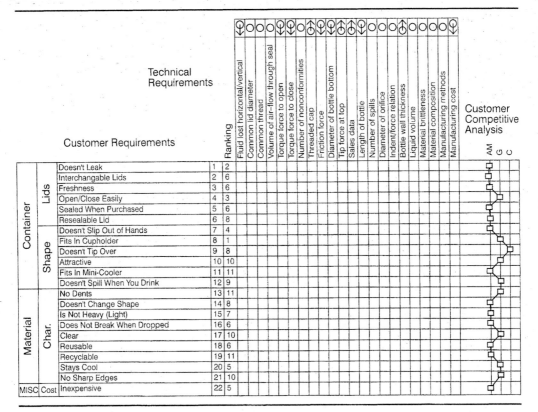

Figure 4.7 Direction of Improvement

If no correlation exists, then the box remains empty.
If there is a negative correlation, the box is marked with a minus sign.

8. *Determine the correlation between the technical requirements.* The team members recorded the correlation between the different technical requirements in the roof of the QFD house. This triangular table shows the relationship between each of the technical requirements (Figure 4.10). Once again, they used the same notations:

A strong positive correlation is denoted by the value 9 or a filled-in circle.
A positive correlation is denoted by the value 3 or an open circle.
A weak correlation is denoted by the value 1 or a triangle.
If no correlation exists, then the box remains empty.
If there is a negative correlation, the box is marked with an X.

9. *Compare the technical performance with that of competitors.* At this point, AM Corp. compared their abilities to generate the technical requirements with the abilities of their competitors. On the matrix, this information is shown in the competitive technical assessment (Figure 4.11).

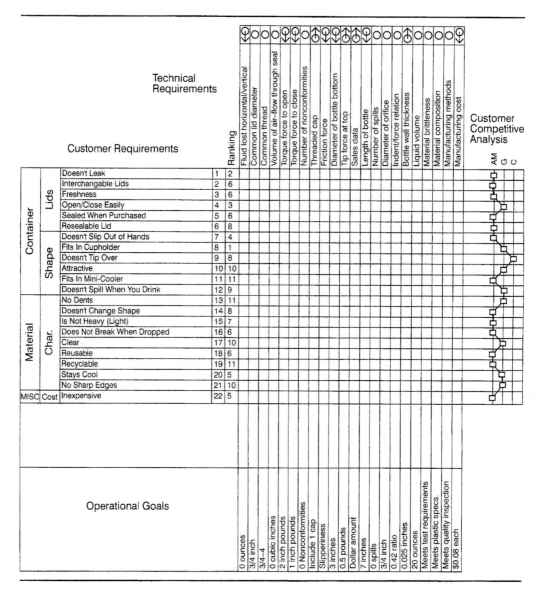

Figure 4.8   Operational Goals

10. *Determine the technical importance.* At this point, the matrix is nearly finished. In order to analyze the information presented, the correlation values for the wants and hows are multiplied by the values from the rankings of the $100 test.

For example; for the first column, a ranking of 2 for "doesn't leak" is multiplied by a value of 9 for "strong correlation," making the total 18. To this value, the ranking of 6 for "sealed when purchased" is multiplied by a value of 1, for "weak correlation." The grand total for the column is 24 (Figure 4.12).

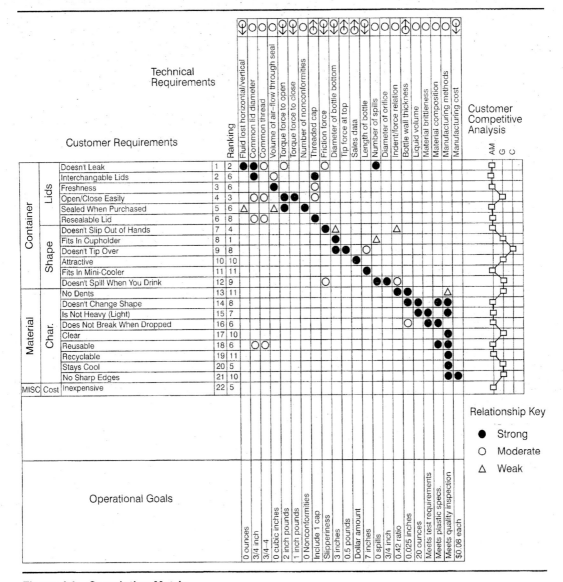

Figure 4.9 Correlation Matrix

11. *Add regulatory and/or internal requirements if necessary.* Here, any rules, regulations, or requirements not set forth by the customer, but by some other agency or government, were identified and recorded (Figure 4.12).

12. *Analyze the QFD matrix.* What did the customer want? How is this supported by customer rankings and competitive comparisons? How well is the competition doing? How does our company compare? Where will our company's emphasis need to be?

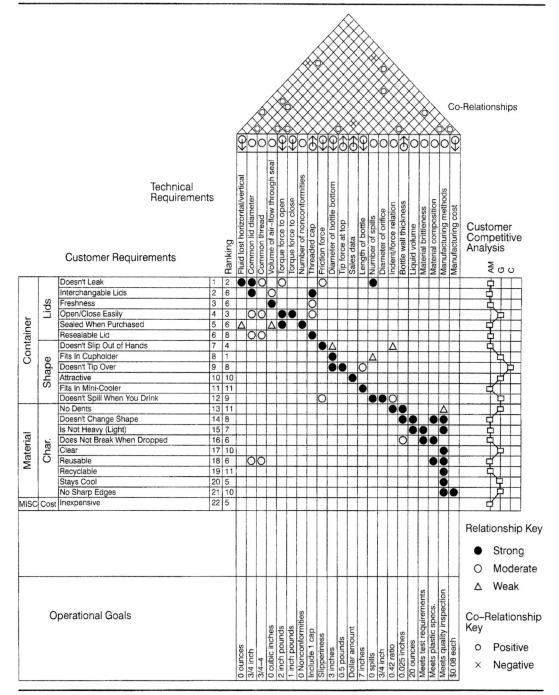

Figure 4.10   Co-relationships

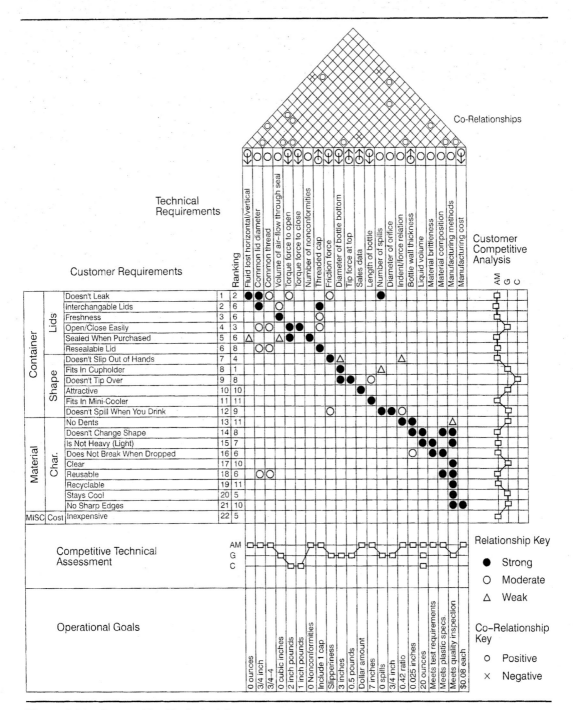

Figure 4.11   Competitive Technical Assessment

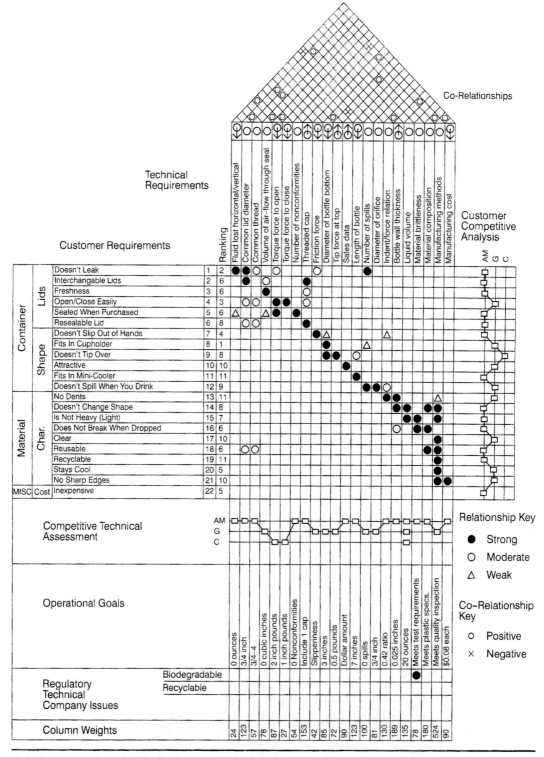

Figure 4.12   Column Weights and Regulatory Issues

AM Corp. studied the matrix they created and came to the following conclusions. In order to satisfy their customers and maintain a competitive advantage, they will have to focus their efforts on designing a sports drink bottle that:

Fits into a standard cup holder in a vehicle, that is, the base must not exceed 3 in.
Steps must be taken to ensure that the bottle does not leak at any time in any position. The technical requirements associated with this requirement are: the lid diameter must be no larger than ¾ in., there must be 4 threads per cap, and the cap must be reapplied at 1 in.-lb of force.
To meet the customer requirement that the bottle be easy to open and close, the new bottle design must require no more than 2 in.-lb of force to open and 1 in.-lb of force to close.
The design of the bottle must be such that it does not slip out of the drinker's hand easily. For this reason, the bottle diameter should be no smaller than 3 in. The type of plastic utilized must have the appropriate coefficient of friction.

BENCHMARKING

Six Sigma organizations often compare their performance against that of another firm in order to learn how they are performing in the marketplace. This act of comparing is called *benchmarking*. During a benchmarking process, a company compares its performance against a set of standards or against the performance of best-in-its-class companies. Judgments are made based on visual observations by the reviewers, interviews with those directly involved, and factual documentation. With the information provided by the comparison, a company can determine how and where to improve its own performance. Though companies may choose different aspects of their operations to benchmark, typical areas to benchmark include procedures, operations, processes, quality-improvement efforts, and marketing and operational strategies.

Benchmarking can be done at several levels of complexity. Some companies choose to conduct a benchmarking assessment at the perception level. A *perception benchmark assessment* focuses on internal issues, seeking to answer questions related to what the people within the company think about themselves, the management, the company, or the quality improvement process.

A *compliance benchmark assessment* verifies a company's compliance with established requirements and standards. The information gathered will answer questions about how a company is currently performing against the published standards, indicating where compliance to standards needs improvement.

A third type of benchmarking assessment investigates the effectiveness of a system a company has designed and implemented. An *effectiveness benchmark assessment* verifies that a company complies with the requirements and has effective systems in place to ensure that the requirements are being fulfilled.

The fourth type of benchmarking, a *continuous improvement benchmark assessment*, verifies that continuous improvement is an integral and permanent facet of an organization. It judges whether the company is providing lip service to process improvement issues or putting systems into place that support continual improvement on a day-to-day basis.

Six Sigma organizations use benchmarking to compare their key measures of performance with those of others in order to determine where improvement opportunities exist. Companies planning a benchmarking assessment should carefully consider the motivating factors. Specifically, why is the company planning to do this and what do they hope to learn? Those beginning a benchmarking assessment program should have plans in place to use the information generated by the comparison. A major pitfall of benchmarking is the failure to use the results of benchmarking to support a larger improvement strategy.

The following steps are usually facets of benchmarking.

1. *Determine the focus.* At the beginning of a benchmarking experience, those involved must determine what aspect of their company will be the focus of the study. The focus may be based on customer requirements, on standards, or on a general continuous improvement process. Information gathered during the benchmarking experience should support the organization's overall mission, goals, and objectives. Be aware that benchmarking and gathering information about processes is of greater value than focusing on metrics. The narrow focus on metrics can lead to stumbling over apples-and-oranges comparisons, while the focus on processes encourages improvement and adoption of new methods. To be of greater value, benchmarking should be a tool used to support a larger strategic objective.

2. *Understand your organization.* Critical to any process is defining and understanding all aspects of a situation. Individuals involved in the process need to develop an understanding of their company. To create a plan and conduct the process, information concerning the external customers, internal customers, and their major inputs and outputs is vital to achieve an understanding of the system under study. Often this step receives less attention than it should. Since people working for the company are performing the benchmarking assessment, the company is a known entity. Avoid the tendency to treat this step trivially. Use flowcharts to describe the processes involved. These will greatly enhance everyone's understanding of the system to be studied during benchmarking.

3. *Determine what to measure.* Once an understanding of the systems present in a company has been gained, it is time to determine the measures of performance. These measures will allow those conducting the benchmarking assessment to judge the performance of the company. This is the time to define what is truly critical for the company to remain competitive. These critical factors for success will be supported by standards for procedures, processes, and behaviors. Benchmarking will pinpoint questions to be answered and issues to be resolved, as well as processes and procedures to be improved. It is important to identify the questions pertinent to the company's particular operations. A well-developed list of items to be benchmarked will result in more consistent assessments and comparisons.

4. *Determine whom (or what, in the case of other benchmarks) to benchmark against.* Choices for whom to benchmark against should be made by considering the

activities and operations under investigation, the size of the company, the number and types of customers, the types of transactions, even the locations of facilities. Careful attention should be paid to selecting appropriate companies. Similarities in size and types of transactions or products may be more important in some instances than selecting a competitor. For instance, the bursar's office at a university may choose to benchmark against successful banking operations, not other universities' bursar's offices. A manufacturing company studying inventory control may be interested in the inventory control activities of a mail-order catalog operation. If the company is interested in beginning a quest for ISO 9000 certification, then the company might systematically select areas within its own operations to compare against the standard in order to check for compliance.

5. *Benchmark.* The areas of the company that have been chosen for the benchmarking assessment should be notified prior to beginning the process. The authorization to proceed with the process should be obtained and notification should come from the highest levels of the company to ensure cooperation. During the benchmarking process, investigators collect and analyze data pertaining to the measures established in step 3. Performance measures and standards that are critical to the success of the company are used to study the company. Investigators are charged with the duty of verifying compliance to the performance measures and standards. The ability to perform to those measures and standards is judged. Compliance can be verified on the basis of interviews of those involved and direct observation of the process.

6. *Improve performance.* Once the data and information have been gathered, a report summarizing the significant strengths and weaknesses of the area under study is created. In this report, the gap between the existing and the desired levels of performance is documented. A good report will focus on patterns of standards violations and elements missing from a strong system. The report does not need to detail each of the observations made by the investigators. It should not be a list of all the infractions seen.

In a successful benchmarking experience, the final report becomes a working document to aid the continuous improvement process. The information gathered in this report is used to investigate root causes, solve them, reduce process variation, and establish systems to prevent the occurrence of nonconformities.

SUMMARY

Through the use of quality function deployment and benchmarking, Six Sigma organizations take the customer information they have gathered, translate it into organizational actions, and disseminate this information throughout the organization. How do Six Sigma organizations capture the voice of the customer?

They ask them.

Is your organization hearing voices?

σ ■ *Take Away Tips*

1. Customer value perceptions are not the same as customer satisfaction perceptions.
2. Value refers to a product's or service's attributed or relative worth or usefulness.
3. Value is judged by a consumer each time they trade something of worth in order to acquire the product or service.
4. Customer satisfaction centers around how they felt the last time they bought a product or service from a company. It is a comparison between customer expectations and customer experience.
5. Six Sigma organizations study their processes from their customers' point of view.
6. QFD enables an organization to capture the voice of the customer.
7. QFDs translate customer's whats into an organization's hows.
8. During a benchmarking process, a company compares its performance against a set of standards or against the performance of best-in-field companies.
9. Benchmarking enables organizations to determine how and where to improve their own performance. ■

Chapter Questions

1. Why would an organization want to be effective at maintaining a customer focus?
2. What must an organization do to maintain a customer focus?
3. What are the benefits of maintaining a customer focus?
4. Using an example from personal experience, describe the difference between satisfaction and perceived value.
5. Describe the principal parts of a quality function deployment matrix.
6. How is each of the principal parts of a QFD matrix created? What does each part hope to provide to the users?
7. Why would a company choose to use a QFD?
8. Describe how you would begin creating a QFD.
9. Describe the steps involved in benchmarking.
10. Why would a company be interested in benchmarking? What would they hope to gain from a benchmarking assessment?

5

Teams

Much has been written about the "two pillars" of the Toyota production system—just-in-time and automation—designed by the late Taiichi Ohno. Although this remarkable combination played a large role in creating the efficiency and success of the Toyota Motor Company, these technological breakthroughs aren't the whole story. The fine-tuning that made the Toyota production system really work came not from upper management, nor from the engineers, but from the shop floor in the form of employee suggestions—over 20 million ideas in the last 40 years.

> *Yuzo Yasuda, 40 Years, 20 Million Ideas:*
> *The Toyota Suggestion System*

The whole employee involvement process springs from asking all your workers the simple question, "What do you think?"

> *Donald Peterson,*
> *Former Chairman of Ford Motor Co.*

▓ Objectives:

1. To discuss the importance of education and training
2. To introduce the topic of motivating employees
3. To introduce the concept of change management
4. To discuss the role of teams in a Six Sigma organization ▓

53

EDUCATION AND TRAINING

Six Sigma organizations employ effective people. These employees are the ones who perform their jobs well and understand how their job fits into the overall scheme of providing products and services to customers. Their knowledge, skills, and efforts are invaluable to the firm. Six Sigma organizations tap into the knowledge and skills of their employees to improve company competitiveness.

Six Sigma organizations take care to ensure that employees have the appropriate education and training that enables them to perform their job requirements at a level that supports the ultimate customer's needs, wants, and expectations. Part of this education and training includes information about how quality, cost, schedule, and profit expectations for their jobs affect customer satisfaction. Through regular feedback employees monitor the impact that their job has on each of these concepts.

Two of Dr. Deming's 14 points, *Institute training on the job* and *Institute a vigorous program of education and self-improvement* focus on education and training. Training refers to job-related skill training and is usually a combination of on-the-job training and classroom-type instruction. Compared to training, education provides individuals with a broader base of knowledge. This allows individuals to look at a situation from other viewpoints. The education an individual receives may not be immediately applicable to the activities they are currently performing.

Six Sigma employees are provided with the appropriate job-related skills training to give them the skills and knowledge set needed to excel in their jobs. One key skill that Six Sigma organizations make sure their employees have is problem-solving. Employees are trained to isolate the root causes of problems, utilize Six Sigma tools to gain improvements, and lock in the gains they achieve to make the improvements permanent. Chapter 8 covers basic problem-solving and introduces many root cause analysis Six Sigma tools. Follow-up or refresher training is also key to skill acquisition and retention. This type of training enables employees to maintain higher skill and performance levels by refamiliarizing employees with the best practices and eliminating poor habits.

MOTIVATING EMPLOYEES

Employees come to work to do a good job. They want a job that allows them to use their knowledge, skills, and abilities so that they can take pride in their work. Six Sigma leaders recognize these traits in their employees and build on them to motivate their people. If people don't come to work to do a bad job, why do things go wrong? Why are products produced and services provided that are unsatisfactory? Usually, faulty systems are at the root of the problem. Dr. Deming warned that if employees must utilize faulty systems, they will not be able to help performing poorly. As one of Dr. Deming's 14 points says, leadership must *remove barriers that rob people of their right to pride of workmanship*. Employees often face difficulties in performing their jobs that can only be removed by leadership. Six Sigma organizations recognize that it is leadership's responsibility to design and maintain non-faulty systems, thus allowing employees to work at their greatest level of productivity.

Changing conditions in the marketplace put pressure on organizations to make modifications to the way they do business. Leadership must communicate to the employees the desired change and motivate individuals to make the change. Dr. Deming once said that "*Nothing will happen without change. Your job as a leader is to manage the change necessary.*" Change is rarely easy. People resist change because humans are control-oriented and when their environments are disrupted, they perceive that they have lost the ability to control their lives. Some people are more resistant to change than others. Resistance can be based on the individual's frame of reference, their individual values, emotions, knowledge, and behavior.

Making change in any organization can be difficult if not impossible without the involvement and cooperation of the employees. It only takes moments to proclaim a new culture or a new method, but it takes a great deal longer to get people to act differently. Six Sigma leaders recognize that employees mold their behavior according to their interpretations of the signals leadership sends them. These signals may come as policies, requests, edicts, or from the day-to-day actions taken by leadership. Because actions speak louder than words, communicating through leadership actions and examples is paramount to changing behavior. To maximize the change process, Six Sigma leaders ensure that the worker/machine/computer interface, as well as the worker-to-worker interface, is compatible with the needs, capabilities, and limitations of the worker. Further, Six Sigma organizations ensure that the reward system matches the desired expectations in order to change behavior. Alignment must exist between rewards, expectations, leadership actions, and customer needs.

 SIX SIGMA TOOLS AT WORK

Making the Change

It is easy to tell someone else they have to change. But change isn't easy. Try to change one thing about yourself. Consider exercising more, eating healthier, or breaking an undesirable habit. To help with the change process, consider the following points and questions.

What is the desired end result? Can you picture it? To change, a person must understand what the ultimate outcome of that change will be.

What actions will you take to make the change? To change, a person takes a series of actions that produce a result that moves the individual toward the desired outcome. This result may be seen and interpreted as either positive or negative. Based on the interpretation of the result, the person modifies his or her attitude and acts differently the next time in order to produce a more appropriate result.

What is the time frame for the change? Change takes time, yet if no timetable exists, a person is likely to say "I'll get to that tomorrow." Effective change takes place when the person works toward the change according to a schedule.

How will you stay motivated? To change, it is necessary to stay motivated. Often, it is not easy to maintain the motivation and direction required to bring about change.

How will you know you have changed? What will your indicators be? A person needs to have some sort of feedback that enables them to understand how they are progressing toward the desired outcome. Otherwise, they may not recognize when the change is complete.

In the future, use these questions to guide you when making a change.

SIX SIGMA TEAMS

Many types of teams exist, including:

Management teams comprised of heads of departments to do strategic planning;

Cross-functional teams with representatives from a large variety of areas for the design or development of complex systems;

Self-directed work teams made up of employees grouped by complementary skills in order to carry out production processes;

Project or problem-solving teams, temporary groups of individuals from the appropriate functional areas with the necessary skills to work on a specific task, play a critical role in Six Sigma organizations.

Six Sigma project teams are given the task of investigating, analyzing, and finding a solution to problems. Project teams consist of people who have been given a mandate to focus on a particular process, area, or problem. Generally, this team is composed of those closest to the problem as well as a few individuals from middle management who have the power to effect change. The team may consist of people from a variety of departments depending on the problem facing them. The team may even include an outside vendor or a representative from the customer base. Upon resolution of the problem, the team will be disbanded or reorganized to focus on another project.

Henry Ford, founder of Ford Motor Corporation, said:

Coming together is the beginning. Keeping together is progress. Working together is success.

Six Sigma organizations recognize that teams are crucial to solving issues and problems facing the organization. Like Henry Ford, they also realize that teams do not always coalesce into highly functional entities without help. There are several stages of team development. Recognizing that teams experience growth throughout their existence helps leaders guide and direct team activities.

During the first stage, the team forms. This *formation* stage is usually experienced in the first few meetings. During this time, the team establishes its goals and objectives. It also determines the ground rules for team performance. For teams to work well, leadership must set clear goals that are aligned with the mission and strategic direction of the firm. When leadership sets the direction, the team is much more focused and tends not to get bogged down in the problem-selection process. The team must know the scope and boundaries that it must work within. Leadership must communicate how the team's progress and performance will be measured.

Oftentimes, following their formation, teams experience a rocky period where team members work out their individual differences. This is the time that the team gets acquainted with each other's idiosyncrasies and the demands of the project. During this *stormy* stage, the goals and scope of the team may be questioned. Since a team is composed of a group of individuals who are united by a common goal, the best teamwork will occur when the individuals focus on the team's objectives rather than personal motives. While working together, team members must understand and agree on the goals of the team. They must establish and adhere to team ground rules for behavior and performance expectations. To ensure harmony in the team, all members must participate and the responsibilities and duties must be fairly distributed. This means that each team member must understand what his/her role is in the completion of the project. Knowledge of how internal or external constraints affect the project is also helpful. Team members must possess a variety of skills, including problem-solving skills, planning skills, facilitation and communication skills, and feedback and conflict management skills.

The third stage of team development occurs when the team starts to work together smoothly. It is during this *performing* stage that things get accomplished. To be successful, teams need the appropriate skills in a supportive organizational culture and the authority to do the job that they have been asked to do. Leadership can do a lot to rid the team of the barriers that inhibit its performance. These barriers include: inadequate release time, territorial behavior from involved functional areas, lack of training, inadequate support systems, lack of guidance or direction, and lack of recognition. Senior leadership's sincere interest and support in the resolution of the problem is evidenced by their willingness to commit money and time for training in problem-solving and facilitation. In any case, senior leadership must monitor and encourage their teams to solve problems. The teams will quickly become unmotivated if the solutions they propose are consistently turned down or ignored. Leadership support will be obvious in management's visibility, diagnostic support, recognition, and limited interference.

As the team finishes its project, the final stage occurs, *concluding*. During this phase, team members draw the project to its conclusion, verify the results, and disband the team. Several key events take place during this time. The team, having taken action, perhaps by implementing a solution to a problem, must verify that what they planned to do got done and what they did actually worked. Teams are not finished when they have proposed a plan of action; teamwork is finished when the plans have been acted on and the results judged effective. Until then, the team cannot be disbanded.

SUMMARY

Six Sigma organizations engage in a continuous cycle of learning and training. To support this cycle of continuous improvement, Six Sigma organizations design recognition and reward systems that motivate their employees. These rewards are aligned with customer needs, wants, and expectations as identified in the strategic plan and supported leadership actions.

σ ■ *Take Away Tips*

1. Six Sigma organizations follow good human resource practices.
2. Six Sigma organizations provide employees with the knowledge and skills they need to do their jobs well in order to provide value for the customer.
3. Change isn't easy, an individual must be motivated to change.
4. Leaders are responsible for managing change.
5. Leaders are responsible for removing the barriers that prevent their employees from performing well.
6. Six Sigma organizations utilize teams to solve problems and enhance processes.
7. Participants on Six Sigma teams can expect their talents, skills, and personality types to be appreciated and used to their best advantage. ■

Chapter Questions

1. Describe the difference between education and training. Why is it important to have both?

2. Describe a situation where you received (or did not receive) job skill training. Was it adequate? Why? Why not? What would you have done differently?

3. Describe a situation where you received (or did not receive) an educational experience. Was it adequate? Why? Why not? What would you have done differently?

4. Describe a situation where a leader motivated you. What did he or she do? How did you react? Why?

5. Describe a change you were required to make. How did it go? What did the change accomplish? How was it accomplished? What motivated you?

6. Describe the phases of team development.

7. For each of the phases of team development, provide an example from your own experience describing how your team got through the phase.

8. How will you guide people who work for you or with you through a change process?

9. How will you motivate the people who work for or with you?

10. What types of activities do Six Sigma teams work on? What process do they use to do problem-sloving?

6

Project Management

How do you eat an elephant?
One bite at a time.

Unknown

■ Objectives:

1. To introduce the topic of project management
2. To familiarize the reader with project proposals
3. To familiarize the reader with project plans
4. To familiarize the reader with project schedules
5. To introduce the concept of Gantt charts
6. To introduce the concept of PERT charts
7. To introduce the concept of Critical Path Method

SIX SIGMA PROJECTS

Essentially, Six Sigma is about results, enhancing profitability through improved quality and efficiency. Six Sigma projects are chosen based on their ability to contribute to the bottom line on a company's income statement by being connected to the strategic plans, objectives, and goals of the corporation. Projects are essential in order for a Six Sigma organization to set their strategic plans in motion. By identifying projects that support meeting the goals and objectives established in the plan, an organization can more toward its ultimate vision of world-class performance.

PROJECT CHARACTERISTICS

Six Sigma projects have three basic characteristics: performance, cost, and time. Performance refers to what the project seeks to accomplish. Unlike day-to-day activities, projects are unique, one-time occurrences created to fulfill specific goals for the organization. Cost refers to the resources needed to complete a project. Most projects must be completed with a limited set of resources. These resources may be related to people, skills, time, money, equipment, facilities, or knowledge. Projects are complex and typically involve a variety of people from a number of areas within an organization. Projects normally have a specific time frame for completion with beginnings and endings clearly defined. Tasks within a project are sequenced, with one phase or activity being completed before another begun.

PROJECT SELECTION

Six Sigma projects are easy to identify, since the Six Sigma methodology seeks to reduce the variability present in processes, eliminate sources of waste, and focus on customer and environmental issues. Projects that do not directly tie to customer issues or financial results are often difficult to sell to management. When choosing a Six Sigma project, care should be taken to avoid poorly defined objectives or metrics. Key business metrics include revenue dollars, labor rates, fixed and variable unit costs, gross margin rates, operating margin rates, inventory costs, general and administrative expenses, cash flow, warranty costs, product liability costs, and cost avoidance.

Six Sigma organizations select projects based on the project's ability to contribute to one or all three of the following: customer perceived value and satisfaction, the organization's financial strength, or operational necessities. For customer-focused organizations, many projects will be selected based on their ability to increase customer value, satisfaction, and retention. Projects may be chosen in order to enable the organization to maintain its competitive edge. These projects may involve the development of a new product or service or an extension to a product line or the development of a product- or service-enhancing feature. These projects will ultimately enhance an organization's financial success. Some projects are operational necessities like meeting government regulations or the repair or replacement of aging equipment. Regardless of the reasons behind a project being selected, effective organizations recognize that a project must be financially sound and provide a payback for their investment.

SIX SIGMA TOOLS AT WORK

Computer Technology Transition and Upgrade Project Selection

Max's Munchies recently invited vendors to submit proposals for a technological upgrade of all of its desktop and laptop computers for all of its nationwide locations. The project has been titled Computer Technology Transition and Upgrade.

Max's Munchies maintains manufacturing facilities in 4 cities and sales offices in 12. The majority of the computers, 1600 in all, are located at the manufacturing facilities. The sales offices have 400 more. The company uses two computer platforms, desktops and laptops. Though these are limited to a narrow range of models, one of the goals of the Computer Technology Transition and Upgrade project is to create more uniformity company wide by selecting a single desktop model and a single laptop model. The company has selected the desired operating system and software applications that these computers must run.

PROJECT PROPOSALS

A project proposal is a document that provides clear information concerning the goals and objectives that a particular project hopes to achieve. Along with this information, the project proposal discusses how the project supports the overall mission, goals, and objectives of the organization. An effective Six Sigma project proposal provides readers with insight into what needs to be accomplished and how it will get accomplished. Through the use of clearly stated mission, deliverables, goals, and objectives associated with the project, proposals sell the project. As an introduction, proposals provide background information about the need for the project. They contain a description or overview of the expectations of the project, including details about the technical aspects of the project. Essential tasks are outlined and delineated. A thorough project proposal will contain information concerning financial requirements, time constraints, and administrative and logistical support for the project. The proposal contains information about the key individuals associated with the project, including the identity of the project manager. Basic areas of performance responsibility are assigned. Tentative schedules and budgets are established. Figure 6.1 gives a brief summary of the typical components of a project proposal.

The project proposal creates a general understanding of:

- What is needed
- What is going to be done
- Why it is going to be done
- Who is going to do it
- When it will be done
- Where it will be done
- How it will be done

The Project Proposal

General Project Description

Provide a detailed description of the project that includes a statement of
the project goals. Describe the major project subsystems or deliverables.
Include a preliminary layout design if applicable. Address any special
client requirements, including how they will be met.

- What is the purpose of the project?
- What is the scope of the project?
- Why should the project be selected?
- What is the life cycle (time from beginning to end) of the project?
- What is the complexity level of the project?
- Is there anything that makes the project unique?
- What measures will be used to judge the project's performance?

Implementation Plan

The implementation plan section contains a brief description listing the
major components of the project, with time estimates for each component.
This section also includes preliminary cost estimates and a preliminary
schedule for the major project components.

- What are the project deliverables?
- How will these deliverables be met?
- What level of risk is associated with the project?
- What are the costs associated with the project?
- What are the time estimates for the components of the project?

Logistic Support and Administration

This section describes the facilities, equipment, and skills that are needed
for the entire project.

- What difficulties may be encountered during the construction or
  implementation phase of the project?
- What contingency plans exist?
- Who will be the project manager?
- Who else will be necessary to help with this project?

**Figure 6.1   Project
Proposal Guidelines**

ESTABLISHING CLEAR PROJECT GOALS AND OBJECTIVES

Effective project proposals state clear project goals. Project goals are established for
three reasons:

To state what must be accomplished to complete the mission
To create commitment and agreement about the project goals among participants
To create clarity of focus for the project.

Six Sigma project managers recognize the importance of establishing clear goals and objectives for a project. They are careful to make sure that anyone working on the project, regardless of the level of their involvement, understands and supports these goals and objectives. Six Sigma project goals are stated in terms of the users' needs. Key questions to ask in order to ensure that a project proposal has a customer focus and clear project goals include:

Who are the end users?
What does the end user want from the project?
What does the end user say the project should do?

An effective goal statement is specific, measurable, agreed upon, realistic, and time-framed. When goals are specific, they are so well-defined that anyone with a basic knowledge of the project can understand them and recognize what the project is trying to accomplish. Measurable goals allow those involved in the project to judge how the project is progressing toward its mission. Agreement among project participants about the overall goals of a project is critical because without it, the project has little chance of achieving success. Participants include, but are not limited to, customers, leadership, and affected departments and individuals. Given that a project is to be accepted based on its ability to meet the mission, goals, and objectives of an organization, insisting that a project be realistic seems unnecessary. Here the word realistic refers to the need to be aware of the time frame established for the project, as well as the manpower and financing available to the project. Limited resources, whether time or money, or unrealistic expectations given the time, money, and talent available, are detrimental to a project. When a project is realistic, it is achievable given the resources, knowledge, and time available. Projects are selected to support the overall objectives of an organization. If a project is not completed within established time periods, chances are the organization has missed an opportunity for success. For this reason, it is critical that the project goals have clearly stated time frames for accomplishment of the project.

Project objectives are the specific tasks required to accomplish the project goals. Project objectives clearly align with and support the project goals. In some instances, several project objectives will be necessary to ensure the organization accomplishes a specific goal. They define who is responsible for accomplishing the goal, what resources are necessary, and what inputs will be needed. As with project goals, project objectives must also be specific, measurable, agreed upon, realistic, and time-framed.

Establishing clear goals with supporting objectives help Six Sigma project managers keep projects on track. Project managers use these goals and objectives as a way to reinforce the commitment of individuals to the project and the team. Well-written goals and objectives enhance communication, keeping everyone associated with a project aware of their role and what they need to do in order to keep the project on track. Goals and objectives also make it easy to see how far the project has progressed and what still needs to be done. Project proposals are submitted to organizational leadership who will judge each project based on its ability to help the organization meet its mission of achieving world-class performance.

SIX SIGMA TOOLS AT WORK

Computer Technology Transition and Upgrade Project Goals and Objectives

Max's Munchies has been working with vendors to clearly define the mission, goals, and objectives of the Computer Technology Transition and Upgrade project. The request for proposals sent to vendors states the mission as:

> *to upgrade all desktop and laptop computers to new models so the company can process more advanced applications in accounting, computer-aided design, and new business systems.*

This mission is supported by the following goals and objectives.

Goal: Upgrade existing computers

Supporting objectives:

- Specify a single desktop and laptop model that runs the appropriate software
- Install appropriate software on the new computers

Goal: Remove existing computers

Supporting objectives:

- Delete software on the old computers
- Dispose of existing computers in an environmentally friendly manner

Goal: Exchange of all computers in 15 weeks

Supporting objective:

- Handle the logistics of the exchange with the users

PROJECT PLANS

Once a proposal has been accepted, it becomes the framework or foundation of a project plan. Project plans are significantly more detailed than project proposals. Projects have three interrelated objectives: meeting the budget, finishing on schedule, and meeting the performance specifications. A good project plan enables an organization to accomplish all three. Though a project plan may be modified several times during a project, effective project plans remain key to organizational success. Project plans provide information about:

- Mission and deliverables
- Specific goals and objectives supporting the mission and its deliverables
- Tasks required to meet the goals and objectives
- Technicalities of who, what, where, when, why, and how

The Project Plan

The Project Plan

In the project plan the mission and deliverables are clarified. The plan also identifies the who, what, where, when, why, and how aspects of the project. The plan details how the project will be accomplished.

Project Plan Elements

- Overview (the mission and the deliverables; what will the final outcome will be?)
- Objectives (specific objectives supporting the mission)
- General Approach (technicalities of who, what, where, when, why, how)
- Contractual Aspects (specifics of who is required to do what)
- Schedules (what time is needed to support each aspect of the plan)
- Resources (what is needed to support each aspect of the plan)
- Personnel (who is needed to support each aspect of the plan)
- Evaluation Measures (performance, effectiveness, cost; how will the project be kept on track?)
- Potential Problems (what could go wrong? how will it be dealt with?)

Figure 6.2 Project Plan Guidelines

- Schedules—the time needed to support each aspect of the plan
- Resources—what is needed to support each aspect of the plan
- Cost analysis
- Value analysis
- Personnel—who is needed to support each aspect of the plan
- Personnel—responsibilities and assignments
- Evaluation measures for keeping the project on track
- Risk analysis—what could go wrong and how it will be dealt with
- Project change management process

Figure 6.2 gives a brief summary of the typical components of a project plan.

 SIX SIGMA TOOLS AT WORK

Computer Technology Transition and Upgrade Project Plan

The contractor whose proposal was accepted for the Computer Technology Transition and Upgrade project submitted the following project plan.

PROJECT MISSION
Contractor is responsible for developing and deploying a process for the replacement of all 2,000 computers—laptop and desktop—in a manner that minimizes user

and productivity disruption. This includes retrieving the old equipment from the user, setting up the new equipment for the user by loading saved files and new software, and disposing of the old equipment. This service must be accomplished in 15 weeks from the start date.

PROJECT GOALS AND SUPPORTING OBJECTIVES

The specific duties of the contractor are as follows:

Goal: Preparation Services

Objectives:

1. Assist Max's Munchies with the process of receiving and warehousing new computers. Max's Munchies will provide computer hardware and software and network cable connections.
2. Assist Max's Munchies in receiving old computers from users.
3. Perform the work on-site. This includes setup and connection of server cabling and tabletop equipment placement. Space where the contractor can perform the upgrade and exchange must be provided at each Max's Munchies location. Contractor's equipment must be utilized as much as possible during the changeover procedure.

Goal: Deployment Services

Objectives:

1. Burn a CD of the user's data from the old PC for backup. Provide to user.
2. Data transfer from user's old computer to new computer.
3. Load hardware and software onto new computers.
4. Maintain records of the asset exchange with the user.
5. Provide "morning after" assistance to users following setup.
6. Provide a Help Desk while the new computers are being deployed.

Goal: Remediation Services

Objectives:

1. Remove all data/computer programs from old computers before disposal.
2. Dispose of all old computers in an environmentally friendly manner.

Goal: Project Control

Information about project control is provided in a later example.

Goal: Schedule

The mission is to be accomplished in 15 weeks. The schedule is provided in a later Six Sigma Tools at Work feature.

Measures of Performance

- Price based on per computer cost
- Number of user difficulties experienced during changeover

- Amount of user downtime hours
- Time to effect changeover
- Changeovers per shift

Contingency Plans

Five extra computers have been planned for during rollout in case the count of computers exceeds 2,000.

Extra staffing will be available in case the rates of changeover are not high enough.

PROJECT SCHEDULES

Six Sigma project planners need to know how much time is available to complete the project. It is also helpful to know whether or not any flexibility exists with this deadline. Schedules convert a project plan into an operating timetable. This timetable is used to monitor and control project activity by showing the relationships among dates, times, activities/tasks, and people. For some people, combining longer term project expectations with pressing day-to-day activities is often detrimental to the completion of a project. There is always the tendency to put the project off just a little longer because of the perception that more time will be available in the future. Project schedules help remind people of the importance of working on the project on a regular basis.

In order to create a schedule, the following must be known: the tasks, the order in which they must be completed, when they must be completed, and the rate at which they can be completed. To schedule a project, the tasks and activities associated with a project plan are laid out according to the time they will take to complete. Once a list of activities has been created, time estimates for each activity are derived. Starting with the project due date, the activities are stepped backwards in time, eventually reaching a start date as all the activities are accounted for. Realistic time estimates need to be created in order to determine how much total time it will take to complete the activities and tasks associated with a project. As the project progresses, it is not unusual for technical difficulties to arise. These often take longer than originally planned to solve. In other cases, materials and manpower are unavailable or late resulting in changes to schedules and task sequencing that throw off time estimates.

Monitoring a project schedule is often done through the use of checkpoints and milestones. Milestones represent long-term or major events that have been or need to be completed for a project. To reach a milestone, a series of smaller activities or tasks will have taken place. Projects unfold as a logical sequence of activities take place or tasks are completed, therefore, the relationship between these activities is critical to any project. When taken out of order, these activities or tasks waste time and effort. Checkpoints are smaller points throughout a project that are used to judge how far the project is toward completion.

SIX SIGMA TOOLS AT WORK

Computer Technology Transition and Upgrade Project Schedule

The contractor whose project proposal was accepted for the Computer Technology Transition and Upgrade project submitted the following schedule with their project plan.

SCHEDULE

Major milestones and deployment rates are as follows. This schedule outlines the time frame and pace of activity.

Phase one: Project Preparation and Pilot Rollout

Week 1   Contractor's Project Manager begins.
Week 2   Pilot rollout begins: 10 PCs per day exchanged. Goal: 50 for the week.
Week 3   Pilot rollout continues: 12 PCs per day exchanged. Goal: 60 for the week.
Week 4   Pause for review of rollout. Some rollout will occur as necessary for
              priority needs (estimate 20 for the week).
                    Phase one checkpoint: 130
                    Phase one milestone: 130

Phase two: Rollout

Week 5   Main rollout begins. 20/day, 100 for the week.
Week 6   Main rollout: 25/day, 125 for the week.
Week 7   Main rollout: 30/day, 150 for the week.
Week 8   Main rollout: 30/day, 150 for the week.
                    Phase two checkpoint: 525
                    Phase two milestone: 655

Phase three: Rollout

Week 9   Main rollout: 40/day, 200 for the week.
Week 10   Main rollout: 40/day, 200 for the week.
Week 11   Main rollout: 40/day, 200 for the week.
Week 12   Main rollout: 40/day, 200 for the week.
                    Phase three checkpoint: 800
                    Phase three milestone: 1,455

Phase four: Wind-down

Week 13   Main rollout: 40/day, 200 for the week.
Week 14   Main rollout: 40/day, 200 for the week.
Week 15   Finishing activities: 30/day, 150 for the week.
                    Phase four total: 550
                    Phase four milestone: 2,005

Gantt charts, the Program Evaluation and Review Technique (PERT), and the Critical Path Method (CPM) are excellent tools for monitoring the complex links of activities associated with a project. Available on Microsoft Project, these charts are invaluable when scheduling a project. A Gantt chart, shown in Figure 6.3 for the Computer Technology Transition and Upgrade Project, enables the user to keep track of the flow and completion of various tasks associated with a project. The chart promotes the identification and assignment of clear-cut tasks while enabling users to visualize the passing of time. Divisions on the chart represent both an amount of time and a task to be done. A line drawn horizontally through a space shows the amount of work actually done compared to the amount of work scheduled to be done.

A PERT chart improves upon a Gantt chart by showing the relationships between tasks (Figure 6.4). Unlike the Gantt chart, which is a list of tasks, the PERT chart enables the project to be viewed as an integrated whole. Because it coordinates and synchronizes many tasks, it is well designed to handle complex projects. To create a PERT network:

1. Compile a list of events/tasks/activities.
2. Determine the relationships between the activities (predecessors, successors).
3. Begin constructing the diagram from the end, working back to the beginning. The key events/tasks/activities identified in step 1 are placed on the diagram between the nodes. Related nodes, those with predecessors and successors, are linked as shown in Figure 6.5.

 SIX SIGMA TOOLS AT WORK

Creating a PERT Network

The successful contractor for Max's Munchies Computer Technology Transition and Upgrade project submitted the following PERT Network with their project plan. To create the network, they completed the following steps:

1. Compile a list of events/tasks/activities.

- Set up work area
- Order computers
- Hire people to perform exchange/upgrade
- Train people to perform exchange/upgrade
- Phase 1
- Phase 2
- Phase 3
- Phase 4
- Set up equipment
- Test equipment

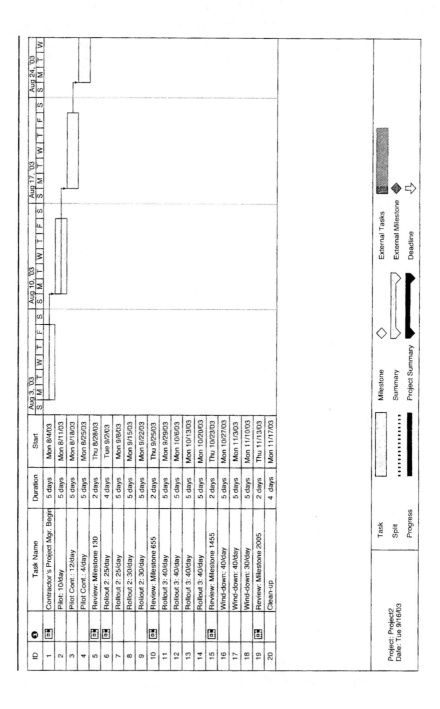

ID		Task Name	Duration	Start
1	▣	Contractor's Project Mgr. Begin	5 days	Mon 8/4/03
2		Pilot: 10/day	5 days	Mon 8/11/03
3		Pilot Cont.: 12/day	5 days	Mon 8/18/03
4		Pilot Cont.: 4/day	5 days	Mon 8/25/03
5	▣	Review: Milestone 130	2 days	Thu 8/28/03
6	▣	Rollout 2: 25/day	4 days	Tue 9/2/03
7		Rollout 2: 25/day	5 days	Mon 9/8/03
8		Rollout 2: 30/day	5 days	Mon 9/15/03
9		Rollout 2: 30/day	5 days	Mon 9/22/03
10	▣	Review: Milestone 655	2 days	Thu 9/25/03
11		Rollout 3: 40/day	5 days	Mon 9/29/03
12		Rollout 3: 40/day	5 days	Mon 10/6/03
13		Rollout 3: 40/day	5 days	Mon 10/13/03
14		Rollout 3: 40/day	5 days	Mon 10/20/03
15	▣	Review: Milestone 1455	2 days	Thu 10/23/03
16		Wind-down: 40/day	5 days	Mon 10/27/03
17		Wind-down: 40/day	5 days	Mon 11/3/03
18		Wind-down: 30/day	5 days	Mon 11/10/03
19	▣	Review: Milestone 2005	2 days	Thu 11/13/03
20		Clean-up	4 days	Mon 11/17/03

Project: Project2
Date: Tue 9/16/03

Task
Split
Progress

Milestone
Summary
Project Summary

External Tasks
External Milestone
Deadline

70

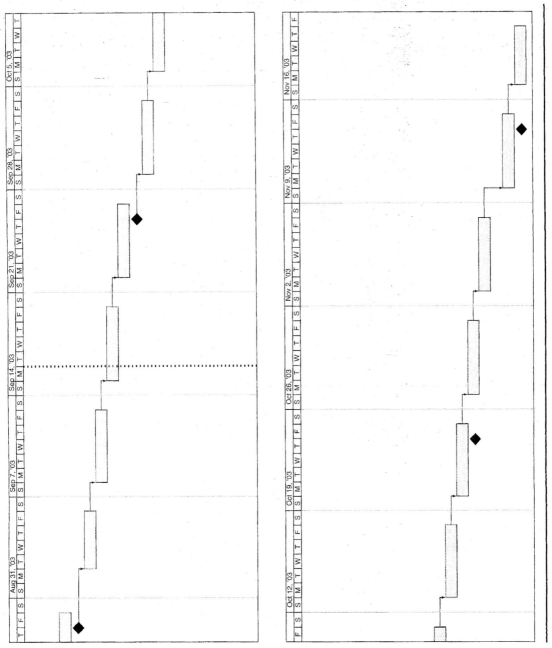

Figure 6.3 Gantt Chart

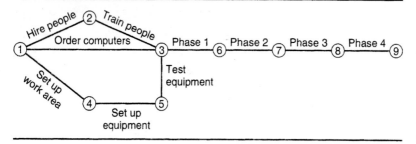

Figure 6.4   PERT Network

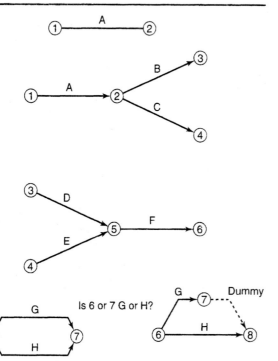

Figure 6.5   Common Network Structures

2. Determine the relationships between the activities (predecessors, successors).

Task	Predecessor
Set up work area (a)	—
Order computers (b)	—
Hire people to perform exchange/upgrade (c)	—
Train people to perform exchange/upgrade (d)	c
Phase 1 (e)	a, b, c, d, i
Phase 2 (f)	e
Phase 3 (g)	e, f
Phase 4 (h)	e, f, g
Set up equipment (i)	a
Test equipment (j)	a, i

3. Begin constructing the diagram from the end, working back to the beginning. The key events/tasks/activities identified in step 1 are placed on the diagram between the nodes as shown in Figure 6.4.

CPM builds on PERT by adding the concept of cost per unit time. CPM gets its name from its ability to determine the longest series of interrelated events that must be completed in a project, the critical path. To use this chart, both the times and the costs associated with the activities must be estimated. The following Six Sigma Tools at Work feature describes the creation of a CPM.

 SIX SIGMA TOOLS AT WORK

Creating a CPM

The steps to create a critical path begin much the same as creating a PERT network. Building on the previous example, to finish the CPM, follow these steps:

1. Compile a list of tasks/activities.
2. Determine the relationships between the activities (predecessors, successors; see Figure 6.6).
3. Determine the costs and times associated with the activities (Figure 6.6).
4. Begin constructing the diagram from the end, working back to the beginning (Figure 6.7).
5. Add up each of the individual paths to determine the critical path. The critical path for this example is 1-3-6-7-8-9 and equals 28 weeks. The other paths are 1-4-5-6-7-8-9 (24 weeks) and 1-2-3-6-7-8-9 (26 weeks)

Task	Predecessor	Weeks		Cost	
		Normal	Crash	Normal	Crash
Set up work area (a)	—	2	2	$25	0
Order computers (b)	—	13	7	$20	$5/wk
Hire people to perform exchange/upgrade (c)	—	6	3	$12	$6/wk
Train people to perform exchange/upgrade (d)	c	5	4	$25	$10/wk
Phase 1 (e)	a, b, c, d, i	4	3	$100	$20/wk
Phase 2 (f)	e	4	3	$100	$20/wk
Phase 3 (g)	e, f	4	3	$100	$30/wk
Phase 4 (h)	e, f, g	3	2	$100	$40/wk
Set up equipment (i)	a	5	4	$13	$2/wk
Test equipment (j)	a, i	2	1	$10	$3/wk

Figure 6.6   Precedents, Timing, and Costs (1000)

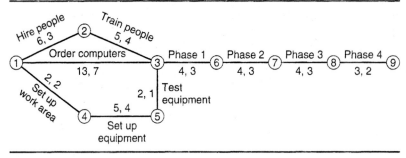

Figure 6.7   CPM

If the speed of the project needs to be increased for any reason, then the path can be "crashed" or shortened by determining which activities can be done more quickly. The critical path method also reveals the cost of doing each of these activities more quickly. For instance, if Max's Munchies wishes to complete the project in less than 28 weeks, they must decide whether or not to speed up the ordering of the computers or one of the four phases. Each week of increased speed in order processing will cost them $5,000 compared to increasing the speed of the actual transition at a cost of between $20,000 and $40,000.

PROJECT BUDGETING

Budgets are plans for allocating and monitoring the use of scarce resources. They set the overall estimates for the costs associated with a project. For budgets to be realistic, it is critical that the people actually closest to the work take part in determining the time and money needed for a project. In order to create a budget, the key activities taking place are studied and the time and money they need to be completed is estimated as best as possible. A complete budget will have information about any income or revenue expected during the life of the project, all expenses related to the project, and cash flow projections and their timing. Budgets are not arbitrary; effort should be taken to ensure that realistic cost and timing information has been found. Budgets should be monitored throughout the life of a project in order to keep project costs on track. Variances should be reported as soon as they are found. These variances can point to problems and recommended actions necessary to keep the project on target. Budgets can enable those working on a project to be aware of how their actions add or take away from the end result of the project.

PROJECT CONTINGENCY PLANS AND CHANGE CONTROL SYSTEMS

Projects, due to their very nature, are complex. For every project, there is a risk of failure. Organizing a project into manageable sections can reduce the fear of failure as well as the potential for failure. Effective project managers don't forget to ask: "What if?" They work with their project team members to identify potential activities or events that may derail a project. Contingency plans are created to ensure that the project team is ready to handle potential problems. While all problems cannot be foreseen, a project plan that includes contingency plans keeps the team flexible and aware that they may be asked to make adjustments to their project plan some time during its lifetime.

Effective project managers recognize that clients make changes to the project as it progresses. All project proposals and plans should contain a description of how requests for changes in the project's plan, budget, schedule, or performance deliverables will be handled. An effective change control system will have steps in place that review the requested changes for both content and procedure and identify how the change will impact the project. This impact must be reflected in adjustments to the project's performance objectives, the schedule, and the budget. Once accepted, change orders become part of the overall project plan. Part of the job of a change control system is to clearly communicate any changes to any person or part of the project affected by the change. The best way to ensure that this critical communication occurs is to have all changes approved in writing by all appropriate representatives of the impacted areas. Ultimately, the change should only be made if its benefits outweigh the costs of implementing the change.

PROJECT CONTROL

Throughout a project, effective project managers monitor the progress a project is making toward completion. Performance, cost, and time—the three aspects of a project—all need to be monitored and controlled in order to ensure project success. Performance of the project refers to the end result and the steps taken to get to it. The performance of a project may be affected by unexpected technical problems, quality or reliability problems, or insurmountable technical difficulties. For instance, a building may have its completion delayed because the foundation must be redone due to technical problems with the concrete being used. Performance of a project may also be affected by insufficient resources brought about by poor planning, logistical problems, or underestimating. Some performance problems may be brought about by the project's end user. The end user may have made a variety of changes to the original specifications for the project.

Project control and monitoring involves gathering and appraising information on how the project's activities compare with the project plan. Actual progress is tracked against the performance measures established in the project plan. These performance measures help a project manager assess how time, money, and other resources have been used to produce the expected outcomes. Many reasons exist why costs need to be monitored during a project. Technical difficulties may require more resources than originally planned. Client-related changes in specifications may have changed the scope of the work significantly, thus affecting the total costs of the project. Or the budget may have been inadequate in the first place due to inadequate estimates, poor projections for inflation, or additional costs due to client-related changes. Costs can also get out of control when the project costs are not watched closely and when corrective cost control is not exercised in time.

By closely monitoring the performance measures associated with the project, an alert project manager can be prepared to respond quickly to deviations in order to keep the project on track and under control. Though very few projects have not had their goals and objectives modified in some way or another from their beginning to their end, careful project control enables a project manager to minimize the effects of these changes on the overall project.

 SIX SIGMA TOOLS AT WORK

Computer Technology Transition and Upgrade Project Control

The project plan submitted by the contractor contained this section detailing project control goals and objectives.

GOAL: PROJECT CONTROL

Objectives:

1. The contractor will provide a project manager who is responsible for the entire scope of the project and the direction of the contractor's personnel involved in the project. This individual will be the single point of contact.
2. The contractor's project manager will develop the schedule and logistical planning for the Computer Technology Transition and Upgrade project. The schedule will include milestones based on the number of computers to be upgraded. The milestones will become the basis for the forecast on each phase of the project. The schedule will include resource planning indicating the level of staffing necessary to achieve project milestones.
3. The contractor's project manager will schedule and oversee all phases on the Computer Technology Transition and Upgrade project.
4. The contractor's project manager will supervise on-site personnel directly or have assigned supervisory person(s) during periods of critical processes.
5. The contractor's project manager will participate in review and problem-solving meetings scheduled over the course of the project.
6. The contractor will create processes and procedures that meet the objectives of schedule, user satisfaction in the equipment exchange, and inventory control.

PROJECT MANAGERS

An effective Six Sigma project manager achieves the desired results within budget and on time and according to the desired standards. Effective project managers realize that in order to accomplish what needs to be done on time and within budget, they must take time to plan their projects. Once a good plan has been created, effective project managers manage their plan.

Unlike functional managers, project managers are generalists with knowledge and experience in a wider variety of areas. A project manager is responsible for organizing, directing, planning, and controlling the events associated with a project. They deal with budgets and schedules. Responsibility for the project rests on their shoulders and they must understand what needs to be done, when it must be done, and where the resources will come from. Throughout a project, the manager will be the one who must clarify misunderstandings, calm upset clients, leaders, and team members, and meet the client's demands while keeping the project on time and within budget. Project managers are responsible for finding the necessary resources, motivating personnel, dealing with problems as they arise, and making project goal trade-offs. In essence, an effective project manager is an individual who does whatever is necessary to keep the project on schedule, within budget, and able to meet performance expectations. Project managers must be prepared to make adjustments to schedules, budgets, and resources in order to deal with the unexpected. For this reason, they must be good at recognizing the early signs of problems and be able to cope with stressful situations. As discussed under the heading of project plans, effective project managers utilize the checkpoints, activities, and time estimates established in the project plan to guide those working on the project. Following a clearly laid out project schedule with clearly delineated responsibilities enables effective project managers to keep their projects on track in terms of time, performance, and cost. Clear project plans enable the effective project manager to direct people both individually and as a team.

Project managers manage people as well as projects. To do this, effective project managers schedule frequent progress reports. These meetings allow the project managers to react quickly when they recognize that a difficulty has arisen. Effective meetings are essential when working on a project.

Due to the very nature of a project, the people associated with a project are temporary, and the project work they do is often in addition to their regular jobs. If this is the case, how does a project manager maintain the commitment and involvement of these individuals in order to get the project done? A project manager must motivate these individuals. This can be done in a variety of ways, including increasing the person's visibility in the organization. In other words, make sure people working on the project are recognized for their work and what they have accomplished. Project managers also have it within their power to create interesting and challenging possibilities for their team members. As discussed in the chapter on teams, people are much more motivated to perform when their assigned tasks enable them to use and stretch the talents, skills, and knowledge they already possess. Another powerful tool a project manager possesses is praise. People like being recognized publicly and privately for a job well done.

SUMMARY

Projects, when chosen because they support the overall goals and objectives of an organization, fulfill the strategic plan and move the organization toward its vision and mission. Without projects, organizations lack a long term vision and instead focus solely on doing day-to-day activities. Conversely, poorly managed projects are costly for an organization. A project that does not achieve its goals and objectives, or one that is not aligned with the goals and objectives of the organization, wastes time, money, and other resources.

σ ■ *Take Away Tips*

1. Six Sigma organizations recognize that projects managed by people with good project management skills are crucial to the success of an organization.
2. Six Sigma organizations select projects that support the organization's mission and goals.
3. Projects have three objectives: performance, cost, and schedule.
4. Project proposals are the documents that sell a project. They concentrate on the goals and objectives that a project hopes to achieve.
5. Project goals create clarity of focus for a project.
6. Project plans provide details related to how a project will be accomplished, including:

   - Mission and deliverables
   - Goals and objectives
   - Tasks
   - Technicalities
   - Schedules
   - Resources
   - Cost analysis
   - Value analysis
   - Personnel
   - Evaluation measures
   - Risk analysis
   - Change management process

7. Project plans should include contingencies.
8. Gantt charts show the flow and completion of tasks within a project.
9. PERT charts show the relationships between tasks in a complex project.
10. CPM builds on PERT by adding the concept of cost per unit time. ■

Chapter Questions

1. Why are project management skills important to apply in order to be effective?

2. Describe the three basic project characteristics in terms of a project you have worked on.

3. Why is completing a project like eating an elephant?

4. How is a project selected to be worked on?

5. What are the components of an effective project proposal?

6. Consider a project you are working on either at work or at school. Using the guidelines presented in this chapter, write a project proposal. Why should your project proposal be accepted? Are the reasons for selecting your project apparent in your proposal?

7. What are the components of an effective project plan?

8. Consider a project you are working on either at work or school. Using the guidelines presented in this chapter, write a project plan. Are the project's goals and objectives clearly stated? How do you know?

9. Create a Gantt chart for a project you are working on either at work or at school.

10. What differentiates a Gantt chart from a PERT chart from a CPM?

11. A not-for-profit organization is interested in buying caramels and selling them to raise money. Create a PERT chart for the following information.

		Weeks		Cost	
Task	Predecessor	Normal	Crash	Normal	Crash
Design ads (a)	—	2	2	$250	0
Order stock (b)	—	12	8	$200	$35/wk
Organize salespeople (c)	—	6	3	$120	$60/wk
Place ads (d)	a	3	2	$25	$10/wk
Select distribution sites (e)	c	4	3	$100	$20/wk
Assign distribution sites (f)	c, e	4	3	$100	$10/wk
Distribute stock to salespeople (g)	c, e, f	2	1	$100	$25/wk
Sell caramels (h)	e, f, g	5	3	$100	$40/wk

12. Complete a CPM for the information in Question 11.

13. The leaders of the project in Question 12 want to speed up their project by three weeks. What would be the most cost effective way of accomplishing that?

14. What does it mean to keep a project under control? How is a project controlled?

15. What are contingency plans? Why is it important to have contingency plans?

16. What is a change control system? How are they structured? What are they used for?

17. What does it take to be an effective project manager?

7

Measures and Metrics

If you don't drive your business, you will be driven out of business.

B. C. Forbes

■ **Objectives:**

1. To show the link between achieving Six Sigma performance levels and the use of measures
2. To familiarize the reader with the design of measures and metrics
3. To familiarize the reader with the costs of poor quality ■

81

MEASURES AND SIX SIGMA

Very simply, what gets measured gets done. For that reason, measures play a significant role in Six Sigma organizations. Six Sigma organizations recognize that if they cannot measure, they cannot manage. They understand that measures tell them how they are progressing toward their strategic goals and objectives. They know that if they do not have sufficient information about a process, product, or service, they cannot control it. And if a process cannot be controlled, the organization is at the mercy of chance. Six Sigma organizations manage their employees, processes, scheduling, production cycle times, supplier partnerships, shipping, and service contracts far better than their competition. Effective performance measurement systems are used for understanding, aligning, and improving performance at all levels and in all parts of the organization.

Metrics or measures are indicators of performance. Properly designed measures, by comparing past results with current performance, enable leaders to answer the questions, *"How are we doing?"* and *"How do we know how well we are doing?"* Leaders of Six Sigma projects use key process input variables (KPIV) and key process output variables (KPOV) as measures of performance to ensure alignment between the organization's mission, objectives, and strategic plan. KPIVs and KPOVs are the measures of performance that define a Six Sigma project's success numerically by linking it to the strategic plan as well as the organization's bottom line. Key business metrics include revenue dollars, labor rates, fixed and variable unit costs, gross margin rates, operating margin rates, inventory costs, general and administrative expenses, cash flow, warranty costs, product liability costs, and cost avoidance.

 SIX SIGMA TOOLS AT WORK

Justifying a Project

Queensville Manufacturing Corporation creates specialty packaging for automotive industry suppliers. The project team has been working to improve a particularly tough packaging problem involving transporting finished transmissions to the original equipment manufacturer (OEM). Company management has told the team that several key projects, including theirs, are competing for funding. In order to improve the chances of their project being selected, the team developed strong metrics to show how investment in their project will result in significant cost savings and improved customer satisfaction through increased quality. After brainstorming about this project, the team developed the following list of objectives and metrics for their project:

By retrofitting Packaging Machine A with a computer guidance system the following will improve:

Capacity:

KPOV: Downtime reduction from 23% to 9% daily
        (downtime cannot be completely eliminated due to product changeovers)

KPIV: Resource consumption reduction

20% less usage of raw materials such as cardboard and shrink-wrap due to an improved packaging arrangement allowing five transmissions per package instead of four previously achieved

Customer satisfaction:

KPOV: Improved delivery performance

Improved packaging arrangement integrates better with customer production lines saving 35% of customer production time

KPIV: Reduced space required for in-process inventory

Improved packaging arrangement allowing five transmissions per package instead of four previously achieved saving 10% of original factory floor space usage

KPOV: Reduced defect levels due to damage from shipping

Improved packaging arrangement provides better protection during shipment saving 80% of damage costs

Revenue:

KPIV: Reduced costs

$600,000 by the third quarter of the following fiscal year given a project completion date of the fourth quarter of this fiscal year

KPOV: Reduced lost opportunity cost

Increased customer satisfaction will result in an increased number of future orders

This project was selected as a focus for Six Sigma improvement because it could be justified by the impact it would have on overall organization performance.

Any organization recognizes the importance of working on activities that enhance bottom line performance. Leaders use measures of performance to select appropriate Six Sigma projects. Good measures of performance are designed based on what is valued by the organization and its customers. Well-designed measures encompass the priorities and values of both. Essentially, performance measures enable an organization to answer the following questions about a Six Sigma project:

- How well is something performing its intended purpose?
- Is the organization able to measure the impact of the changes being made?
- How does the organization know it has allocated its assets correctly?

Well-constructed measures are aligned with strategic goals of the organization as well as their customers' priorities. Willingness to use measures increases when performance measures are relevant to the organization operationally and, where applicable, to the individual personally. Usability is also a function of understandability. This makes measures that are clearly written and focused more powerful than ones that are oblique or lengthy.

Schedule/Delivery Performance
Throughput
Quality
Downtime
Idle Time
Expediting Costs
Inventory Levels
Work-in-Process Levels
Safety, Environment, Cleanliness, Order
Use of Space
Frequency of Material Movement

Figure 7.1   Process Measures

Measures of performance can be found in two categories: processes and results. Processes exist to get work done. They are the activities that must take place in order to produce a product or provide a service. Since processes are how organizations do the work that they do, process measures monitor operational activities or how the work is done (Figure 7.1).

Results relate to both organizations and their customers. To an organization, results are the objectives the organization wants to achieve. From a customer point of view, results represent what they hope to obtain by doing business with the organization, whether it be a product or a service. Performance measures related to organizational results focus on strategic intent (Figure 7.2). Performance measures related to customer results concentrate on the attributes of products and services (Figure 7.3). Products and services are created by the organization and purchased by customers. Products can be tangible manufactured items or information products such as reports, invoices, designs, or courses. Services received by customers are even more varied. Organizations may provide anything from information to dental work to entertainment products like movies, games, or amusement park rides.

Measures need to be integrated and utilized throughout the entire organization. Traditionally, organizations have focused their attention on measures related to the financial aspects of doing business, such as revenues, profits, and earnings. Effective

Market Share
Repeat/Retained Customers
Product Line Growth
Name Recognition
Customers/Employees Ratio
Pretax Profit

**Figure 7.2   Organizational Results
Performance Measures Focused
on Strategic Intent**

Scrap
Rework
Downtime
Repair Costs
Warranty Claims
Complaints
Liability Costs

**Figure 7.3   Customer Results
Performance Measures
Related to Product or Service
Attributes**

organizations realize that the outcomes, processes, products, and services of their business must be measured. Figure 7.4 provides some traditional measures as well as a broader range of measures.

The Balanced Scorecard method, introduced by Robert Kaplan and David Norton, goes beyond financial measures and integrates measures from four areas. These measures focus on key business processes and are aligned into a few manageable indicators of performance so that management is able to quickly access the short-term and long-term health of the organization. The Balanced Scorecard combines and categorizes process and results measures into four areas: Customer Focus, Internal Processes, Learning and Growth, and Financial Analysis.

When designing measures related to Customer Focus, the emphasis is on connecting with the customer, determining what the customer is interested in achieving, and using that information to translate the mission and strategy statements into specific market-based and customer-based objectives. In other words, what must the organization deliver to its customers to achieve high degrees of satisfaction, retention, acquisition, and eventually, market share? What is the organization going to do for its customers that will make them want to buy from the organization time and time again? These measures identify and monitor the level of value propositions the organization delivers to targeted customers and market segments. *Value propositions are the attributes that the product or service has that meets customer needs, wants, and expectations.* They are indicators that the customers are satisfied. These measures are in three categories:

1. Product or service attributes related to functionality, price, and quality
2. Customer relationship attributes such as delivery, response time, convenient access, responsiveness, and long-term commitment
3. Image and reputation attributes which are more intangible factors that attract a customer

Traditional Measures	Overall Organization Measures
Revenues	Employee Satisfaction, Growth, and Development
Profits	
Growth	Customer Survey Results
Earnings	Number of Completed Improvement Projects
Return on Investment (ROI)	
Sales Revenue	Cost of Poor Quality (COPQ) Reduction
Total Expenses	Vendor Quality Rating
Number of Customers	Return on Process Improvement Investment
Number of Repeat Buyers	
Payroll as a Percent of Sales	Safety, Environment, Cleanliness, Order
Number of Customers per Employee	Condition and Maintenance of Equipment/Tools
Number of Customer Complaints	
Complaint Resolution Rating	
Schedule Achievement	

Figure 7.4   Traditional and Broader Performance Measures

Internal Processes measures study the effectiveness and efficiency of the processes performed by the organization in order to fulfill customer requirements. When designing these measures, effective organizations identify the internal processes that are most critical for achieving customer and shareholder objectives. Once these key processes have been identified, measures are developed that concentrate on monitoring the improvement efforts in the areas of quality, response time, and cost. This information is used to determine if the current processes serve the customer effectively, if these are the best processes, and if they are operating at their best.

Learning and Growth measures monitor the individual and group innovation and learning occurring within an organization. These measures focus on the ability of the organization to enhance the capability of their people, systems, and organizational processes. Recognizing that this is a long-term effort, emphasis is placed on the development of employee capabilities, the development of information system capabilities, and employee motivation, retention, productivity, and satisfaction. These measures are used to judge whether or not the organization has employees who have sufficient information and the right equipment to do their jobs well. The measures also serve those interested in finding out whether or not employees are involved in the decisions affecting them, and how much recognition and support employees receive. They can also be used to evaluate employee skills and competencies and compare this information with what employees will need in the future. These measures can also be used to monitor the morale and climate within the organization.

Financial Analysis measures are perhaps the measures with which people are the most familiar. These measures track the organization's performance in the financial arena. These measures are focused on monitoring financial performance. Examples of financial measure include revenue levels, cost levels, productivity, asset utilization, and investment risk. Examples of each of the four types of measures are provided in Figure 7.5.

 SIX SIGMA TOOLS AT WORK

Indicators or Measures of Performance

Leaders of PM Printing and Design created their strategic plan in order to communicate to their employees the importance of creating and maintaining a customer-focused process orientation as they improve the way they do business. Their indicators or measures of performance reflect this desire.

Customer Measures

Results measures	Overall customer satisfaction (KPOV)
	Market share (KPOV)
	■ Number of customers
	■ Number of repeat customers
	■ Number of new customers
Process measures:	Time to complete customer order (KPIV)

Financial Measures

Results measures: Cost per printed unit (impression) (KPOV)
Profitability (KPOV)
Return on investment (KPOV)

Process measures: Cost avoidance (performing work in-house versus contracting work) (KPIV)

Internal Measures

Results measures: Improvements in hours paid vs. hours billed (KPIV)

Process measures: Improvements in job turnaround time (KPIV) (cycle time reduction/removal of non–value-added activities)

Improvements in billing lag time (KPIV) (cycle time reduction/removal of non–value-added activities)

Improvements in first time through quality (KPIV) (reduction in rework/scrap)

Learning and Growth Measures

Results measures: Improvements in employee retention (KPIV)

Process measures: Progress toward cross-training goals for critical processes as identified by customers (KPIV)

Financial Measures

Sales Revenues
Total Expenses
Pretax Profit
Return on Investment

Customer Measures

Number of Customers
Number of Repeat Buyers
Customer Survey Results
Number of Customer Complaints
Complaint Resolution Rating
Name Recognition
Price Differentials
On-Time Delivery
Response Time

Internal Measures

Payroll as a Percent of Sales
Number of Customers per Employee
Cost of Poor Quality
Employee Survey Results
Throughput Yield
Quality Level
Product/Service Cost
Productivity
Employee Morale

Learning and Growth Measures

Number of Teams
Number of Completed Projects
Number of Percentage of Employees
    Involved
Number and Percentage of Employees
    Involved in Educational Opportunities

Figure 7.5   Measures of Performance

Measures are not without their pitfalls. The number of measures used by an organization must be reasonable in order to be effective. It is critical to determine what needs to be measured and why it needs to be measured before designing a measure of performance. Measures for measurement's sake must be avoided. Too many measures, or unfocused measures, lead to hesitation in the users. Care must be taken to establish meaningful and actionable measures. For instance, if the measure is stated as "Improve contact with customers," there is little room for defining what is actually being measured or the effectiveness of activities designed to enhance contact with the customers. Measures need to be specific and quantitative in order to be effective. For example, "Visit five customer accounts per month" or "Decrease scrap on Line 2 by 5% in six months" is significantly more specific and actionable as well as more measurable when compared to the generic statements "improve contact" or "reduce waste." It is also critical to ensure that the right things are being measured. Sometimes the choice is made to measure the easy actions rather than the important actions. This leads to measures that are merely counts of actions rather than indicators of business opportunities. In other cases, measures may be too abstract. Though the measure may sound good on paper, it cannot be achieved because few understand what it means. One key question to ask is, "If only one item, parameter, type of result, and so on, could be measured in order to assess the performance of the organization at a given level, what would it be?"

When developing measures, consider the following:

> What does the organization need to know?
> What is currently being measured?
> How does what the organization needs to know compare with what is currently being measured?
> How is this information being captured?
> Is the information currently being captured useful?
> Is the information currently being captured being used?
> What old measures can be deleted?
> What new measures are appropriate?
> Do the identified, selected, and measured factors reflect what the customers need, require, and expect?
> Are these measurements being captured over time?
> Are these selected factors actionable within the organization?
> Can the impact of the changes made be measured?
> Have the organization's assets been allocated correctly?

Measures must be defined in objective terms. The best measures are easy to express as a numerical value. Valuable measures show progress toward the milestones of strategic goals and objectives. Measures are useful and effective when those using them can identify how the measure enables them to make better decisions in relation to their day-to-day activities.

SIX SIGMA TOOLS AT WORK

Measures of Patient Care

In response to customer complaints about substandard treatment, hospitals are taking steps to measure patient satisfaction and make improvements based on this information. To create more patient-centered care, hospitals need to understand patient experiences by looking at processes from the patients' point of view. Measuring patient-centered care is more complex than the traditional measures of performance that hospitals have used in the past, requiring a new set of performance measures. The new measures of performance focus on more subjective patient issues, such as how patients feel about the way they are treated, and how kindness and courtesy of the staff affected their experience. Previously, most of the measures have focused on safety and quality standards, such as how many infections were contracted during patient hospital stays, or the number of heart-bypass surgeries or C-sections a hospital performs in a year. Though there is a tendency to view the "soft stuff" as unimportant, more and more hospitals are developing measures of performance that focus on the patient. These patient-care focused measures of performance may include how well-informed of their condition and treatment patients felt they were, the patient's physical comfort and pain relief, the emotional support they received, the respect they received for their preferences and expressed needs, and how well hospitals prepared them for caring for themselves at home. Hospitals use this information to improve the level of care they offer their patients. Some examples of measures of performance are given in Figure 7.6.

Financial Measures

Total Expenses
Return on Investment (ROI)

Customer Measures

Number of Patients Treated
Patient Survey Results
Number of Patient/Customer
 Complaints
Complaint Resolution Rating
Kindness Rating
Staff Courtesy Rating
Patient Information Availability
Patient Comfort Rating
Patient Pain Relief
Patient Readmittance Rate

Internal Measures

Medicine-Dispensing Error Rate
Number of Patients per Employee
Length of Stay
Quality Level
Safety Rating
Number of Surgeries
Infection Rates

Learning and Growth Measures

Number of Teams
Number of Completed Projects
Number of Percentage of Employees
 Involved
Number and Percentage of Employees
 Involved in Educational Opportunities

Figure 7.6   Measures of Performance for a Hospital

COSTS OF QUALITY

Products and services featuring what the customer wants at a competitive price will result in increased market share and therefore higher revenue for a company. Companies whose products and processes are defect-free enjoy the benefits of faster cycle times, lower warranty costs, and reduced scrap and rework costs. These lead to lower total cost for the product or service, which leads to more competitive pricing, which results in higher revenue for the company. Six Sigma organizations manage their processes to improve the bottom lines on their income statements. Investigating the costs associated with quality provides managers with an effective method to judge the economics and viability of a quality-improvement system. Quality costs serve as a baseline and a benchmark for selecting improvement projects.

 SIX SIGMA TOOLS AT WORK

Costs of Quality

Over a 17-year period, airlines have been trying to reduce the number of lost bags (Figure 7.7). As of the year 2006, the average number of lost bags per 1000 passengers was 6.0. This means that 99.994% of the passengers and their luggage arrive at the same airport at the same time. Why would an airline company be interested in improving operations from 99.994%? Why isn't this good enough? What are the costs of quality in this situation?

In the case of lost luggage, the types of quality costs are numerous. For instance, if a passenger is reunited with their luggage after it arrives on the next flight, the costs of quality include passenger inconvenience, loss of customer goodwill, and perhaps the cost of a gesture of goodwill on the part of the airline in the form of vouchers for meals or flight ticket upgrades.

As the scenario becomes more complex, a wider array of quality costs exist. For example, if an airline must reunite 100 bags with their owners per day at a hub airport such as Atlanta or New York, the costs can be enormous. The expenses associated with having airline employees track, locate, and reroute lost bags might run as high as 40 person-hours per day at $20/hour for a cost of $800/day. Once located, the luggage must be delivered to the owners, necessitating baggage handling and delivery charges. If a delivery service were to charge $1 per mile for the round-trip, in larger cities, the average cost of delivering that bag to a customer might be $50. One hundred deliveries per day at $50 per delivery equals $5,000. Just these two costs total to $5,800/day or $2,117,000 per year! This doesn't include the cost of reimbursing customers for incidental expenses while they wait for their bags, the costs of handling extra paperwork to settle lost bag claims, loss of customer goodwill, and negative publicity. Add to this figure the costs associated with bags that are truly lost ($1,250 for domestic flights and $9.07 per pound of checked luggage for international travelers) and the total climbs even higher. And these figures are merely the estimated cost at a single airport for a single airline!

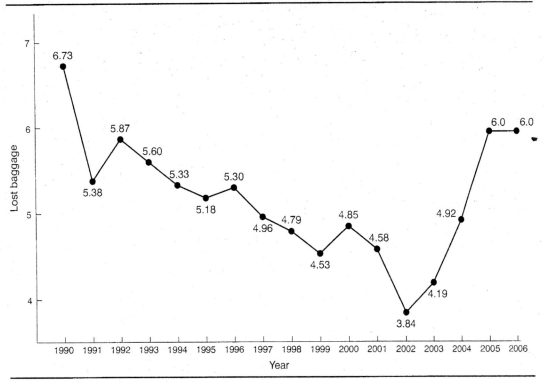

Figure 7.7   Mishandled Luggage (per 1000 Passengers)
SOURCE: K. Choquetter, "Claim Increase for Lost Baggage Still up in the Air," *USA Today*, March 17, 1998, and www.dot.gov/airrconsumer.

Consider the more intangible effects of being a victim of lost luggage. If customers view airline baggage handling systems as a black hole where bags get sucked in only to resurface sometime later, somewhere else, if at all, then consumers will be hesitant to check bags. If the ever-increasing amount of carry-on luggage people board the plane with is any indication, fears of lost luggage do exist. Carry-on baggage presents its own problems, from dramatically slowing the process of loading and unloading of the plane, to shifting in-flight and falling on an unsuspecting passenger when the overhead bins are opened during (or after) the flight, to blocking exits from the airplane in an emergency. These costs, such as fees for delayed departure from the gate or liability costs, can be quantified and calculated into a company's performance and profit picture. Is it any wonder that airlines have been working throughout the past decade to reduce the number of lost bags?

Quality costs can originate from anywhere within a company. Any time a process is performed incorrectly, quality costs are incurred. Costs of quality, poor-quality cost, and cost of poor quality are all terms used to describe the costs associated with providing a quality product or service. *A **quality cost** is considered to be any cost that a company* *incurs to ensure that the quality of the product or service is perfect. Quality costs are the portion of the operating costs brought about by providing a product or service that does not conform to performance standards. Quality costs are also costs associated with the prevention of poor quality.* The most commonly listed costs of quality include scrap, rework, and warranty costs. As Figure 7.8 shows, these easily identified quality costs are merely the tip of the iceberg. Quality costs can be measured and tracked. These measures can be used to guide improvement efforts.

Prevention Costs

Prevention costs *are those costs that occur when a company is performing activities designed to prevent poor quality in products or services.* Prevention costs are often seen as front-end costs designed to ensure that the product or service is created to meet customer requirements. Examples of such costs are design reviews, education and training, supplier selection and capability reviews, and process improvement projects. Prevention efforts try to determine the root causes of problems and eliminate them at the source so reccurrences do not happen. The initial investment in improving processes is more

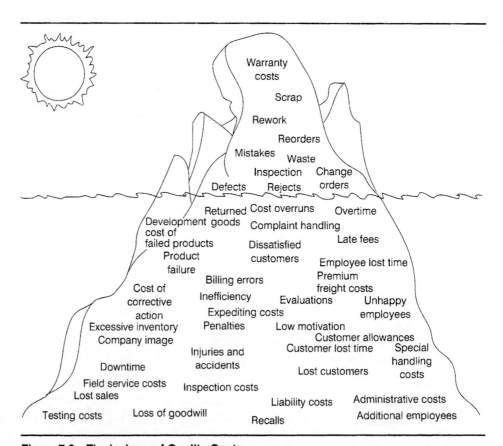

Figure 7.8   The Iceberg of Quality Costs

than compensated by the resulting cost savings. Preventing the nonconformity before it is manufactured or prepared to serve the customer is the least costly approach to providing a quality product or service.

Appraisal Costs

Appraisal costs are the costs associated with measuring, evaluating, or auditing products or services to make sure that they conform to specifications or requirements. Appraisal costs are the costs of evaluating the product or service during the production of the product or the providing of the service to determine if, in its unfinished or finished state, it is capable of meeting the requirements set by the customer. Appraisal activities are necessary in an environment where product, process, or service problems are found. Appraisal costs can be associated with raw materials inspection, work-in-process (activities-in-process for the service industries) evaluation, or finished product reviews. Examples of appraisal costs include incoming inspection, work-in-process inspection, final inspection or testing, material reviews, and calibration of measuring or testing equipment. When the quality of the product or service reaches high levels, then appraisal costs can be reduced.

Failure Costs

Failure costs occur when the complete product or service does not conform to customer requirements. Two types exist: internal and external. *Internal failure costs are those costs associated with product nonconformities or service failures found before the product is shipped or the service is provided to the customer.* Internal failure costs are the costs of correcting the situation. The failure costs may take the form of scrap, rework, remaking, reinspection, or retesting. *External failure costs are the costs that occur when a nonconforming product or service reaches the customer.* External failure costs include the costs associated with customer returns and complaints, warranty claims, product recalls, or product liability claims. Since external failure costs have the greatest impact on the corporate pocketbook, they must be reduced to zero. Because they are highly visible, external costs often receive the most attention. Unfortunately, internal failure costs may be seen as necessary evils in the process of providing good-quality products or services to the consumer. Nothing could be more false. Doing the work twice, through rework or scrap, is not a successful strategy for operating in today's economic environment.

Intangible Costs

How a customer views a company and its performance will have a definite impact on long-term profitability. *Intangible costs—hidden costs associated with providing a nonconforming product or service to a customer—involve the company's image.* Intangible costs of poor quality, because they are difficult to identify and quantify, are often left out of quality cost determinations. They must not be overlooked or disregarded. Is it

Prevention Costs

Quality planning
Quality program administration
Supplier-rating program administration
Customer requirements/expectations
   market research
Product design/development reviews
Quality education programs
Equipment and preventive maintenance

Appraisal Costs

In-process inspection
Incoming inspection
Testing/inspection equipment
Audits
Product evaluations

Failure Costs

Internal:

Rework
Scrap
Repair
Material-failure reviews
Design changes to meet customer
   expectations
Corrective actions
Making up lost time
Rewriting a proposal
Stocking extra parts
Engineering change notices

External:

Returned goods
Corrective actions
Warranty costs
Customer complaints
Liability costs
Penalties
Replacement parts
Investigating complaints

Intangible Costs

Customer dissatisfaction
Company image
Lost sales
Loss of customer goodwill
Customer time loss
Offsetting customer dissatisfaction

Figure 7.9   Categories of Quality Costs

possible to quantify the cost of missing an important deadline? What will be the impact of quality problems or schedule delays on the company's image? Intangible costs of quality can be three or four times as great as the tangible costs of quality. Even if these costs can only be named, and no quantifiable value can be placed on them, it is important for decision makers to be aware of their existence.

The four types of quality costs are interrelated. In summary, **total quality costs** *are considered to be the sum of prevention costs, appraisal costs, failure costs, and intangible costs.* Figure 7.9 shows some of the quality costs from Figure 7.8 in their respective categories.

In the struggle to meet the three conflicting goals of quality, cost, and delivery, identifying and quantifying quality costs helps ensure that quality does not suffer. When quality costs are discussed as a vague entity, their importance in relation to cost and delivery is not understood. By quantifying quality costs, all individuals producing a product or providing a service understand what it will cost if quality suffers. Six Sigma organizations understand that true cost reduction occurs when the root causes of nonconformities are recognized and eliminated. Once quantified, quality costs can be used to determine which projects will allow for the greatest return on investment and which projects have been most effective at improving processes, lowering failure rates, and reducing appraisal costs. Once cost of quality data has been measured and tabulated, this data can be used to select quality improvement projects as well as to identify the most costly aspects of a specific problem. Quality cost information can be used to guide improvement.

SUMMARY

Six Sigma organizations, through the use of performance measures, select projects that are tied to customer requirements and business results. These measures help optimize overall business results by balancing cost, quality, features, and availability considerations for products and their production.

 ## Take Away Tips

1. The measurement phase of any problem-solving process should require a complete evaluation of key process variables.
2. Measurement systems allow Six Sigma organizations to perform a gap analysis, studying the difference between actual to planned progress, by:

   - Determining that a gap exists between desired and actual performance.
   - Determining the root cause of the gap.
   - Determining the necessary corrective action to eliminate the root cause of the gap.
   - Determining whether or not the corrective actions eliminated the root cause and closed the gap between the actual and desired performance.

3. Quality costs can be used as justification for actions taken to improve products and services.
4. Identifying quality costs will allow management to judge improvement investments and profit contributions. ▓

Chapter Questions

1. Now that you have read the chapter, what does B. C. Forbes mean by, "If you don't drive your business, you will be driven out of business"?
2. How do effective organizations use performance measures?
3. What is the difference between process and results measures?
4. Why is an effective performance measurement system necessary?

5. What performance measures does the organization you work for use?

6. How does your organization use performance measures?

7. Create a set of measures, based on the Balanced Scorecard and the Six Sigma Tools at Work feature Indicators or Measures of Performance on page 86–87, for a fast food restaurant.

8. Create a set of measures, based on the Balanced Scorecard and the Six Sigma Tools at Work feature Indicators or Measures of Performance on pages 86–87, for a movie theater.

9. What is a prevention cost? How can it be recognized? Describe where prevention costs can be found.

10. What is an appraisal cost? How can it be recognized? Describe where appraisal costs can be found.

11. What are the two types of failure costs? How can they be recognized? Describe where these costs can be found.

12. Describe the relationships among prevention costs, appraisal costs, and failure costs. Where should a company's efforts be focused? Why?

13. How are quality costs used for decision making?

14. What should a quality cost system emphasize?

15. What are the benefits of having, finding, or determining quality costs?

8

Problem-Solving Using Design, Measure, Analyze, Improve, Control

Have you ever been lost? What is the first thing you need to do before proceeding? If you answered "find out where you are," then you realize the importance of knowing your current status in order to get to your desired destination. Six Sigma is about knowing where you are and where you are going.

■ Objectives:

1. To understand and utilize the Define, Measure, Analyze, Improve, Control problem solving process in order to learn to ask the right questions, present information clearly, and make judgments based on the information
2. To understand and utilize a variety of techniques for effective problem diagnosis and problem solving
3. To learn to diagnose and analyze problems that cause variation in the manufacturing, process, and service industries ■

PROBLEM-SOLVING

Problem-solving, the isolation and analysis of a problem and the development of a permanent solution, is an integral part of the Six Sigma methodology. To achieve the desired Six Sigma levels of performance, people need to be trained in correct problem-solving procedures. Six Sigma practitioners recognize that in order to locate and eliminate the root cause of a problem, problem-solving should follow a logical, systematic method. Other, less structured attempts at problem-solving run the risk of attempting to eliminate the symptoms associated with the problem rather than eliminating the problem at its source. Six Sigma problem-solving efforts focus on finding root causes. Proposed solutions prevent a recurrence of the problem. Controls are put in place to monitor the solution. Teamwork, coordinated and directed problem solving, problem-solving techniques, and statistical training are all part of ensuring that problems are isolated, analyzed, and corrected. The Six Sigma methodology uses the problem-solving

---

Define (Plan)

1. Identify the problem/project
2. Define the requirements
3. Establish goals

Measure (Plan)

4. Gather information about the current process
5. Define and measure key process steps and inputs
    a. Select appropriate metrics: key process output variables (KPOV)
    b. Determine how these metrics will be tracked over time
    c. Determine current baseline performance of project/process
    d. Determine the key process input variables (KPIV) that drive the key process output variables (KPOV)

Analyze (Plan)

6. Identify potential root causes of the problem
7. Validate the cause and effect relationship
    a. Determine what changes need to be made to the key process input variables in order to positively affect the key process output variables

Improve (Do)

8. Implement the solutions to address the root causes of the problem
9. Test solutions
    a. Determine if the changes have positively affected the KPOVs
10. Measure results

Control (Study, Act)

11. Evaluate and monitor improvements
    a. If the changes made result in performance improvements, establish control of the KPIVs at the new levels; if the changes have not resulted in performance improvement, return to step 5 and make the appropriate changes
12. Establish standard operating procedures

Figure 8.1   Six Sigma Problem-Solving Steps

steps: define, measure, analyze, improve, control (DMAIC). As Figure 8.1 shows, the generic steps for Six Sigma project implementation follow the Plan-Do-Study-Act problem-solving cycle espoused by Drs. Deming and Shewhart.

DEFINE

In problem solving, Six Sigma's DMAIC steps place a strong emphasis on studying the current conditions and planning how to approach a problem. At this stage, problem-solvers seek to identify the problem or project, define the requirements, and establish the goals to be achieved. Information concerning the problem(s) may have come from a number of different sources, departments, employees, or customers. Management involvement and commitment is crucial to the success of any major problem-solving process. Management should participate in the recognition and identification of problems, since they are ultimately responsible for selecting Six Sigma projects.

Once a problem situation has been recognized and before the problem is attacked, the Six Sigma improvement team is created. This team will be given the task of investigating, analyzing, and finding a solution to the problem situation within a specified time frame. This problem-solving team consists of people who have knowledge of the process or problem under study. Generally, this team is composed of those closest to the problem as well as a few individuals from middle management with enough power to effect change.

 SIX SIGMA TOOLS AT WORK

Plastics and Dashes: Identify the Problem

Plastics and Dashes Inc. (P&D) supplies instrument panels and other plastic components for automobile manufacturers. Recently their largest customer informed them that there have been an excessive number of customer complaints and warranty claims concerning the P&D instrument panel. The warranty claims have amounted to over $200,000, including the cost of parts and labor. In response to this problem, Plastics and Dashes' management has initiated a corrective action request (Figure 8.2) and formed an improvement team to investigate. The steps they will take to solve this problem are detailed in the Six Sigma Tools at Work features throughout this chapter.

MEASURE

Once a project has been identified, Six Sigma teams gather information about the existing process. During this phase of problem-solving, critical information is obtained about the key metrics including key process input and output variables. This information is tracked over time and is used to identify potential root causes of the problem. Several tools can aid in this process including check sheets, Pareto diagrams, process flow diagrams, cause and effect diagrams, why-why diagrams, and force field diagrams.

CORRECTIVE/PREVENTIVE ACTION REQUEST

TO DEPARTMENT/VENDOR:	INSTRUMENT PANEL
DATE:	8/31/2004
ORIGINATOR:	R. SMITH

FINDING/NONCONFORMITY: CUSTOMER WARRANTY CLAIMS FOR INSTRUMENT PANEL 360ID ARE EXCESSIVE FOR THE TIME PERIOD 1/1/04–8/1/04

APPARENT CAUSE: CLAIMS ARE HIGH IN NUMBER AND CITE ELECTRICAL PROBLEMS AND NOISE/LOOSE COMPONENTS

ASSIGNED TO: M. COOK   DATE RESPONSE DUE: 10/1/04
ASSIGNED TO: Q. SHEPHERD   DATE RESPONSE DUE: 10/1/04

IMMEDIATE CORRECTIVE ACTION: REPLACE COMPONENTS AS NEEDED; REPLACE ENTIRE DASH AT NO COST TO CUSTOMER IF NECESSARY

ROOT CAUSE:

PREVENTIVE ACTION:

EFFECTIVE DATE:

ASSIGNEE	DATE	ASSIGNEE	DATE
QUALITY ASSURANCE	DATE	R. SMITH ORIGINATOR	8/3/2004 DATE

COMMENTS/AUDIT/REVIEW: SATISFACTORY ☐   UNSATISFACTORY ☐

NAME	DATE

Figure 8.2   Plastics and Dashes: Corrective Action Request Form

Technique: Check Sheets

Several techniques exist to help team members determine the true nature of their problem. The most basic of these is the check sheet. A check sheet is a data-recording device, essentially a list of categories. As events occur in these categories; a check or mark is placed on the check sheet in the appropriate category. Given a list of items or events, the user of a check sheet marks down the number of times a particular event or item occurs. In essence, the user checks off occurrences. Check sheets are often used in conjunction with other quality assurance techniques. Be careful not to confuse a check sheet with a checklist. The latter lists all of the important steps or actions that need to take place, or things that need to be remembered.

 SIX SIGMA TOOLS AT WORK

Plastics and Dashes: Check Sheets

The problem-solving team at Plastics and Dashes has a great deal of instrument panel warranty information to sort through. In order to gain a better understanding of the situation, they have decided to investigate the key process output variable of warranty claims from the preceding six months. A check sheet has been chosen to record the types of claims and to determine how many of each type exists.

To create a check sheet, they first brainstormed a list of potential warranty problems. The categories they came up with include: loose instrument panel components, noisy instrument panel components, electrical problems, improper installation of the instrument panel or its components, inoperative instrument panel components, and warped instrument panel. The check sheet created from this list will be used by the investigators to record the types of warranty problems. As the investigators make their determination, a mark is made in the appropriate category of the check sheet (Figure 8.3). Once all the warranty information has been

Loose instrument panel components	///// ///// ///// ///// ///// ///// //
Noisy instrument panel components	///// ///// /////
Electrical problems	///// ///
Improper installation of the instrument panel or its components	///// ///// /////
Inoperative instrument panel components	///// ///// //
Warped instrument panel	/////
Other	

Figure 8.3   Plastics and Dashes: Warranty Panel Information Partially Completed Data Recording Check Sheet

reviewed, these sheets will be collected and turned over to the team to be tallied. The information from these sheets will help the team focus their problem-solving efforts.

Technique: Pareto Analysis

One very useful Six Sigma tool is Pareto Analysis. The **Pareto chart** is a graphical tool for ranking causes of problems from the most significant to the least significant. Dr. Juran popularized the Pareto principle for use in problem identification. First identified by Vilfredo Pareto, a 19th century engineer and economist, the Pareto principle, also known as the 80–20 rule, originally pointed out that the greatest portion of wealth in Italy was concentrated in a few families. Dr. Juran, stating that 80% of problems come from 20% of causes, used Pareto's work to encourage management to focus their improvement efforts on the 20% "vital few." Pareto charts are a graphical display of the 80–20 rule. These charts are applicable to any problem that can be separated into categories of occurrences.

While the split is not always 80–20, the Pareto chart is a visual method of identifying which problems are most significant. Pareto charts allow users to separate the vital few problems from the trivial many. The use of Pareto charts also limits the tendency of people to focus on the most recent problems rather than on the most important problems.

A Pareto chart is constructed using the following steps:

1. Select the subject for the chart. This can be a particular product line exhibiting problems, or a department, or a process.
2. Determine what data need to be gathered. Determine if numbers, percentages, or costs are going to be tracked. Determine which nonconformities or defects will be tracked.
3. Gather data related to the quality problem. Be sure that the time period during which data will be gathered is established.
4. Use a check sheet to gather data. Record the total numbers in each category. Categories will be the types of defects or nonconformities.
5. Determine the total number of nonconformities and calculate the percent of the total in each category.
6. Determine the costs associated with the nonconformities or defects.
7. Select the scales for the chart. The y axis scales are typically the number of occurrences, number of defects, dollar loss per category, or percent. The x axis usually displays the categories of nonconformities, defects, or items of interest.
8. Draw a Pareto chart by organizing the data from the largest category to the smallest. Include all pertinent information on the chart.
9. Analyze the chart or charts. The largest bars represent the vital few problems. If there does not appear to be one or two major problems, recheck the categories to determine if another analysis is necessary.

σ SIX SIGMA TOOLS AT WORK

Plastics and Dashes: Constructing a Pareto Chart

At Plastics and Dashes, the team members working on the instrument panel warranty issue have decided to begin their investigation by creating a Pareto chart.

Step 1 Select the Subject for the Chart. The subject of the chart is the key process output variable: instrument panel warranty claims.

Step 2 Determine What Data Need to Be Gathered. The data to be used to create the chart are the different reasons customers have brought their cars in for instrument panel warranty work. Cost information on instrument panel warranty work is also available.

Step 3 Gather the Data Related to the Quality Problem. The team has determined it is appropriate to use the warranty information for the preceding six months. Copies of warranty information have been distributed to the team.

Step 4 Make a Check Sheet of the Gathered Data and Record the Total Numbers in Each Category. Based on the warranty information, the team has chosen the following categories for the x axis of the chart: loose instrument panel components, noisy instrument panel components, electrical problems, improper installation of the instrument panel or its components inoperative instrument panel components, and warped instrument panels (refer to Figure 8.3).

Step 5 Determine the Total Number of Nonconformities and Calculate the Percent of the Total in Each Category. From the six months of warranty information, they also have the number of occurrences for each category:

1.	Loose instrument panel components	355	41.5%
2.	Noisy instrument panel components	200	23.4%
3.	Electrical problems	110	12.9%
4.	Improper installation of the instrument panel or its components	80	9.4%
5.	Inoperative instrument panel components	65	7.6%
6.	Warped instrument panel	45	5.2%

Warranty claims for instrument panels total 855.

Step 6 Determine the Costs Associated with the Nonconformities or Defects. The warranty claims also provided cost information associated with each category.

1.	Loose instrument panel components	$115,000
2.	Noisy instrument panel components	$25,000
3.	Electrical problems	$55,000
4.	Improper installation of the instrument panel or its components	$10,000
5.	Inoperative instrument panel components	$5,000
6.	Warped instrument panel	$1,000

Step 7 Select the Scales for the Chart. The team members have decided to create two Pareto charts, one for number of occurrences and the other for costs. On each chart, the *x* axis will display the warranty claim categories. The *y* axis will be scaled appropriately to show all the data.

Step 8 Draw a Pareto Chart by Organizing the Data from the Largest Category to the Smallest. The Pareto charts are shown in Figures 8.4 and 8.5. A Pareto chart for percentages could also be created.

Step 9 Analyze the Charts. When analyzing the charts, it is easy to see that the most prevalent warranty claim is loose instrument panel components. It makes sense that loose components might also be noisy and the Pareto chart (Figure 8.4) reflects this, noisy instrument panel components being the second most frequently occurring warranty claim. The second chart, in Figure 8.5, tells a slightly different story. The category "loose instrument panel components" has the highest costs; however, "electrical problems" has the second-highest costs.

At this point, although all the warranty claims are important, the Pareto chart has shown that efforts should be concentrated on investigating the causes of loose instrument panel components. Solving this warranty claim would significantly affect warranty numbers and costs.

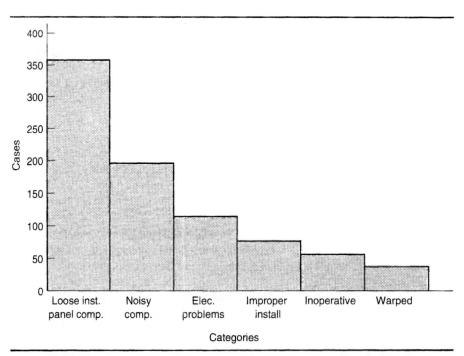

Figure 8.4   Plastics and Dashes: Instrument Panel Problems by Warranty Claim Type

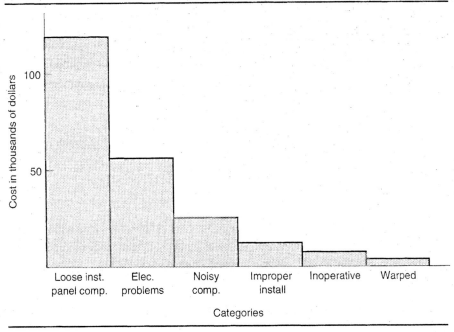

Figure 8.5   Plastics and Dashes: Costs of Instrument Panel Problems by Warranty Type

Technique: Process Maps

Process maps are powerful communication tools that provide a clear understanding of how business is conducted within the organization. Identifying and writing down the process in pictorial form helps people understand just how they do the work that they do. Creating a process map enables Six Sigma improvement teams to understand the current process and how it is performed. They can use this map to evaluate operations and identify the activities that have been added to the process over time in order to adapt older processes to changes in the business. Once changes have been proposed, process maps are equally powerful for communicating the proposed changes to the process.

Process maps are known by many names including flowcharts, process flowcharts, and process flow diagrams. A **process map** is a graphical representation of all the steps involved in an entire process or a particular segment of a process (Figure 8.6). Diagramming the flow of a process or system aids in understanding it. Flowcharting is effectively used in the first stages of problem-solving because the charts enable those studying the process to quickly understand what is involved in a process from start to finish. Problem-solving team members can clearly see what is being done to a product or provided by a service at the various stages in a process. Process flowcharts clarify the routines used to serve customers. Problem or non–value-added activities nested within a process are easily identified by using a flowchart.

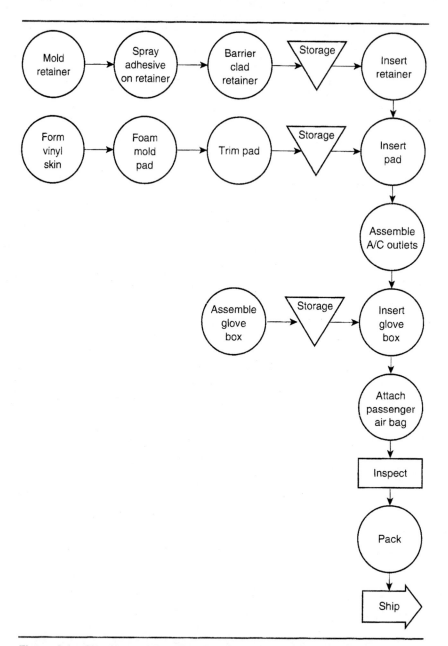

Figure 8.6 Plastics and Dashes: Glove Box Assembly Flowchart

Process maps are fairly straightforward to construct. The steps to creating such charts are the following:

1. Define the process boundaries. For the purpose of the chart, determine where the process begins and ends.

2. Define the process steps. Use brainstorming to identify the steps for a new process. For existing processes actually observe the process in action.
3. Sort the steps into the order of their occurrence in the process.
4. Place the steps in appropriate flowchart symbols (Figure 8.7) and create the chart.
5. Evaluate the steps for completeness, efficiency, and possible problems such as non–value-added activities.

Because processes and systems are often complex, in the early stages of flowchart construction, removable 3-by-5-inch sticky notes placed on a large piece of paper or board allow creators greater flexibility when creating and refining a flowchart. When the chart is complete, a final copy can be made utilizing the correct symbols. The symbols can either be placed next to the description of the step or they can surround the information.

A variation on the traditional process flowchart is the deployment flowchart. When a deployment flowchart is created, job or department titles are written across the top of the page and the activities of the process that occur in that job or department are written underneath that heading (Figure 8.8). Flowcharts can also be constructed with pictures for easier understanding (Figure 8.9). When used as routing sheets, it is not unusual to see process flowcharts such as those in Figures 8.10 and 8.11

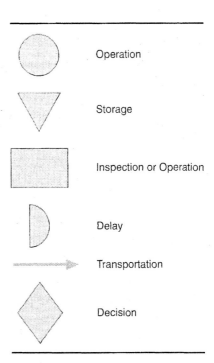

Operation

Storage

Inspection or Operation

Delay

Transportation

Decision

Figure 8.7   Flowchart Symbols

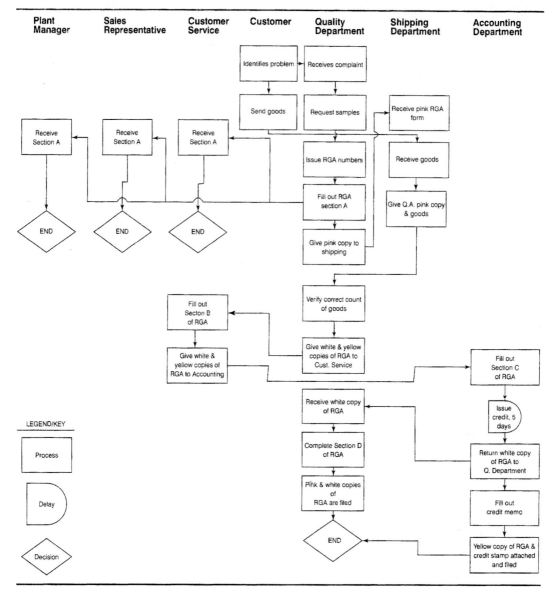

Figure 8.8   Deployment Process Flowchart for Return Goods Authorization (RGA) Forms

which include additional details like process activities, operator self-inspection notes, and specifications.

During the flowcharting process, members of the problem-solving team gain a greater understanding of their process. They will also begin to identify possible causes of problems within the process. It is now time to more clearly identify those possible measures within the process.

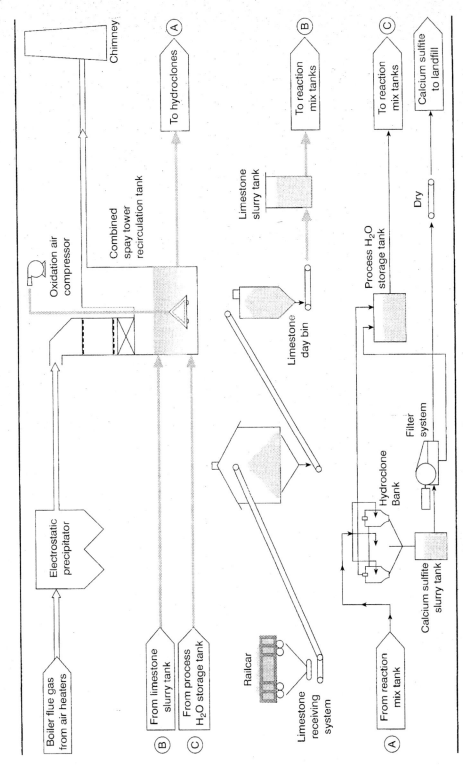

Figure 8.9   Flue Gas Desulfurization Process

109

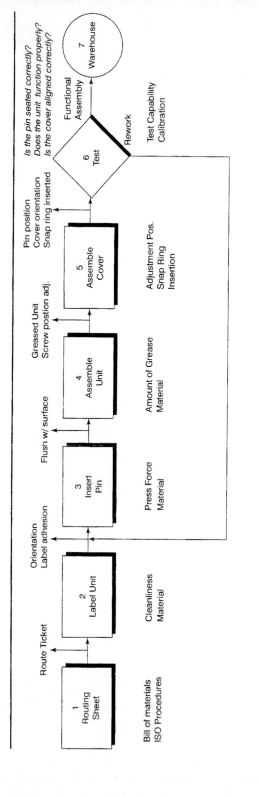

Figure 8.10 Process Flowchart with Instructions and Specifications

110

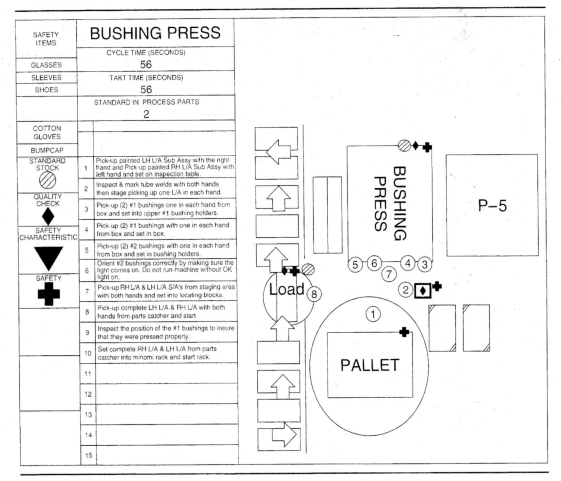

SAFETY ITEMS	BUSHING PRESS	
	CYCLE TIME (SECONDS)	
GLASSES	56	
SLEEVES	TAKT TIME (SECONDS)	
SHOES	56	
	STANDARD IN PROCESS PARTS	
	2	
COTTON GLOVES		
BUMPCAP		
STANDARD STOCK	1	Pick-up painted LH L/A Sub Assy with the right hand and Pick-up painted RH L/A Sub Assy with left hand and set on inspection table.
	2	Inspect & mark tube welds with both hands then stage picking up one L/A in each hand.
QUALITY CHECK	3	Pick-up (2) #1 bushings one in each hand from box and set into upper #1 bushing holders.
	4	Pick-up (2) #1 bushings with one in each hand from box and set in box.
SAFETY CHARACTERISTIC	5	Pick-up (2) #2 bushings with one in each hand from box and set in bushing holders.
	6	Orient #2 bushings correctly by making sure the light comes on. Do not run machine without OK light on.
SAFETY	7	Pick-up RH L/A & LH L/A S/A's from staging area with both hands and set into locating blocks.
	8	Pick-up complete LH L/A & RH L/A with both hands from parts catcher and start.
	9	Inspect the position of the #1 bushings to insure that they were pressed properly.
	10	Set complete RH L/A & LH L/A from parts catcher into minomi rack and start rack.
	11	
	12	
	13	
	14	
	15	

Figure 8.11   Bushing Press Process Map

 SIX SIGMA TOOLS AT WORK

Plastics and Dashes: Creating a Flowchart

To help determine the current baseline performance of the process, the instrument panel warranty team created a flowchart of the instrument panel assembly process.

Step 1 Define the Process Steps. First, the team members brainstormed the steps in the assembly process. They double-checked their steps by observing the actual process. They wrote down each step on 3-by-5-inch sticky notes.

Step 2 Sort the Steps into the Order of their Occurrence in the Process. After reconciling their observations with their brainstorming efforts, the team sorted the steps into the order of their occurrence.

> **Step 3** Place the Steps in Appropriate Flowchart Symbols. With the steps in the correct order, it was a simple task to add the appropriate flowchart symbols and create the chart (refer to Figure 8.6).
>
> **Step 4** Evaluate the Steps for Completeness, Efficiency, and Possible Problems. The team reviewed the finished chart for completeness. Several team members were unaware of the complete process. Because it creates a greater understanding of the process, this diagram will be helpful during later problem-solving efforts.

ANALYZE

During the Analyze phase of problem-solving, Six Sigma teams focus on identifying potential root causes of the problem they are working on. They also seek to validate a cause and effect relationship between the key process input variables and the key process output variables. This analysis enables the team to identify the vital few root causes of the problem.

Technique: Brainstorming

In order to identify potential root causes of problems, Six Sigma improvement teams often turn to brainstorming. *The purpose of **brainstorming** is to generate a use of problems, opportunities, or ideas from a group of people.* Everyone present at the session should participate. The discussion leader must ensure that everyone is given an opportunity to comment and add ideas. Critical to brainstorming is that no arguing, no criticism, no negativism, and no evaluation of the ideas, problems, or opportunities take place during the session. It is a session devoted purely to the generation of ideas.

The length of time allotted to brainstorming varies; sessions may last from 10 to 45 minutes. Some team leaders deliberately keep the meetings short to limit opportunities to begin problem solving. A session ends when no more items are brought up. The result of the session will be a list of ideas, problems, or opportunities to be tackled. After being listed, the items are sorted and ranked by category, importance, priority, benefit, cost, impact, time, or other considerations.

 SIX SIGMA TOOLS AT WORK

Plastics and Dashes: Brainstorming

The team at Plastics and Dashes Inc. conducted a further study of the causes of loose instrument panel components. Their investigation revealed that the glove box in the instrument panel was the main problem area (Figure 8.12). In order to better understand why the glove box might be loose, the team assembled to brainstorm the key process input variables associated with the glove box.

JERRY: I think you all know why we are here today. Did you all get the opportunity to review the glove box information? Good. Well, let's get started by concentrating on the relationship between the glove box and the instrument panel. I'll list the ideas on

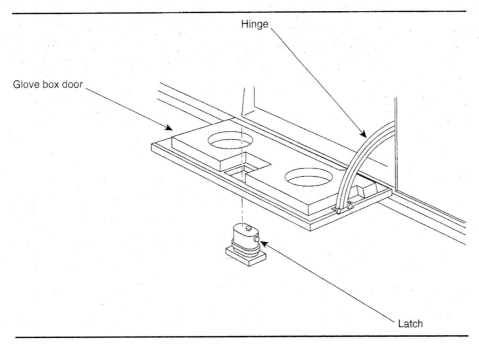

Figure 8.12   Plastics and Dashes: Glove Box

the board here, while you folks call them out. Remember, we are not here to evaluate ideas. We'll do that next.

SAM: How about the tightness of the latch?

FRANK: Of course the tightness of the latch will affect the fit between the glove box and the instrument panel! Tell us something we don't know.

JERRY: Frank, have you forgotten the rules of a brainstorming session? No criticizing. Sam, can you expand on your concept?

SAM: I was thinking that the positioning of the latch as well as the positioning of the hinge would affect the tightness of the latch.

JERRY: Okay. (Writes on board.) Tightness of Latch, Positioning of Latch, Positioning of Hinge. Any other ideas?

SUE: What about the strength of the hinge?

JERRY: (Writes on board.) Strength of Hinge.

SHARON: What about the glove box handle strength?

FRANK: And the glove box handle positioning?

JERRY: (Writes on board.) Glove Box Handle Strength. Glove Box Handle Positioning.

The session continues until a variety of key process input variables have been generated (Figure 8.13). After no more ideas surface or at subsequent meetings, discussion and clarification of the ideas can commence.

Positioning of the Glove Box
Strength of the Glove Box
Tightness of the Latch
Positioning of the Latch
Strength of the Latch
Positioning of the Hinge
Strength of the Hinge
Glove Box Handle Strength
Glove Box Handle Positioning
Glove Box Construction Materials

Figure 8.13 Key Process Input Variables Associated with the Glove Box

Technique: Cause-and-Effect Diagrams

Another excellent method of identifying potential root causes is the cause-and-effect diagram. The *cause-and-effect diagram* is also called the Ishikawa diagram after Kaoru Ishikawa, who developed it, or the fish-bone diagram because the completed diagram resembles a fish skeleton. A chart of this type will help *identify causes for nonconforming or defective products or services*. This chart is useful in a brainstorming session because it organizes the ideas that are presented. Problem-solvers benefit from using the chart by being able to separate a large problem into manageable parts. The problem or effect is clearly identified on the right-hand side of the chart, and the potential causes of the problem are organized on the left-hand side. The cause-and-effect diagram also allows the session leader to logically organize the possible causes of the problem and to focus on one area at a time. Not only does the chart permit the display of causes of the problem, it also shows subcategories related to those causes.

To construct a cause-and-effect diagram.

1. Clearly identify the effect or the problem. The succinctly stated effect or problem statement is placed in a box at the end of a line.
2. Identify the causes. Discussion ensues concerning the potential causes of the problem. To guide the discussion, attack just one possible cause area at a time. General topic areas are usually methods, materials, machines, people, environment, and information, although other areas can be added as needed. Under each major area, subcauses related to the major cause should be identified. Brainstorming is the usual method for identifying these causes.
3. Build the diagram. Organize the causes and subcauses in diagram format.
4. Analyze the diagram. At this point, solutions will need to be identified. Decisions will also need to be made concerning the cost-effectiveness of the solution as well as its feasibility.

σ SIX SIGMA TOOLS AT WORK

Plastics and Dashes: Constructing a Cause-and-Effect Diagram

As the Plastics and Dashes Inc. instrument panel warranty team continued its investigation, it was determined that defective latches were causing most of the warranty claims associated with the categories of loose instrument panel components and noise. The Six Sigma improvement team would like to identify potential root causes of defective latches.

Step 1 Identify the Effect or Problem. The team identified the problem as defective latches.

Step 2 Identify the Causes. Rather than use the traditional methods, materials, machines, people, environment, and information, this team felt that the potential areas to search for causes related directly to the latch. For that reason, they chose these potential causes: broken, misadjusted, binds, inoperative, loose.

Step 3 Build the Diagram. The team brainstormed root causes for each category (Figure 8.14).

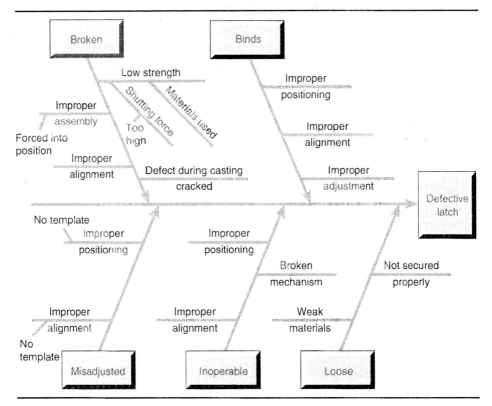

Figure 8.14   Plastics and Dashes: Cause-and-Effect Diagram

Step 4 Analyze the Diagram. The team discussed and analyzed the diagram. After much discussion, they came to the following conclusions. Latches that were either broken, misadjusted, or inoperable or those that bind have two root causes in common: improper alignment and improper positioning. Latches that were loose or broken had a root cause of low material strength (those materials supporting the latch were low in strength). From their findings, the team determined that there were three root causes associated with defective latches: improper alignment, improper positioning, and low material strength.

Technique: Why-Why Diagram

An excellent technique for identifying the root cause(s) of a problem is to ask "Why" five times. *Why-why diagrams organize the thinking of a problem-solving group and illustrate a chain of symptoms leading to the true cause of a problem.* By asking "why" five times, the problem-solvers are stripping away the symptoms surrounding the problem and getting to the true cause of the problem. At the end of a session it should be possible to make a positively worded, straightforward statement defining the true problem to be investigated.

Developed by group consensus, the why-why diagram flows from left to right. The diagram starts on the left with a statement of the problem to be resolved. Then the group is asked why this problem might exist. The responses will be statements of causes that the group believes contribute to the problem under discussion. There may be only one cause or there may be several. Causes can be separate or interrelated. Regardless of the number of causes or their relationships, the causes should be written on the diagram in a single, clear statement. "Why" statements should be supported by facts as much as possible and not by hearsay or unfounded opinions. Figure 8.15 shows a why-why diagram the Plastics and Dashes problem-solving team completed for instrument panel warranty costs.

This investigation is continued through as many levels as needed until a root cause is found for each of the problem statements, original or developed during the discussions. Frequently five levels of "why" are needed to determine the root cause. In the end, this process leads to a network of reasons the original problems occurred. The ending points indicate areas that need to be addressed to resolve the original problem. These become the actions the company must take to address the situation. Why-why diagrams can be expanded to include notations concerning who will be responsible for action items and when the actions will be completed.

Technique: Scatter Diagrams

*The **scatter diagram** is a graphical technique that is used to analyze the relationship between two different variables.* Two sets of data are plotted on a graph. The independent variable—i.e., the variable that can be manipulated—is recorded on the x axis. The dependent variable, the one being predicted, is displayed on the y axis. From this diagram, the user can determine if a connection or relationship exists between the two

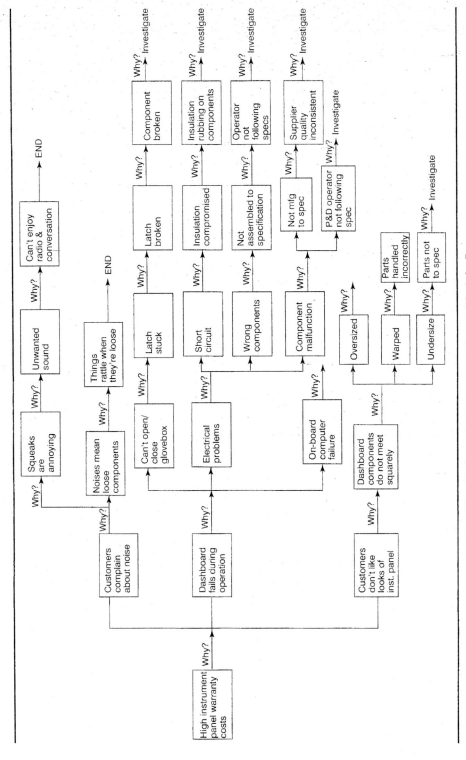

Figure 8.15 Plastics and Dashes: Why-Why Diagram for Instrument Panel, Work-in-Progress

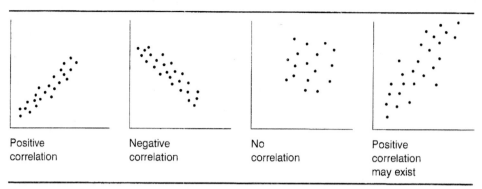

Figure 8.16   Scatter Diagram Interpretations

variables being compared. If a relationship exists, then steps can be taken to identify process changes that affect the relationship. Figure 8.16 shows different interpretations of scatter diagrams.

To construct a scatter diagram, use these steps:

1. Select the characteristic, the independent variable, you wish to study.
2. Select the characteristic, the dependent variable, that you suspect affects the independent variable.
3. Gather the data about the two characteristics.
4. Draw, scale, and label the horizontal and vertical axes.
5. Plot the points.
6. Interpret the scatter diagram to see if there is a relationship between the two characteristics.

 SIX SIGMA TOOLS AT WORK

Creating a Scatter Diagram

Shirley is the setup operator in the shrink-wrap area. In this area, 5-ft-by-5-ft cartons of parts are sealed with several layers of plastic wrap before being loaded on the trucks for shipment. Shirley's job is to load the plastic used in the shrink-wrapping operation onto the shrink-wrap machine, set the speed at which the unit will rotate, and set the tension level on the shrink-wrap feeder. To understand the relationship between the tension level on the feeder and the speed of the rotating mechanism, Shirley has created a scatter diagram.

The rotator speed is most easily controlled, so she has placed the most typically used speed settings (in rpm) on the x axis. On the y axis, she places the number of tears (Figure 8.17).

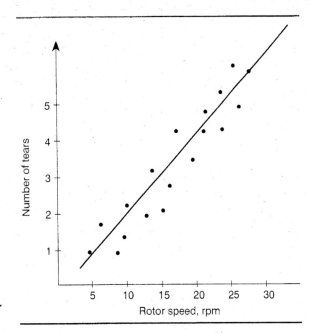

Figure 8.17 Scatter Diagram

The diagram reveals a positive correlation: As the speed increases, the number of tears increases. From this information, Shirley now knows that the tension has to be reduced in order to prevent the wrap from tearing. Using the diagram, Shirley is able to determine the optimal speed for the rotor and the best tension setting.

IMPROVE

Once the root cause of the problem has been identified, it is time to propose and implement potential solutions. The chosen solution should address the root causes of the problem and should be tested to ensure that it does truly solve the problem. By analyzing the data gathered, the project team can choose the best solution for the problem. The solution should be judged against four general criteria:

1. The solution should be chosen on the basis of its potential to prevent a recurrence of the problem. A quick or short-term fix to a problem will only mean that time will be wasted in solving this problem again when it recurs in the future.
2. The solution should address the root cause of the problem. A quick or short-term fix that focuses on correcting the symptoms of a problem will waste time because the problem will recur in the future.
3. The solution should be cost-effective. The most expensive solution is not necessarily the best solution for the company's interests. Solutions may necessitate determining the company's future plans for a particular process or

product. Major changes to the process, system, or equipment may not be an appropriate solution for a process or product that will be discontinued in the near future. Technological advances will need to be investigated to determine if they are the most cost-effective solutions.

4. The solution should be capable of being implemented within a reasonable amount of time. A timely solution to the problem is necessary to relieve the company of the burden of monitoring the current problem and its associated quick fixes.

ⓒ SIX SIGMA TOOLS AT WORK

Plastics and Dashes: Glove Box Solutions

Through the use of why-why and cause-and-effect diagrams, the team was able to identify the root causes of the glove box latch problem as improper alignment, improper positioning, and low material strength. They decided to make the following changes part of their solution:

1. Redesign the glove box latch. This solution was chosen to counteract low material strength.
2. Reposition the glove box door, striker, and hinge. This solution was chosen to counteract improper positioning and alignment. They also hoped this change would eliminate potential squeaks and rattles.
3. Reinforce the glove box latch. This solution was chosen to counteract breakage. By increasing the material at the latch position on the glove box door, they hoped to eliminate breakage. They also decided to use a stronger adhesive to reinforce the rivets securing the latch to the door.

Implementing the solution is often done by members of the problem-solving team. Critical to ensuring the success of the solution implementation is assigning responsibilities to specific individuals and holding them accountable for accomplishing the task. Knowing who will be doing what and when will help ensure that the project stays on track.

Sometimes implementing solutions is complicated by a variety of factors, including conflicting departmental needs, costs, or priorities. Using a force-field analysis can help identify the issues affecting the implementation of a solution.

Technique: Force-Field Analysis

A *force-field analysis* is a chart that helps teams separate the driving forces and the restraining forces associated with a complex situation. These easy-to-develop diagrams help a team determine the positive or driving forces that are encouraging improvement of the process as well as the forces that restrain improvement. Teams may also choose to use force-field analysis as a source of discussion issues surrounding a particular problem or opportunity. Once the driving and restraining forces have been identified, the team can discuss how to enhance the driving forces and remove the restraining forces.

 SIX SIGMA TOOLS AT WORK

Plastics and Dashes: Using Force-Field Analysis

Though the Six Sigma team isolated the root causes of the glove box latch problems, there is some resistance from management to implement the necessary changes. The team has decided to use a force-field analysis to counter this resistance.

The team began by brainstorming the driving forces behind the change. Then they changed direction and brainstormed all the reasons why management might not want to make the change. Having completed these two sides of the diagram, the team identified ways to enhance the driving forces and minimize the effects of the restraining forces. Then the team got busy and completed the steps in the action plan. Figure 8.18 presents the completed force-field diagram. Note the numbers

---

Glove Box Latch Line Improvements

Driving Forces	Restraining Forces
Less rework (1)	Time to retool line (1)
Lower costs (1)	Cost to retool line (1)
Less scrap (1)	Time to retrain employees (1)
Quicker throughput (1, 2)	Poor understanding of need
Improved customer satisfaction (4)	for improvement (5)
Less inspection (1, 2, 4)	
Fewer non–value-added activities (2)	
Improved reputation (4)	
Increased business (4)	
Loss of customers (3)	

Action Plan

1. Perform cost/benefit analysis on rework, scrap, and customer dissatisfaction costs versus costs required to solve the problem
2. Perform analysis to determine cost savings associated with removal of non–value-added activities
3. Contact customers to assess risk of losing business
4. Use measures of performance to determine whether or not the implementation is effective
5. Present information from action plan steps 1–4 to management to improve their understanding of the need for improvement.

Figure 8.18   Plastics and Dashes; Force-Field Analysis

in the table represent the link between the action plans and the driving or restraining force.

After listening to the results of action plan steps 1–4, management has a clearer understanding of the issues involved in making the improvements to the glove box line. They have decided to go ahead with the improvements.

CONTROL

Once a solution has been implemented, during the control phase of the DMAIC cycle, steps are taken to evaluate and monitor the improvements. At this time, decisions are made to adopt the change, abandon it, make adjustments, or if necessary, repeat the problem-solving cycle. If the solution proves to be viable, it is made part of the standard operating procedures in order to ensure that the problem does not resurface.

This phase of the DMAIC process exists to ensure that the new controls and procedures stay in place. It is easy to believe that the "new and better" method should be utilized without fail; however, in any situation where a change has taken place, there is a tendency to return to old methods, controls, and procedures. Widespread active involvement in improvement projects helps ensure successful implementation of new methods. Extensive training and short follow-up training sessions are also helpful in ingraining the new method. Follow-up checks must be put in place to prevent problem recurrences from lapses to old routines and methods.

 SIX SIGMA TOOLS AT WORK

Plastics and Dashes: Evaluating the Solution

The instrument panel warranty team implemented their solutions and used the measures of performance developed earlier to study the solutions in order to determine whether or not the changes were working. Their original measures of performance were warranty costs and number and type of warranty claims. The Pareto chart in Figure 8.19 provides information about warranty claims made following the changes. When this figure is compared to Figure 8.4 showing warranty claims before the problem-solving team went into action, the improvement is obvious. Warranty costs declined in proportion to the decreased number of claims, to just under $25,000. A process measure also tracked the length of time to implement the changes, a very speedy five days.

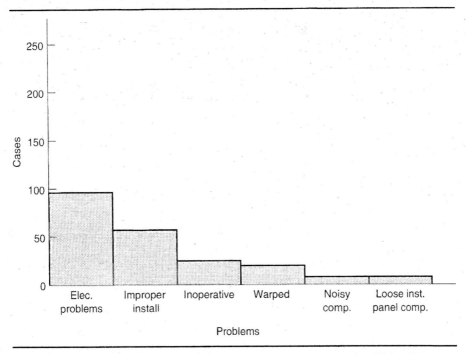

Figure 8.19   Plastics and Dashes: Pareto Chart of Instrument Panel Problems by Warranty Claim Type

SUMMARY

Improvement projects are easy to identify. A review of operations will reveal many opportunities for improvement. Any sources of waste, such as warranty claims, overtime, scrap, or rework, as well as production backlogs or areas in need of more capacity, are potential projects. Even small improvements can lead to a significant impact on the organization's financial statement. Having completed one project, others wait for the same problem-solving process.

σ   Take Away Tips

1. Problem solving is the isolation and analysis of a problem and the development of a permanent solution. Problem solving should be logical and systematic.
2. The following are the Six Sigma problem-solving steps

   1. Identify the problem/project
   2. Define the requirements
   3. Establish goals
   4. Gather information about the current process
   5. Define and measure key process steps and inputs
      a. Select appropriate metrics: key process output variables (KPOV)

   b. Determine how these metrics will be tracked over time
   c. Determine current baseline performance of project/process
   d. Determine the key process input variables (KPIV) that drive the key process output variables (KPOV)
6. Identify potential root causes of the problem
7. Validate the cause-and-effect relationship
   a. Determine what changes need to be made to the key process input variables in order to positively affect the key process output variables
8. Implement the solution to address the root causes of the problem
9. Test solutions
   a. Determine if the changes have positively affected the KPOVs.
10. Measure results
11. Evaluation and monitor improvements
    a. If the changes made result in performance improvements, establish control of the KPIVs at the new levels. If the changes have not resulted in performance improvement, return to step 5 and make the appropriate changes.
12. Establish standard operating procedures

3. The following are techniques used in problem-solving: brainstorming, Pareto analysis, why-why diagrams, flowcharts, force-field analysis, cause-and-effect diagrams, check sheets, and scatter diagrams.
4. Problem solvers are tempted to propose solutions before identifying the root cause of the problem and performing an in-depth study of the situation. Adhering to a problem-solving method avoids this tendency.
5. Brainstorming is designed for idea generation. Ideas should not be discussed or criticized during a brainstorming session.
6. Flowcharts are powerful tools that allow problem-solvers to gain in-depth knowledge of the process.
7. Cause-and-effect diagrams enable problem-solvers to identify the root causes of succinctly stated problems.
8. Steps must be taken to ensure that the new methods or changes to the process are permanent.
9. Don't be afraid to apply the techniques you know. ■

Chapter Questions

1. An orange juice producer has found that the fill weights (weight of product per container) of several of its orange juice products do not meet specifications. If the problem continues, unhappy customers will stop buying their product. Outline the steps that they should take to solve this problem. Provide as much detail as you can.

2. Bicycles are being stolen at a local campus. Campus security is considering changes in bike rack design, bike parking restrictions, and bike registrations to try to reduce thefts. Thieves have been using hacksaws and bolt cutters

to remove locks from the bikes. Create a problem statement for this situation. How will an improvement team use the problem statement?

3. A pizza company with stores located city wide uses one order call-in phone number for the entire city. Callers, regardless of their address, can phone XXX-1111 to place an order. Based on the caller's phone number, an automated switching service directs the call to the appropriate store.

   On a recent Friday evening, the pizza company lost as many as 15,000 orders when a malfunctioning mechanical device made calls to their phone number impossible. From about 5:30 to 8 P.M., when callers hoping to place an order phoned, they were met with either silence or a busy signal. This is not the first time this malfunction has occurred. Just two weeks earlier, the same problem surfaced. The pizza company and the company that installed the system are working to ensure the situation doesn't repeat itself. They believe a defective call switch is to blame.

   Based on what you have learned in this chapter, why is a structured problem-solving process critical to the success of finding and eliminating the problem? What steps do you recommend they follow?

4. During the past month, a customer-satisfaction survey was given to 200 customers at a local fast-food restaurant. The following complaints were lodged:

Complaint	Number of Complaints
Cold Food	105
Flimsy Utensils	20
Food Tastes Bad	10
Salad Not Fresh	94
Poor Service	15
Food Greasy	9
Lack of Courtesy	5
Lack of Cleanliness	25

Create a Pareto chart with this information.

5. A local bank is keeping track of the different reasons people phone the bank. Those answering the phones place a mark on their check sheet in the rows most representative of the customers' questions. Given the following check sheet, make a Pareto diagram:

Credit Card Payment Questions	245
Transfer Call to Another Department	145
Balance Questions	377
Payment Receipt Questions	57
Finance Charge Questions	30
Other	341

Comment on what you would do about the high number of calls in the "Other" column.

6. Once a Pareto chart has been created, what steps would you take to deal with the situation given in Question 5 in your quality-improvement team?

7. Review Question 3. What are two measures of performance that can be used to determine if the changes they make are effective?

8. Review Question 5. What are two measures of performance that can be used to determine if the changes they make are effective?

9. Brainstorm 10 reasons why a computer might malfunction.

10. Brainstorm 10 reasons why a customer may not feel the service was adequate at a department store.

11. Create a why-why diagram for how you ended up taking this particular class.

12. A mail order company has a goal of reducing the amount of time a customer has to wait in order to place an order. Create a why-why diagram about waiting on the telephone. Once you have created the diagram, how would you use it?

13. WP Uniforms provides a selection of lab coats, shirts, trousers, uniforms, and outfits for area businesses. For a fee, WP Uniforms will collect soiled garments once a week, wash and repair these garments, and return them the following week while picking up a new batch of soiled garments.

    At WP Uniforms, shirts are laundered in large batches. From the laundry, these shirts are inspected, repaired, and sorted. To determine if the process can be done more effectively, the employees want to create a flow chart of the process. They have brainstormed the following steps and placed them in order. Create a flowchart with their information. Remember to use symbols appropriately.

Shirts arrive from laundry.	Ask: Is shirt beyond cost-effective
Pull shirts from racks.	repair?
Remove shirts from hangers.	Discard shirt if badly damaged.
Inspect.	Sort according to size.
Ask: Does shirt have holes or	Fold shirt.
other damage?	Place in proper storage area.
Make note of repair needs.	Make hourly count.

14. Coating chocolate with a hard shell began with M&Ms during World War II. Coated candies were easier to transport because the coating prevented them from melting. Making coated candies is an interesting process. First the chocolate centers are formed in little molds. These chocolate centers are then placed in a large rotating drum that looks a bit like a cement mixer. Temperature controls on the drum maintain a low enough temperature to prevent the chocolate from softening. While rolling around in the

drum, the chocolates are sprayed with sugary liquid that hardens into the white candy shell. Since the chocolates are constantly rotating, they do not clump together while wet with the sugary liquid. Once the white candy shell has hardened, a second, colored, sugar liquid is sprayed into the drum. Once the color coating dries, the colored candies are removed from the drum by pouring them onto a conveyor belt where each candy fits into one of thousands of candy shaped depressions. The belt vibrates gently to seat the candies into the depressions. Once they are organized on the belt, they proceed through a machine that gently imprints a maker's mark onto each candy with edible ink. Map this process.

15. A customer placed a call to a mail order catalog firm. Several times the customer dialed the phone and received a busy signal. Finally, the phone was answered electronically, and the customer was told to wait for the next available operator. Although it was a 1-800 number, he found it annoying to wait on the phone until his ear hurt. Yet he did not want to hang up for fear he would not be able to get through to the firm again. Using the problem statement "What makes a customer wait?" as your base, brainstorm to create a cause-and-effect diagram. Once you have created the diagram, how would you use it?

16. Create cause-and-effect diagrams for (a) a car that won't start, (b) an upset stomach, and (c) a long line at the supermarket.

17. Create a force-field diagram for Question 2 concerning bike thefts.

18. Create a force-field diagram for a restaurant where customers are waiting more than 10 minutes for their food.

Statistics

If things were done right just 99.9 percent of the time, then we'd have to accept

- *One hour of unsafe drinking water per month*
- *Two unsafe plane landings per day at O'Hare International Airport in Chicago*
- *16,000 pieces of mail lost by the U.S. Postal Service every hour*
- *20,000 incorrect drug prescriptions per year*
- *500 incorrect surgical operations each week*
- *22,000 checks deducted from the wrong bank accounts per hour*
- *32,000 missed heartbeats per person per year*

Original source unknown

■ Objectives:

1. To review basic statistical concepts
2. To understand how to graphically and analytically study a process by using statistics
3. To know how to create and interpret a frequency diagram and a histogram
4. To know how to calculate the mean, median, mode, range, and standard deviation for a given set of numbers
5. To understand the importance of the normal curve and the central limit theorem in quality assurance
6. To know how to find the area under a curve using the standard normal probability distribution (Z tables)
7. To understand how to interpret the information analyzed ■

Statistics, the collection, tabulation, analysis, interpretation, and presentation of numerical data, provides a viable method of supporting or clarifying a Six Sigma project. The Six Sigma methodology uses correctly collected, analyzed, and interpreted statistical information to understand and predict process behavior. The five aspects of statistics—collection, tabulation, analysis, interpretation, and presentation—are equally important when analyzing a process. Once gathered and analyzed, statistical data can be used to aid in decisions about making process changes or pursuing a particular course of action.

POPULATIONS VERSUS SAMPLES

Statistics can be gathered by studying either the entire collection of values associated with a process or only a portion of the values. A **population** is *a collection of all possible elements, values, or items associated with a situation*. A population can contain a finite number of things or it may be nearly infinite. As the size of a population increases, studying that population becomes unwieldy unless sampling can be used. A **sample** is *a subset of elements or measurements taken from a population*. A doctor's office may wish to sample 10 insurance claim forms per week to check the forms for completeness. A manufacturer of toothpaste may check the weight of a dozen tubes per hour to ensure that the tubes are filled correctly. A sample will represent the population as long as the sample is random and unbiased. In a *random sample*, each item in the population has the same opportunity to be selected.

 SIX SIGMA TOOLS AT WORK

Taking a Sample

An outlet store has just received a shipment of 1,000 shirts sealed in cardboard boxes. The store had ordered 800 white shirts and 200 blue. The store manager wishes to check that there actually are 20 percent blue shirts and 80 percent white shirts. He doesn't want to open all of the boxes and count all of the shirts, so he has decided to sample the population. Table 9.1 shows the results of 10 random samples of 10 shirts each.

A greater number of blue shirts is found in some samples than in others. However, when the results are compiled, the blue shirts comprise 19 percent, very close to the desired value of 20 percent. The manager of the outlet store is pleased to learn that the samples have shown that there are approximately 20 percent blue shirts and 80 percent white.

An example of biased sampling could occur on the manufacturing floor. If, when an inspector receives a skid of goods, that inspector always samples from the top layer and takes a part from each of the four corners of the skid, the sample is biased. The parts in the rest of the skid have not been considered. Furthermore, operators observing this behavior may choose to place only the best-quality product in those corners.

Table 9.1   A Sampling of Shirts

Sample Number	Sample Size	Number of White Shirts	Number of Blue Shirts	Percentage of Blue Shirts
1	10	8	2	20
2	10	7	3	30
3	10	8	2	20
4	10	9	1	10
5	10	10	0	0
6	10	7	3	30
7	10	8	2	20
8	10	9	1	10
9	10	8	2	20
10	10	7	3	20
Total	100	81	19	19

The inspector has biased the sample because it is not random and does not represent all of the parts of the skid. The inspector is receiving an incorrect impression about the quality in the entire skid.

Unbiased samples depend on other features besides randomness. Conditions surrounding the population should not be altered in any way from sample to sample. The sampling method can also undermine the validity of a sample. Ensure the validity of a sample by asking such questions as

> How was the problem defined?
> What was studied?
> How many items were sampled?
> How was the sample taken?
> How often?
> Have conditions changed?

DATA COLLECTION

Two types of statistics exist: deductive and inductive. Also known as *descriptive statistics*, **deductive statistics** *describe a population or complete group of data*. When describing a population using deductive statistics, the investigator must study each entity within the population. This provides a great deal of information about the population, product, or process, but gathering the information is time-consuming. Imagine contacting each man, woman, and child in the United States, all 300 million of them, to conduct the national census!

When the quantity of the information to be studied is too great, inductive statistics are used. **Inductive statistics** *deal with a limited amount of data or a representative sample* *of the population.* Once samples are analyzed and interpreted, predictions can be made concerning the larger population of data. Quality assurance (and the U.S. census) relies primarily on inductive statistics. Properly gathered and analyzed, sample data provides a wealth of information.

Two types of statistical data can be collected. **Variables data,** *those quality characteristics that can be measured,* are treated differently from **attribute data,** *those quality characteristics that are observed to be either present or absent, conforming or nonconforming.* While both variables and attribute data can be described by numbers, attribute data are countable, not measurable.

Variables data tend to be continuous in nature. When data are **continuous,** *the measured value can take on any value within a range.* The range of values that the measurements can take on will be set by the expectations of the users or the circumstances surrounding the situation. For example, a manufacturer might wish to monitor the thickness of a part. During the course of the day, the samples may have values of 0.399, 0.402, 0.401, 0.400, 0.401, 0.403, and 0.398 inch.

Discrete data consist of distinct parts. In other words, when measured, **discrete data** *will be countable using whole numbers.* For example, the number of frozen vegetable packages found on the shelf during an inventory count—ten packages of frozen peas, eight packages of frozen corn, 22 packages of frozen Brussels sprouts—is discrete, countable data. Since vegetable packages can only be sold to customers when the packages are whole and unopened, only whole-numbered measurements will exist; continuous measurements would not be applicable in this case. Attribute data, since the data are seen as being either conforming or not conforming to specifications, are primarily discrete data.

A statistical analysis begins with the gathering of data about a process or product. Sometimes raw data gathered from a process take the form of ungrouped data. **Ungrouped data** *are easily recognized because when viewed, it appears that the data are without any order.* **Grouped data,** on the other hand, *are grouped together on the basis of when the values were taken or observed.* Consider the following Six Sigma Tools at Work feature.

 SIX SIGMA TOOLS AT WORK

Grouping Data

A company manufactures various parts for automobile transmissions. One part, a clutch plate, resembles a flat round plate with four keyways stamped into it (Figure 9.1). Recently, the customer brought to the manufacturer's attention the fact that not all of the keyways are being cut out to the correct depth. The manufacturer asked the operator to measure each keyway in five parts every 15 minutes and record the measurements. Table 9.2 shows the results. When management started to analyze and interpret the data they were unable to do so. Why?

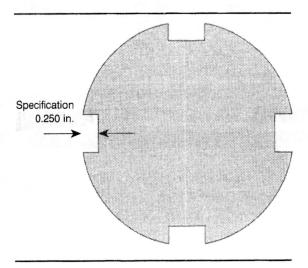

Specification
    0.250 in.

Figure 9.1   Clutch Plate

Table 9.2   Clutch Plate Ungrouped Data (in inches)

0.247	0.245	0.271
0.254	0.260	0.276
0.268	0.278	0.268
0.261	0.260	0.230
0.231	0.224	0.243
0.241	0.224	0.225
0.252	0.222	0.232
0.258	0.242	0.254
0.266	0.244	0.242
0.226	0.277	0.248
0.263	0.222	0.236
0.242	0.260	0.262
0.242	0.249	0.223
0.264	0.250	0.240
0.218	0.251	0.222
0.216	0.255	0.261
0.266	0.247	0.244
0.266	0.250	0.249
0.218	0.235	0.226
0.269	0.258	0.232
0.260	0.251	0.250
0.241	0.245	0.248
0.250	0.239	0.252
0.246	0.248	0.251

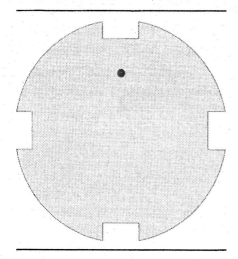

Figure 9.2   Clutch Plate with Mark

Table 9.3   Clutch Plate Grouped Data (in inches)

	Keyway 1	Keyway 2	Keyway 3	Keyway 4
Subgroup 1	0.250	0.261	0.250	0.240
Subgroup 2	0.251	0.259	0.249	0.242
Subgroup 3	0.250	0.258	0.251	0.245
Subgroup 4	0.249	0.257	0.250	0.243
Subgroup 5	0.250	0.262	0.250	0.244
Subgroup 6	0.251	0.260	0.249	0.245
Subgroup 7	0.251	0.258	0.250	0.241
Subgroup 8	0.250	0.259	0.249	0.247
Subgroup 9	0.250	0.257	0.250	0.245
Subgroup 10	0.249	0.256	0.251	0.244
Subgroup 11	0.250	0.260	0.250	0.243
Subgroup 12	0.251	0.258	0.251	0.244
Subgroup 13	0.250	0.257	0.250	0.245
Subgroup 14	0.250	0.256	0.249	0.246
Subgroup 15	0.250	0.257	0.250	0.246

An investigation of this raw, ungrouped data reveals that there is no way to determine which measurements belong with which keyway. Which keyway is too deep? Too shallow? It is not possible to determine the answer.

To rectify this situation, during the stamping process, the manufacturer placed a small mark below one of the keyways (Figure 9.2). The mark labels that keyway as number 1. Clockwise around the part, the other keyways are designated 2, 3, and 4. The mark does not affect the use of the part. The operator was asked to measure the keyway depths again, five parts every 15 minutes (Table 9.3).

By organizing the data according to keyway, it could then be determined that keyway number 2 is too deep, and keyway number 4 is too shallow.

MEASUREMENTS: ACCURACY, PRECISION, AND MEASUREMENT ERROR

The validity of a measurement comes not only from the selection of a sample size and an understanding of the group of data being measured, it also depends on the measurements themselves and how they were taken. Measurement error occurs while the measurements are being taken and recorded. **Measurement error** *is considered to be the difference between a measured value and the true value.* The error that occurs is one either of accuracy or of precision. **Accuracy** *refers to how far from the actual or real value the measurement is.* **Precision** *is the ability to repeat a series of measurements and get the same value each time.* Precision is sometimes referred to as **repeatability.**

Figure 9.3a pictures the concept of accuracy. The marks average to the center target. Figure 9.3b, with all of the marks clustered together, shows precision. Figure 9.3c describes a situation in which both accuracy and precision exist. The following Six Sigma Tools at Work feature and Figures 9.4, 9.5, and 9.6 illustrate the concepts of accuracy and precision.

σ SIX SIGMA TOOLS AT WORK

Accuracy and Precision

Accuracy and precision describe the location and the spread of the data. Look at Figures 9.4, 9.5, and 9.6 showing the data from the Clutch Plate example. When compared, the difference in the keyways' accuracy and precision becomes apparent. The data for keyways 1 and 3 exhibit greater accuracy than that for keyways 2 and 4. Note how the data for keyways 1 and 3 are concentrated around the target specification of 0.250 inch. The data values for keyway 2 are greater than the desired target specification and those for keyway 4 are smaller. Notice, too, the difference in precision. Data for keyways 1 and 3 are precise, tightly grouped around the target. Data values for keyways 2 and 4 are not only far away from the target, they are also more spread out, less precise. Changes to this stamping process must be twofold, improving both the accuracy and the precision.

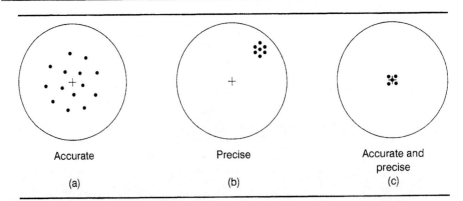

Accurate	Precise	Accurate and precise
(a)	(b)	(c)

Figure 9.3   Accuracy and Precision

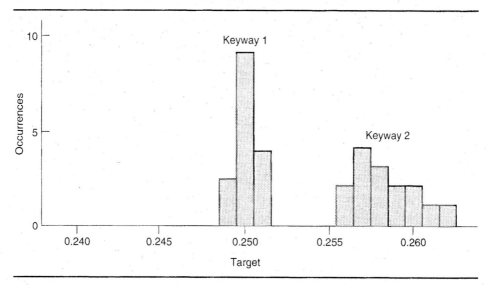

Figure 9.4   Data for Keyways 1 and 2 Comparing Accuracy and Precision

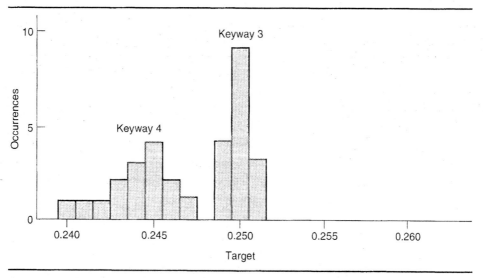

Figure 9.5   Data for Keyways 3 and 4 Comparing Accuracy and Precision

Measurement errors may contribute to the lack of accuracy and precision. Measurement errors are not always the fault of the individual performing the measuring. In any situation, several sources of error exist, including environment, people, and machine error. Environmental problems, such as with dust, dirt, temperature, and water, cause measurement errors by disturbing either the products or the measuring tools.

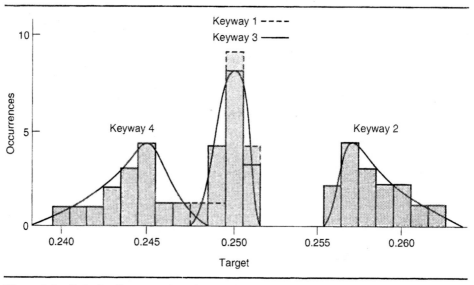

Figure 9.6   Data for Keyways 1 and 3 Are Both Accurate and Precise While Data for Keyways 2 and 4 Are Not

Significant figures and associated rounding errors affect the viability of a measurement. **Significant figures** *are the numerals or digits in a number, excluding any leading zeros used to place the decimal point.* Zeros following a digit—for example, 9.700—are significant if they have truly been measured. When working a statistical problem, you should use only the number of digits that the measuring devices are able to provide. If a micrometer reads to three decimal places, then all mathematical calculations should be worked to no more than three decimal places. With today's computers and calculators, there is a temptation to use all the numbers that appear on the screen. Since the measuring device may not have originally measured to that many decimal places, the number should be rounded to the original number of significant figures. Calculations are performed and then rounded to the number of significant figures present in the value with the smallest number of significant figures. When rounding, round to the next highest number if the figure is a 5 or greater. If the figure is 4 or below, round down. Consider the following examples:

$$23.59 \div 3.8 = 6.2 \quad \text{(3.8 has fewest significant figures)}$$
$$3{,}456 \div 12.3 = 281 \quad \text{(12.3 has three significant figures)}$$
$$3.2 \times 10^2 + 6{,}930 = 7.3 \times 10^3 \quad \text{(3.2} \times 10^2 \text{ has two significant figures)}$$
$$6{,}983 \div 16.4 = 425.79268 = 426 \text{ when rounded}$$

Human errors associated with measurement errors can be either unintentional or intentional. Unintentional errors result from poor training, inadequate procedures, or incomplete or ambiguous instructions. These types of errors can be minimized by good planning, training, and supervision. Intentional errors are rare and are usually related to poor attitudes; they will require improving employee relations and individual guidance to solve.

DATA ANALYSIS: GRAPHICAL

A thorough statistical analysis of the data that has been gathered involves three aspects: graphical, analytical, and interpretive. A variety of different graphical methods exist, including the frequency diagram and the histogram.

Frequency Diagrams

A *frequency diagram* shows the number of times each of the measured values occurred when the data were collected. This diagram shows at a glance which values occur the most frequently as well as the spread of the data. To create a frequency diagram, the following steps are necessary:

1. Collect the data. Record the measurements or counts of the characteristics of interest.
2. Count the number of times each measurement or count occurs.
3. Construct the diagram by placing the counts or measured values on the x axis and the frequency or number of occurrences on the y axis. The x axis must contain each possible measurement value from the lowest to the highest, even if a particular value does not have any corresponding measurements. A bar is drawn on the diagram to depict each of the values and the number of times the value occurred in the data collected.
4. Interpret the frequency diagram. Study the diagrams you create and think about the diagram's shape, size, and location in terms of the desired target specification. We will learn more about interpreting frequency diagrams later in the chapter.

 SIX SIGMA TOOLS AT WORK

Constructing a Frequency Diagram

To respond to customer issues, the engineers involved in the clutch plate problem are studying the thickness of the part. To gain a clearer understanding of incoming material thickness, they plan to create a frequency diagram.

Step 1 Collect the Data. The first step is performed by the operator, who randomly selects five parts each hour, measures the thickness of each part, and records the values (Table 9.4).

Table 9.4   Clutch Plate Thickness: Sums and Averages

						SX$_i$	X
Subgroup 1	0.0625	0.0626	0.0624	0.0625	0.0627	0.3127	0.0625
Subgroup 2	0.0624	0.0623	0.0624	0.0626	0.0625	0.3122	0.0624
Subgroup 3	0.0622	0.0625	0.0623	0.0625	0.0626	0.3121	0.0624
Subgroup 4	0.0624	0.0623	0.0620	0.0623	0.0624	0.3114	0.0623
Subgroup 5	0.0621	0.0621	0.0622	0.0625	0.0624	0.3113	0.0623
Subgroup 6	0.0628	0.0626	0.0625	0.0626	0.0627	0.3132	0.0626
Subgroup 7	0.0624	0.0627	0.0625	0.0624	0.0626	0.3126	0.0625
Subgroup 8	0.0624	0.0625	0.0625	0.0626	0.0626	0.3126	0.0625
Subgroup 9	0.0627	0.0628	0.0626	0.0625	0.0627	0.3133	0.0627
Subgroup 10	0.0625	0.0626	0.0628	0.0626	0.0627	0.3132	0.0626
Subgroup 11	0.0625	0.0624	0.0626	0.0626	0.0626	0.3127	0.0625
Subgroup 12	0.0630	0.0628	0.0627	0.0625	0.0627	0.3134	0.0627
Subgroup 13	0.0627	0.0626	0.0628	0.0627	0.0626	0.3137	0.0627
Subgroup 14	0.0626	0.0626	0.0625	0.0626	0.0627	0.3130	0.0626
Subgroup 15	0.0628	0.0627	0.0626	0.0625	0.0626	0.3132	0.0626
Subgroup 16	0.0625	0.0626	0.0625	0.0628	0.0627	0.3131	0.0626
Subgroup 17	0.0624	0.0626	0.0624	0.0625	0.0627	0.3126	0.0625
Subgroup 18	0.0628	0.0627	0.0628	0.0626	0.0630	0.3139	0.0627
Subgroup 19	0.0627	0.0626	0.0628	0.0625	0.0627	0.3133	0.0627
Subgroup 20	0.0626	0.0625	0.0626	0.0625	0.0627	0.3129	0.0626
Subgroup 21	0.0627	0.0626	0.0628	0.0625	0.0627	0.3133	0.0627
Subgroup 22	0.0625	0.0626	0.0628	0.0625	0.0627	0.3131	0.0626
Subgroup 23	0.0628	0.0626	0.0627	0.0630	0.0627	0.3138	0.0628
Subgroup 24	0.0625	0.0631	0.0630	0.0628	0.0627	0.3141	0.0628
Subgroup 25	0.0627	0.0630	0.0631	0.0628	0.0627	0.3143	0.0629
Subgroup 26	0.0630	0.0628	0.0620	0.0628	0.0627	0.3142	0.0628
Subgroup 27	0.0630	0.0628	0.0631	0.0628	0.0627	0.3144	0.0629
Subgroup 28	0.0632	0.0632	0.0628	0.0631	0.0630	0.3153	0.0631
Subgroup 29	0.0630	0.0628	0.0631	0.0632	0.0631	0.3152	0.0630
Subgroup 30	0.0632	0.0631	0.0630	0.0628	0.0628	0.3149	0.0630
						9.3981	

Step 2 Count the Number of Times Each Measurement Occurs. A check sheet, or tally sheet is used to make this step easier (Figure 9.7).

Step 3 Construct the Diagram. The count of the number of times each measurement occurred is placed on the *y* axis. The values, between 0.0620 and 0.0632, are each marked on the *x* axis. The completed frequency diagram is shown in Figure 9.8.

Step 4 Interpret the Frequency Diagram. This frequency distribution is nearly symmetrical, but there is only one occurrence of the value 0.0629. The engineers should definitely investigate why this is so.

0.0620	/
0.0621	//
0.0622	//
0.0623	////
0.0624	++++ ++++ //
0.0625	++++ ++++ ++++ ++++ ++++ /
0.0626	++++ ++++ ++++ ++++ ++++ ++++
0.0627	++++ ++++ ++++ ++++ ++++ //
0.0628	++++ ++++ ++++ ++++ ///
0.0629	/
0.0630	++++ ++++ /
0.0631	++++ //
0.0632	////

Figure 9.7   Clutch Plate Thickness Tally Sheet

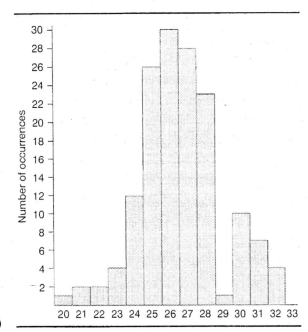

Figure 9.8   Clutch Plate Thickness Frequency Distribution (Coded 0.06)

Histograms

Histograms and frequency diagrams are very similar. The most notable difference between the two is that on a histogram the data are grouped into cells. Each cell contains a range of values. This grouping of data results in fewer cells on the graph than with a frequency diagram. The x axis scale on a histogram will indicate the cell midpoints rather than individual values. The following Six Sigma Tools at Work feature details the construction of a histogram.

 SIX SIGMA TOOLS AT WORK

Constructing a Histogram

The engineers working with the thickness of the clutch plate have decided to create a histogram to aid in their analysis of the process. They are following these steps:

Step 1 Collect the Data and Construct a Tally Sheet. The engineers will use the data previously collected (Table 9.3) as well as the tally sheet created during the construction of the frequency diagram (Figure 9.7).

Step 2 Calculate the Range. The **range**, *represented by the letter R, is calculated by subtracting the lowest observed value from the highest observed value.* In this case, 0.0620 is the lowest value and 0.0632 is the highest:

$$\text{Range} = R = X_h - X_l$$

where

$$R = \text{range}$$
$$X_h = \text{highest number}$$
$$X_l = \text{lowest number}$$
$$R = 0.0632 - 0.0620 = 0.0012$$

Step 3 Create the Cells. In a histogram, data are combined into cells. Cells are composed of three components: cell intervals, cell midpoints, and cell boundaries (Figure 9.9). **Cell midpoints** *identify the centers of cells. A* **cell interval** *is the distance between the cell midpoints. The* **cell boundary** *defines the limits of the cell.*

Cell Intervals Odd-numbered cell intervals are often chosen for ease of calculation. For example, if the data were measured to one decimal place, then the cell intervals could be 0.3, 0.5, 0.7, or 0.9. If the gathered data were measured to three decimal places, then the cell intervals to choose from would be 0.003, 0.005, 0.007, and 0.009. (The values of 1, 0.1, and 0.001 are not chosen for a histogram because they result in the creation of a frequency diagram.) For this example, because the data were measured to four decimal places, the cell interval could be 0.0003, 0.0005, 0.0007, or 0.0009.

Cell interval choice plays a large part in the size of the histogram created. To determine the number of cells, the following formula is used:

$$h = \frac{R}{i} + 1$$

where

$$h = \text{number of cells}$$
$$i = \text{cell interval}$$
$$R = \text{range}$$

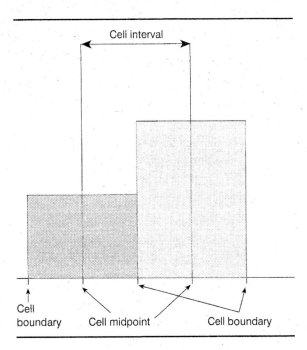

Figure 9.9   Histogram
Cell Description

Since both i, the cell interval, and h, the number of cells, are unknown, creators of histograms must choose values for one of them and then solve for the other. For our example, if we choose a cell interval of 0.0003,

$$h = \frac{0.0012}{0.0003} + 1$$

$$h = 5$$

The histogram created will contain 5 cells.
    For a cell interval value of 0.0005:

$$h = \frac{0.0012}{0.0005} + 1$$

$$h = 3$$

For a cell interval value of 0.0007:`

$$h = \frac{0.0012}{0.0007} + 1$$

$$h = 3$$

As the cell interval gets larger, the number of cells necessary to hold all the data and make a histogram decreases. When deciding the number of cells to use, it is sometimes helpful to follow this rule of thumb:

    For fewer than 100 pieces of data, use 4 to 9 cells.
    For 100 to 500 pieces of data, use 8 to 17 cells.
    For 500 or more, use 15 to 20 cells.

Another helpful rule of thumb exists for determining the number of cells in a histogram. Use the square root of n (represented as $\sqrt{n}$), where n is the number of data points, as an approximation of the number of cells needed.

For this example, we will use a cell interval of 0.0003. This will create a histogram that provides enough spread to analyze the data.

Cell Midpoints   When constructing a histogram, it is important to remember two things: (1) Histograms must contain all of the data; (2) one particular value cannot fit into two different cells. Cell midpoints are selected to ensure that these problems are avoided. To determine the midpoint values that anchor the histogram, use either one of the following two techniques.

The simplest technique is to choose the lowest value measured. In this example, the lowest measured value is 0.0620. Other midpoint values are determined by adding the cell interval of 0.0003 to 0.0620 first and then adding it to each successive new midpoint. If we begin at 0.0620, we find the other midpoints at 0.0623, 0.0626, 0.0629, and 0.0632. If the number of values in the cell is high and the distance between the cell boundaries is not large, the midpoint is the most representative value in the cell.

Cell Boundaries   The cell size, set by the boundaries of the cell, is determined by the cell midpoints and the cell interval. Locating the cell boundaries, or the limits of the cell, allows the user to place values in a particular cell. To determine the lower cell boundary, divide the cell interval by 2 and subtract that value from the cell midpoint. To calculate the lower cell boundary for a cell with a midpoint of 0.0620, the cell interval is divided by 2:

$$0.0003 \div 2 = 0.00015$$

Then, subtract 0.00015 from the cell midpoint,

$$0.0620 - 0.00015 = 0.06185, \text{ the first lower boundary}$$

To determine the upper cell boundary for a midpoint of 0.0620, add the cell interval to the lower cell boundary:

$$0.06185 + 0.0003 = 0.06215$$

The lower cell boundary of one cell is the upper cell boundary of another. Continue adding the cell interval to each new lower cell boundary calculated until all the lower cell boundaries have been determined.

Note that the cell boundaries are a half decimal value greater in accuracy than the measured values. This is to help ensure that values can be placed in only one cell of a histogram. In our example, the first cell will have boundaries of 0.06185 and 0.06215. The second cell will have boundaries of 0.06215 and 0.06245. Where would a data value of 0.0621 be placed? Obviously in the first cell. Cell intervals, with their midpoint values starting at 0.0620, are shown in Figure 9.10.

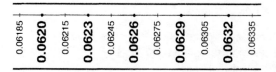

Figure 9.10   Cell Boundaries and Midpoints

Step 4 Label the Axes. Scale and label the horizontal axis according to the cell midpoints determined in Step 3. Label the vertical axis to reflect the amount of data collected, in counting numbers.

Step 5 Post the Values. The final step in the creation of a histogram is to post the values from the check sheet to the histogram. The *x* axis is marked with the cell midpoints and, if space permits, the cell boundaries. The cell boundaries are used to guide the creator when posting the values to the histogram. On the *y* axis, the frequency of those values within a particular cell is shown. All the data must be included in the cells (Figure 9.11).

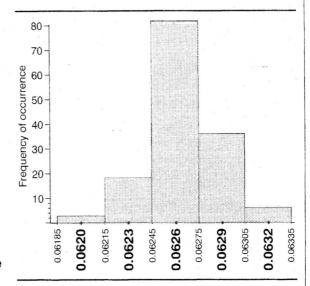

Figure 9.11   Clutch Plate Thickness Histogram

Step 6 Interpret the Histogram. As we can see in Figure 9.11, the data are grouped around 0.0626 and are somewhat symmetrical. In the following sections, we will study histogram shapes, sizes, and locations when compared to a desired target specification. We will also utilize measures such as means, modes, and medians to create a clear picture of where the data are grouped (the central tendency of the data). Standard deviations and ranges will be used to measure how the data are dispersed around the mean. These statistical values will be used to fully describe the data comprising a histogram.

Shape, location, and spread are the characteristics used to describe a distribution (Figure 9.12).

Shape: Symmetry, Skewness, Kurtosis Shape   *Symmetry, skewness, and kurtosis shape refers to the form that the values of the measurable characteristics take on when plotted or graphed.* Tracing a smooth curve over the tops of the rectangular areas used when

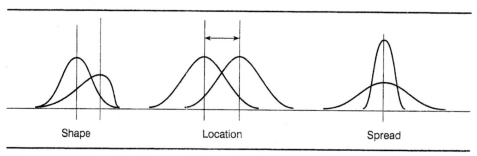

Shape	Location	Spread

Figure 9.12   Shape, Location, and Spread

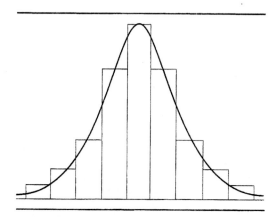

Figure 9.13   Symmetrical Histogram with Smooth Curve Overlay

graphing a histogram clarifies the shape of a histogram for the viewer (Figure 9.13). Identifiable characteristics include **symmetry**, or, in the case of lack of symmetry, **skewness** of the data; **kurtosis**, or *peakedness of the data;* and **modes**, *the number of peaks in the data.*

When a distribution is **symmetrical**, *the two halves are mirror images of each other.* The two halves correspond in size, shape, and arrangement (Figure 9.13). When a distribution is not symmetrical, it is considered to be skewed (Figure 9.14). With a *skewed distribution, the majority of the data are grouped either to the left or the right of a center value, and on the opposite side a few values trail away from the center. When a distribution is* **skewed to the right,** *the majority of the data are found on the left side of the figure, with the tail of the distribution going to the right.* The opposite is true for a distribution that is **skewed to the left**.

Kurtosis describes the peakedness of the distribution. A *distribution with a high peak is referred to as* **leptokurtic;** *a flatter curve is called* **platykurtic** (Figure 9.15). Typically, the kurtosis of a histogram is discussed by comparing it with another distribution. As we will see later in the chapter, skewness and kurtosis can be calculated numerically. Occasionally distributions will display unusual patterns. *If the distribution displays more than one peak, it is considered* **multimodal.** *Distributions with two distinct peaks are called* **bimodal** (Figure 9.16).

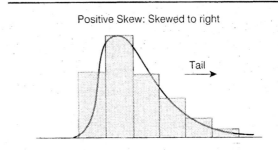

Positive Skew: Skewed to right

Tail →

Negative Skew: Skewed to left

← Tail

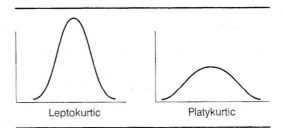

Figure 9.14   Skewness

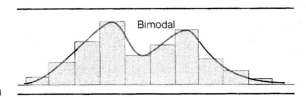

Leptokurtic   Platykurtic

Figure 9.15   Leptokurtic and Platykurtic

Bimodal

Figure 9.16   Bimodal Distribution

 SIX SIGMA TOOLS AT WORK

Analyzing the Histogram

Analyzing Figure 9.11 based on the three characteristics of shape, location, and spread reveals that the clutch plate thickness data are fairly consistent.

The **shape** of the distribution is somewhat symmetrical, though skewed very slightly to the right. The data are unimodal, centering on 0.0626 inch. Since we have no other distributions of the same type of product, we cannot make any comparisons or comments on the kurtosis of the data. **Location,** or where the data are located or gathered, is around 0.0626. If the engineers have specifications of 0.0625 ÷ 0.0003 then the center of the distribution is higher than the desired value. Given the specifications, the **spread** of the data is broader than the desired 0.0622 to 0.0628 at 0.0620 to 0.0632. Further mathematical analysis with techniques covered later in this chapter will give us an even clearer picture of the data.

DATA ANALYSIS: ANALYTICAL

Though shape was easily seen from a picture, the location and spread can be more clearly identified mathematically. Location is described by measures of central tendency: the mean, mode, and median. Spread is defined by measures of dispersion: the range and standard deviation.

Location: Measures of Central Tendency

Averages, medians, and modes are the statistical values that define the center of a distribution. *Since they reveal the place where the data tend to be gathered, these values are commonly called the* **measures of central tendency.**

Mean

The **mean** *of a series of measurements is determined by adding the values together and then dividing this sum by the total number of values.* When this value is calculated for a population, it is referred to as the mean and is signified by μ. When this value is calculated for a sample, it is called the *average* and is signified by $\overline{X}$ (X bar). Means and averages can be used to judge whether or not a group of values is accurate. To calculate the mean of a population, use the following formula:

$$\mu = \frac{X_1 + X_2 + X_3 + \cdots + X_n}{n} = \frac{\sum\limits_{i=1}^{n} X_i}{n}$$

where

$$\mu = \text{mean value of the series of measurements}$$
$$X_1, X_2, \ldots, X_n = \text{values of successive measurements}$$
$$n = \text{number of readings}$$

The same formula can be used to calculate the average associated with a sample. To calculate the average of a sample, use the following formula:

$$\overline{X} = \frac{X_{s1} + X_{s2} + X_{s3} + \cdots + X_{sn}}{n} = \frac{\sum\limits_{i=1}^{n} X_i}{n}$$

where

$\overline{X}$ = average value of the sample measurements
$X_{s1}, X_{s2}, \ldots, X_{sn}$ = values of sample measurements
n = number of readings

 SIX SIGMA TOOLS AT WORK

Determining the Mean

Averages for each of the subgroups for the thicknesses of the clutch plate can be calculated.

1. Calculate the sum of each set of subgroup values:

Subgroup 1:
$$\sum X_1 = 0.0625 + 0.0626 + 0.0624 + 0.0625 + 0.0627$$
$$= 0.3127$$

2. Calculate the subgroup average by dividing the sum by the number of samples in the subgroup ($n = 5$):

Subgroup 1:
$$\overline{X} = \frac{0.0625 + 0.0626 + 0.0624 + 0.0625 + 0.0627}{5}$$
$$= \frac{0.3127}{5}$$
$$= 0.0625$$

From earlier in the chapter, Table 9.4 gives a list of the sums and averages calculated for this example. Once the averages for each subgroup have been calculated, a grand average for all of the subgroups can be found by dividing the sum of the subgroup sums by the total number of items taken in all of the subgroups (150). A grand average is designated as $\overline{\overline{X}}$ (X double bar):

$$\overline{\overline{X}} = \frac{0.3127 + 0.3122 + 0.3121 + 0.3114 + \cdots + 0.3149}{150}$$
$$= \frac{9.3990}{150}$$
$$= 0.0627$$

Notice that an average of the averages is not taken. Taking an average of the averages will work only when the sample sizes are constant. Use the sums of each of the subgroups to perform the calculation.

Median

The **median** is the value that divides an ordered series of numbers so that there is an equal number of values on either side of the center, or median, value. An ordered series of data has been arranged according to their magnitude. Once the values are placed in order, the median is the value of the number that has an equal number of values to its left and right. In the case of finding a median for an even number of values, the two center values of the ordered set of numbers are added together and the result is divided by 2. Figure 9.17 shows the calculation of several medians.

 SIX SIGMA TOOLS AT WORK

Determining the Median

From the check sheet (Figure 9.7) the median of the clutch plate thickness data can be found. When the data are placed in an ordered series, the center or median number is found to be 0.0626. Each measurement must be taken into account when calculating a median. Do not use solely the cell midpoints of a frequency diagram or a histogram.

23 25 26 27 28 29 25 22 24 24 25 26 25
Unordered set of numbers

22 23 24 24 25 25 25 25 26 26 27 28 29
Ordered set of numbers

Median = 25

1 2 4 1 5 2 6 7
Unordered set of numbers

1 1 2 2 4 5 6 7
Ordered set of numbers

Median = (2 + 4) ÷ 2 = 3

Figure 9.17 Calculating Medians

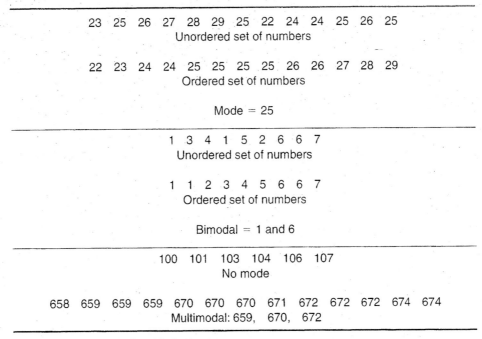

23 25 26 27 28 29 25 22 24 24 25 26 25
Unordered set of numbers

22 23 24 24 25 25 25 25 26 26 27 28 29
Ordered set of numbers

Mode = 25

1 3 4 1 5 2 6 6 7
Unordered set of numbers

1 1 2 3 4 5 6 6 7
Ordered set of numbers

Bimodal = 1 and 6

100   101   103   104   106   107
No mode

658 659 659 659 670 670 670 671 672 672 672 674 674
Multimodal: 659,   670,   672

Figure 9.18   Calculating Modes

Mode

The **mode** *is the most frequently occurring number in a group of values.* In a set of numbers, a mode may or may not occur (Figure 9.18). A set of numbers may also have two or more modes. If a set of numbers or measurements has one mode, it is said to be unimodal. If it has two numbers appearing with the same frequency, it is called bimodal. Distributions with more than two modes are referred to as multimodal. In a frequency distribution or a histogram, the cell with the highest frequency is the mode.

 SIX SIGMA TOOLS AT WORK:

Determining the Mode

The mode can be found for the clutch plate thickness data. The check sheet (Figure 9.7) clearly shows that 0.0626 is the most frequently occurring number. It is tallied 30 times.

The Relationship Among the Mean, Median, and Mode

As measures of central tendency, the mean, median, and mode can be compared with each other to determine where the data are located. Measures of central tendency describe the center position of the data. They show how the data tend to

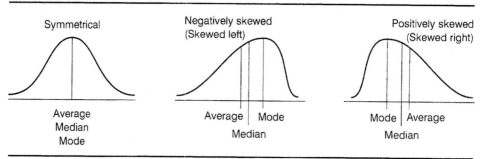

Figure 9.19   Comparison of Mean, Mode and Median

build up around a center value. When a distribution is symmetrical, the mean, mode, and median values are equal. For a skewed distribution, the values will be different (Figure 9.19). Comparing the mean (average), mode, and median determines whether or not a distribution is skewed and, if it is, in which direction.

 SIX SIGMA TOOLS AT WORK:

Seeing the Relationship

Knowing the average, median, and mode of the clutch plate data provides information about the symmetry of the data. If the distribution is symmetrical, the average, mode, and median values will be equal. A skewed distribution will have different values. From previous examples, the values for the clutch plate are

$$\text{Average} = 0.0627 \text{ inch}$$
$$\text{Median} = 0.0626 \text{ inch}$$
$$\text{Mode} = 0.0626 \text{ inch}$$

As seen in the frequency diagram (Figure 9.20), the mode marks the peak of the distribution. The average, slightly to the right of the mode and median, pulls the distribution to the right. This slight positive skew is due to the high values for clutch plate thickness that occur in later samples.

Spread: Measures of Dispersion

The range and standard deviation are two measurements that enable the investigator to determine the spread of the data, that is, where the values fall in relation to each other and to the mean. Because these two describe where the data are dispersed on either side of a central value, they are often referred to as measures of dispersion. Used

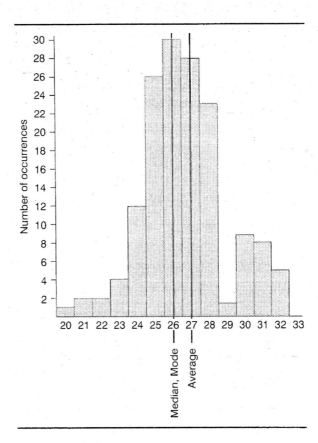

Figure 9.20 Comparison of Mean, Mode, and Median for the Clutch Plate

in conjunction with the mean, mode, and median, these values create a more complete picture of a distribution.

Range

As was pointed out in the discussion of the histogram earlier in this chapter, the *range is the difference between the highest value in a series of values or sample and the lowest value in that same series.* A range value describes how far the data spread. All of the other values in a population or sample will fall between the highest and lowest values:

$$R = X_h - X_l$$

where

R = range
X_h = highest value in the series
X_l = lowest value in the series

σ **SIX SIGMA TOOLS AT WORK:**

Calculating Range Values

The flat round plate data comprises subgroups of sample size five (Table 9.4). For each sample, a range value can be calculated. For example:

Subgroup 1   0.0625   0.0626   0.0624   0.0625   0.0627

Range $= X_h - X_l = 0.0627 - 0.0624 = 0.0003$

Subgroup 2   0.0624   0.0623   0.0624   0.0626   0.0625

Range $= X_h - X_l = 0.0626 - 0.0623 = 0.0003$

The other ranges are calculated in the same manner. These range values are used in the next chapter to study the variation present in the process over time.

Standard Deviation

The range shows where each end of the distribution is located, but it doesn't tell how the data are grouped within the distribution. In Figure 9.21, the three distributions have the same average and range, but all three are different. *The standard deviation shows the dispersion of the data within the distribution.* It describes how the individual values fall in relation to their means, the actual amount of variation present in a set of data. The standard deviation, because it uses all of the measurements taken, provides more reliable information about the dispersion of the data. The range considers only the two extreme values in its calculation, giving no information concerning where the values may be grouped. Since it only considers the highest and lowest values, the range has the disadvantage of becoming a less accurate description of the data as the number of readings or sample values increases. The range is best used with small populations or small sample sizes of less than 10 values. However, since the range is easy to calculate, it is the most frequently used measure of dispersion.

When the measurements have been taken from each and every item in the total population, the standard deviation is calculated through the use of the following formula:

$$\sigma = \sqrt{\frac{\sum_{i=1}^{n}(X_i - \mu)^2}{n}}$$

where

σ = standard deviation of the population
μ = mean value of the series of measurements
$X_i = X_1, X_2, \ldots, X_n$ = values of each reading
n = number of readings

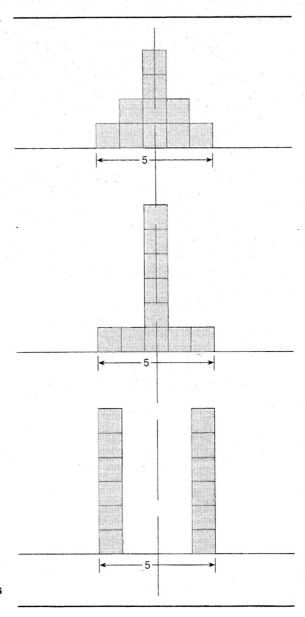

Figure 9.21 Different Distributions with Same Averages and Ranges

The standard deviation of the population is sometimes known as the *root mean square deviation*. When populations increase in size it becomes difficult to calculate without help from a computer.

A smaller standard deviation is desirable because it indicates greater similarity between data values—that is, the data are more precisely grouped. In the case of products, a small standard deviation indicates that the products are nearly alike. As discussed with the Taguchi loss function in Chapter 2, creating products or providing services that are similar to each other is optimal.

When the measurements are taken from items sampled from the entire population, the previous formula is modified to reflect the fact that not every item in the population has been measured. This change is reflected in the denominator. The standard deviation of a sample is represented by the letter s:

$$s = \sqrt{\frac{\sum_{i=1}^{n}(X_i - \overline{X})^2}{n - 1}}$$

where

$$s = \text{standard deviation of the sample}$$
$$\overline{X} = \text{average value of the series of measurements}$$
$$X_i = X_1, X_2, \ldots, X_n = \text{values of each reading}$$
$$n = \text{number of readings}$$

σ SIX SIGMA TOOLS AT WORK:

Determining the Standard Deviation of a Sample

In the case of subgroups comprising the clutch plate data, it is possible to calculate the sample standard deviation for each of the subgroups. For subgroup 1:

$$s_1 = \sqrt{\frac{\Sigma(X_i - \overline{X})^2}{n - 1}}$$

$$= \sqrt{\frac{(0.0624 - 0.0625)^2 + 2(0.0625 - 0.0625)^2 + (0.0626 - 0.0625)^2 + (0.0627 - 0.0625)^2}{5 - 1}}$$

$$= 0.0001$$

Standard deviations for the remaining subgroups can be calculated in the same manner.

Using the Mean, Mode, Median, Standard Deviation, and Range Together

Measures of central tendency and measures of dispersion are critical when describing statistical data. As the following example shows, one without the other creates an incomplete picture of the values measured.

σ SIX SIGMA TOOLS AT WORK

Seeing the Whole Picture I

Two engineers were keeping track of the rate of water pipe being laid by three different crews. Over the past 36 days, the amount of pipe laid per day was recorded and the frequency diagrams shown in Figure 9.22 were created. When they studied the data originally, the two engineers calculated only the mean, mode, and median for each crew.

$$\text{Mean}_1 = 20 \qquad \text{Median}_1 = 20 \qquad \text{Mode}_1 = 20$$
$$\text{Mean}_2 = 20 \qquad \text{Median}_2 = 20 \qquad \text{Mode}_2 = 20$$
$$\text{Mean}_3 = 20 \qquad \text{Median}_3 = 20 \qquad \text{Mode}_3 = 20$$

On the surface, these distributions appear the same. It was not until the range and standard deviation for each of the three pipe-laying crews' work were calculated that the differences became apparent:

$$\text{Range}_1 = 4$$

$$\text{Standard deviation}_1 = 1.03, \text{ rounded to } 1.0$$

$$\sigma = \sqrt{\frac{\begin{array}{c}3(18 - 20)^2 + 7(19 - 20)^2 + 16(20 - 20)^2 \\ + \ 7(21 - 20)^2 + 3(22 - 20)^2\end{array}}{36}}$$

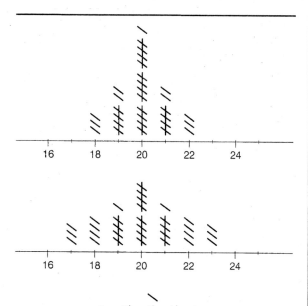

Figure 9.22 Frequency Diagrams of the Amount of Pipe Laid per Day in Feet

Range$_2$ = 6
Standard deviation$_2$ = 1.65, rounded to 1.7

$$\sigma = \sqrt{\dfrac{\begin{array}{c}3(17-20)^2 + 4(18-20)^2 + 6(19-20)^2\\ + 10(20-20)^2 + 6(21-20)^2 + 4(22-20)^2\\ + 3(23-20)^2\end{array}}{36}}$$

Range$_3$ = 10
Standard deviation$_3$ = 2.42, rounded to 2.4

$$\sigma = \sqrt{\dfrac{\begin{array}{c}1(15-20)^2 + 2(16-20)^2 + 3(17-20)^2\\ + 4(18-20)^2 + 5(19-20)^2 + 6(20-20)^2\\ + 5(21-20)^2 + 4(22-20)^2 + 3(23-20)^2\\ + 2(24-20)^2 + 1(25-20)^2\end{array}}{36}}$$

Once calculated, the ranges and standard deviations revealed that significant differences exist in the performance of the three crews. The first crew was much more consistent in the amount of pipe they laid per day.

SIX SIGMA TOOLS AT WORK

Seeing the Whole Picture II

When we combine the analytical calculations with the graphical information from the previous Six Sigma Tools at Work features, we see a more complete picture of the clutch plate data we are studying (Figure 9.11). The grand average, $\overline{\overline{X}}$ = 0.0627 inches, median (0.0626), and mode (0.0626) confirm that the histogram is skewed slightly to the right. Because we know the grand average of the data, we also know that the distribution is not centered on the desired target value of 0.0625 inches. The frequency diagram gives us the critical information that there is only one plate with a thickness of 0.0629 inches. The range of our data is fairly broad; the frequency diagram shows an overall spread of the distribution of 0.0012 inches. In general, through their calculations and diagrams, the engineers have learned that they are making the plates too thick. They have also learned that the machining process is not producing plates of consistent thickness.

Other Measures of Dispersion

Skewness

*When a distribution lacks symmetry, it is considered **skewed**.* A picture of the distribution is not necessary to determine skewness. Skewness can be measured by calculating the following value:

$$a_3 = \dfrac{\sum_{i=1}^{h} f_i(X_i - \overline{X})^3/n}{s^3}$$

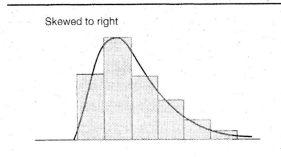

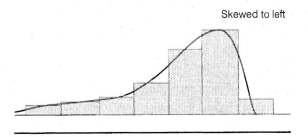

Figure 9.23 Skewness

where

$$a_3 = \text{skewness}$$
$$X_i = \text{individual data values under study}$$
$$\overline{X} = \text{average of individual values}$$
$$n = \text{sample size}$$
$$s = \text{standard deviation of sample}$$
$$f_i = \text{frequency of occurrence}$$

Once determined, the skewness figure is compared with zero. A skewness value of zero means that the distribution is symmetrical. A value greater than zero means that the data are skewed to the right; the tail of the distribution goes to the right. If the value is negative (less than zero), then the distribution is skewed to the left, with a tail of the distribution going to the left (Figure 9.23). The higher the value, the stronger the skewness.

Kurtosis

Kurtosis, the peakedness of the data, is another value that can be calculated:

$$a_4 = \frac{\sum_{i=1}^{h} f_i(X_i - \overline{X})^4/n}{s^4}$$

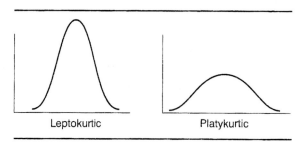

Figure 9.24   Kurtosis

where

a_4 = kurtosis
X_i = individual data values under study
$\overline{X}$ = average of individual values
n = sample size
s = standard deviation of sample

Once calculated, the kurtosis value must be compared with another distribution or with a standard in order to be interpreted. In Figure 9.24, the distribution on the left side is more peaked than that on the right. Its kurtosis value would be larger.

CENTRAL LIMIT THEOREM

Much of statistical process control is based on the use of samples taken from a population of items. The central limit theorem enables conclusions to be drawn from the sample data and applied to a population. The **central limit theorem** states that a group of sample averages tends to be normally distributed; as the sample size n increases, this tendency toward normality improves. The population from which the samples are taken does not need to be normally distributed for the sample averages to tend to be normally distributed (Figure 9.25). In the field of quality, the central limit theorem supports the use of sampling to analyze the population. The mean of the sample averages will approximate the mean of the population. The variation associated with the sample averages will be less than that of the population. It is important to remember that it is the sample *averages* that tend toward normality, as the following Six Sigma Tools at Work feature shows.

 SIX SIGMA TOOLS AT WORK

Using the Central Limit Theorem

Roger and Bill are trying to settle an argument. Roger says that averages from a deck of cards will form a normal curve when plotted. Bill says they won't. They decide to try the following exercise involving averages. They are going to follow these rules:

1. They will randomly select five cards from a well-shuffled deck and write down the values (Figure 9.26). (An ace is worth 1 point, a jack 11, a queen 12, and a king 13.)

2. They will record the numerical values on a graph (Figure 9.26).
3. They will calculate the average for the five cards.
4. They will graph the results of step 3 on a graph separate from that used in step 2 (Figure 9.27).
5. They will then replace the five cards in the deck.
6. They will shuffle the deck.
7. They will repeat this process 50 times.

Figure 9.26 displays the results of steps 1 and 2. Since the deck was well shuffled and the selection of cards from the deck was random, each card had the same chance of being selected—1/52. The fairly uniform distribution of values in the frequency diagram in Figure 9.26 shows that each type of card was selected approximately the same number of times. The distribution would be even more uniform if a greater number of cards had been drawn.

Figure 9.27 graphs the results of step 4. Notice that as the number of averages recorded increases, the results look more and more like a normal curve. As predicted by the central limit theorem, the distribution of the sample averages in the final diagram in Figure 9.27 is approximately normal. This has occurred even though the original distribution was not normal.

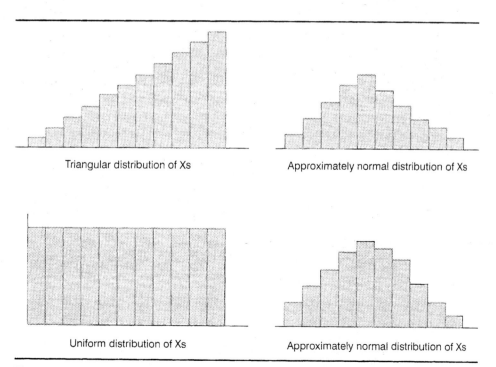

Triangular distribution of Xs   Approximately normal distribution of Xs

Uniform distribution of Xs   Approximately normal distribution of Xs

Figure 9.25   Nonnormal Distributions and Their Plots of Averages

1	11	13	10	12	7	10.6	26	8	10	1	9	10	7.6
2	1	7	12	9	3	6.4	27	9	13	2	2	2	5.6
3	9	5	12	1	11	7.6	28	12	4	12	3	13	8.8
4	11	5	7	9	12	8.8	29	12	4	7	6	9	7.6
5	7	12	13	7	4	8.6	30	1	12	3	12	11	7.8
6	11	9	5	1	13	7.8	31	12	3	10	11	6	8.4
7	1	4	13	12	13	8.6	32	3	5	10	2	7	5.4
8	13	3	2	6	12	7.2	33	9	1	2	3	11	5.2
9	2	4	1	10	13	6.0	34	6	8	6	13	9	8.4
10	4	5	12	1	9	6.2	35	2	12	5	10	4	6.6
11	2	5	7	7	11	6.4	36	6	4	8	9	12	7.8
12	6	9	8	2	12	7.4	37	9	13	3	10	1	7.2
13	2	3	6	11	11	6.6	38	2	1	13	7	5	5.6
14	2	6	9	11	13	8.2	39	10	11	5	12	13	10.2
15	6	8	8	9	1	6.4	40	13	2	8	2	11	7.2
16	3	4	12	1	6	5.2	41	2	10	5	4	11	6.4
17	8	1	8	6	10	6.6	42	10	4	12	7	11	8.8
18	5	7	6	8	8	6.8	43	13	13	7	1	10	8.8
19	2	5	4	10	1	4.4	44	9	10	7	11	11	9.6
20	5	7	12	7	8	7.8	45	6	7	8	7	4	6.4
21	9	1	3	6	12	6.2	46	1	4	12	11	13	8.2
22	1	13	9	3	6	6.4	47	9	11	8	1	11	8.0
23	4	5	13	5	7	6.8	48	8	13	10	13	4	9.6
24	3	7	9	8	10	7.4	49	12	11	11	2	3	7.8
25	1	7	6	6	1	4.2	50	2	12	5	11	9	7.8

```
 1  ||||  ||||  ||||  ||||  ||
 2  ||||  ||||  ||||  ||||
 3  ||||  ||||  ||||
 4  ||||  ||||  ||||  |
 5  ||||  ||||  ||||  |
 6  ||||  ||||  ||||  |||
 7  ||||  ||||  ||||  ||||  |
 8  ||||  ||||  ||||  |
 9  ||||  ||||  ||||  ||||  |
10  ||||  ||||  ||||  ||
11  ||||  ||||  ||||  ||||  |||
12  ||||  ||||  ||||  ||||  ||||
13  ||||  ||||  ||||  ||||  ||
```

Figure 9.26 Numerical Values of Cards and Frequency Distribution

NORMAL FREQUENCY DISTRIBUTION

The normal frequency distribution, the familiar bell-shaped curve (Figure 9.28), is commonly called a *normal curve*. A **normal frequency distribution** *is described by the normal density function:*

$$f(x) = \frac{1}{\sigma\sqrt{2\pi}}\, e^{-(x-\mu)^2/2\sigma^2} \qquad -\infty < x < \infty$$

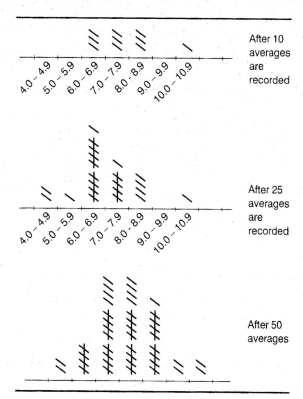

Figure 9.27 Distribution of Sample Averages

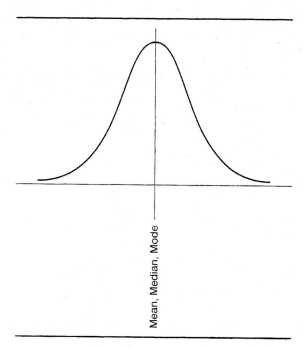

Figure 9.28 The Normal Curve

where

$$\pi \approx 3.14159$$
$$e \approx 2.71828$$

The normal frequency distribution has six distinct features:

1. A normal curve is symmetrical about μ, the central value.
2. The mean, mode, and median are all equal.
3. The curve is unimodal and bell-shaped.
4. Data values concentrate around the mean value of the distribution and decrease in frequency as the values get further away from the mean.
5. The area under the normal curve equals 1. One hundred percent of the data are found under the normal curve, 50 percent on the left-hand side, 50 percent on the right.
6. The normal distribution can be described in terms of its mean and standard deviation by observing that 99.73 percent of the measured values fall within ±3 standard deviations of the mean ($\mu \pm 3\sigma$), that 95.5 percent of the data fall within ±2 standard deviations of the mean ($\mu \pm 2\sigma$), and that 68.3 percent of the data fall within ±1 standard deviation ($\mu \pm 1\sigma$). Figure 9.29 demonstrates the percentage of measurements falling within each standard deviation.

These six features combine to create a peak in the center of the distribution, with the number of values decreasing as the measurements get farther away from the mean. As the data fall away toward the horizontal axis, the curve flattens. The tails of the normal distribution approach the horizontal axis and extend indefinitely, never reaching or crossing it.

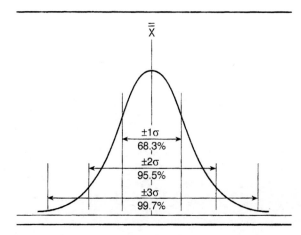

Figure 9.29   Percentage of Measurements Falling Within Each Standard Deviation

While not all symmetrical distributions are normal distributions, these six features are general indicators of a normal distribution. (There is a chi square test for normality. Refer to a statistics text for a complete description of the chi square test.)

Standard Normal Probability Distribution: Z Tables

The area under the normal curve can be determined if the mean and the standard deviation are known. The mean, or in the case of samples, the average, locates the center of the normal distribution. The standard deviation defines the spread of the data about the center of the distribution.

The relationships discussed in features 5 and 6 of the normal frequency distribution make it possible to calculate the percentage of values that fall between any two readings. If 100 percent of the data are under the normal curve, then the amount of product above or below a particular value can be determined. These values may be dimensions like the upper and lower specification limits set by the designer or they can be any value of interest. The formula for finding the area under the normal curve is

$$f(x) = \frac{1}{\sigma\sqrt{2\pi}} e^{-(x-\mu)^2/2\sigma^2} \qquad -\infty < x < \infty$$

where

$$\pi \approx 3.14159$$
$$e \approx 2.71828$$

This formula can be simplified through the use of the standard normal probability distribution table (Appendix 1). This table uses the formula

$$f(Z) = \frac{1}{\sqrt{2\pi}} e^{-Z^2/2}$$

where

$$Z = \frac{X_i - \overline{X}}{s} = \text{standard normal value}$$
$$X_i = \text{individual X value of interest}$$
$$\overline{X} = \text{average}$$
$$s = \text{standard deviation}$$

This formula also works with population means and population standard deviations:

$$Z = \frac{X_i - \mu}{\sigma_{\overline{x}}} = \text{standard normal value}$$

where

$$X_i = \text{individual X value of interest}$$
$$\mu = \text{population mean}$$
$$\sigma_{\bar{x}} = \text{population standard deviation} = \frac{\sigma}{\sqrt{n}}$$

Z is used with the table in Appendix 1 to find the value of the area under the curve, which represents a percentage or proportion of the product or measurements produced. If Z has a positive value, then it is to the right of the center of the distribution and X_i is larger than $\bar{X}$. If the Z value is negative, then it is on the left side of the center and X_i is smaller than $\bar{X}$.

To find the area under the normal curve associated with a particular X_i, use the following procedure:

1. Use the information on normal curves to verify that the measurements are normally distributed.
2. Use the mean, standard deviation, and value of interest in the formula to calculate Z.
3. Find the Z value in the table in Appendix 1.
4. Use the table to convert the Z values to the area of interest.
5. Convert the area of interest value from the table to a percentage by multiplying by 100.

The table in Appendix 1 is a left-reading table, meaning that it will provide the area under the curve from negative infinity up to the value of interest (Figure 9.30). These values will have to be manipulated to find the area greater than the value of interest or between two values. Drawing a picture of the situation in question and shading the area of interest often helps clarify the Z calculations. Values of Z should be rounded to two decimal places for use in the table. Interpolation between values can also be performed.

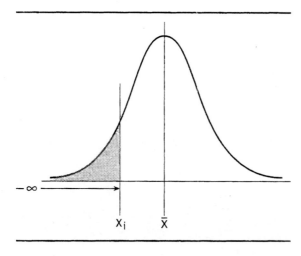

Figure 9.30   Normal Curve for Left-Reading Z Table

SIX SIGMA TOOLS AT WORK

Using Standard Normal Probability Distribution

The engineers working with the clutch plate thickness data have determined that their data approximates a normal curve. They would like to determine what percentage of parts from the samples taken are below 0.0624 inch and above 0.0629 inch.

1. From the data in Table 9.3, they calculated an average of 0.0627 and a standard deviation of 0.00023. They used the Z tables to determine the percentage of parts under 0.0624 inch thick. In Figure 9.31 the area of interest is shaded.

$$Z = \frac{0.0624 - 0.0627}{0.00023} = -1.30$$

From Appendix 1: Area = 0.0968

or 9.68 percent of the parts are thinner than 0.0624 inch.

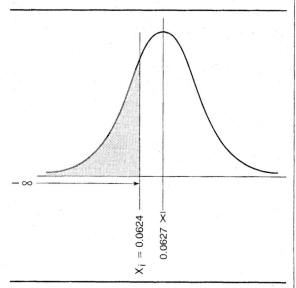

Figure 9.31   Area Under the Curve, X_i = 0.0624

2. When determining the percentage of the parts that are 0.0629 inch thick or thicker, it is important to note that the table in Appendix 1 is a left-reading table. Since the engineers want to determine the percentage of parts thicker than 0.0629 (the area shaded in Figure 9.32), they will have to subtract the area up to 0.0629 from 1.00.

$$Z = \frac{0.0629 - 0.0627}{0.00023} = 0.87$$

Area = 0.8079

or 80.79 percent of the parts are *thinner* than 0.0629 inch. However, they want the percentage of parts that are *thicker* than 0.0629 inch. To find this

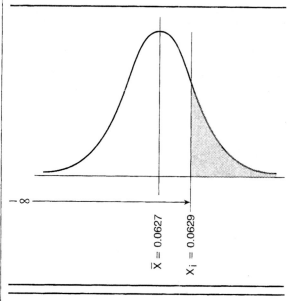

$\bar{X} = 0.0627$

$X_i = 0.0629$

Figure 9.32   Area Under the Curve, $X_i = 0.0629$

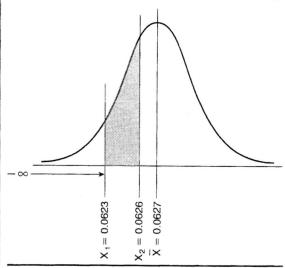

$X_1 = 0.0623$

$X_2 = 0.0626$

$\bar{X} = 0.0627$

Figure 9.33   Area Under the Curve Between 0.0623 and 0.0626

area they must subtract the area from 1.0 (remember: 100 percent of the parts fall under the normal curve):

$$1.00 - 0.8079 = 0.1921$$

or 19.21 percent of the parts are thicker than 0.0629 inch.

3. The engineers also want to find the percentage of the parts between 0.0623 and 0.0626 inch thick: The area of interest is shaded in Figure 9.33. In this problem the engineers must calculate two areas of interest, one for those parts 0.0623 inches thick or thinner and the other for those parts 0.0626 inch thick or thinner. The area of interest for those parts 0.0623 inch and thinner will be subtracted from the area of interest for 0.0626 inch and thinner.

First solve for parts 0.0623 inch or thinner:

$$Z_1 = \frac{0.0623 - 0.0627}{0.00023} = -1.74$$

$$\text{Area}_1 = 0.0409$$

or 4.09 percent of the parts are 0.0623 inches or thinner.
Then solve for parts 0.0626 inches or thinner:

$$Z_2 = \frac{0.0626 - 0.0627}{0.00023} = -0.44$$

$$\text{Area}_2 = 0.3300$$

or 33 percent of the parts are 0.0626 inches or thinner. Subtracting these two areas will determine the area in between:

$$0.3300 - 0.0409 = 0.2891$$

or 28.91 percent of the parts fall between 0.0623 and 0.0626 inches.

Confidence Intervals

When samples in a subgroup are averaged and the standard deviation calculated, these values are called point estimates. As a result of the central limit theorem, as long as they are random and unbiased samples, these subgroup sample averages can serve as estimators of the population mean. Determining whether or not the sample average is a good approximation of the population mean depends upon the spread of the sample data, the standard deviation of the distribution of the subgroup. The standard deviation, or standard error (SE), indicates the amount of error that will exist when the subgroup average is used to estimate the population mean.

Confidence interval testing is a technique that enables us to determine how well the subgroup average approximates the population mean. This straightforward calculation will enable us to make statements like: "there is a 95% probability that the sample average is a good estimator of the population mean" or "there is a 90% probability that the population mean is between X_1 and X_2." To determine X_1 and X_2, the endpoints for the confidence interval, use the formula:

$$\overline{X} \pm \frac{Z_{(\alpha/2)}(\sigma)}{\sqrt{n}}$$

where

$\overline{X}$ = sample average
n = number of samples
σ = population standard deviation
s = standard deviation (also $\sigma_{(n-1)}$)

α = probability that the population mean is not in the interval (alpha risk)

$1 - \alpha$ = probability the population mean is in the interval

$Z_{(\alpha/2)}$ = value from the Z table in Appendix 1 with an area of $\alpha/2$ to its right.

⬡ SIX SIGMA TOOLS AT WORK

Confidence Interval Calculation Using α

Manufacturing medical devices requires the ability to meet close tolerances. For a particularly critical machine setup, the manufacturing engineer conducted two runoffs for an injection molding machine. The first runoff, in which all of the molded parts were measured, the population mean was 0.800 mm with a population standard deviation, σ, of 0.007. From the second runoff, only 50 parts were sampled and their measurements taken. These randomly selected samples of parts have an average length of 0.822 mm and a standard deviation of 0.010. The manufacturing engineer would like to know, with 95% confidence, the interval values for the population mean for the second runoff.

$$0.822 \pm \frac{1.96(0.007)}{\sqrt{50}}$$

$$0.822 \pm 0.002$$

where

$\overline{X} = 0.822$

$n = 50$

$\sigma = 0.007$

$\alpha = 0.05$

$1 - 0.05 = 0.95$

$Z_{(\alpha/2)}$ = value from the Z table in Appendix 1 with an area of 0.025 to its right.
The interval is (0.820, 0.824). The engineer can be 95% confident that the population mean is between these two values.

The above formula, using the Z table, is considered a reasonable approximation if $n \geq 30$. For smaller sample sizes there is not an easy method to determine if the population is normal. Under these circumstances, the t distribution is used.

$$\overline{X} \pm \frac{t_{(\alpha/2)}(s)}{\sqrt{n}}$$

where

$\overline{X}$ = sample average

n = number of samples

s = standard deviation (also $\sigma_{(n-1)}$)

α = probability that the population mean is not in the interval (alpha risk)

$1 - \alpha$ = probability the population mean in the interval

$t_{(\alpha/2)}$ = value from the t table

df = degrees of freedom (n -- 1), the amount of data used by the measure of dispersion

The t value compensates for our lack of information about σ. The smaller the sample size, the more doubt exists, and the larger t must be. This t value is selected based on the degrees of freedom in the system, n -- 1. Values for the t distribution appear in Appendix 3.

 SIX SIGMA TOOLS AT WORK

Confidence Interval Calculation Using the t Distribution

Two machines have recently been installed at a manufacturing plant. In order to determine if additional noise dampening devices are needed, an industrial hygienist has taken several noise exposure measurements at a water jet cutting work center and a conventional stamping machine. He would like to determine with 90% confidence that these samples represent the mean noise exposure expected to be experienced by workers. The values represent the percentage of allowable daily dose. A value of 50% during an 8 hour shift represents 85 dB.

For the water jet cutting work center, the ratios recorded were $X_1 = 0.45$, $X_2 = 0.47$, and $X_3 = 0.44$, resulting in an $\overline{X} = 0.45$ and s = 0.015. The water jet noise value is calculated below.

$$0.45 \pm \frac{2.920(0.015)}{\sqrt{3}}$$

where

$$\overline{X} = 0.45$$
$$n = 3$$
$$s = 0.015$$
$$\alpha = 0.10$$
$$1 - \alpha = 0.90$$
$$t_{(\alpha/2)} = 2.920$$
$$df = 3 - 1 = 2$$

The interval is (0.425, 0.475). The hygienist can be 90% confident that the population mean is between these two values for the water jet cutting work center. Since these values are below the legal permissible decibel levels, no additional noise dampening is required.

For the conventional stamping machine, the ratios recorded were $X_1 = 0.55$, $X_2 = 0.75$, and $X_3 = 0.57$, resulting in an $\overline{X} = 0.62$ and s = 0.11.

$$0.62 \pm \frac{2.920(0.11)}{\sqrt{3}}$$

where

$$\overline{X} = 0.62$$
$$n = 3$$
$$s = 0.11$$
$$\alpha = 0.10$$
$$1 - \alpha = 0.90$$
$$t_{(\alpha/2)} = 2.920$$
$$df = 2$$

The interval is (0.43, 0.81). The hygienist can be 90% confident that the population mean is between these two values. Note that due to its large standard deviation, this is a much broader spread than the other interval. This broad interval includes values that are above the legal permissible decibel levels, and therefore, additional noise dampening is required.

SUMMARY

Frequency diagrams and histograms graphically depict the processes or occurrences under study. Means, modes, medians, standard deviations, and ranges are powerful tools used to describe processes statistically. Because of the central limit theorem, users of statistical information can form conclusions about populations of items based on the sample statistics.

 ■ *Take Away Tips*

1. Accuracy and precision are of paramount importance in quality assurance.
2. Histograms and frequency diagrams are similar. Unlike a frequency diagram, a histogram will group the data into cells.
3. Histograms are constructed using cell intervals, cell midpoints, and cell boundaries.
4. The analysis of histograms and frequency diagrams is based on shape, location, and spread.
5. Shape refers to symmetry, skewness, and kurtosis.
6. The location or central tendency refers to the relationship between the mean (average), mode, and median.
7. The spread or dispersion of data is described by the range and standard deviation.
8. Skewness describes the tendency of data to be gathered either to the left or right side of a distribution. When a distribution is symmetrical, skewness equals zero.
9. Kurtosis describes the peakedness of data. Leptokurtic distributions are more peaked than platykurtic ones.
10. A normal curve can be identified by the following five features: It is symmetrical about a central value. The mean, mode, and median are all equal. It is unimodal and bell-shaped. Data cluster around the mean value of the distribution and then fall away toward the horizontal axis. The area under the normal curve equals 1; 100 percent of the data is found under the normal curve.

11. In a normal distribution 99.73 percent of the measured values fall within ± 3 standard deviations of the mean ($\mu \pm 3\sigma$); 95.5 percent of the data fall within ± 2 standard deviations of the mean ($\mu \pm 2\sigma$); and 68.3 percent of the data fall within ± 1 standard deviation ($\mu \pm 1\sigma$).

12. The area under a normal curve can be calculated using the Z table and its associated formula. ▧

σ ▧ Formulas

$$R = X_h - X_l$$

$$\mu \text{ or } \overline{X} = \frac{X_1 + X_2 + X_3 + \ldots + X_n}{n} = \frac{\Sigma X_i}{n}$$

$$\sigma = \sqrt{\frac{\Sigma(X_i - \mu)^2}{n}}$$

$$s = \sqrt{\frac{\Sigma(X_i - \overline{X})^2}{n - 1}}$$

$$a_3 = \frac{\Sigma f_i(X_i - \overline{X})^3/n}{s^3}$$

$$a_4 = \frac{\Sigma f_i(X_i - \overline{X})^4/n}{s^4}$$

$$f(x) = \frac{1}{\sigma\sqrt{2\pi}} e^{-\frac{(x-\mu)^2}{2\sigma^2}} \qquad -\infty < x < \infty$$

where

$$\pi \approx 3.14159$$
$$e \approx 2.71828$$

$$f(Z) = \frac{1}{\sqrt{2\pi}} e^{-\frac{Z^2}{2}}$$

$$Z = \frac{X_i - \overline{X}}{s}$$

$$Z = \frac{X_i - \mu}{\sigma}$$

Chapter Questions

1. Describe the concepts of a sample and a population.

2. Describe a situation that is accurate, one that is precise, and one that is both. A picture may help you with your description.

3. Make a frequency distribution of the following data. Is this distribution bimodal? Multimodal? Skewed to the left? Skewed to the right? Normal?

   225, 226, 227, 226, 227, 228, 228, 229, 222, 223, 224, 226, 227, 228, 225, 221, 227, 229, 230

4. NB Plastics uses injection molds to produce plastic parts that range in size from a marble to a book. Parts are pulled off the press by one operator and passed on to another member of the team to be finished or cleaned up. This often involves trimming loose material, drilling holes, and painting. After a batch of parts has completed its cycle through the finishing process, a sample of five parts is chosen at random and certain dimensions are measured to ensure that each part is within certain tolerances. This information (in mm) is recorded for each of the five pieces and evaluated. Create a frequency diagram. Are the two operators trimming off the same amount of material? How do you know?

   Part Name: Mount
   Critical Dimension: 0.654 ± 0.005
   Tolerance: ±0.001
   Method of Checking: Caliper

Date	Time	Press	Oper	Samp 1	Samp 2	Samp 3	Samp 4	Samp 5
9/20/92	0100	#1	Jack	0.6550	0.6545	0.6540	0.6540	0.6545
9/20/92	0300	#1	Jack	0.6540	0.6540	0.6545	0.6545	0.6545
9/20/92	0500	#1	Jack	0.6540	0.6540	0.6540	0.6540	0.6535
9/20/92	0700	#1	Jack	0.6540	0.6540	0.6540	0.6540	0.6540
9/21/92	1100	#1	Mary	0.6595	0.6580	0.6580	0.6595	0.6595
9/21/92	1300	#1	Mary	0.6580	0.6580	0.6585	0.6590	0.6575
9/21/92	1500	#1	Mary	0.6580	0.6580	0.6580	0.6585	0.6590
9/22/92	0900	#1	Mary	0.6575	0.6570	0.6580	0.6585	0.6580

5. Create a histogram with the data in Question 4. Describe the distribution's shape, spread, and location.

6. Make a histogram of the following sample data:
   225, 226, 227, 226, 227, 228, 228, 229, 222, 223, 224, 226, 227, 228, 225, 221, 227, 229, 230, 225, 226, 227, 229, 228, 224, 223, 222, 225, 226, 227, 224, 223, 222, 228, 229, 225, 226

7. A manufacturer of CDs has a design specification for the width of the CD of 120 ± 0.3 mm. Create a histogram using the following data. Describe the distribution's shape, spread, and location.

Measurement	Tally
119.4	///
119.5	////
119.6	///// /
119.7	///// //
119.8	///// /////
119.9	///// ///
120.0	///// //
120.1	/////
120.2	////

8. What is meant by the following expression: the central tendency of the data?

9. What is meant by the following expression: measures of dispersion?

10. Find the mean, mode, and median of the following numbers: 34, 35, 36, 34, 32, 34, 45, 46, 45, 43, 44, 43, 34, 30, 48, 38, 38, 40, 34.

11. Using the following sample data, calculate the mean, mode, and median:

1.116	1.122	1.125
1.123	1.122	1.123
1.133	1.125	1.118
1.117	1.121	1.123
1.124	1.136	1.122
1.119	1.127	1.122
1.129	1.125	1.119
1.121	1.124	
1.128	1.122	

12. For the data from Question 4, determine the mean, mode, median, standard deviation, and range. Use these values to describe the distribution. Compare this mathematical description with the description you created for the histogram problem.

13. For the CD data of Question 7, determine the mean, mode, median, standard deviation, and range. Use these values to describe the distribution. Compare this mathematical description with the description you created in Question 7.

14. If the average wait time is 12 minutes with a standard deviation of 3 minutes, determine the percentage of patrons who wait less than 15 minutes for their main course to be brought to their tables.

15. The thickness of a part is to have an upper specification of 0.925 and a lower specification of 0.870 mm. The average of the process is currently

0.917 with a standard deviation of 0.005. Determine the percentage of product above 0.93 mm.

16. The Rockwell hardness of specimens of an alloy shipped by your supplier varies according to a normal distribution with mean 70 and standard deviation 3. Specimens are acceptable for machining only if their hardness is greater than 65. What percentage of specimens will be acceptable?

17. If the mean value of the weight of a particular brand of dog food is 20.6 lb and the standard deviation is 1.3, assume a normal distribution and calculate the amount of product produced that falls below the lower specification value of 19.7 lb.

18. For the CD data from Question 7, determine what percentage of the CDs produced are above and below the specifications of 120 ± 0.3 mm.

19. NB Manufacturing has ordered the construction of a new machine to replace an older machine in a machining cell. Now that the machine has been built, a runoff is to be performed. The diameters on the test pieces were checked for runout. From the 32 parts sampled, the average was 0.0015 with a standard deviation of 0.0008. The engineers would like to know, with 90% confidence, the interval values for the population mean.

20. An automotive manufacturer has selected ten car seats in order to study the Rockwell hardness of the seat recliner mechanism. A sample of 8 has an average of 44.795 and a standard deviation of 0.402. At a 95% confidence level, what is the interval for the population mean?

10

Variable Control Charts

When suppliers experienced difficulties inserting diodes, resistors, and capacitors in the circuit boards without shattering them, the Six Sigma team used control charts to study variation in the supplier's manufacturing process. Control charts pointed to the problem: the original hole size specification for the circuit board was too small.

Paraphrased from Six Sigma
Report on Business Magazine, October 1997

▓ Objectives:

1. To understand the concept of variation
2. To understand the difference between assignable causes and chance causes
3. To learn how to construct control charts for variables, either $\overline{X}$ and R charts or $\overline{X}$ and s charts
4. To recognize when a process is under control and when it is not
5. To understand the importance of the R and s charts when interpreting variable control charts
6. To know how to revise a control chart in which assignable causes have been identified and corrected ▓

INTRODUCTION

The only shortcoming in a histogram analysis is its failure to show process performance over time. Let's take a look at the data in Table 10.1. When these averages are graphed in a histogram, the result closely resembles a normal curve (Figure 10.1a). Graphing the averages by subgroup number, according to when they were produced, gives a different impression of the data (Figure 10.1b). From the chart, it appears that the thickness of the clutch plate is increasing as production continues. This was not evident during the creation of the histogram or an analysis of the average, range, and

Table 10.1   Clutch Plate Thickness: Sums and Averages

						ΣX_i	$\bar{X}$
Subgroup 1	0.0625	0.0626	0.0624	0.0625	0.0627	0.3127	0.0625
Subgroup 2	0.0624	0.0623	0.0624	0.0626	0.0625	0.3122	0.0624
Subgroup 3	0.0622	0.0625	0.0623	0.0625	0.0626	0.3121	0.0624
Subgroup 4	0.0624	0.0623	0.0620	0.0623	0.0624	0.3114	0.0623
Subgroup 5	0.0621	0.0621	0.0622	0.0625	0.0624	0.3113	0.0623
Subgroup 6	0.0628	0.0626	0.0625	0.0626	0.0627	0.3132	0.0626
Subgroup 7	0.0624	0.0627	0.0625	0.0624	0.0626	0.3126	0.0625
Subgroup 8	0.0624	0.0625	0.0625	0.0626	0.0626	0.3126	0.0625
Subgroup 9	0.0627	0.0628	0.0626	0.0625	0.0627	0.3133	0.0627
Subgroup 10	0.0625	0.0626	0.0628	0.0626	0.0627	0.3132	0.0626
Subgroup 11	0.0625	0.0624	0.0626	0.0626	0.0626	0.3127	0.0625
Subgroup 12	0.0630	0.0628	0.0627	0.0625	0.0627	0.3134	0.0627
Subgroup 13	0.0627	0.0626	0.0628	0.0627	0.0626	0.3137	0.0627
Subgroup 14	0.0626	0.0626	0.0625	0.0626	0.0627	0.3130	0.0626
Subgroup 15	0.0628	0.0627	0.0626	0.0625	0.0626	0.3132	0.0626
Subgroup 16	0.0625	0.0626	0.0625	0.0628	0.0627	0.3131	0.0626
Subgroup 17	0.0624	0.0626	0.0624	0.0625	0.0627	0.3126	0.0625
Subgroup 18	0.0628	0.0627	0.0628	0.0626	0.0630	0.3139	0.0627
Subgroup 19	0.0627	0.0626	0.0628	0.0625	0.0627	0.3133	0.0627
Subgroup 20	0.0626	0.0625	0.0626	0.0625	0.0627	0.3129	0.0626
Subgroup 21	0.0627	0.0626	0.0628	0.0625	0.0627	0.3133	0.0627
Subgroup 22	0.0625	0.0626	0.0628	0.0625	0.0627	0.3131	0.0626
Subgroup 23	0.0628	0.0626	0.0627	0.0630	0.0627	0.3138	0.0628
Subgroup 24	0.0625	0.0631	0.0630	0.0628	0.0627	0.3141	0.0628
Subgroup 25	0.0627	0.0630	0.0631	0.0628	0.0627	0.3143	0.0629
Subgroup 26	0.0630	0.0628	0.0620	0.0628	0.0627	0.3142	0.0628
Subgroup 27	0.0630	0.0628	0.0631	0.0628	0.0627	0.3144	0.0629
Subgroup 28	0.0632	0.0632	0.0628	0.0631	0.0630	0.3153	0.0631
Subgroup 29	0.0630	0.0628	0.0631	0.0632	0.0631	0.3152	0.0630
Subgroup 30	0.0632	0.0631	0.0630	0.0628	0.0628	0.3149	0.0630
						9.3981	

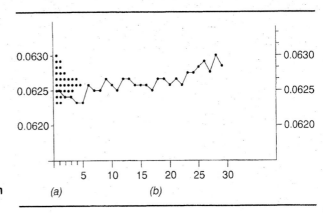

Figure 10.1 Chart with Histogram   (a)   (b)

standard deviation. A control chart enhances the analysis of the process by showing how that process is performing over time. Using statistical control charting creates a feedback loop enabling Six Sigma organizations to improve their processes, products, and services.

Control charts serve two basic functions:

1. As decision-making tools. They provide an economic basis for making a decision as to whether to investigate for potential problems, to adjust the process, or to leave the process alone.
   a. Control charts provide information for timely decisions concerning recently produced items. If an out-of-control condition is shown by the control chart, then a decision can be made about sorting or reworking the most recent production.
   b. Control chart information is used to determine the process capability, or the level of quality the process is capable of producing. Samples of completed product can be statistically compared with the process specifications. This comparison provides information concerning the process's ability to meet the specifications set by the product designer.
2. As problem-solving tools. They point out where improvement is needed.
   a. Control chart information can be used to help locate and investigate the causes of the unacceptable or marginal quality. By observing the patterns on the chart the investigator can determine what adjustments need to be made.
   b. During daily production runs, the operator can monitor machine production and determine when to make the necessary adjustments to the process or when to leave the process alone to ensure quality production.

Variation

Variation, *where no two items or services are exactly the same,* exists in all processes. Although it may take a very precise measuring instrument or a very astute consumer to notice the variation, any process in nature will exhibit variation. Understanding variation and its causes results in better decisions.

 SIX SIGMA TOOLS AT WORK

Understanding Variation

An industrial engineering department is seeking to decrease the amount of time it takes to perform a printer assembly operation. An analysis of the methods used by the operators performing the assembly has revealed that one of the operators completes the assembly in 75 percent of the time it takes another operator performing the same assembly operation. Further investigation determines that the two operators use parts produced on different machines. The histograms in Figure 10.2 are based on measurements of the parts from the two different processes. In Figure 10.2*b* the spread of the process is considerably smaller, enabling the faster operator to assemble the parts much more quickly and with less effort. The slower operator must try a part in the assembly, discard the part if it doesn't fit, and try another part. Repeating the operation when the parts do not fit has made the operator much less efficient. This operator's apparent lack of speed is actually caused by the process and is not the fault of the operator. Had management not investigated variation in the process, they might have made incorrect judgments about the operator's performance. Instead, they realize that management intervention will be necessary to improve production at the previous operation and produce parts with less variation.

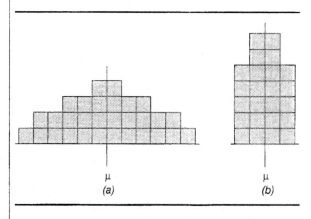

μ
(a)

μ
(b)

Figure 10.2 Histograms of Part Measurements from Two Machines

Several types of variation are tracked with statistical methods. These include:

1. Within-piece variation, or the variation within a single item or surface. For example, a single square yard of fabric may be examined to see if the color varies from one location to another.
2. Piece-to-piece variation, or the variation that occurs among pieces produced at approximately the same time. For example, in a production run filling gallon jugs with milk, when each of the milk jugs is checked after the filling station, the fill level from jug to jug will be slightly different.
3. Time-to-time variation, or the variation in the product produced at different times of the day—for example, the comparison of a part that has been stamped at the beginning of a production run with the part stamped at the end of a production run.

Chance and Assignable Causes

Chance, or **common causes**, *are small random changes in the process that cannot be avoided.* These small differences are due to the inherent variation present in all processes. They consistently affect the process and its performance day after day, every day. Variation of this type is only removable by making a change in the existing process. Six Sigma organizations realize that removing chance causes from a system usually involves management intervention.

Assignable causes *are variations in the process that can be identified as having a specific cause.* Assignable causes are causes that are not part of the process on a regular basis. This type of variation arises because of specific circumstances. Sources of variation can be found in the process itself, the materials used, the operator's actions, or the environment. Examples of factors that can contribute to process variation include tool wear, machine vibration, and work-holding devices. Changes in material thickness, composition, or hardness are sources of variation. Operator actions affecting variation include overadjusting the machine, making an error during the inspection activity, changing the machine settings, or failing to properly align the part before machining. Environmental factors affecting variation include heat, light, radiation, and humidity.

Control Charts for Variables

Control charts enable those studying a process to analyze the variation present. To create a control chart, samples, arranged into subgroups, are taken during the process. The averages of the subgroup values are plotted on the control chart. The **centerline** ($\bar{\bar{C}}$) *of this chart shows where the process average is centered, the central tendency of the data.* The **upper control limit (UCL)** and **lower control limit (LCL)**, *calculated based on* ± 3 σ, *describe the spread of the process* (Figure 10.3). In other words, we can expect future production to fall between these ± 3 σ limits 99.73 percent of the time, providing the process does not change and is under control.

Instead of waiting until an entire production run is complete or until the product reaches the end of the assembly line, management can have critical part dimensions checked and charted throughout the process. If a part or group of parts has been made incorrectly, production can be stopped, adjusted, or otherwise modified to produce parts correctly.

Variables are the measurable characteristics of a product or service. Examples of variables include the height, weight, or length of a part. One of the most commonly used variable chart combinations in statistical process control is the combination of the $\overline{X}$ and R charts. Typical $\overline{X}$ and R charts are shown in Figure 10.3. $\overline{X}$ and R charts are used together to determine the distribution of the subgroup averages of sample measurements

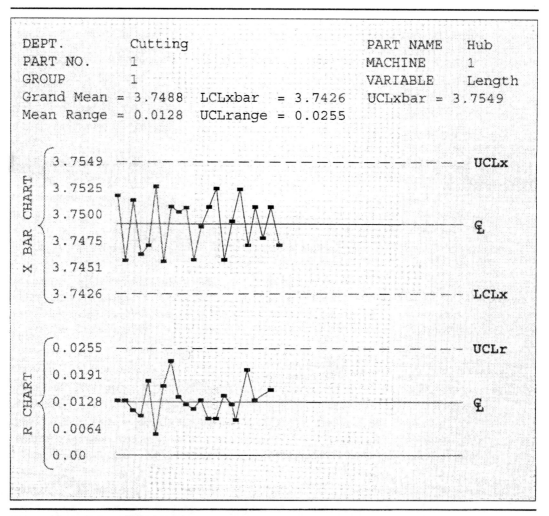

Figure 10.3 Typical $\overline{X}$ and R Chart

taken from a process. The importance of using these two charts in conjunction with each other will become apparent shortly.

$\overline{X}$ and R Charts

The $\overline{X}$ chart is used to monitor the variation of the subgroup averages that are calculated from the individual sampled data. Averages rather than individual observations are used on control charts because average values will indicate a change in the amount of variation much faster than will individual values. Control limits on this chart are used to evaluate the variation from one subgroup to another.

The following steps and examples explain the construction of an $\overline{X}$ chart.

1. Define the Problem

In any situation it is necessary to determine what the goal of monitoring a particular quality characteristic or group of characteristics is. Control charts can be placed on a process to help determine where the true source of the problem is located.

 SIX SIGMA TOOLS AT WORK

Defining the Problem

An assembly area has been experiencing serious delays in the construction of computer printers. As a Six Sigma Black Belt, you have been asked to determine the cause of these delays and fix the problems as soon as possible. You convened a meeting involving those closest to the assembly problems. Representatives from production, supervision, manufacturing engineering, industrial engineering, quality assurance, and maintenance created a cause-and-effect diagram showing the potential causes for the assembly difficulties (Figure 10.4). Discussions during the meeting revealed that the shaft which holds the roller in place could be the major cause of assembly problems.

2. Select the Quality Characteristic to Be Measured

Variable control charts are based on measurements. The characteristics selected for measurement should be ones that affect product or service performance. Characteristic choice depends on whether or not the process is being monitored for within-piece variation, piece-to-piece variation, or variation over time. Product or service characteristics such as length, height, viscosity, color, temperature, and velocity are typically used in manufacturing settings. Delivery times, checkout times, and service times are examples of characteristics chosen in a service industry.

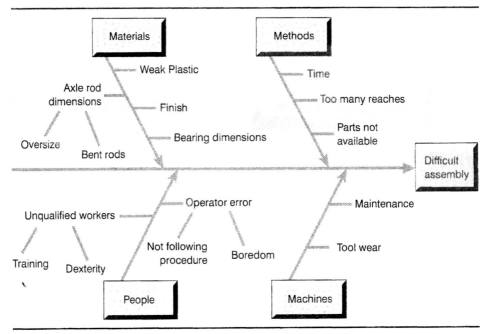

Figure 10.4   Printer Assembly: Cause-and-Effect Diagram

σ SIX SIGMA TOOLS AT WORK

Identifying the Quality Characteristic

As the Six Sigma project meeting described in the earlier Six Sigma Tools at Work feature continues, further investigation reveals that the length of the shaft is hindering assembly operations. The characteristic to measure has been identified as piece-to-piece variation in the length of the shafts. To begin to study the situation, measurements of the lengths of the shafts will be sampled.

---

3. Choose a Rational Subgroup Size to Be Sampled

Subgroups, and the samples composing them, must be homogeneous. A *homogeneous subgroup will have been produced under the same conditions, by the same machine, the same operator, the same mold, and so on.* Homogeneous lots can also be designated by equal time intervals. Samples should be taken in an unbiased, random fashion. They should be representative of the entire population. The letter n is used to designate the number of samples taken within a subgroup. When constructing $\overline{X}$ and R charts, keep the subgroup sample size constant for each subgroup taken.

Decisions concerning the specific size of the subgroup—n, or the number of samples—require judgment. Sampling should occur frequently enough to detect changes in the process. Ask how often is the system expected to change. Examine the process and identify the factors causing change in the process. To be effective, sampling must occur as often as the system's most frequently changing factor. Once the number and frequency of sampling have been selected, they should not be changed unless the system itself has changed.

Realistically, sampling frequency must balance the value of the data obtained with the costs of taking the samples. Sampling is usually more frequent when control charts are first used to monitor the process. As process improvements are made and the process stabilizes, the frequency of sampling and subgroup size can be decreased.

When gathering sample data, it is important to have the following information in order to properly analyze the data:

1. *Who* will be collecting the data?
2. *What* aspect of the process is to be measured?
3. *Where* or at what point in the process will the sample be taken?
4. *When* or how frequently will the process be sampled?
5. *Why* is this particular sample being taken?
6. *How* will the data be collected?
7. *How many* samples will be taken (subgroup size)?

Some other guidelines to be followed include:

- The larger the subgroup size, the more sensitive the chart becomes to small variations in the process average. This will provide a better picture of the process since it allows the investigator to detect changes in the process quickly.
- While a larger subgroup size makes for a more sensitive chart, it also increases inspection costs.
- Destructive testing may make large subgroup sizes unfeasible. For example, it would not make sense for a fireworks manufacturer to test each and every one of its products.
- Subgroup sizes smaller than four do not create a representative distribution of subgroup averages. Subgroup averages are nearly normal for subgroups of four or more even when sampled from a nonnormal population.
- When the subgroup size exceeds 10, the standard deviation (s) chart, rather than the range (R) chart, should be used. For large subgroup sizes, the s chart gives a better representation of the true dispersion or true differences between the individuals sampled than does the R chart.

 SIX SIGMA TOOLS AT WORK

Selecting Subgroup Sample Size

The production from the machine making the shafts is consistent at 150 per hour. Since the process is currently exhibiting problems, your team has decided to take a sample of five measurements every 10 minutes from the production. The values for the day's production run are shown in Figure 10.5.

4. Collect the Data

To create a control chart, an amount of data sufficient to accurately reflect the statistical control of the process must be gathered. A minimum of 20 subgroups of sample size n = 4 is suggested. Each time a subgroup of sample size n is taken, an average is calculated for the subgroup. To do this, the individual values are recorded, summed, and then divided by the number of samples in the subgroup. This average, $\overline{X}_i$, is then plotted on the control chart.

DEPT.	Roller		PART NAME	Shaft	
PART NO.	1		MACHINE	1	
GROUP	1		VARIABLE	length	

Subgroup	1	2	3	4	5
Time	07:30	07:40	07:50	08:00	08:10
Date	07/02/95	07/02/95	07/02/95	07/02/95	07/02/95
1	11.95	12.03	12.01	11.97	12.00
2	12.00	12.02	12.00	11.98	12.01
3	12.03 ①	11.96	11.97	12.00	12.02
4	11.98	12.00	11.98	12.03	12.03
5	12.01	11.98	12.00	11.99	12.02
$\overline{X}$	11.99 ②	12.00	11.99	11.99	12.02
Range	0.08 ③	0.07	0.04	0.06	0.03

Subgroup	6	7	8	9	10
Time	08:20	08:30	08:40	08:50	09:00
Date	07/02/95	07/02/95	07/02/95	07/02/95	07/02/95
1	11.98	12.00	12.00	12.00	12.02
2	11.98	12.01	12.01	12.02	12.00
3	12.00	12.03	12.04	11.96	11.97
4	12.01	12.00	12.00	12.00	12.05
5	11.99	11.98	12.02	11.98	12.00
$\overline{X}$	11.99	12.00	12.01	11.99	12.01
Range	0.03	0.05	0.04	0.06	0.08

Subgroup	11	12	13	14	15
Time	09:10	09:20	09:30	09:40	09:50
Date	07/02/95	07/02/95	07/02/95	07/02/95	07/02/95
1	11.98	11.92	11.93	11.99	12.00
2	11.97	11.95	11.95	11.93	11.98
3	11.96	11.92	11.98	11.94	11.99
4	11.95	11.94	11.94	11.95	11.95
5	12.00	11.96	11.96	11.96	11.93
$\overline{X}$	11.97	11.94	11.95	11.95	11.97
Range	0.05	0.04	0.05	0.06	0.07

Subgroup	16	17	18	19	20
Time	10:00	10:10	10:20	10:30	10:40
Date	07/02/95	07/02/95	07/02/95	07/02/95	07/02/95
1	12.00	12.02	12.00	11.97	11.99
2	11.98	11.98	12.01	12.03	12.01
3	11.99	11.97	12.02	12.00	12.02
4	11.96	11.98	12.01	12.01	12.00
5	11.97	11.99	11.99	11.99	12.01
X̄	11.98	11.99	12.01	12.00	12.01
Range	0.04	0.05	0.03	0.06	0.03

Subgroup	21
Time	10:50
Date	07/02/95
1	12.00
2	11.98
3	11.99
4	11.99
5	12.02
X̄	12.00
Range	0.04

$$R = 0.05 = 12.02 - 11.97$$

$$\frac{12.00 + 11.98 + 11.99 + 11.96 + 11.97}{5} = 11.98$$

Figure 10.5   Values for a Day's Production

Collecting Data

A sample of size n = 5 is taken at 10-minute intervals from the process making shafts. As shown in Figure 10.5, a total of 21 subgroups of sample size n = 5 have been taken. Each time a subgroup sample is taken, the individual values are recorded [Figure 10.5, (1)], summed, and then divided by the number of samples taken to get the average for the subgroup [Figure 10.5, (2)]. This subgroup average is then plotted on the control chart [Figure 10.6, (1)].

5. Determine the Trial Centerline for the X̄ Chart

The centerline of the control chart is the process average. It would be the mean, μ, if the average of the population measurements for the entire process were known. Since the value of the population mean μ cannot be determined unless all of the parts being produced are measured, in its place the grand average of the subgroup averages, $\overline{\overline{X}}$ (X double bar, covered previously in Chapter 9), is used. The grand average, or $\overline{\overline{X}}$ is

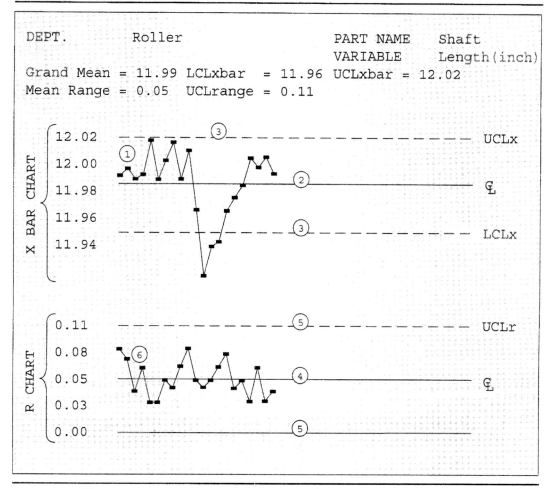

Figure 10.6 X̄ and R Control Charts for Roller Shaft Length

calculated by summing all the subgroup averages and then dividing by the number of subgroups. This value is plotted as the centerline of the X̄ chart:

$$\overline{\overline{X}} = \frac{\sum\limits_{i=1}^{m} \overline{X}_i}{m}$$

where

$\overline{\overline{X}}$ = average of the subgroup averages
$\overline{X}_i$ = average of the ith subgroup
m = number of subgroups

6. Determine the Trial Control Limits for the X̄ Chart

Control limits are established at ±3 standard deviations from the centerline for the process using the following formulas:

$$UCL_{\overline{X}} = \overline{\overline{X}} + 3\sigma_{\overline{x}}$$
$$LCL_{\overline{X}} = \overline{\overline{X}} - 3\sigma_{\overline{x}}$$

where

UCL = upper control limit of the $\overline{X}$ chart
LCL = lower control limit of the $\overline{X}$ chart
$\sigma_{\overline{x}}$ = population standard deviation of the subgroup averages

The population standard deviation σ is needed to calculate the upper and lower control limits. Since control charts are based on sample data, Dr. Shewhart developed a good approximation of $3\sigma_{\overline{x}}$ using the product of an A_2 factor multiplied by $\overline{R}$, the average of the ranges. The $A_2\overline{R}$ combination uses the sample data for its calculation. $\overline{R}$ is calculated by summing the values of the individual subgroup ranges and dividing by the number of subgroups m:

$$\overline{R} = \frac{\sum\limits_{i=1}^{m} R_i}{m}$$

where

$\overline{R}$ = average of the ranges
R_i = individual range values for the sample
m = number of subgroups

A_2, the factor that allows the approximation $A_2\overline{R} \approx 3\sigma_{\overline{x}}$ to be true, is selected based on the subgroup sample size n. See Appendix 2 for the A_2 factors.

Upon replacement, the formulas for the upper and lower control limits become

$$UCL_{\overline{X}} = \overline{\overline{X}} + A_2\overline{R}$$
$$LCL_{\overline{X}} = \overline{\overline{X}} - A_2\overline{R}$$

After calculating the control limits, we place the centerline $\overline{\overline{X}}$ and the upper and lower control limits (UCL and LCL, respectively) on the chart. The upper and lower control limits are shown by dashed lines. The grand average, or $\overline{\overline{X}}$, is shown by a solid line. The control limits on the $\overline{X}$ chart will be symmetrical about the central line.

 SIX SIGMA TOOLS AT WORK

Calculating the $\overline{X}$ Chart Centerline and Control Limits

Construction of an $\overline{X}$ chart begins with the calculation of the centerline $\overline{\overline{X}}$. Using the 21 subgroups of sample size n = 5 provided in Figure 10.5, we calculate $\overline{\overline{X}}$ by summing all the subgroup averages based on the individual samples taken and then dividing by the number of subgroups, m:

$$\overline{\overline{X}} = \frac{11.99 + 12.00 + 11.99 + \cdots + 12.00}{21}$$
$$= \frac{251.77}{21} = 11.99$$

This value is plotted as the centerline of the $\overline{X}$ chart [Figure 10.6, (2)].

$\overline{R}$ is calculated by summing the values of the individual subgroup ranges (Figure 10.5) and dividing by the number of subgroups, m:

$$\overline{R} = \frac{0.08 + 0.07 + 0.04 + \cdots + 0.04}{21}$$

$$= \frac{1.06}{21} = 0.05$$

The A_2 factor for a sample size of five is selected from the table in Appendix 2. The values for the upper and lower control limits of the $\overline{X}$ chart are calculated as follows:

$$UCL_{\overline{X}} = \overline{\overline{X}} + A_2\overline{R}$$
$$= 11.99 + 0.577(0.05) = 12.02$$
$$LCL_{\overline{X}} = \overline{\overline{X}} - A_2\overline{R}$$
$$= 11.99 - 0.577(0.05) = 11.96$$

Once calculated, the upper and lower control limits (UCL and LCL, respectively) are placed on the chart [Figure 10.6, (3)].

7. Determine the Trial Control Limits for the R Chart

When an $\overline{X}$ chart is used to evaluate the variation in quality from subgroup to subgroup, the range chart is a method of determining the amount of variation among the individual samples. The importance of the range chart is often overlooked. Without the range chart, or the standard deviation chart to be discussed later, it would not be possible to fully understand process capability. Where the $\overline{X}$ chart shows the average of the individual subgroups, giving the viewer an understanding of where the process is centered, the range chart shows the spread or dispersion of the individual samples within the subgroup. If the product displays a wide spread or a large range, then the individuals being produced are not similar to each other. The optimal situation from a quality perspective is when the parts are grouped closely around the process average. This situation will yield a small value for both the range and the standard deviation, meaning that the measurements are very similar to each other. $\overline{R}$, the centerline of the R chart, is calculated as:

$$\overline{R} = \frac{\sum\limits_{i=1}^{m} R_i}{m}$$

To create the upper and lower control limits for the $\overline{R}$ chart the average of the subgroup ranges ($\overline{R}$) multiplied by the D_3 and D_4 factors is used:

$$UCL_R = D_4\overline{R}$$
$$LCL_R = D_3\overline{R}$$

Along with the value of A_2, the values of D_3 and D_4 are found in the table in Appendix 2. These values are selected on the basis of the subgroup sample size n.

The control limits, when displayed on the R chart, should theoretically be symmetrical about the centerline ($\overline{R}$). However, because range values cannot be negative, a value of zero is given for the lower control limit with sample sizes of six or less. This results in an R chart that is asymmetrical. As with the $\overline{X}$ chart, control limits for the R chart are shown with a dashed line. The centerline is shown with a solid line.

 SIX SIGMA TOOLS AT WORK

Calculating the R Chart Centerline and Control Limits

Constructing an R chart is similar to creating an $\overline{X}$ chart. To begin the process, individual range values are calculated for each of the subgroups by subtracting the highest value in the subgroup from the lowest value [Figure 10.5, (3)]. Once calculated, these individual range values (R_i) are plotted on the R chart [Figure 10.6, (6)].

To determine the centerline of the R chart, individual range (R_i) values are summed and divided by the total number of subgroups to give $\overline{R}$ [Figure 10.6, (4)].

$$\overline{R} = \frac{0.08 + 0.07 + 0.04 + \cdots + 0.04}{21}$$

$$= \frac{1.06}{21} = 0.05$$

With n = 5, the values of D_3 and D_4 are found in the table in Appendix 2. The control limits for the R chart are calculated as follows:

$$UCL_R = D_4\overline{R}$$
$$= 2.114(0.05) = 0.11$$
$$LCL_R = D_3\overline{R}$$
$$= 0(0.05) = 0$$

The control limits are placed on the R chart [Figure 10.6, (5)].

---

8. Examine the Process: Control Chart Interpretation

Correct interpretation of control charts is essential to managing a process. Understanding the sources and potential causes of variation is critical to good management decisions. Managers must be able to determine if the variation present in a process is indicating a trend that must be dealt with or is merely random variation natural to the process. Misinterpretation can lead to a variety of losses, including

- Blaming people for problems that they cannot control
- Spending time and money looking for problems that do not exist
- Spending time and money on process adjustments or new equipment that are not necessary
- Taking action where no action is warranted

■ Asking for worker-related improvements where process or equipment improvements need to be made first

Once the performance of a process is predictable, there is a sound basis for making plans and decisions concerning the process, the system, and its output. Costs to manufacture the product or provide the service become predictable.

State of Process Control   *A process is considered to be in a state of control, or **under** **control**, when the performance of the process falls within the statistically calculated control limits and exhibits only chance, or common, causes.* When a process is under control it is considered stable and the amount of future variation is predictable. A stable process does not necessarily meet the specifications set by the designer nor exhibit minimal variation; a stable process merely has a predictable amount of variation.

Six Sigma practiners appreciate the benefits of a stable process with predictable variation. When the process performance is predictable there is a rational basis for planning. It is fairly straightforward to determine costs associated with a stable process. Quality levels from time period to time period are predictable. When changes, additions, or improvements are made to a stable process, the effects of the change can be determined quickly and reliably.

When an assignable cause is present, the process is considered unstable, out of control, or beyond the expected normal variation. In an unstable process the variation is unpredictable, meaning that the magnitude of the variation could change from one time period to another. Six Sigma practiners need to determine whether the variation that exists in a process is common or assignable. To treat an assignable cause as a chance cause could result in a disruption to a system or a process that is operating correctly except for the assignable cause. To treat chance causes as assignable causes is an ineffective use of resources because the variation is inherent in the process.

When a system is subject to only chance causes of variation, 99.73 percent of the parts produced will fall within $\pm 3\sigma$. This means that if 1,000 subgroups are sampled, 997 of the subgroups will have values within the upper and lower control limits. Based on the normal curve, a control chart can be divided into three zones (Figure 10.7).

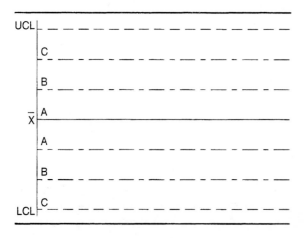

Figure 10.7   Zones on a Control Chart

Zone A is ±1 standard deviation from the centerline and should contain approximately 68.3 percent of the calculated sample averages or ranges. Zone B is ±2 standard deviations from the centerline and should contain 27.2 percent (95.5 percent − 68.3 percent) of the points. Zone C is ±3 standard deviations from the centerline and should contain only approximately 4.2 percent of the points (99.7 percent − 95.5 percent). With these zones as a guide, a control chart exhibits a state of control when:

1. Two-thirds of the points are near the center value.
2. A few of the points are on or near the center value.
3. The points appear to float back and forth across the centerline.
4. The points are balanced (in roughly equal numbers) on both sides of the centerline.
5. There are no points beyond the control limits.
6. There are no patterns or trends on the chart.

While analyzing $\overline{X}$ and R charts, take a moment to study the scale of the range chart. The spread of the upper and lower control limits will reveal whether or not a significant amount of variation is present in the process. This clue to the amount of variation present may be overlooked if the R chart is checked only for patterns or out-of-control points.

Identifying Patterns   A process that is not under control or is unstable displays patterns of variation. Patterns signal the need to investigate the process and determine if an assignable cause can be found for the variation. Figures 10.8 through 10.14 display a variety of out-of-control conditions and give some reasons why those conditions may exist.

Trends or Steady Changes in Level   A trend is a steady, progressive change in the location where the data are centered on the chart. Figure 10.8 displays a downward trend on the R chart. Note that the points were found in the upper half of the control chart at the beginning of the process and on the lower half of the chart at the end. The key to identifying a trend or steady change in level is to recognize that the points are slowly and steadily working their way from one level of the chart to another.

A trend may appear on the $\overline{X}$ chart because of tool or die wear, a gradual deterioration of the equipment, a buildup of chips, a slowly loosening work-holding device, a breakdown of the chemicals used in the process, or some other gradual change. R chart trends could be due to changes in worker skills, shifting work-holding devices, or wearout. Improvements would lead to less variation; increases in variation would reflect a decrease in skill or a change in the quality of the incoming material.

An oscillating trend would also need to be investigated (Figure 10.9). In this type of trend the points oscillate up and down for approximately 14 points or more. This could be due to a lack of homogeneity, perhaps a mixing of the output from two machines making the same product.

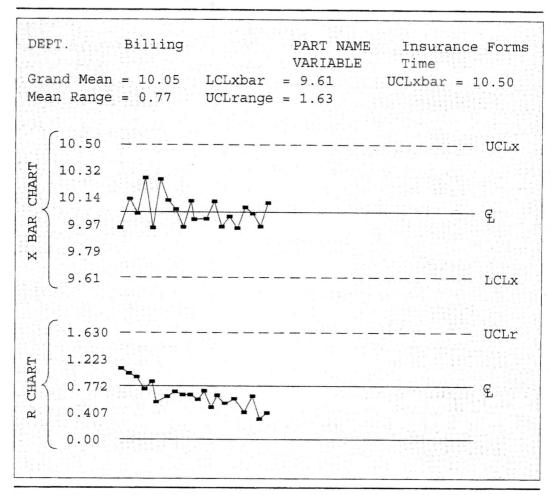

DEPT.   Billing   PART NAME   Insurance Forms
                                    VARIABLE   Time
Grand Mean = 10.05   LCLxbar = 9.61   UCLxbar = 10.50
Mean Range = 0.77   UCLrange = 1.63

Figure 10.8   Control Chart with Grand Mean = 10.05

Change, Jump, or Shift in Level   Figure 10.10 displays what is meant by a change, jump, or shift in level. Note that the process begins at one level (Figure 10.10a) and jumps quickly to another level (Figure 10.10b) as the process continues to operate. This change, jump, or shift in level is fairly abrupt, unlike a trend described above. A change, jump, or shift can occur either on the $\overline{X}$ or R chart or on both charts. Causes for sudden shifts in level tend to reflect some new and fairly significant difference in the process. When investigating a sudden shift or jump in level, look for significant changes that can be pinpointed to a specific moment in time. For the $\overline{X}$ chart, causes include new machines, dies, or tooling; the minor failure of a machine part; new or inexperienced workers; new batches of raw material; new production methods; or changes to the process settings. For the R chart, potential sources of jumps or shifts in level causing a change in the process variability or spread include a new or

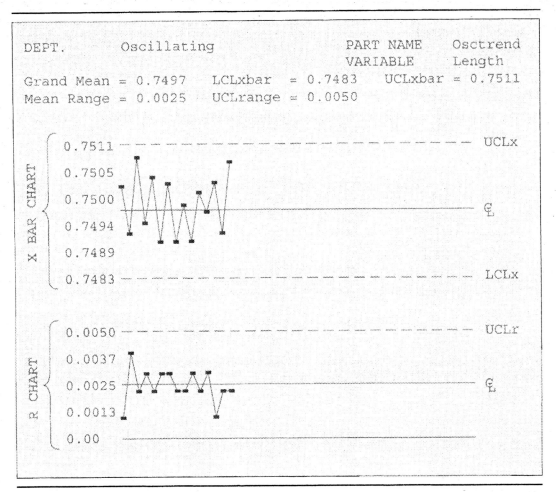

DEPT.   Oscillating   PART NAME   Osctrend
                                        VARIABLE   Length
Grand Mean = 0.7497   LCLxbar = 0.7483   UCLxbar = 0.7511
Mean Range = 0.0025   UCLrange = 0.0050

Figure 10.9   An Oscillating Trend

inexperienced operator, a sudden increase in the play associated with gears or work-holding devices, or greater variation in incoming material.

Runs   A process can be considered out of control when there are unnatural runs present in the process. Imagine tossing a coin. If two heads occur in a row, the onlooker would probably agree that this occurred by chance. Even though the probability of the coin landing with heads showing is 50-50, no one expects coin tosses to alternate between heads and tails. If, however, an onlooker saw someone toss six heads in a row, that onlooker would probably be suspicious that this set of events is not due to chance. The same principle applies to control charts. While the points on a control chart do not necessarily alternate above and below the centerline in a chart that is under control, the points are normally balanced above and below the centerline.

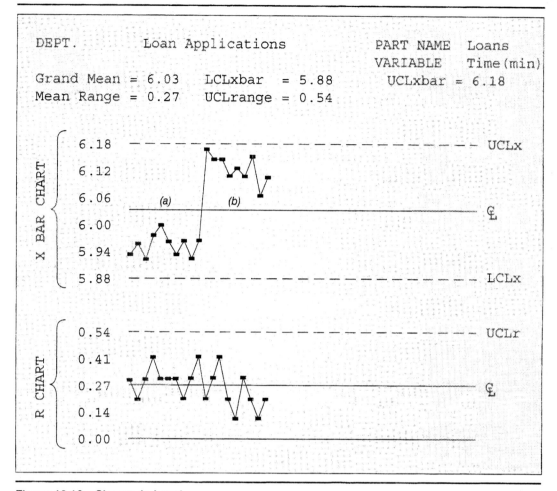

Figure 10.10   Change in Level

A cluster of seven points in a row above or below the centerline would be improbable and would likely have an assignable cause. The same could be said for situations where 10 out of 11 points or 12 out of 14 points are located on one side or the other of the centerline (Figure 10.11). A run may also be considered a trend if it displays increasing or decreasing values.

Runs on the $\bar{X}$ chart can be caused by temperature changes; tool or die wear; gradual deterioration of the process; or deterioration of the chemicals, oils, or cooling fluids used in the process. Runs on the R chart (Figure 10.12) signal a change in the process variation. Causes for these R chart runs could be a change in operator skill, either an improvement or a decrement, or a gradual improvement in the homogeneity of the process because of changes in the incoming material or changes to the process itself.

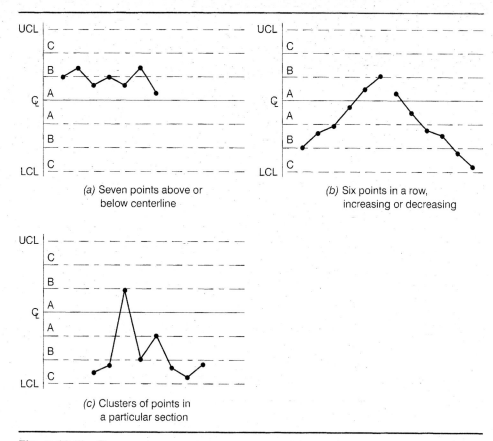

(a) Seven points above or below centerline

(b) Six points in a row, increasing or decreasing

(c) Clusters of points in a particular section

Figure 10.11   Runs

Recurring Cycles   Recurring cycles are caused by systematic changes related to the process. When investigating what appears to be cycles (Figure 10.13) on the chart, it is important to look for causes that will change, vary, or cycle over time. For the $\overline{X}$ chart, potential causes are tool or machine wear conditions, an accumulation and then removal of chips or other waste material around the tooling, maintenance schedules, periodic rotation of operators, worker fatigue, periodic replacement of cooling fluid or cutting oil, or changes in the process environment such as temperature or humidity. Cycles on an R chart are not as common; an R chart displays the variation or spread of the process, which usually does not cycle. Potential causes are related to lubrication cycles and operator fatigue.

Cycles can be difficult to locate because the entire cycle may not be present on a single chart. The frequency of inspection could potentially cause a cycle to be overlooked. For example, if the cycle occurs every 15 minutes and samples are taken only every 30 minutes, then it is possible for the cycle to be overlooked.

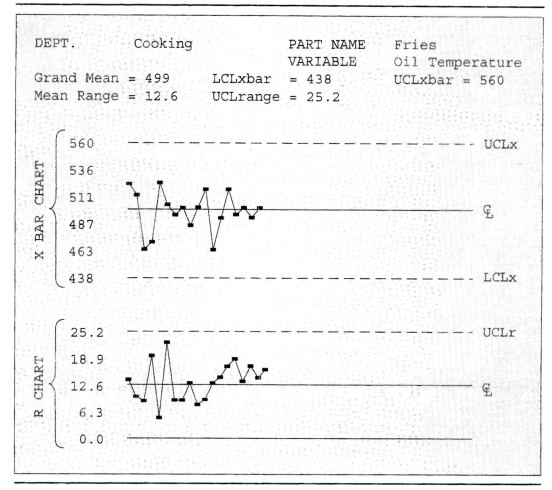

Figure 10.12   Run of Points Above the Centerline of the R Chart

Two Populations   When a control chart is under control, approximately 68 percent of the sample averages will fall within $\pm 1\sigma$ of the centerline. When a large number of the sample averages appear near or outside the control limits, two populations of samples might exist. "Two populations" refers to the existence of two (or more) sources of data.

On an $\overline{X}$ chart, the different sources of production might be due to the output of two or more machines being combined before sampling takes place. It might also occur because the work of two different operators is combined or two different sources of raw materials are brought together in the process. A two-population situation means that the items being sampled are not homogeneous (Figure 10.14). Maintaining the homogeneity of the items being sampled is critical for creating and using control charts.

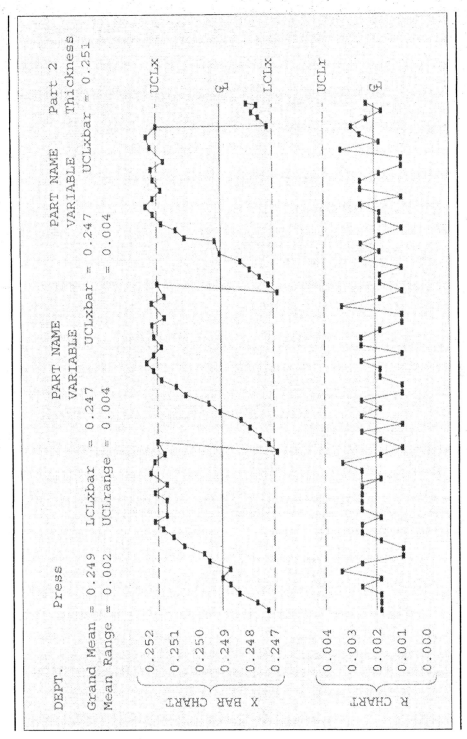

Figure 10.13 Cycle in Part Thickness

197

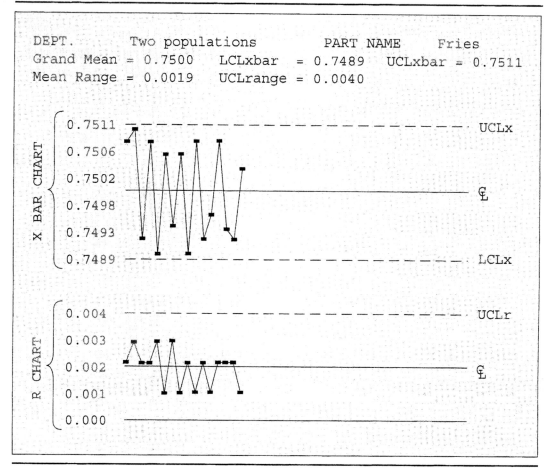

Figure 10.14   Two Populations

This type of pattern on an R chart signals that different workers are using the same chart or that the variation is due to the fact that raw materials are coming from different suppliers.

9. Revise the Charts

There are two circumstances under which the control chart is revised and new limits calculated. Existing calculations can be revised if a chart exhibits good control and any changes made to improve the process are permanent. When the new operating conditions become routine and no out-of-control signals have been seen, the chart may be revised. The revisions provide a better estimate of the population standard deviation, representing the spread of all of the individual parts in the process. With this value, a better understanding of the entire process can be gained.

Control limits are also revised if patterns exist, provided that the patterns have been identified and eliminated. Once the causes have been determined, investigated, and corrected in such a way that they will not affect the process in the future, the control chart can be revised. The new limits will reflect the changes and improvements made to the process. In both cases the new limits are used to judge the process behavior in the future.

The following four steps are taken to revise the charts.

A. Interpret the Original Charts   The R chart reflects the stability of the process and should be analyzed first. A lack of control on the R chart shows that the process is not producing parts that are very similar to each other. The process is not precise. If the R chart exhibits process control, study the $\overline{X}$ chart. Determine if cycles, trends, runs, two populations, mistakes, or other examples of lack of control exist. If both the $\overline{X}$ and R charts are exhibiting good control, proceed to step D. If the charts display out-of-control conditions, then continue to step B.

 SIX SIGMA TOOLS AT WORK

Examining the Control Charts

Returning to the computer printer roller shaft example, an examination of the $\overline{X}$ and R charts begins by investigating the R chart, which displays the variation present in the process. Evidence of excessive variation would indicate that the process is not producing consistent product. The R chart (Figure 10.15) exhibits good control. The points are evenly spaced on both sides of the centerline and there are no points beyond the control limits. There are no unusual patterns or trends in the data. Given these observations, it can be said that the process is producing parts of similar dimensions.

Next the $\overline{X}$ chart is examined. An inspection of the $\overline{X}$ chart reveals an unusual pattern occurring at points 12, 13, and 14. These measurements are all below the lower control limit. When compared with other samples throughout the day's production, the parts produced during the time when samples 12, 13, and 14 were taken were much shorter than parts produced during other times in the production run. A glance at the R chart reveals that the range of the individual measurements taken in the samples is small, meaning that the parts produced during samples 12, 13, and 14 are all similar in size. An investigation into the cause of the production of undersized parts needs to take place.

B. Isolate the Cause   If either the $\overline{X}$ or R chart is not exhibiting good statistical control, find the cause of the problem. Problems shown on the control chart may be removed only if the causes of those problems have been isolated and steps have been taken to eliminate them.

C. Take Corrective Action   Take the necessary steps to correct the causes associated with the problems exhibited on the chart. Once the causes of variation have been removed from the process, these points may be removed from the control chart and the calculations revised.

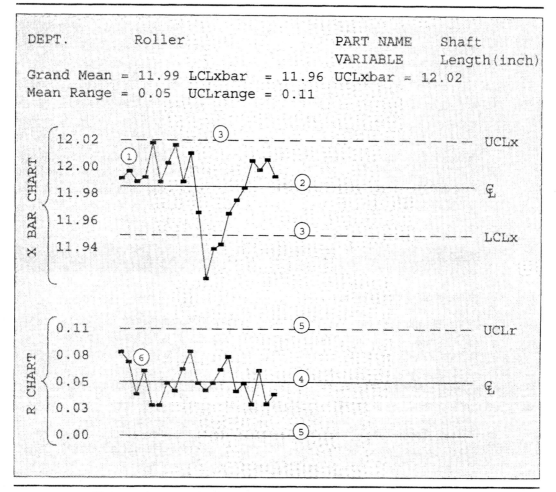

DEPT.   Roller   PART NAME   Shaft
                                           VARIABLE   Length(inch)
Grand Mean = 11.99 LCLxbar = 11.96 UCLxbar = 12.02
Mean Range = 0.05   UCLrange = 0.11

Figure 10.15 X̄ and R Control Charts for Roller Shaft Length

σ SIX SIGMA TOOLS AT WORK

A Further Examination of the Control Charts

An investigation into the differences in shaft lengths has been conducted. The X̄ and R charts aid the investigators by allowing them to isolate when the differences were first noticed. Since the R chart (Figure 10.15) exhibits good control, the investigators are able to concentrate their attention on possible causes for a consistent change in shaft length for those three subgroups. Their investigation reveals that the machine settings had been bumped during the loading of the machine. For the time being, operators are being asked to check the control panel settings after loading the machine. To take care of the problem for the long term, manufacturing engineers are looking into possible design changes to protect the controls against accidental manipulation.

D. Revise the Chart   To determine the new limits against which the process will be judged in the future, it is necessary to remove any undesirable points, the causes of which have been determined and corrected, from the charts. The criteria for removing points are based on finding the cause behind the out-of-control condition. If no cause can be found and corrected, then the points *cannot* be removed from the chart. Groups of points, runs, trends, and other patterns can be removed in the same manner as removing individual points. In the case of charts that are exhibiting good statistical control, the points removed will equal zero and the calculations will continue from there.

Two methods can be used to discard the data. When it is necessary to remove a subgroup from the calculations, it can be removed from only the out-of-control chart or it can be removed from both charts. In the first case, when an $\overline{X}$ value must be removed from the $\overline{X}$ control chart, its corresponding R value is *not* removed from the R chart, and vice versa. In this text, the points are removed from *both* charts. This second approach has been chosen because the values on both charts are interrelated. The R chart values describe the spread of the data on the $\overline{X}$ chart. Removing data from one chart or the other negates this relationship.

The formulas for revising both the $\overline{X}$ and R charts are as follows:

$$\overline{\overline{X}}_{new} = \frac{\Sigma\overline{X} - \overline{X}_d}{m - m_d}$$

$$R_{new} = \frac{\Sigma R - R_d}{m - m_d}$$

where

$$\overline{X}_d = \text{discarded subgroup averages}$$
$$m_d = \text{number of discarded subgroups}$$
$$R_d = \text{discarded subgroup ranges}$$

The newly calculated values of $\overline{\overline{X}}$ and $\overline{R}$ are used to establish updated values for the centerline and control limits on the chart. These new limits reflect that improvements have been made to the process and future production should be capable of meeting these new limits. The formulas for the revised limits are:

$$\overline{\overline{X}}_{new} = \overline{X}_0 \qquad \overline{R}_{new} = R_0$$
$$\sigma_0 = R_0/d_2$$
$$UCL_{\overline{X}} = \overline{X}_0 + A\sigma_0$$
$$LCL_{\overline{X}} = \overline{X}_0 - A\sigma_0$$
$$UCL_R = D_2\sigma_0$$
$$LCL_R = D_1\sigma_0$$

where d_2, A, D_1, and D_2 are factors from the table in Appendix 2.

σ SIX SIGMA TOOLS AT WORK

Revising the Control Limits

Since a cause for the undersized parts has been determined for the values for 12, 13, and 14, they can be removed from the calculations for the $\overline{X}$ and R chart. The points removed from calculations remain on the chart; but they are crossed out. The new or revised limits will be used to monitor future production. The new limits will extend from the old limits, as shown in Figure 10.16.

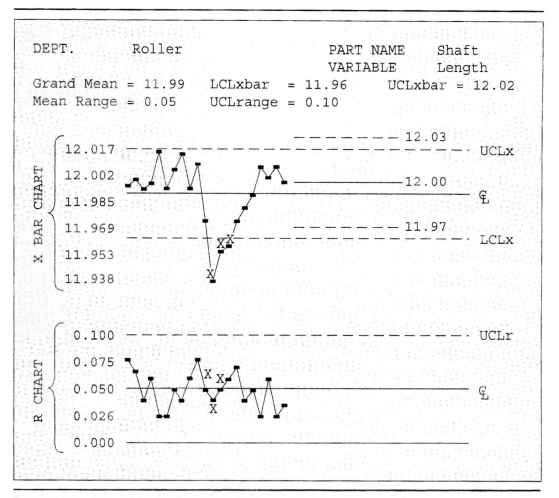

Figure 10.16   Extension of Limits on a Chart

Revising the calculations is performed as follows:

$$\overline{\overline{X}}_{new} = \overline{X}_0 = \frac{\sum\limits_{i=1}^{m} \overline{X} - \overline{X}_d}{m - m_d}$$

$$= \frac{251.77 - 11.94 - 11.95 - 11.95}{21 - 3}$$

$$= 12.00$$

$$\overline{R}_{new} = R_0 = \frac{\sum\limits_{i=1}^{m} R - R_d}{m - m_d}$$

$$= \frac{1.06 - 0.04 - 0.05 - 0.06}{21 - 3}$$

$$= 0.05$$

Calculating the σ_0 for the process, when n = 5,

$$\sigma_0 = \frac{R_0}{d_2} = \frac{0.05}{2.326} = 0.02$$

$$UCL_{\overline{X}} = 12.00 + 1.342(0.02) = 12.03$$

$$LCL_{\overline{X}} = 12.00 - 1.342(0.02) = 11.97$$

$$UCL_R = 4.918(0.02) = 0.10$$

$$LCL_R = 0(0.02) = 0$$

Achieve the Purpose

Users of control charts are endeavoring to decrease the variation inherent in a process over time. Once established, control charts enable the user to understand where the process is currently centered and what the distribution of that process is. To know this information and not utilize it to improve the process defeats the purpose of creating control charts.

As the process improves, the average should come closer to the center of the specifications. The spread of the data, as shown by the range or the standard deviation, should decrease, the parts produced or services provided become more similar to each other.

$\overline{X}$ and s Charts

The $\overline{X}$ and range charts are used together in order to show both the center of the process measurements (accuracy) and the spread of the data (precision). An alternative combination of charts to show both the central tendency and the dispersion of the data is the $\overline{X}$ and **standard deviation**, or **s, chart**. The s chart is more accurate than the R chart. The subgroup sample standard deviation, or s value, is calculated using all of the data rather than just the high and low values in the sample like the

R chart. So while the range chart is simple to construct, it is most effective when the sample size is less than 10. When the sample size exceeds 10, the range does not truly represent the variation present in the process. Under these circumstances, the s chart is used with the $\overline{X}$ chart.

The combination of $\overline{X}$ and s charts is created by the same methods as the $\overline{X}$ and R charts. The formulas are modified to reflect the use of s instead of R for the calculations.

For the $\overline{X}$ chart,

$$\overline{\overline{X}} = \frac{\sum\limits_{i=1}^{m} \overline{X}_i}{m}$$

$$UCL_{\overline{X}} = \overline{\overline{X}} + A_3 \overline{s}$$

$$LCL_{\overline{X}} = \overline{\overline{X}} - A_3 \overline{s}$$

For the s chart,

$$\overline{s} = \frac{\sum\limits_{i=1}^{m} s_i}{m}$$

$$UCL_s = B_4 \overline{s}$$

$$LCL_s = B_3 \overline{s}$$

where

s_i = standard deviation of the subgroup values
$\overline{s}_i$ = average of the subgroup sample standard deviations
A_3, B_3, B_4 = factors used for calculating 3σ control limits for $\overline{X}$ and s charts using the average sample standard deviation and Appendix 2

As in the $\overline{X}$ and R chart, the revised control limits can be calculated using the following formulas:

$$\overline{X}_0 = \overline{\overline{X}}_{new} = \frac{\sum \overline{X} - \overline{X}_d}{m - m_d}$$

$$s_0 = \overline{s}_{new} = \frac{\sum s - s_d}{m - m_d}$$

and

$$\sigma = s_0 / c_4$$

$$UCL_{\overline{X}} = \overline{X}_0 + A\sigma_0$$

$$LCL_{\overline{X}} = \overline{X}_0 - A\sigma_0$$

$$UCL_s = B_6 \sigma_0$$

$$LCL_s = B_5 \sigma_0$$

where

$$s_d = \text{sample standard deviation of the discarded subgroup}$$
$$c_4 = \text{factor found in Appendix 2 for computing } \sigma_0 \text{ from } \bar{s}$$
$$A, B_5, B_6 = \text{factors found in Appendix 2 for computing the } 3\sigma \text{ process control}$$
$$\text{limits for } \bar{X} \text{ and s charts}$$

 SIX SIGMA TOOLS AT WORK

$\bar{X}$ and s Charts

This Six Sigma Tools at Work Feature uses the roller shaft data except that the range has been replaced by s, the sample standard deviation. A sample of size n = 5 is taken at intervals from the process making shafts (Figure 10.17). A total of 21 subgroups of measurements is taken. Each time a sample is taken, the individual values are recorded [Figure 10.17, (1)], summed, and then divided by the number of samples taken to get the average [Figure 10.17, (2)]. This average is then plotted on the control chart [Figure 10.18, (1)]. Note that in this example, the values for $\bar{X}$ and s have been calculated to three decimal places for clarity.

Using the 21 samples provided in Figure 10.17, we can calculate $\bar{\bar{X}}$ by summing all the averages from the individual samples taken and then dividing by the number of subgroups:

$$\bar{\bar{X}} = \frac{251.76}{21} = 11.99$$

This value is plotted as the centerline of the $\bar{X}$ chart [Figure 10.18, (2)]. This is the centerline of the s chart [Figure 10.18, (4)].

Individual standard deviations are calculated for each of the subgroups by utilizing the formula for calculating standard deviations [Figure 10.17, (3)]. Once calculated, these values are plotted on the s chart [Figure 10.18, (6)].

The value of the grand standard deviation average is calculated by summing the values of the sample standard deviations [Figure 10.17, (3)] and dividing by the number of subgroups m:

$$\bar{s} = \frac{0.031 + 0.029 + 0.016 + \cdots + 0.015}{21} = \frac{0.414}{21} = 0.02$$

The A_3 factor for a sample size of five is selected from the table in Appendix 2. The values for the upper and lower control limits of the $\bar{X}$ chart are calculated as follows:

$$UCL_{\bar{X}} = \bar{\bar{X}} + A_3\bar{s}$$
$$= 11.99 + 1.427(0.02) = 12.02$$
$$LCL_{\bar{X}} = \bar{\bar{X}} - A_3\bar{s}$$
$$= 11.99 - 1.427(0.02) = 11.96$$

Once calculated, the upper and lower control limits (UCL and LCL, respectively) are placed on the chart [Figure 10.18, (3)].

With $n = 5$, the values of B_3 and B_4 are found in the table in Appendix 2. The control limits for the s chart are calculated as follows:

$$UCL_s = B_4\bar{s}$$
$$= 2.089(0.02) = 0.04$$
$$LCL_s = B_3\bar{s}$$
$$= 0(0.02) = 0$$

The control limits are placed on the s chart [Figure 10.18, (5)].

DEPT.	Roller		PART NAME	Shaft
PART NO.	1		MACHINE	1
GROUP	1		VARIABLE	length

Subgroup	1	2	3	4	5
Time	07:30	07:40	07:50	08:00	08:10
Date	07/02/95	07/02/95	07/02/95	07/02/95	07/02/95
1	11.95	12.03	12.01	11.97	12.00
2	12.00	12.02	12.00	11.98	12.01
3	12.03 ①	11.96	11.97	12.00	12.02
4	11.98	12.00	11.98	12.03	12.03
5	12.01	11.98	12.00	11.99	12.02
X̄	11.99 ②	12.00	11.99	11.99	12.02
s	0.031③	0.029	0.016	0.023	0.011
Subgroup	6	7	8	9	10
Time	08:20	08:30	08:40	08:50	09:00
Date	07/02/95	07/02/95	07/02/95	07/02/95	07/02/95
1	11.98	12.00	12.00	12.00	12.02
2	11.98	12.01	12.01	12.02	12.00
3	12.00	12.03	12.04	11.96	11.97
4	12.01	12.00	12.00	12.00	12.05
5	11.99	11.98	12.02	11.98	12.00
X̄	11.99	12.00	12.01	11.99	12.01
s	0.013	0.018	0.017	0.023	0.030
Subgroup	11	12	13	14	15
Time	09:10	09:20	09:30	09:40	09:50
Date	07/02/95	07/02/95	07/02/95	07/02/95	07/02/95
1	11.98	11.92	11.93	11.99	12.00
2	11.97	11.95	11.95	11.93	11.98
3	11.96	11.92	11.98	11.94	11.99
4	11.95	11.94	11.94	11.95	11.95
5	12.00	11.96	11.96	11.96	11.93
X̄	11.97	11.94	11.95	11.95	11.97
s	0.019	0.018	0.019	0.023	0.029

Subgroup	16	17	18	19	20
Time	10:00	10:10	10:20	10:30	10:40
Date	07/02/95	07/02/95	07/02/95	07/02/95	07/02/95
1	12.00	12.02	12.00	11.97	11.99
2	11.98	11.98	12.01	12.03	12.01
3	11.99 ①	11.97	12.02	12.00	12.02
4	11.96	11.98	12.01	12.01	12.00
5	11.97	11.99	11.99	11.99	12.01
$\overline{X}$	11.98	11.999	12.01	12.00	12.01
s	0.016 ②	0.019	0.011	0.022	0.011

Subgroup	21	③
Time	10:50	
Date	07/02/95	
1	12.00	
2	11.98	
3	11.99	
4	11.99	
5	12.02	
$\overline{X}$	12.00	
s	0.015	

$$\frac{12.00 + 11.98 + 11.99 + 11.96 + 11.97}{5} = 11.98$$

$$\sqrt{\frac{(12 - 11.98)^2 + (11.98 - 11.98)^2 + (11.99 - 11.98)^2 + (11.96 - 11.98)^2 + (11.97 - 11.98)^2}{5 - 1}} = 0.016$$

Figure 10.17   Shafts, Averages, and Standard Deviations

The s chart (Figure 10.18) exhibits good control. The points are evenly spaced on both sides of the centerline and there are no points beyond the control limits. There are no unusual patterns or trends in the data. Given these observations, it can be said that the process is producing parts of similar dimensions.

Next the $\overline{X}$ chart is examined. Once again, an inspection of the $\overline{X}$ chart reveals the unusual pattern occurring at points 12, 13, and 14. These measurements are all below the lower control limit. When compared with other samples throughout the day's production, the parts produced during the time that samples 12, 13, and 14 were taken were much smaller than parts produced during other times in the production run. As before, this signals that an investigation into the cause of the production of undersized parts needs to take place.

Since a cause for the undersized parts was determined in the previous example, these values can be removed from the calculations for the $\overline{X}$ chart and s chart. The revised limits will be used to monitor future production. The new limits will extend from the old limits.

Revising the calculations is performed as follows:

$$\overline{\overline{X}}_{new} = \overline{X}_0 = \frac{\Sigma\overline{X} - \overline{X}_d}{m - m_d}$$

$$= \frac{251.76 - 11.94 - 11.95 - 11.95}{21 - 3}$$

$$= 12.00$$

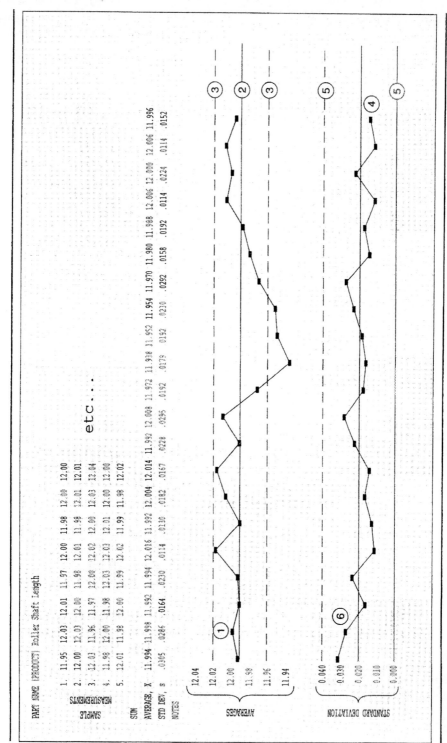

Figure 10.18 $\overline{X}$ and s Control Charts for Roller Shaft Length

208

$$\bar{s}_{new} = s_0 = \frac{\Sigma s - s_d}{m - m_d}$$

$$= \frac{0.414 - 0.0179 - 0.0192 - 0.0230}{21 - 3}$$

$$= 0.02$$

Calculating σ_0

$$\sigma_0 = \frac{s_0}{c_4} = \frac{0.02}{0.9400} = 0.02$$

$$UCL_{\bar{X}} = 12.00 + 1.342(0.02) = 12.03$$

$$LCL_{\bar{X}} = 12.00 - 1.342(0.02) = 11.97$$

$$UCL_s = 1.964(0.02) = 0.04$$

$$LCL_s = 0(0.02) = 0$$

SUMMARY

Control charts are easy to construct and use in studying a process, whether that process is in a manufacturing or service environment. Control charts indicate areas for improvement. Once the root cause has been identified, changes can be proposed and tested, and improvements can be monitored through the use of control charts. Through the use of control charts, similar gains can be realized in the manufacturing sector. Users of control charts report savings in scrap, including material and labor; lower rework costs; reduced inspection; higher product quality; more consistent part characteristics; greater operator confidence; lower troubleshooting costs; reduced completion times; faster deliveries; and others.

σ ▓ *Take Away Tips*

1. Control charts enhance the analysis of a process by showing how that process performs over time. Control charts allow for early detection of process changes.
2. Control charts serve two basic functions: They provide an economic basis for making a decision as to whether to investigate for potential problems, adjust the process, or leave the process alone; and they assist in the identification of problems in the process.
3. Variation, differences between items, exists in all processes. Variation can be within-piece, piece-to-piece, and time-to-time.
4. The $\bar{X}$ chart is used to monitor the variation in the average values of the measurements of groups of samples. Averages rather than individual observations are used on control charts because average values will indicate a change in the amount of variation much faster than individual values will.

5. The $\overline{X}$ chart, showing the central tendency of the data, is always used in conjunction with either a range or a standard deviation chart.

6. The R and s charts show the spread or dispersion of the data.

7. The centerline of a control chart shows where the process is centered. The upper and lower control limits describe the spread of the process.

8. A homogeneous subgroup is essential to the proper study of a process. Certain guidelines can be applied in choosing a rational subgroup.

9. Common, or chance, causes are small random changes in the process that cannot be avoided. Assignable causes are large variations in the process that can be identified as having a specific cause.

10. A process is considered to be in a state of control, or under control, when the performance of the process falls within the statistically calculated control limits and exhibits only common, or chance, causes. Certain guidelines can be applied for determining by control chart when a process is under control.

11. Patterns on a control chart indicate a lack of statistical control. Patterns may take the form of changes or jumps in level, runs, trends, or cycles or may reflect the existence of two populations or mistakes.

12. The steps for revising a control chart are (a) examine the chart for out-of-control conditions; (b) isolate the causes of the out-of-control condition; (c) eliminate the cause of the out-of-control condition; and (d) revise the chart, using the formulas presented in the chapter. Revisions to the control chart can take place only when the assignable causes have been determined and eliminated. ■

σ ■ Formulas

Average and Range Charts

$\overline{X}$ chart:

$$\overline{\overline{X}} = \frac{\sum\limits_{i=1}^{m} \overline{X}_i}{m}$$

$$UCL_{\overline{X}} = \overline{\overline{X}} + A_2\overline{R}$$

$$LCL_{\overline{X}} = \overline{\overline{X}} - A_2\overline{R}$$

R chart:

$$\overline{R} = \frac{\sum\limits_{i=1}^{m} R_i}{m}$$

$$UCL_R = D_4\overline{R}$$

$$LCL_R = D_3\overline{R}$$

Revising the charts:

$$\bar{X} = \bar{\bar{X}}_{new} = \frac{\sum\limits_{i=1}^{m} \bar{X} - \bar{X}_d}{m - m_d}$$

$$UCL_{\bar{X}} = \bar{X}_0 + A\sigma_0$$

$$LCL_{\bar{X}} = \bar{X}_0 - A\sigma_0$$

$$\sigma_0 = R_0/d_2$$

$$\bar{R}_{new} = \frac{\sum\limits_{i=1}^{m} R - R_d}{m - m_d}$$

$$UCL_R = D_2\sigma_0$$

$$LCL_R = D_1\sigma_0$$

Average and Standard Deviation Charts

$\bar{X}$ chart:

$$\bar{\bar{X}} = \frac{\sum\limits_{i=1}^{m} \bar{X}_i}{m}$$

$$UCL_{\bar{X}} = \bar{\bar{X}} + A_3\bar{s}$$

$$LCL_{\bar{X}} = \bar{\bar{X}} - A_3\bar{s}$$

s chart:

$$\bar{s} = \frac{\sum\limits_{i=1}^{m} s_i}{m}$$

$$UCL_s = B_4\bar{s}$$

$$LCL_s = B_3\bar{s}$$

Revising the charts:

$$X_0 = \bar{\bar{X}}_{new} = \frac{\sum\limits_{i=1}^{m} \bar{X} - \bar{X}_d}{m - m_d}$$

$$s_0 = \bar{s}_{new} = \frac{\sum\limits_{i=1}^{m} s - s_d}{m - m_d}$$

$$\sigma_0 = s_0/c_4$$
$$UCL_{\overline{X}} = \overline{X}_0 + A\sigma_0$$
$$LCL_{\overline{X}} = \overline{X}_0 - A\sigma_0$$
$$UCL_s = B_6\sigma_0$$
$$LCL_s = B_5\sigma_0$$

Chapter Questions

1. Describe the difference between chance and assignable causes.

2. A large bank establishes $\overline{X}$ and R charts for the time required to process applications for its charge cards. A sample of five applications is taken each day. The first four weeks (20 days) of data give

$$\overline{\overline{X}} = 16 \text{ min} \quad \overline{s} = 3 \text{ min} \quad \overline{R} = 7 \text{ min}$$

Based on the values given, calculate the centerline and control limits for the $\overline{X}$ and R charts.

3. The data below are $\overline{X}$ and R values for 25 samples of size n = 4 taken from a process filling bags of fertilizer. The measurements are made on the fill weight of the bags in pounds.

Subgroup Number	$\overline{X}$	Range	Subgroup Number	$\overline{X}$	Range
1	50.3	0.73	14	50.8	0.70
2	49.6	0.75	15	50.0	0.65
3	50.8	0.79	16	49.9	0.66
4	50.9	0.74	17	50.4	0.67
5	49.8	0.72	18	50.5	0.68
6	50.5	0.73	19	50.7	0.70
7	50.2	0.71	20	50.2	0.65
8	49.9	0.70	21	49.9	0.60
9	50.0	0.65	22	50.1	0.64
10	50.1	0.67	23	49.5	0.60
11	50.2	0.65	24	50.0	0.62
12	50.5	0.67	25	50.3	0.60
13	50.4	0.68			

Set up the $\overline{X}$ and R charts on this process. Interpret the charts. Does the process seem to be in control? If necessary, assume assignable causes and revise the trial control limits. If the average fill of the bags is to be 50.0 pounds, how does this process compare?

4. The data below are $\overline{X}$ and R values for 12 samples of size n = 5. They were taken from a process producing bearings. The measurements are made on the inside diameter of the bearing. The data have been coded from 0.50; in other words, a measurement of 0.50345 has been recorded as 345. Range values are coded from 0.000; that is, 0.00013 is recorded as 13.

Subgroup Number	$\overline{X}$	Range
1	345	13
2	347	14
3	350	12
4	346	11
5	350	15
6	345	16
7	349	14
8	348	13
9	348	12
10	354	15
11	352	13
12	355	16

Set up the $\overline{X}$ and R charts on this process. Does the process seem to be in control? Why or why not? If necessary, assume assignable causes and revise the trial control limits.

5. Describe how both an $\overline{X}$ and R or s chart would look if they were under normal statistical control.

6. Why is the use and interpretation of an R or s chart so critical when examining an $\overline{X}$ chart?

7. Create an $\overline{X}$ and R chart for the clutch plate information in Table 10.1 on page 176. You will need to calculate the range values for each subgroup. Calculate the control limits and centerline for each chart. Graph the data with the calculated values. Beginning with the R chart, how does the process look?

8. RM Manufacturing makes thermometers for use in the medical field. These thermometers, which read in degrees Celsius, are able to measure temperatures to a level of precision of two decimal places. Each hour, RM Manufacturing tests eight randomly selected thermometers in a solution that is known to be at a temperature of 3°C. Use the following data to create and interpret an $\overline{X}$ and R chart. Based on the desired thermometer reading of 3°, interpret the results of your plotted averages and ranges.

Subgroup	Average Temperature	Range	Subgroup	Average Temperature	Range
1	3.06	0.10	9	3.00	0.09
2	3.03	0.09	10	3.03	0.14
3	3.10	0.12	11	2.96	0.07
4	3.05	0.07	12	2.99	0.11
5	2.98	0.08	13	3.01	0.09
6	3.00	0.10	14	2.98	0.13
7	3.01	0.15	15	3.02	0.08
8	3.04	0.09			

9. The environmental safety engineer at a local firm is keeping track of the air particulate readings for four separate areas within the plant. Create an $\overline{X}$ and s chart for the average amount of particulates found at the time of each sample (read down the columns for each particular time, n = 4). Interpret the chart. What is the drawback of constructing the chart based on the times the samples were taken versus the location in the plant that the samples were taken?

Initial Particulates Readings

DATE	4/15			4/16			4/17		
TIME	8:00 AM	4:00 PM	12:00 AM	8:00 AM	4:00 PM	12:00 AM	8:00 AM	4:00 PM	12:00 AM
NORTH PIT	300	350	480	365	400	470	410	375	500
SOUTH PIT	440	470	495	405	505	560	445	440	575
EAST PIT	275	300	360	300	300	325	260	295	355
WEST PIT	350	360	400	360	360	390	325	360	405

DATE	4/18			4/19			4/20		
TIME	8:00 AM	4:00 PM	12:00 AM	8:00 AM	4:00 PM	12:00 AM	8:00 AM	4:00 PM	12:00 AM
NORTH PIT	320	350	475	335	410	490	420	385	485
SOUTH PIT	485	505	545	415	520	575	430	440	520
EAST PIT	330	320	370	270	320	345	280	315	375
WEST PIT	225	370	410	350	370	400	335	370	415

DATE	4/21			4/22			4/23		
TIME	8:00 AM	4:00 PM	12:00 AM	8:00 AM	4:00 PM	12:00 AM	8:00 AM	4:00 PM	12:00 AM
NORTH PIT	290	330	450	310	390	390	325	400	495
SOUTH PIT	430	520	510	435	440	560	485	540	450
EAST PIT	285	315	350	295	305	330	250	265	360
WEST PIT	350	360	400	360	360	390	340	325	400

10. Using the information in Question 9, create an $\overline{X}$ and s chart based on the daily average for each location in the plant (read across the columns for each pit, n = 3). Interpret the chart. What is the drawback of constructing the chart based on the location from which the samples were taken versus constructing a chart based on the times at which the samples were taken?

Process Capability

How do we know the process will generate products or services that meet the customer's specifications?

■ Objectives:

1. To gain an understanding of the relationship between individual values and their averages
2. To understand the difference between specification limits and control limits
3. To learn to calculate and interpret the process capability indices: C_p, C_r, and C_{pk} ■

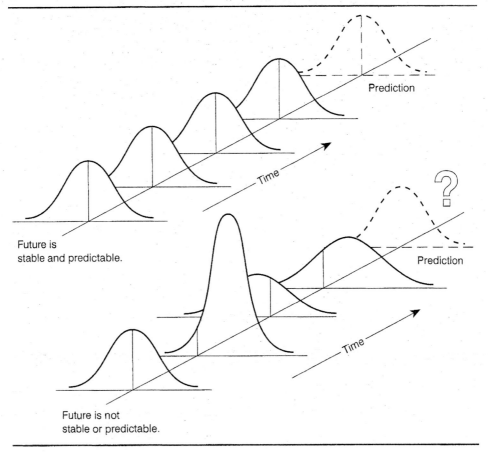

Figure 11.1   Future Predictions

Process capability refers to the ability of a process to produce products or provide services capable of meeting the specifications set by the customer or designer. As discussed in previous chapters, variation affects a process and may prevent the process from producing products or services that meet customer specifications. Reducing process variability and creating consistent quality both increase the viability of predictions of future process performance (Figure 11.1).

Manufacturers of products and providers of services can use process capability concepts to assist in decisions concerning product or process specifications, appropriate production methods, equipment to be used, and time commitments.

INDIVIDUAL VALUES COMPARED WITH AVERAGES

Process capability is based on the performance of individual products or services against specifications. Information from samples helps determine the behavior of individuals in a process.

A relationship exists between subgroup sample averages and individual values. Table 11.1 repeats the tally of individual and average values of clutch plate thickness data from Table 10.1. With this actual production line data, two frequency diagrams have been created in Figure 11.2. One frequency diagram is constructed of individual values; the other is made up of subgroup averages. Both distributions are approximately normal. The important difference to note is that individual values spread much more widely than their averages. When the two diagrams are compared, the averages are grouped closer to the center value than are the individual values, as described by the central limit theorem. Average values smooth out the highs and lows associated with individuals. This comparison will be important to keep in mind when comparing the behavior of averages and control limits with that of individual values and specification limits (Figure 11.3).

Table 11.1   Clutch Plate Thickness: Sums and Averages

						$\sum X_i$	$\bar{X}$	$\bar{R}$
Subgroup 1	0.0625	0.0626	0.0624	0.0625	0.0627	0.3127	0.0625	0.0003
Subgroup 2	0.0624	0.0623	0.0624	0.0626	0.0625	0.3122	0.0624	0.0003
Subgroup 3	0.0622	0.0625	0.0623	0.0625	0.0626	0.3121	0.0624	0.0004
Subgroup 4	0.0624	0.0623	0.0620	0.0623	0.0624	0.3114	0.0623	0.0004
Subgroup 5	0.0621	0.0621	0.0622	0.0625	0.0624	0.3113	0.0623	0.0004
Subgroup 6	0.0628	0.0626	0.0625	0.0626	0.0627	0.3132	0.0626	0.0003
Subgroup 7	0.0624	0.0627	0.0625	0.0624	0.0626	0.3126	0.0625	0.0003
Subgroup 8	0.0624	0.0625	0.0625	0.0626	0.0626	0.3126	0.0625	0.0002
Subgroup 9	0.0627	0.0628	0.0626	0.0625	0.0627	0.3133	0.0627	0.0003
Subgroup 10	0.0625	0.0626	0.0628	0.0626	0.0627	0.3132	0.0626	0.0003
Subgroup 11	0.0625	0.0624	0.0626	0.0626	0.0626	0.3127	0.0625	0.0002
Subgroup 12	0.0630	0.0628	0.0627	0.0625	0.0627	0.3134	0.0627	0.0005
Subgroup 13	0.0627	0.0626	0.0628	0.0627	0.0626	0.3137	0.0627	0.0002
Subgroup 14	0.0626	0.0626	0.0625	0.0626	0.0627	0.3130	0.0626	0.0002
Subgroup 15	0.0628	0.0627	0.0626	0.0625	0.0626	0.3132	0.0626	0.0003
Subgroup 16	0.0625	0.0626	0.0625	0.0628	0.0627	0.3131	0.0626	0.0003
Subgroup 17	0.0624	0.0626	0.0624	0.0625	0.0627	0.3126	0.0625	0.0003
Subgroup 18	0.0628	0.0627	0.0628	0.0626	0.0630	0.3139	0.0627	0.0004
Subgroup 19	0.0627	0.0626	0.0628	0.0625	0.0627	0.3133	0.0627	0.0003
Subgroup 20	0.0626	0.0625	0.0626	0.0625	0.0627	0.3129	0.0626	0.0002
Subgroup 21	0.0627	0.0626	0.0628	0.0625	0.0627	0.3133	0.0627	0.0003
Subgroup 22	0.0625	0.0626	0.0628	0.0625	0.0627	0.3131	0.0626	0.0003
Subgroup 23	0.0628	0.0626	0.0627	0.0630	0.0627	0.3138	0.0628	0.0004
Subgroup 24	0.0625	0.0631	0.0630	0.0628	0.0627	0.3141	0.0628	0.0006
Subgroup 25	0.0627	0.0630	0.0631	0.0628	0.0627	0.3143	0.0629	0.0004
Subgroup 26	0.0630	0.0628	0.0629	0.0628	0.0627	0.3142	0.0628	0.0003
Subgroup 27	0.0630	0.0628	0.0631	0.0628	0.0627	0.3144	0.0629	0.0004
Subgroup 28	0.0632	0.0632	0.0628	0.0631	0.0630	0.3153	0.0631	0.0004
Subgroup 29	0.0630	0.0628	0.0631	0.0632	0.0631	0.3152	0.0630	0.0004
Subgroup 30	0.0632	0.0631	0.0630	0.0628	0.0628	0.3149	0.0630	0.0004
						9.3981		

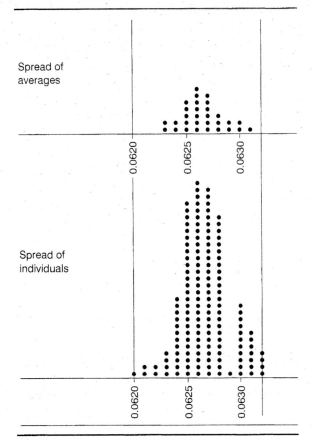

Figure 11.2   Normal Curves for Individuals and Averages

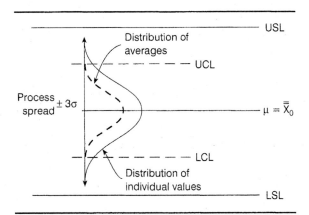

Figure 11.3   Comparison of the Spread of Individual Values with Averages

ESTIMATION OF POPULATION SIGMA FROM SAMPLE DATA

The larger the sample size, n, the more representative the sample average, $\overline{X}$, is of the mean of the population, μ. In other words, $\overline{X}$ becomes a more reliable estimate of μ as the sample size is increased. The ability of $\overline{X}$ to approximate μ is measured by the expression $\sigma/\sqrt{n}$, the standard error of the mean. It is possible to estimate the spread of the population of individuals using the sample data. This formula shows the relationship between the population standard deviation (σ) and the standard deviation of the subgroup averages ($\sigma_{\overline{X}}$):

$$\sigma_{\overline{X}} = \frac{\sigma}{\sqrt{n}}$$

where

$\sigma_{\overline{X}}$ = standard deviation of subgroup averages
σ = population standard deviation
n = number of observations in each subgroup

The population standard deviation, σ, is determined by measuring the individuals. This necessitates measuring every value. To avoid complicated calculations, if the process can be assumed to be normal, the population standard deviation can be estimated from either the standard deviation associated with the sample standard deviation (s) or the range (R):

$$\hat{\sigma} = \frac{\overline{s}}{c_4} \quad \text{or} \quad \hat{\sigma} = \frac{\overline{R}}{d_2}$$

where

$\hat{\sigma}$ = estimate of population standard deviation
$\overline{s}$ = sample standard deviation calculated from subgroup samples
$\overline{R}$ = average range of subgroups
c_4 as found in Appendix 2
d_2 as found in Appendix 2

Because of the estimators (c_4 and d_2), these two formulas will yield similar but not identical values for $\hat{\sigma}$. Dr. Shewhart confirmed that the standard deviation of subgroup sample means is the standard deviation of individual samples divided by the square root of the subgroup size. He did this by drawing, at random from a large bowl, numbered, metal lined, disk-shaped tags. He used this information to determine the estimators c_4 and d_2.

CONTROL LIMITS VERSUS SPECIFICATION LIMITS

A process is in control only when its process centering and the amount of variation present in the process remains constant over time. If both are constant, then the behavior of the process will be predictable. As discussed in Chapter 10, a process under control exhibits the following characteristics:

1. Two-thirds of the points are near the center value.
2. A few of the points are close to the center value.
3. The points float back and forth across the centerline.
4. The points are balanced (in roughly equal numbers) on both sides of the centerline.
5. There are no points beyond the control limits.
6. There are no patterns or trends on the chart.

It is important to note that a process in statistical control will not necessarily meet specifications as established by the customer. There is a difference between a process conforming to specifications and a process performing within statistical control.

Established during the design process or from customer requests, specifications communicate what the customers expect, want, or need from the process. Specifications can be considered the voice of the customer.

Control limits are the voice of the process. The centerline on the $\overline{X}$ chart represents process centering. The R and s chart limits represent the amount of variation present in the process. Control limits are a prediction of the variation that the process will exhibit in the near future. The difference between specifications and control limits is that specifications relay wishes and control limits tell of reality.

Occasionally, creators of control charts inappropriately place specification limits on control charts. Processes are unaware of specifications; they perform to the best of their capabilities. Unfortunately, specification limits on control charts encourage users to adjust the process on the basis of them instead of on the true limits of the process, the control limits. The resulting miscued changes can potentially disrupt the process and increase process variation.

As Figure 11.2 shows, the spread of individual values is wider than the spread of the averages. For this reason, control limits cannot be compared directly with specification limits. An $\overline{X}$ chart does not reflect how widely the individual values composing the plotted averages spread. This is one reason why an R or s chart is always used in conjunction with the $\overline{X}$ chart. The spread of the individual data can be seen only by observing what is happening on the R or s chart. If the values on the R or s chart are large, then the variation associated with the average is large. Figure 11.4 shows a control chart created using the concepts from Chapter 10 and the values in Table 11.1. The $\overline{X}$'s are circled. Individual values shown as X's are also plotted on this chart. Note where the individual values fall in relation to the control limits established for the process. The individuals spread more widely than the averages and follow the pattern established by the R chart. Studying the R chart in conjunction with the $\overline{X}$ chart can significantly increase the understanding of how the process is performing.

For explanatory purposes, both control limits and specification limits appear on the charts in Figure 11.5, a practice not to be followed in industry. The variation in Figure 11.5, top chart, exceeds control limits marking the expected process variation but not the specification limits. While the process is out of control, for the time being the customer's needs are being met. The process in Figure 11.5, bottom chart,

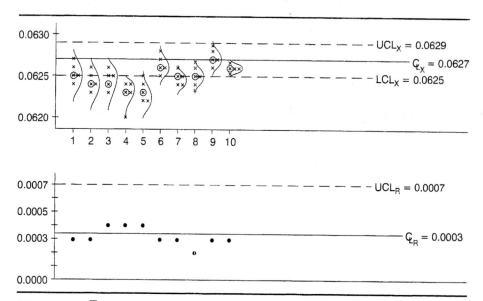

Figure 11.4   X̄ and R Chart Showing Averages and Individuals

is under control and within the control limits, but the specification limits do not correspond with the control limits. This situation reveals that the process is performing to the best of its abilities, but not well enough to meet the specifications set by the customer.

σ SIX SIGMA TOOLS AT WORK

Using the X̄ and R Charts to Assess the Process

A Six Sigma team has been studying the results of a tensile strength test. To better understand the process performance and the spread of the individual values that compose the averages, they have overlaid the R chart pattern on the X̄ chart. To do this easily, they divided the X̄ chart into three sections (Figure 11.6) chosen on the basis of how the data on the X̄ chart appear to be grouped. X̄ values in section A are centered at the mean and are very similar. In section B, the X̄ values are above the mean and more spread out. Section C values have a slight downward trend.

Studying the sections on the R chart reveals that the spread of the data is changing (Figure 11.6). The values in section A have an average amount of variation, denoted by the normal curve corresponding to section A. Variation increases in section B, resulting in a much broader spread on the normal curve (B). The significant decrease in variation in section C is shown by the narrow, peaked distribution. The R chart describes the spread of the individuals on the X̄ chart.

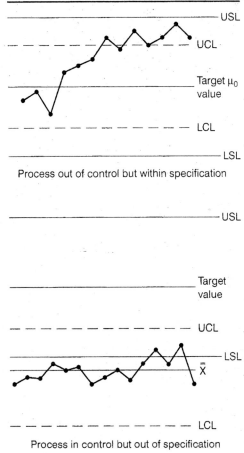

Figure 11.5 For Explanation Purposes Only, These Charts Show Control Limits versus Specification Limits

THE 6σ SPREAD VERSUS SPECIFICATION LIMITS

The spread of the individuals in a process, 6σ, is the measure used to compare the realities of production with the desires of the customers. The process standard deviation is based on either s or R from control chart data:

$$\hat{\sigma} = \frac{\bar{s}}{c_4} \quad \text{or} \quad \hat{\sigma} = \frac{\bar{R}}{d_2}$$

where

$\hat{\sigma}$ = estimate of population standard deviation
$\bar{s}$ = sample standard deviation calculated from process
$\bar{R}$ = average range of subgroups calculated from process
c_4 as found in Appendix 2
d_2 as found in Appendix 2

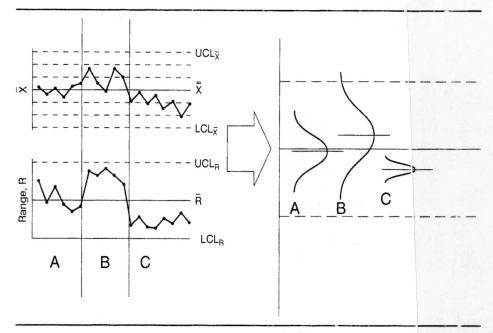

Figure 11.6   Overlaying the R Chart Pattern on the X̄ Chart

Remember, because of the estimators (c_4 and d_2), these two formulas will yield similar but not identical values for $\hat{\sigma}$.

Specification limits, the allowable spread of the individuals, are compared with the 6σ spread of the process to determine how capable the process is of meeting the specifications. Three different situations can exist when specifications and 6σ are compared: (1) the 6σ process spread can be less than the spread of the specification limits; (2) the 6σ process spread can be equal to the spread of the specification limits; (3) the 6σ process spread can be greater than the spread of the specification limits.

Case I: $6\sigma < USL - LSL$ This is the most desirable case. Figure 11.7 illustrates this relationship. The control limits have been placed on the diagram, as well as the spread of the process averages (dotted line). The 6σ spread of the process individuals is shown by the solid line. As expected, the spread of the individual values is greater than the spread of the averages; however, the values are still within the specification limits. The 6σ spread of the individuals is less than the spread of the specifications. This allows for more room for process shifts while staying within the specifications. Notice that even if the process drifts out of control (Figure 11.7b), the change must be dramatic before the parts are considered out of specification.

Case II: $6\sigma = USL - LSL$ In this situation, 6σ is equal to the tolerance (Figure 11.8a). As long as the process remains in control and centered, with no change in process variation, the parts produced will be within specification. However, a shift in the process mean (Figure 11.8b) will result in the production of parts that are

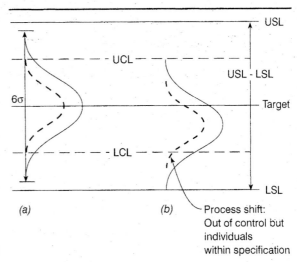

**Figure 11.7 Case I:
6σ < USL − LSL**

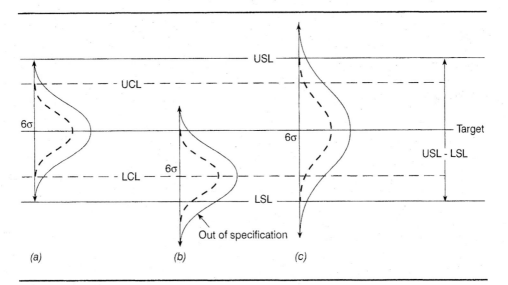

Figure 11.8 Case II: 6σ = USL − LSL

out of specification. An increase in the variation present in the process also creates an
out-of-specification situation (Figure 11.8c).

Case III: 6σ > USL − LSL Any time that the 6σ spread is greater than the tolerance spread, an undesirable situation exists (Figure 11.9a). Even though the process
is exhibiting only natural patterns of variation, it is incapable of meeting the specifications set by the customer. To correct this problem, management intervention will be
necessary in order to change the process to decrease the variation or to recenter the

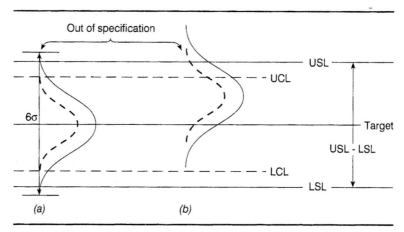

Figure 11.9   Case III: $6\sigma >$ USL $-$ LSL

process if necessary. The capability of the process cannot be improved without changing the existing process. To achieve a substantial reduction in the standard deviation or spread of the data, management will have to authorize the utilization of different materials, the overhaul of the machine, the purchase of a new machine, the retraining of the operator, or other significant changes to the process. Other, less desirable approaches to dealing with this problem are to perform 100 percent inspection on the product, increase the specification limits, or shift the process average so that all of the nonconforming products occur at one end of the distribution (Figure 11.9b). In certain cases, shifting the process average can eliminate scrap and increase the amount of rework, thus saving scrap costs by increasing rework costs.

CALCULATING PROCESS CAPABILITY INDICES

Process capability indices are mathematical ratios that quantify the ability of a process to produce products within the specifications. The capability indices compare the spread of the individuals created by the process with the specification limits set by the customer or designer. The 6σ spread of the individuals can be calculated for a new process that has not produced a significant number of parts or for a process currently in operation. In either case, a true 6σ value cannot be determined until the process is under control, as described by the $\overline{X}$ and R charts or $\overline{X}$ and s charts. If the process is not stable, the calculated values may not be representative of the true process capability.

Calculating $6\hat{\sigma}$

Assuming the process is under statistical control, we use one of the two following methods to calculate $6\hat{\sigma}$ of a new process:

1. Take at least 20 subgroups of sample size 4 for a total of 80 measurements.
2. Calculate the sample standard deviation, s_i, for each subgroup.

3. Calculate the average sample standard deviation, $\bar{s}$:

$$\bar{s} = \frac{\sum\limits_{i=1}^{m} s_i}{m}$$

where

$$s_i = \text{standard deviation for each subgroup}$$
$$m = \text{number of subgroups}$$

4. Calculate the estimate of the population standard deviation:

$$\hat{\sigma} = \frac{\bar{s}}{c_4}$$

where c_4 is obtained from Appendix 2.

5. Multiply the population standard deviation by 6.

 SIX SIGMA TOOLS AT WORK

Calculating $6\hat{\sigma}$

The Six Sigma team monitoring a process making roller shafts for printers wish to calculate $6\hat{\sigma}$ using the data in Table 11.2. They have 21 subgroups of sample size 5 for a total of 105 measurements, more than the 80 recommended.

They calculate the sample standard deviation, s_i, for each subgroup (Table 11.2). From these values they calculate the average sample standard deviation, $\bar{s}$:

$$\bar{s} = \frac{\sum\limits_{i=1}^{m} s_i}{m} = \frac{0.031 + 0.029 + \cdots + 0.015}{21}$$

$$= \frac{0.414}{21} = 0.02$$

The next step involves calculating the estimate of the population standard deviation:

$$\hat{\sigma} = \frac{\bar{s}}{c_4} = \frac{0.02}{0.9400} = 0.021$$

The value of c_4 is obtained from Appendix 2 and is based on a sample size of 5. As the final step they multiply the population standard deviation by 6:

$$6\hat{\sigma} = 6(0.021) = 0.126$$

This value can be compared with the spread of the specifications to determine how the individual products produced by the process compare with the specifications set by the designer.

Table 11.2   X̄ and s Values of Roller Shafts

Subgroup Number	X₁					X̄	s
1	11.950	12.000	12.030	11.980	12.010	11.994	0.031
2	12.030	12.020	11.960	12.000	11.980	11.998	0.029
3	12.010	12.000	11.970	11.980	12.000	11.992	0.016
4	11.970	11.980	12.000	12.030	11.990	11.994	0.023
5	12.000	12.010	12.020	12.030	12.020	12.016	0.011
6	11.980	11.980	12.000	12.010	11.990	11.992	0.013
7	12.000	12.010	12.030	12.000	11.980	12.004	0.018
8	12.000	12.010	12.040	12.000	12.020	12.014	0.017
9	12.000	12.020	11.960	12.000	11.980	11.992	0.023
10	12.020	12.000	11.970	12.050	12.000	12.008	0.030
11	11.980	11.970	11.960	11.950	12.000	11.972	0.019
12	11.920	11.950	11.920	11.940	11.960	11.938	0.018
13	11.980	11.930	11.940	11.950	11.960	11.952	0.019
14	11.990	11.930	11.940	11.950	11.960	11.954	0.023
15	12.000	11.980	11.990	11.950	11.930	11.970	0.029
16	12.000	11.980	11.970	11.960	11.990	11.980	0.016
17	12.020	11.980	11.970	11.980	11.990	11.988	0.019
18	12.000	12.010	12.020	12.010	11.990	12.006	0.011
19	11.970	12.030	12.000	12.010	11.990	12.000	0.022
20	11.990	12.010	12.020	12.000	12.010	12.006	0.011
21	12.000	11.980	11.990	11.990	12.020	11.996	0.015

A second method of calculating $6\hat{\sigma}$ is to use the data from a control chart. Once again, it is assumed that the process is under statistical control, with no unusual patterns of variation.

1. Take the past 20 subgroups, sample size of 4 or more.
2. Calculate the range, R, for each subgroup.
3. Calculate the average range, $\overline{R}$:

$$\overline{R} = \frac{\sum\limits_{i=1}^{m} R_i}{m}$$

where

$$R_i = \text{individual range values for the subgroups}$$
$$m = \text{number of subgroups}$$

4. Calculate the estimate of the population standard deviation, $\hat{\sigma}$:

$$\hat{\sigma} = \frac{\overline{R}}{d_2}$$

where d_2 is obtained from Appendix 2.

5. Multiply the population standard deviation by 6.

Using more than 20 subgroups will improve the accuracy of the calculations.

SIX SIGMA TOOLS AT WORK

Calculating 6σ

The Six Sigma team used the data in Table 11.1 to calculate $6\hat{\sigma}$ for the clutch plate. Thirty subgroups of sample size 5 and their ranges are used to calculate the average range, $\bar{R}$:

$$\bar{R} = \frac{\sum_{i=1}^{m} R_i}{m} = \frac{0.0003 + 0.0003 + \cdots + 0.0004}{21}$$

$$= 0.0003$$

Next, the engineers calculate the estimate of the population standard deviation, $\hat{\sigma}$:

$$\hat{\sigma} = \frac{\bar{R}}{d_2} = \frac{0.0003}{2.326} = 0.0001$$

Using a sample size of 5, they take the value for d_2 from Appendix 2. To determine $6\hat{\sigma}$, they multiply the population standard deviation by 6:

$$6\hat{\sigma} = 6(0.0001) = 0.0006$$

They now compare this value with the specification limits to determine how well the process is performing.

The Capability Index

Once calculated, the σ values can be used to determine several indices related to process capability. The **capability index C_p** is the ratio of tolerance (USL − LSL) and $6\hat{\sigma}$:

$$C_p = \frac{USL - LSL}{6\hat{\sigma}}$$

where

$$C_p = \text{capability index}$$
$$USL - LSL = \text{upper specification limit} - \text{lower specification limit, or tolerance}$$

The capability index is interpreted as follows: If the capability index is larger than 1.00, a Case I situation exists (Figure 11.7a). This is desirable. The greater this value, the better. If the capability index is equal to 1.00, then a Case II situation exists (Figure 11.8a). This is not optimal, but it is feasible. If the capability index is less than 1.00, then a Case III situation exists (Figure 11.9a). Values of less than 1 are undesirable and reflect the process's inability to meet the specifications.

SIX SIGMA TOOLS AT WORK

Finding the Capability Index I

The clutch plate from the earlier Six Sigma Tools at Work feature has specification limits of 0.0625 ± 0.0003. The upper specification limit is 0.0628 and the lower specification limit is 0.0622. To calculate C_p:

$$C_p = \frac{USL - LSL}{6\hat{\sigma}} = \frac{0.0628 - 0.0622}{0.0006}$$
$$= 1.0$$

A value of 1.0 means that the process is just capable of meeting the demands placed on it by the customer's specifications. To be on the safe side, changes will need to occur to improve the process performance.

 SIX SIGMA TOOLS AT WORK

Finding the Capability Index II

The Six Sigma team monitoring the roller shaft process want to calculate its C_p. They use specification limits of USL = 12.05, LSL = 11.95:

$$C_r = \frac{USL - LSL}{6\hat{\sigma}} = \frac{12.05 - 11.95}{0.126}$$
$$= 0.794$$

This process is not capable of meeting the demands placed on it. Improvements will need to take place to meet the customer's expectations.

The Capability Ratio

Another indicator of process capability is called the **capability ratio.** This ratio is similar to the capability index, though it reverses the numerator and the denominator. It is defined as

$$C_r = \frac{6\hat{\sigma}}{USL - LSL}$$

A capability ratio less than 1 is the most desirable situation. The larger the ratio, the less capable the process is of meeting specifications. Be aware that it is easy to confuse the two indices. The most commonly used index is the capability index.

C_{pk}

The centering of the process is shown by C_{pk}. As shown by the Taguchi loss function described in Chapter 2, a process operating in the center of the specifications set by the designer is usually more desirable than one that is consistently producing parts to

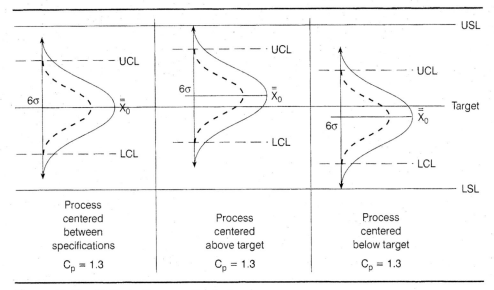

Figure 11.10 Shifts in Process Centering

the high or low side of the specification limits. In Figure 11.10, all three distributions have the same C_p index value of 1.3. Though each of these processes has the same capability index, they represent three different scenarios. In the first situation the process is centered as well as capable. In the second, a further upward shift in the process would result in an out-of-specification situation. The reverse holds true in the third situation. C_p and C_r do not take into account the centering of the process. *The ratio that reflects how the process is performing in terms of a nominal, center, or target value is C_{pk}.* C_{pk} can be calculated using the following formula:

$$C_{pk} = \frac{Z(min)}{3}$$

where Z(min) is the smaller of

$$Z(USL) = \frac{USL - \overline{X}}{\hat{\sigma}}$$

$$or \ Z(LSL) = \frac{\overline{X} - LSL}{\hat{\sigma}}$$

When $C_{pk} = C_p$ the process is centered. Figure 11.11 illustrates C_p and C_{pk} values for a process that is centered and one that is off center. The relationships between C_p and C_{pk} are as follows:

1. When C_p has a value of 1.0 or greater, the process is producing product capable of meeting specifications.
2. The C_p value does not reflect process centering.
3. When the process is centered, $C_p = C_{pk}$.

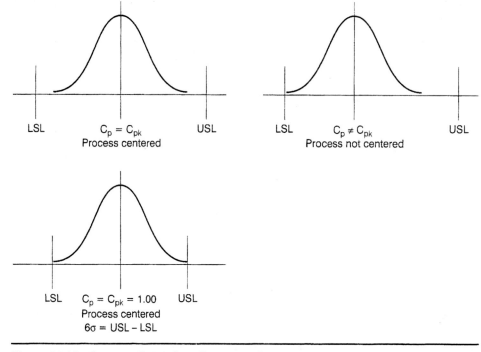

Figure 11.11   Process Centering: C_p versus C_{pk}

4. C_{pk} is always less than or equal to C_p.
5. When C_p is greater than or equal to 1.0 and C_{pk} has a value of 1.00 or more, it indicates the process is producing product that conforms to specifications.
6. When C_{pk} has a value less than 1.00, it indicates the process is producing product that does not conform to specifications.
7. A C_p value of less than 1.00 indicates that the process is not capable.
8. A C_{pk} value of zero indicates the process average is equal to one of the specification limits.
9. A negative C_{pk} value indicates that the average is outside the specification limits.

SIX SIGMA TOOLS AT WORK

Finding C_{pk}

Determine the C_{pk} for the roller shaft values. The average, $\overline{X}$, is equal to 11.990.

$$C_{pk} = \frac{Z(min)}{3}$$

where

$$Z(min) = \text{smaller of } \frac{(USL - \overline{X})}{\hat{\sigma}} \text{ or } \frac{(\overline{X} - LSL)}{\hat{\sigma}}$$

$$Z(USL) = \frac{(12.050 - 11.990)}{0.021} = 2.857$$

$$Z(LSL) = \frac{(11.990 - 11.950)}{0.021} = 1.905$$

$$C_{pk} = \frac{1.905}{3} = 0.635$$

A C_{pk} value of less than 1 means that the process is not capable. Because the C_p value (0.794) and the C_{pk} value (0.635) are not equal, the process is not centered between the specification limits.

 SIX SIGMA TOOLS AT WORK

Calculating C_{pk}

To determine the C_{pk} for the clutch plate:

$$C_{pk} = \frac{Z(min)}{3} = \frac{1}{3} = 0.3333$$

where

$$Z(USL) = \frac{0.0628 - 0.0627}{0.0001} = 1$$

$$Z(LSL) = \frac{0.0627 - 0.0622}{0.0001} = 5$$

The C_{pk} value of 0.3333 is less than 1 and not equal to $C_p = 1$. The process is not centered between the specification limits.

SUMMARY

Process capability indices are used to judge how consistently the process is performing. These indices provide a great deal of information concerning process centering and the ability of the process to meet specifications. Process capability indices can guide the improvement process toward uniformity about a target value.

σ ■ Take Away Tips

1. Process capability refers to the ability of a process to meet the specifications set by the customer or designer.
2. Individuals in a process spread more widely around a center value than do the averages.
3. Specification limits are set by the designer or customer. Control limits are determined by the current process.
4. $6\hat{\sigma}$ is the spread of the process or process capability.
5. C_p, the capability index, is the ratio of the tolerance (USL $-$ LSL) and the process capability ($6\hat{\sigma}$).
6. C_r, the capability ratio, is the ratio of the process capability (6σ) and the tolerance (USL $-$ LSL).
7. C_{pk} is the ratio that reflects how the process is performing in relation to a nominal, center, or target value. ■

σ ■ Formulas

$$\hat{\sigma} = \frac{\bar{s}}{c_4}$$

$$\hat{\sigma} = \frac{\bar{R}}{d_2}$$

Capability Indices

$$C_p = \frac{USL - LSL}{6\hat{\sigma}}$$

$$C_r = \frac{6\hat{\sigma}}{USL - LSL}$$

$$C_{pk} = \frac{Z(min)}{3}$$

where Z(min) is the smaller of Z(USL) = $(USL - \bar{X})/\hat{\sigma}$ or Z(LSL) = $(\bar{X} - LSL)/\hat{\sigma}$.

Chapter Questions

1. What do control limits represent? What do specification limits represent? Describe the three cases that compare specification limits to control limits.
2. Why can a process be in control but not be capable of meeting specifications?

3. A hospital is using $\overline{X}$ and R charts to record the time it takes to process patient account information. A sample of five applications is taken each day. The first four weeks' (20 days') data give the following values:

$$\overline{\overline{X}} = 16 \text{ min} \quad \overline{R} = 7 \text{ min}$$

If the upper and lower specifications are 21 minutes and 13 minutes, respectively, calculate $6\hat{\sigma}$, C_p, and C_{pk}. Interpret the indices.

4. For the data in Question 3 of Chapter 10, calculate $6\hat{\sigma}$, C_p, and C_{pk}. Interpret the indices. The specification limits are 50 ± 0.5.

5. Stress tests are used to study the heart muscle after a person has had a heart attack. Timely information from these stress tests can help doctors prevent future heart attacks. The team investigating the turnaround time of stress tests has managed to reduce the amount of time it takes for a doctor to receive the results of a stress test from 68 to 32 hours on average. The team had a goal of reducing test turnaround times to between 30 and 36 hours. Given that the new average test turnaround time is 32 hours, with a standard deviation of 1, and $n = 9$, calculate and interpret C_p and C_{pk}.

6. Hotels use statistical information and control charts to track their performance on a variety of indicators. Recently a hotel manager has been asked whether or not his team is capable of maintaining scores between 8 and 10 (on a scale of 1 to 10) for "overall cleanliness of room." The most recent data has a mean of 8.624, a standard deviation of 1.446, and $n = 10$. Calculate and interpret C_p and C_{pk}.

7. The Tasty Morsels Chocolate Company tracks the amount of chocolate found in its chocolate bars. The target is 26 grams and the upper and lower specifications are 29 and 23 grams, respectively. If their most recent $\overline{X}$ has a centerline of 25 and the R chart has a centerline of 2, and $n = 4$, is the process capable? Calculate and interpret C_p and C_{pk}.

8. From the information in Question 7 of Chapter 10, calculate $6\hat{\sigma}$, C_p, and C_{pk}. Interpret the indices. The specification limits are 3 ± 0.05.

9. For the data in Question 10 of Chapter 10, use $\overline{s}/c_4$ to calculate $6\hat{\sigma}$, C_p, and C_{pk}. Interpret the indices. Specifications: 400 ± 150 particulates per million.

10. A quality analyst is checking the process capability associated with the production of struts, specifically the amount of torque used to tighten a fastener. Twenty-five samples of size 4 have been taken. These were used to create $\overline{X}$ and R charts. The values for these charts are as follows. The upper and lower control limits for the $\overline{X}$ chart are 74.80 Nm and 72.37 Nm, respectively. $\overline{\overline{X}}$ is 73.58 Nm. $\overline{R}$ is 1.66. The specification limits are 80 Nm $\pm$ 10. Calculate $6\hat{\sigma}$, C_p, and C_{pk}. Interpret the values.

12

Probability

Did you know that if 30 people are gathered together, the probability of two of them sharing a birthday is 70%?

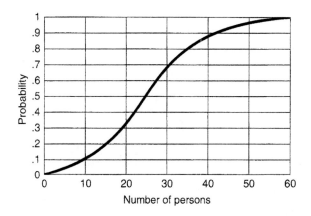

The Likelihood of Sharing a Birthday

■ Objectives:

1. To become familiar with seven probability theorems
2. To become familiar with the discrete probability distributions: hypergeometric, binomial, and Poisson
3. To review the normal continuous probability distribution ■

Probability is the chance that something will happen. Probabilities quantify the chance that an event will occur. A person's first exposure to probability theory usually occurs early in life in the form of the coin toss. A fair coin is tossed and the winner is the person who correctly predicts whether the coin will land face up or face down. After observing the way the coin lands a number of times, a pattern emerges: approximately half of the tosses land face up, half face down. In future coin tosses, whenever a pattern inconsistent with this 50-50 split emerges, we wonder if the coin is "fair."

Six Sigma practitioners use probability to understand the chance that a tool will break, that a line will clog, that a person will be late for an appointment, or that a service will not be performed on time.

PROBABILITY THEOREMS

The probability of an occurrence is written as $P(A)$ *and is equal to*

$$P(A) = \frac{\text{number of occurrences}}{\text{total number of possibilities}} = \frac{s}{n}$$

 SIX SIGMA TOOLS AT WORK

Determining Probabilities

During a production run, two test parts are mixed in with a box of 25 good parts. During an inspection, the probability of randomly selecting one of the test parts is

$$P(\text{selecting a test part}) = \frac{2}{27}$$

A 104-key computer keyboard has been disassembled and the keys have been placed in a paper sack. If all of the keys, including the function keys, number keys, and command keys, are in the bag, what is the probability that one of the 12 function keys will be drawn randomly from the bag?

$$P(\text{selecting one of the 12 function keys}) = \frac{12}{104}$$

Theorem 1: Probability Is Expressed as a Number Between 0 and 1:

$$0 \le P(A) \le 1$$

If an event has a probability value of 1, then it is a certainty that it will happen; in other words, there is a 100 percent chance the event will occur. At the other end of the spectrum, if an event will not occur, then it will have a probability value of 0. In between the certainty that an event will definitely occur or not occur, probabilities exist defined by the ratio of desired occurrences to the total number of occurrences.

Theorem 2: The Sum of the Probabilities of the Events in a Situation Is Equal to 1.00:

$$\sum P_i = P(A) + P(B) + \cdots + P(N) = 1.00$$

 SIX SIGMA TOOLS AT WORK

The Sum of the Probabilities

A manufacturer of piston rings receives raw materials from three different suppliers. In the stockroom there are currently 20 steel rolls from supplier A, 30 rolls of steel from supplier B, and another 50 rolls from supplier C. From these 100 rolls of steel in the stockroom, a machinist will encounter the following probabilities in selecting steel for the next job:

$$P(\text{steel from supplier A}) = 20/100 = 0.20 \text{ or } 20\%$$
$$P(\text{steel from supplier B}) = 30/100 = 0.30 \text{ or } 30\%$$
$$P(\text{steel from supplier C}) = 50/100 = 0.50 \text{ or } 50\%$$

And from Theorem 2:

$$P(\text{steel from A}) + P(\text{steel from B}) + P(\text{steel from C}) = 0.20 + 0.30 + 0.50$$
$$= 1.00$$

Theorem 3: If P(A) Is the Probability That Event A Will Occur, Then the Probability That A Will Not Occur Is

$$P(A') = 1.00 - P(A)$$

 SIX SIGMA TOOLS AT WORK

Determining the Probability that an Event Will Not Occur

Currently, the stockroom contains steel rolls from only suppliers A and B. There are 20 rolls from supplier A and 30 rolls from supplier B. If the roll selected was from supplier A, what is the probability that a roll from supplier B was not selected?

$$P(A') = 1.00 - P(A)$$

where

$$P(A) = P(\text{selecting a roll from supplier A}) = \frac{20}{50} = 0.40$$

Then

$$P(A') = P(\text{selecting a roll from supplier B}) = 1.00 - 0.40 = 0.60$$

Events are considered **mutually exclusive** if they cannot occur simultaneously. Mutually exclusive events can happen only one at a time. When one event occurs it prevents the other from happening. Rolling a die and getting a 6 is an event mutually exclusive of getting any other value on that roll of the die.

Theorem 4: For Mutually Exclusive Events, the Probability That Either Event A or Event B Will Occur Is the Sum of Their Respective Probabilities:

$$P(A \text{ or } B) = P(A) + P(B)$$

Theorem 4 is called "the additive law of probability." Notice that the "or" in the probability statement is represented by a "+" sign.

 SIX SIGMA TOOLS AT WORK

Probability in Mutually Exclusive Events II

At the piston ring factory, a machine operator visits the raw materials holding area. If 20 percent of the steel comes from supplier A, 30 percent from supplier B, and 50 percent from supplier C, what is the probability that the machinist will randomly select steel from either supplier A or supplier C?

$$P(\text{steel from supplier A}) = 0.20$$
$$P(\text{steel from supplier B}) = 0.30$$
$$P(\text{steel from supplier C}) = 0.50$$

Since the choice of steel from supplier A precludes choosing either supplier B or C, and vice versa, these events are mutually exclusive. Applying Theorem 4, we have

$$P(\text{steel from A or steel from C}) = P(A) + P(C)$$
$$= 0.20 + 0.50$$
$$= 0.70$$

Events are considered **nonmutually exclusive events** when they may occur simultaneously. If both can happen, then Theorem 4 must be modified to take into account the overlapping area where both events can occur simultaneously. For instance, in a deck of cards the King, Queen, and Jack of diamonds are both diamonds and red face cards (Figure 12.1).

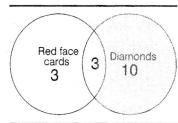

Figure 12.1   Venn Diagram

Theorem 5: When Events A and B Are Not Mutually Exclusive Events, the Probability That Either Event A or Event B or Both Will Occur Is

$$P(A \ or \ B \ or \ both) = P(A) + P(B) - P(both)$$

σ SIX SIGMA TOOLS AT WORK

Probability in Nonmutually Exclusive Events

The manager of a local job shop is trying to determine what routings parts make the most often through the plant. Knowing this information will help the manager plan machine usage. The manager has uncovered the following information:

$$P(\text{part requires plating}) = 0.12$$
$$P(\text{part requires heat-treating}) = 0.29$$

Parts that need plating may also need heat-treating. Therefore these events are not mutually exclusive, and

$$P(\text{part requires both plating and heat-treating}) = 0.07$$

The manager would like to know the probability that the part will require either plating or heat-treating. Applying Theorem 5:

P(part requires plating or heat-treating)

= P(part requires plating) + P(part requires heat-treating)

− P(part requires both plating and heat-treating)

= 0.29 + 0.12 − 0.07

= 0.34

It is not unusual for one outcome or event to affect the outcome of another event. *When the occurrence of one event alters the probabilities associated with another event, these events are considered* **dependent.**

Theorem 6: If A and B Are Dependent Events, the Probability That Both A and B Will Occur Is

$$P(A \ and \ B) = P(A) \times P(B|A)$$

In this theorem, the occurrence of B is dependent on the outcome of A. This relationship between A and B is represented by $P(A|B)$. The vertical bar ($|$) is translated as "given that." The probability that both A and B will occur is the probability that A will occur multiplied by the probability that B will occur, given that A has already occurred.

When events are **independent,** *one event does not influence the occurrence of another.* The result of one outcome or event is unaffected by the outcome of another event. Mathematically, events are considered independent if the following are true:

$$P(A|B) = P(A) \quad \text{and} \quad P(B|A) = P(B) \quad \text{and} \quad P(A \text{ and } B) = P(A) \times P(B)$$

Theorem 7: If A and B Are Independent Events, Then the Probability That Both A and B Will Occur Is

$$P(A \text{ and } B) = P(A) \times P(B)$$

This is often referred to as a joint probability, meaning that both A and B can occur at the same time.

 SIX SIGMA TOOLS AT WORK

Probability in Independent Events

A local mail order catalog business employs 200 people in the packaging and shipping departments. The personnel department maintains the records shown in Table 12.1. Questions have arisen concerning whether there has been a tendency to place female workers in the packaging department instead of in the shipping department. Management feels that there is no relationship between being female and working in the packaging department. In other words, they feel that these two events are independent. A quick probability calculation can enable the firm to determine whether this is true.

If an employee is selected at random from the 200 total employees, what is the probability that the employee works for the packaging department?

$$P(\text{Packaging}) = 80/200 = 0.4$$

If the employee selected is female, what is the probability that the employee works in the packaging department?

$$P(\text{packaging}|\text{female}) = \frac{P(\text{female and packaging})}{P(\text{female})} = \frac{32/200}{80/200} = 0.4$$

Independence can be established if the following are true:

$$P(\text{packaging}|\text{female}) = P(\text{packaging})$$
$$0.4 = 0.4$$

	Department		
Sex	**Packaging**	**Shipping**	**Total**
Female	32	48	80
Male	48	72	120
Total	80	120	200

Table 12.1   Employee Records

and
$$P(\text{female}|\text{packaging}) = P(\text{female})$$
$$\frac{32/200}{80/200} = 0.4$$
and from Table 12.1, it can be seen that
$$P(\text{female and packaging}) = P(\text{female}) \times P(\text{packaging})$$
$$32/200 = 80/200 \times 80/200$$
$$0.16 = 0.16$$
Since the three probability comparisons are equal, they are independent.

PERMUTATIONS AND COMBINATIONS

As the number of ways that a particular outcome may occur increases, so does the complexity of determining all possible outcomes. For instance, if a part must go through four different machining operations and for each operation there are several machines available, then the scheduler will have a number of choices about how the part can be scheduled through the process. Permutations and combinations are used to increase the efficiency of calculating the number of different outcomes possible.

A *permutation is the number of arrangements that* n *objects can have when* r *of them are used:*

$$P_r^n = \frac{n!}{(n - r)!}$$

The order of the arrangement of a set of objects is important when calculating a permutation.

 SIX SIGMA TOOLS AT WORK

Calculating a Permutation

At a local manufacturing facility, a scheduler is facing a dilemma. A part must go through the following three different machining operations in order, and for each of these operations there are several machines available. The scheduler's boss has asked him to list all the different ways that the part can be scheduled. The scheduler is reluctant to begin the list because there are so many different permutations. Using the following information, he calculates the number of permutations possible:

Grinding (4 machines): The part must go to two different grinding machines, each set up with different tools.

Heat-treating (3 units): Heat-treating the part takes only one heat treatment unit.

Milling (5 machines): The part must go through three different milling machines, each set up with different tools.

The scheduler knows that order is important, and so the number of permutations for each work center must be calculated. These values will then be multiplied together to determine the total number of schedules possible.
Grinding (four machines selected two at a time):

$$P_r^n = \frac{n!}{(n-r)!} = \frac{4!}{(4-2)!} = 12$$

This can also be found by writing down all the different ways that the two machines can be selected. Remember, order is important:

$$12 \; 13 \; 14 \; 23 \; 24 \; 21 \; 34 \; 32 \; 31 \; 43 \; 42 \; 41$$

Heat-treating (three machines selected one at a time):

$$P_r^n = \frac{n!}{(n-r)!} = \frac{3!}{(3-1)!} = 3$$

Milling (five machines selected three at a time):

$$P_r^n = \frac{n!}{(n-r)!} = \frac{5!}{(5-3)!} = 60$$

Since there are 12 different permutations to schedule the grinding machines, 3 for the heat treatment units, and 20 for the milling machines, the total number of permutations that the scheduler will have to list is $12 \times 3 \times 60 = 2160$!

*When the order in which the items are used is not important, the number of possibilities can be calculated by using the formula for a **combination.** The calculation for a combination uses only the number of elements, with no regard to any arrangement:*

$$C_r^n = \frac{n!}{r!(n-r)!}$$

 SIX SIGMA TOOL AT WORK

Calculating a Combination

A Six Sigma team is being created to deal with a situation at a local chemical company. Two different departments are involved, chemical process engineering and the laboratory. There are seven members of the chemical process engineering group and three of them must be on the committee. The number of different combinations of members from the chemical process engineering group is

$$C_r^n = \frac{n!}{r!(n-r)!} = \frac{7!}{3!(7-3)!} = 35$$

There are five members of the laboratory group and two of them must be on the committee. The number of different combinations of members from the laboratory group is

$$C_r^n = \frac{n!}{r!(n-r)!} = \frac{5!}{2!(5-2)!} = 10$$

For the total number of different arrangements on the committee, multiply the number of combinations from the chemical process engineering group by the number of combinations from the laboratory group:

$$\text{Total} = C_3^7 \times C_2^5 = 35 \times 10 = 350$$

DISCRETE PROBABILITY DISTRIBUTIONS

For a probability distribution to exist, a process must be defined by a random variable for which all the possible outcomes and their probabilities have been enumerated. Discrete probability distributions count attribute data, the occurrence of nonconforming activities or items, or nonconformities on an item.

Hypergeometric Probability Distribution

When a random sample is taken from a small lot size, the hypergeometric probability distribution will determine the probability that a particular event will occur. The hypergeometric is most effective when the sample size is greater than 10 percent of the size of the population ($n/N > 0.1$) and the total number of nonconforming items is known. To use the hypergeometric probability distribution, the population must be finite and samples must be taken randomly, without replacement. The following formula is used to calculate the probability an event will occur:

$$P(d) = \frac{C_d^D C_{n-d}^{N-D}}{C_n^N}$$

$$P(d) = \frac{\dfrac{D!}{d!(D-d)!}\left[\dfrac{(N-D)!}{(n-d)![(N-D)-(n-d)]!}\right]}{\dfrac{N!}{n!(N-n)!}}$$

where

$$
\begin{aligned}
D &= \text{number of nonconforming or defective units in lot} \\
d &= \text{number of nonconforming or defective units in sample} \\
N &= \text{lot size} \\
n &= \text{sample size} \\
N - D &= \text{number of conforming units in lot} \\
n - d &= \text{number of conforming units in sample}
\end{aligned}
$$

The hypergeometric distribution is an exact distribution; the P(d) translates to the probability of exactly d nonconformities. In the numerator, the first combination is the combination of all nonconforming items in the population and in the sample. The second combination is for all of the conforming items in the population and the sample. The denominator is the combination of the total population and the total number sampled.

 SIX SIGMA TOOLS AT WORK

Using the Hypergeometric Probability Distribution

To help train their agents in forgery detection, officials have hidden four counterfeit stock certificates with 11 authentic certificates. What is the probability that the trainees will select one counterfeit certificate in a random sample (without replacement) of three?

$$D = \text{number of counterfeits in lot} = 4$$
$$d = \text{seeking the probability that one counterfeit will be found} = 1$$
$$N = \text{lot size} = 15$$
$$n = \text{sample size} = 3$$
$$N - D = \text{number of authentic certificates in lot} = 11$$
$$n - d = \text{number of authentic certificates in sample} = 2$$

$$P(1) = \frac{C_1^4 C_2^{11}}{C_3^{15}}$$

$$= \frac{\left[\dfrac{4!}{1!(4-1)!}\right]\left[\dfrac{11!}{2!(11-2)!}\right]}{\dfrac{15!}{3!(15-3)!}} = 0.48$$

If the officials were interested in determining the probability of selecting two or fewer of the counterfeit certificates, the result would be

$$P(2 \text{ or fewer}) = P(0) + P(1) + P(2)$$

$$P(0) = \frac{C_0^4 C_{3-0}^{15-4}}{C_3^{15}}$$

$$= \frac{\left[\dfrac{4!}{0!(4-0)!}\right]\left[\dfrac{11!}{3!(11-3)!}\right]}{\dfrac{15!}{3!(15-3)!}} = 0.36$$

$$P(1) = 0.48$$

$$P(2) = \frac{C_2^4 C_{3-2}^{15-4}}{C_3^{15}}$$

$$= \frac{\left[\dfrac{4!}{2!(4-2)!}\right]\left[\dfrac{11!}{1!(11-1)!}\right]}{\dfrac{15!}{3!(15-3)!}} = 0.15$$

The probability of selecting two or fewer counterfeit certificates is

$$P(2 \text{ or fewer}) = P(0) + P(1) + P(2) = 0.48 + 0.36 + 0.15 = 0.99$$

The above probability can also be found by using Theorem 2 and calculating

$$P(2 \text{ or fewer}) = 1 - P(3)$$

What is the probability of selecting all four counterfeits? This can't be calculated because the sample size is only three.

Binomial Probability Distribution

The *binomial probability distribution* was developed by Sir Issac Newton *to categorize the results of a number of repeated trials and the outcomes of those trials.* The "bi" in binomial refers to two conditions: The outcome is either a success or a failure. In terms of a product being produced, the outcome is either conforming or nonconforming. The distribution was developed to reduce the number of calculations associated with a large number of trials containing only two possible outcomes: success (s) or failure (f). Table 12.2 shows how complicated the calculations become as the number of trials held increases.

The binomial probability distribution can be used if two conditions are met:

1. There is a nearly infinite number of items or a steady stream of items being produced.

Number of Trials	Possible Outcomes*
1	s f
2	ss ff sf fs
3	sss fff ssf sff sfs
	fss ffs fsf
4	ssss ffff sfff ssff sffs sssf
	fsss ffss fffs fssf sfsf
	fsfs ssfs sfss ffsf fsff
5	sssss fffff sffff sfffs sffss
	sfsss fssss fsssf fssff fsfff
	sfsfs fsfsf ssfff ssffs ssfss
	ffsss ffssf ffsff ssssf sssff
	fffss ffffs sfsff fsfss sffsf
	fssfs sfssf fsffs ssfsf ffsfs
	fffsf sssfs

Table 12.2 Binomial Distribution: Outcomes Associated with Repeated Trials

*Success = s; failure = f.

2. The outcome is seen as either a success or a failure. Or in terms of a product, it is either conforming or nonconforming. The binomial formula for calculating the probability an event will occur is

$$P(d) = \frac{n!}{d!(n-d)!}p^d q^{n-d}$$

where

d = number of nonconforming units, defectives, or failures sought
n = sample size
p = proportion of nonconforming units, defectives, or failures in population
q = (1 − p) = proportion of good or conforming units or successes in population

This distribution is an exact distribution, meaning that the P(d) translates to the probability of exactly d nonconforming units or failures occurring. The mean of the binomial distribution is μ = np. The standard deviation of the binomial distribution is $\sigma = \sqrt{np(1-p)}$. The binomial distribution tables are found in Appendix 3.

 SIX SIGMA TOOLS AT WORK

Using the Binomial Probability Distribution

The billing department of a local department store sends monthly statements to the store's customers. In order for those statements to reach the customer in a timely fashion, the addresses on the envelopes must be correct. Occasionally errors are made with the addresses. The billing department estimates that errors are made two percent of the time. For this continuous process, in which an error in the address is considered a nonconforming unit, what is the probability that in a sample of size eight, one address will be incorrect?

$$P(d) = \frac{n!}{d!(n-d)!}p^d q^{n-d}$$

where

d = number of nonconforming units sought = 1
n = sample size = 8
p = proportion of population nonconforming = 0.02
q = (1 − p) = proportion of conforming units = 1 − 0.02

$$P(1) = \frac{8!}{1!(8-1)!}0.02^1 \times 0.98^{8-1} = 0.14$$

Cumulative binomial distribution tables are included in Appendix 3. To utilize the appendix, match the sample size (n) with the number of nonconforming/defective units sought (d) and the proportion of nonconforming units/defectives in the population (p). Since this table is cumulative and we are seeking the probability of exactly 1 (P(1)), we must subtract the probability of exactly 0 (P(0)). For this example,

From Appendix 3:

$$P(1) = \text{Cum } P(1) - \text{Cum } P(0)$$
$$= 0.9897 - 0.8508$$
$$= 0.1389 \qquad \text{or } 0.14 \text{ when rounded}$$

d = 1

↓   (n = 8)

p = 0.02	p	0.01	0.02	0.03	0.04	0.05	0.06	0.07
	d							
	0	0.9227	0.8508	0.7837	0.7214	0.6634	0.6096	0.5596
n = 8	→1	0.9973	0.9897	0.9777	0.9619	0.9428	0.9208	0.8965
	2	0.9999	0.9996	0.9987	0.9969	0.9942	0.9904	0.9853

Poisson Probability Distribution

First described by Simeon Poisson in 1837, the **Poisson probability distribution** *quantifies the count of discrete events*. To use the Poisson distribution successfully, it is important to identify a well-defined, finite region known as the *area of opportunity* in which the discrete, independent events may take place. This finite region, or area of opportunity, may be defined as a particular space, time, or product. The Poisson distribution is often used when calculating the probability that an event will occur when there is a large area of opportunity, such as in the case of rivets on an airplane wing. The Poisson distribution is also used when studying arrival-rate probabilities. The formula for the Poisson distribution is

$$P(c) = \frac{(np)^c}{c!} e^{-np}$$

where

np = average count or number of events in sample
c = count or number of events in sample
$e \approx 2.718281$

These calculations can be further simplified by using a Poisson table (Appendix 4). To establish the probability of finding an expected number of nonconformities (c) by using the table, np and c must be known. The Poisson probability distribution is also an exact distribution. $P(c)$ is the probability of exactly c nonconformities. The mean of the Poisson distribution is $\mu = np$. The standard deviation of the Poisson distribution is $\sigma = \sqrt{np}$.

 SIX SIGMA TOOLS AT WORK

Using the Poisson Distribution

The local branch office of a bank is interested in improving staff scheduling during peak hours. For this reason the manager would like to determine the probability that three or more customers will arrive at the bank in any given minute. The average number of customers arriving at the bank in any given minute is two.

P(3 or more customers arriving in any given minute)

$$= P(3) + P(4) + P(5) + P(6) + \cdots$$

Since it is impossible to solve the problem in this fashion, Theorems 2 and 3 must be applied:

P(3 or more customers arriving in any given minute)

$$= 1 - P(2 \text{ or fewer}) - 1 - [P(2) + P(1) + P(0)]$$

By calculation:

$$1 - \left[\frac{(2)^2}{2!} e^{-2} + \frac{(2)^1}{1!} e^{-2} + \frac{(2)^0}{0!} e^{-2} \right]$$

$$1 - [0.271 + 0.271 + 0.135] = 0.323$$

From the table in Appendix 4, np = 2, c = (2 or less). Using the column for cumulative values,

$$1 - 0.677 = 0.323$$

where

np = average number of customers in sample = 2
c = number of customers in sample = 0, 1, 2
e ≈ 2.718281

CONTINUOUS PROBABILITY DISTRIBUTION

Normal Distribution

In situations where the data can take on a continuous range of values, a discrete distribution, such as the binomial, cannot be used to calculate the probability that an event will occur. For these situations, the normal distribution, a continuous probability distribution, should be used. Covered in Chapter 9, this distribution is solved by finding the value of Z and using the Z tables in Appendix 1 to determine the probability an event will occur:

$$Z = \frac{X_i - \overline{X}}{s}$$

where

Z = standard normal value
X_i = value of interest
$\overline{X}$ = average
s = standard deviation

The values in the Z table can be interpreted either as frequencies or as probability values. The mean of the normal is np. The standard deviation of the normal is $\sqrt{npq}$.

SIX SIGMA TOOLS AT WORK

Using the Normal Distribution

A tool on a stamping press is expected to complete a large number of strokes before it is removed and reworked. As a tool wears, the dimensions of the stamped part change. Eventually, the parts are unable to meet specifications. As a tool wears, it is removed from the press and resharpened. For this particular example, a combination of $\overline{X}$ and R charts is being used to monitor part dimensions. The $\overline{X}$ chart tracks the dimension of the part. After it reaches a certain point, the tool is pulled and reground. Those tracking the process have determined that the average number of strokes or parts the tool can complete is 60,000, with a standard deviation of 3,000. Determine the percentage of tools that will require regrinding before 55,000 strokes.

Figure 12.2 shows the normal probability distribution associated with this example. The area in question is shaded.

$$Z = \frac{55,000 - 60,000}{3,000} = -1.67$$

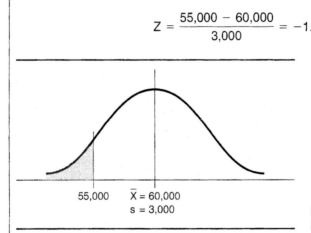

55,000 $\overline{X} = 60,000$
          $s = 3,000$

Figure 12.2   Normal Probability Distribution

From the table in Appendix 1, the area to the left of 55,000 is equal to 0.0475. Only 4.75 percent of the tools will last for fewer than 55,000 strokes.

SUMMARY

Probability, its theorems and distributions, plays an important role in understanding situations. Probability concepts also support the creation of control charts for attributes, which will be covered in the next chapter. The binomial distribution serves as the foundation for control charts for nonconforming units or activities. Control charts for nonconformities have the Poisson distribution as their basis.

σ ■ Take Away Tips

1. Seven theorems exist to explain probability.
2. Discrete and continuous probability distributions exist to describe the probability that an event will occur.
3. The hypergeometric, binomial, and Poisson distributions are all discrete probability distributions.
4. The normal distribution is a continuous probability distribution.
5. The binomial and Poisson distributions can be used to approximate the hypergeometric distribution.
6. The Poisson and normal distributions can be used to approximate the binomial distribution. ■

σ ■ Formulas

$$P(A) = \frac{\text{number of occurences}}{\text{total number of possibilities}} = \frac{s}{n}$$

Theorem 1: Probability Is Expressed as a Number Between 0 and 1:

$$0 \le P(A) \le 1$$

Theorem 2: The Sum of the Probabilities of the Events in a Situation Is Equal to 1.00:

$$\Sigma P_i = P(A) + P(B) + \cdots + P(N) = 1.00$$

Theorem 3: If $P(A)$ Is the Probability That Event A Will Occur, Then the Probability That A Will Not Occur Is

$$P(A') = 1.00 - P(A)$$

Theorem 4: For Mutually Exclusive Events, the Probability That Either Event A or Event B Will Occur Is the Sum of Their Respective Probabilities:

$$P(A \text{ or } B) = P(A) + P(B)$$

Theorem 5: When Events A and B Are Not Mutually Exclusive Events, the Probability That Either Event A or Event B or Both Will Occur Is

$$P(A \text{ or } B \text{ or both}) = P(A) + P(B) - P(\text{both})$$

Theorem 6: If A and B Are Dependent Events, the Probability That Both A and B Will Occur Is

$$P(A \text{ and } B) = P(A) - P(B|A)$$

Theorem 7: If A and B Are Independent Events, Then the Probability That Both A and B Will Occur Is

$$P(A \text{ and } B) = P(A) \times P(B)$$

Permutations

$$P_r^n = \frac{n!}{(n-r)!}$$

Combinations

$$C_r^n = \frac{n!}{r!(n-r)!}$$

Hypergeometric Probability Distribution

$$P(d) = \frac{C_d^D C_{n-d}^{N-D}}{C_n^N}$$

where

D = number of nonconforming or defective units in lot
d = number of nonconforming or defective units in sample
N = lot size
n = sample size
$N - D$ = number of conforming units in lot
$n - d$ = number of conforming units in sample

Binomial Probability Distribution

$$P(d) = \frac{n!}{d!(n-d)!} p^d q^{n-d}$$

where

d = number of nonconforming units, defectives, or failures sought
n = sample size
p = proportion of nonconforming units, defectives, or failures in population
$q = (1 - p)$ = proportion of good or conforming units, or successes, in population

Poisson Probability Distribution

$$P(c) = \frac{(np)^c}{c!} e^{-np}$$

where

np = average count or number of events in sample
c = count or number of events in sample
$e \approx 2.718281$

Normal Distribution

$$Z = \frac{X_i - \overline{X}}{s}$$

using the Z table in Appendix 1.

Approximations

Hypergeometric distribution can be approximated by the binomial when n/N ≤ 0.10.

Hypergeometric distribution can be approximated by the Poisson when n/N ≤ 0.10, p ≤ 0.10, and np ≤ 5.

Binomial distribution can be approximated by the Poisson when the population of the lot is assumed to be infinite, p ≤ 0.10, and np ≤ 5.

Binomial distribution can be approximated by the normal when p nears 0.5 and n ≥ 10.

Chapter Questions

1. The probability of drawing a pink chip from a bowl of different-colored chips is 0.35, the probability of drawing a blue chip is 0.46, the probability of drawing a green chip is 0.15, and the probability of drawing a purple chip is 0.04. What is the probability that a blue or a purple chip will be drawn?

2. At the county fair, the duck pond contains eight yellow ducks numbered 1 to 8, six orange ducks numbered 1 to 6, and ten gray ducks numbered 1 to 10. What is the probability of obtaining an orange duck numbered with a 5? Of obtaining an orange duck? Of obtaining a duck labeled with a 5?

3. If there are five different parts to be stocked but only three bins available, what is the number of permutations possible for five parts taken three at a time?

4. If a manufacturer is trying to put together a sample collection of her product and order is not important, how many combinations can be created with 15 items that will be placed in packages containing five items? If order is important, how many permutations can be created?

5. An assembly plant receives its voltage regulators from two different suppliers: 75 percent come from Hayes Voltage Co. and 25 percent come from Romig Voltage Co. The percentage of voltage regulators from Hayes that perform according to specification is 95 percent. The voltage regulators from Romig perform according to specification only 80 percent of the time. What is the probability that any one voltage regulator received by the plant performs according to spec?

6. Suppose a firm makes couches in four different styles and three different fabrics. Use the table to calculate the probability that a couch picked at random will be made from fabric 1. If the couch is style 1, what is the probability that it will be made from fabric 2? What is the probability that a couch of style 4 will be selected at random? If a couch is made from fabric 3, what is the probability that it is a style 3 couch?

			Fabric	
Style	*F1*	*F2*	*F3*	*Total*
S1	150	55	100	305
S2	120	25	70	215
S3	80	60	85	225
S4	110	35	110	255
Total	460	175	365	1000

7. The owner of a local office supply store has just received a shipment of copy machine paper. As the 15 cases are being unloaded off the truck, the owner is informed that one of the cases contains blue paper instead of white. Before the owner can isolate the case, it is mixed in with the other cases. There is no way to distinguish from the outside of the case which case contains blue paper. Since the cases sell for a different price than individual packages of paper, if the owner opens the case, it cannot be replaced (sold as a case). What is the probability that the manager will find the case that contains blue paper in one of the first three randomly chosen cases?

8. A robot is used to prepare cases of peanut butter for shipment. As the 12 cases are being loaded, two of the cases are dropped. Before the operator can isolate the cases, they are mixed in with the other cases. (This is the end of the production run, so there are no replacement cases.) What is the probability that the operator will find the two broken cases in the first four randomly chosen cases?

9. A lot of ten bottles of medicine has four nonconforming units. What is the probability of drawing two nonconforming units in a random sample of five? What is the probability that one or fewer nonconforming units will be chosen in a sample of five?

10. A steady stream of bolts is sampled at a rate of 6 per hour. The fraction nonconforming in the lot is 0.034. What is the probability that 1 or fewer of the 6 parts will be found nonconforming?

11. An environmental engineer places monitors in a large number of streams to measure the amount of pollutants in the water. If the amount of pollutants exceeds a certain level, the water is considered nonconforming. In the past, the proportion nonconforming has been 0.04. What is the probability that one of the fifteen samples taken per day will contain an excessive amount of pollutants?

12. A steady stream of newspapers is sampled at a rate of 6 per hour. The inspector checks the newspaper for printing legibility. If the first page of the paper is not clearly printed, the paper is recycled. Currently, the fraction nonconforming in the lot is 0.030. What is the probability that 2 of the 6 papers checked will be nonconforming?

13. A receptionist receives an average of 0.9 calls per minute. Find the probability that in any given minute there will be at least one incoming call.

14. If on the average 0.3 customers arrive per minute at a cafeteria, what is the probability that exactly three customers will arrive during a five minute span?

15. A computer software company's emergency call service receives an average of 0.90 calls per minute. Find the probability that in any given minute there will be more than one incoming call.

16. The mean weight of a company's racing bicycles is 9.07 kg, with a standard deviation of 0.40 kg. If the distribution is approximately normal, determine (a) the percentage of bicycles weighing less than 8.30 kg and (b) the percentage of bicycles weighing between 8.00 and 10.10 kg.

17. Multicar accidents often result in fatalities. Across the nation, records are kept of the total number of accidents involving 10 or more vehicles. Over the past 25 years, the average number of accidents involving 10 or more cars is 7 per year. The standard deviation is 4. Assume that the distribution is approximately normal and determine (a) the percentage of years accumulating fewer than 4 multicar accidents and (b) the percentage of years having more than 12 multicar accidents.

13

Attribute Control Charts

Quality is the most important factor in business.

Andrew Carnegie

Objectives:

1. To learn how to construct fraction defective (p) charts for both constant and variable sample sizes
2. To learn how to construct number defective (np) charts
3. To learn how to construct percent defective charts
4. To learn how to construct charts for counts of defects (c charts)
5. To learn how to construct charts for defects per unit (u charts) for both constant and variable sample sizes
6. To understand how to interpret p, np, c, and u charts ■

ATTRIBUTES

Attributes are characteristics associated with a product or service. These characteristics either do or do not exist, and they can be counted. Examples of attributes include the number of leaking containers, of scratches on a surface, of on-time deliveries, or of errors on an invoice. Attribute charts are used to study the stability of processes over time. The most difficult part about collecting attribute data lies in the need to develop precise operational definitions of what is conforming and what is not. There are some disadvantages to using attribute charts. The charts do not provide information to answer questions like: Do several defects exist on the same product? Is the product still usable? Can it be reworked? What is the severity or degree of nonconformance?

CHARTS FOR DEFECTIVE UNITS

Fraction Defective (p) Charts: Constant Sample Size

When the interest is in studying the proportion of products rendered unusable by their defects, a fraction defective (p) chart, a number defective (np) chart, or a percent defective chart should be used. The **fraction defective chart** is based on the binomial distribution and is used to study the proportion of defective products or services being provided. This chart is also known as a fraction nonconforming chart or p chart. A defective product or service is considered unacceptable because of some deviation from an expected level of performance. The product or service can be judged to be either good or bad, correct or incorrect, working or not working. For example, a container is either leaking or it is not, an engine starts or it does not, and an order delivered to a restaurant patron is either correct or incorrect.

Because of the structure of their formulas, p charts can be constructed using either a constant or variable sample size. A p chart for constant sample size is constructed using the following steps:

1. *Gather the data.* In constructing any attribute chart, careful consideration must be given to the process and what characteristics should be studied. The choice of the attributes to monitor should center on the customer's needs and expectations as well as on current and potential problem areas. When gathering the data concerning the attributes under study, identify defective units by comparing the inspected product with the specifications. The number defective (np) is tracked. In some cases, go/no-go gauges are used; in others, pictures of typical conforming and defective products are helpful. In the service industry, details of incorrect bills, faulty customer service, or other performance criteria should be clearly established.

The sample sizes for attribute charts tend to be quite large (for example, n = 250). Large sample sizes are required to maintain sensitivity to detect process performance changes. The sample size should be large enough to include defective items in each subgroup. When process quality is very good, large sample sizes are needed to capture information about the process. When selected, samples must be random and representative of the process.

2. *Calculate p, the fraction defective.* The fraction defective (p) is plotted on a fraction defective chart. As the products or services are inspected, each subgroup will yield a number defective (np). The fraction defective (p), plotted on the p chart, is calculated using n, the number of inspected items, and np, the number of defective items found:

$$p = \frac{np}{n}$$

3. *Plot the fraction defective (p) on the control chart.* Once calculated, the values of p for each subgroup are plotted on the chart. The scale for the p chart should reflect the magnitude of the data.

4. *Calculate the centerline and control limits.* The centerline of the control chart is the average of the subgroup fraction defective. The number defective values are added up and then divided by the total number of samples:

$$\text{Centerline } \bar{p} = \frac{\sum\limits_{i=1}^{n} np}{\sum\limits_{i=1}^{n} n}$$

The control limits for a p chart are found using the following formulas:

$$UCL_p = \bar{p} + 3\frac{\sqrt{\bar{p}(1 - \bar{p})}}{\sqrt{n}}$$

$$LCL_p = \bar{p} - 3\frac{\sqrt{\bar{p}(1 - \bar{p})}}{\sqrt{n}}$$

On occasion, the lower control limit of a p chart may have a negative value. When this occurs, the result of the LCL_p calculation should be rounded up to zero.

5. *Draw the centerline and control limits on the chart.* Using a solid line to denote the centerline and dashed lines for the control limits, draw the centerline and control limits on the chart.

6. *Interpret the chart.* The interpretation of a fraction defective chart is similar in many aspects to the interpretation of a variables control chart. Emphasis is placed on determining if the process is operating within its control limits and exhibiting random variation. The data points on a p chart should flow smoothly back and forth across the centerline. The number of points on each side of the centerline should be balanced, with the majority of the points near the centerline. There should be no patterns in the data, such as trends, runs, cycles, or sudden shifts in level. All of the points should fall between the upper and lower control limits. Points beyond the control limits are immediately obvious and indicate an instability in the process. One difference between the interpretation of a variables

control chart and a p chart is the desirability in the p chart of having points that approach the lower control limits. This makes sense because quality improvement efforts reflected on a fraction defective chart should show that the fraction defective is being reduced, the ultimate goal of improving a process. This favorable occurrence should be investigated to determine what was done right and whether or not there are changes or improvements that should be incorporated into the process on a permanent basis.

The process capability is the $\bar{p}$, the centerline of the control chart.

 SIX SIGMA TOOLS AT WORK

Making a p Chart

Special Plastics, Inc., has been making the blanks for credit cards for a number of years. They use p charts to keep track of the number of defective cards that are created each time a batch of blank cards is run. Use the data in Table 13.1 to create a fraction defective (p) chart.

Step 1 Gather the Data. The characteristics that have been designated for study include blemishes on the card's front and back surfaces, color inconsistencies, white spots or bumps caused by dirt, scratches, chips, indentations, or other flaws. Several photographs are maintained at each operator's workstation to provide a clear understanding of what constitutes a defective product.

Batches of 15,000 blank cards are run each day. Samples of size 500 are randomly selected and inspected. The number of defective units (np) is recorded on data sheets (Table 13.1).

Step 2 Calculate p, the Fraction Defective. After each sample is taken and the inspections are complete, the fraction defective (p) is calculated using n = 500, and np, the number of defective items. (Here we work p to three decimal places.) For example, for the first value,

$$p = \frac{np}{n} = \frac{20}{500} = 0.040$$

The remaining calculated p values are shown in Table 13.1.

Step 3 Plot the Fraction Defective on the Control Chart. As they are calculated, the values of p for each subgroup are plotted on the chart. The p chart in Figure 13.1 has been scaled to reflect the magnitude of the data.

Step 4 Calculate the Centerline and Control Limits. The centerline of the control chart is the average of the subgroup fraction defective. The number of defective values from Table 13.1 are added up and then divided by the total number of samples:

$$\text{Centerline } \bar{p} = \frac{\sum\limits_{i=1}^{n} np}{\sum\limits_{i=1}^{n} n} = \frac{312}{20(500)} = 0.031$$

Subgroup Number	n	np	p
1	500	20	0.040
2	500	21	0.042
3	500	19	0.038
4	500	15	0.030
5	500	18	0.036
6	500	20	0.040
7	500	19	0.038
8	500	28	0.056
9	500	17	0.034
10	500	20	0.040
11	500	19	0.038
12	500	18	0.036
13	500	10	0.020
14	500	11	0.022
15	500	10	0.020
16	500	9	0.018
17	500	10	0.020
18	500	11	0.022
19	500	9	0.018
20	500	8	0.016
	10,000	312	

Table 13.1   Data Sheet: Credit Cards

The control limits for a p chart are found using the following formulas:

$$UCL_p = \bar{p} + 3\frac{\sqrt{\bar{p}(1 - \bar{p})}}{\sqrt{n}}$$

$$= 0.031 + 0.023 = 0.054$$

$$LCL_p = \bar{p} - 3\frac{\sqrt{\bar{p}(1 - \bar{p})}}{\sqrt{n}}$$

$$= 0.031 - 0.023 = 0.008$$

Step 5 Draw the Centerline and Control Limits on the Chart. The centerline and control limits are then drawn on the chart (Figure 13.1), with a solid line denoting the centerline and dashed lines the control limits.

Step 6 Interpret the Chart. The process capability for this chart is $\bar{p}$, 0.031, the centerline of the control chart. Point 8 in Figure 13.1 is above the upper control limit and should be investigated to determine if an assignable cause exists. If one is found, steps should be taken to prevent future occurrences. When the control chart is studied for any nonrandom conditions, such as runs, trends, cycles, or points out of control, connecting the data points can help reveal any patterns. Of great interest is the significant decrease in the fraction defective after point 13. This reflects the installation of a new machine.

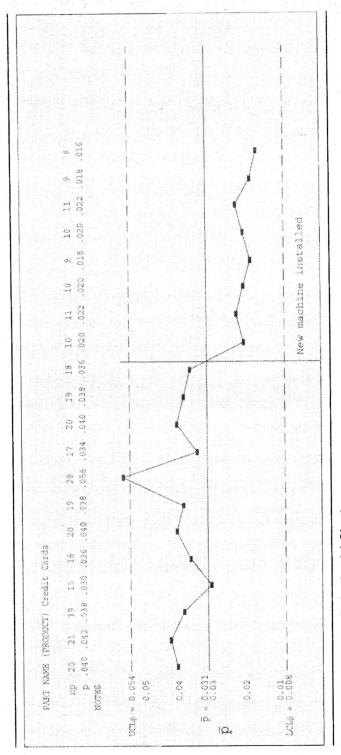

Figure 13.1 Fraction Defective (p) Chart

261

Revising the p Chart

Once an assignable cause has been isolated and the process has been modified to prevent its recurrence, then the centerline and control limits can be recalculated to reflect the changes. The points that have been isolated as due to an assignable cause will be removed from the calculations. To revise the centerline and control limits of a p chart,

$$\bar{p}_{new} = \frac{\sum_{i=1}^{n} np - np_d}{\sum_{i=1}^{n} n - n_d}$$

$$UCL_{p_{new}} = \bar{p}_{new} + 3\frac{\sqrt{\bar{p}_{new}(1 - \bar{p}_{new})}}{\sqrt{n}}$$

$$LCL_{p_{new}} = \bar{p}_{new} - 3\frac{\sqrt{\bar{p}_{new}(1 - \bar{p}_{new})}}{\sqrt{n}}$$

The process capability of the revised chart is the newly calculated $\bar{p}_{new}$.

 SIX SIGMA TOOLS AT WORK

Revising the p Chart

Special Plastics, Inc., has been involved in several quality improvement efforts that have resulted in the change in level seen in Figure 13.1. Recently a new machine has been installed and is currently being used to improve the printing and color consistency. This system safeguards against dirt in the printing ink and prevents white spots from appearing on the cards. Since the new equipment has been installed, the number of defectives cards has decreased (Figure 13.1). Those monitoring the process want to calculate a new centerline and control limits using only the data following the process changes; that is, points 1 through 12 should be removed. Revise the control limits and determine the new process capability:

$$\bar{p}_{new} = \frac{\sum_{i=1}^{n} np - np_d}{\sum_{i=1}^{n} n - n_d} = \frac{312 - 20 - 21 - 19 - 15 - \cdots - 18}{10,000 - 12(500)}$$

$$= 0.020$$

$$UCL_{p_{new}} = \bar{p}_{new} + 3\frac{\sqrt{\bar{p}_{new}(1 - \bar{p}_{new})}}{\sqrt{n}}$$

$$= 0.020 + 3\frac{\sqrt{0.020(1 - 0.020)}}{\sqrt{500}}$$

$$= 0.039$$

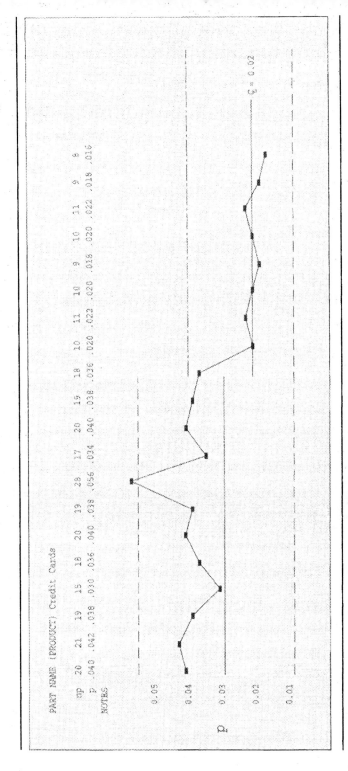

Figure 13.2 Fraction Defective (p) Chart: Revised Limits

$$LCL_{\bar{p}_{new}} = \bar{p}_{new} - 3\frac{\sqrt{\bar{p}_{new}(1-\bar{p}_{new})}}{\sqrt{n}}$$

$$= 0.020 - 3\frac{\sqrt{0.020(1-0.020)}}{\sqrt{500}}$$

$$= 0.001$$

The process capability of the revised chart is 0.020, the newly calculated $\bar{p}_{new}$. In the future, the process will be expected to conform to the new limits shown in Figure 13.2.

Percent Defective Chart

The percent defective chart is a variation on the fraction defective (p) chart. Constructing a *percent defective chart* is very similar to the construction of a fraction defective chart, but here *the p values are changed to a percentage by multiplying by a factor of 100*. The centerline for a percent defective chart is $100\bar{p}$. The control limits are

$$UCL_{100p} = 100\left[\bar{p} + \frac{3\sqrt{\bar{p}(1-\bar{p})}}{\sqrt{n}}\right]$$

$$LCL_{100p} = 100\left[\bar{p} - \frac{3\sqrt{\bar{p}(1-\bar{p})}}{\sqrt{n}}\right]$$

A percent defective chart is interpreted in the same manner as is a fraction defective chart. The process capability of a percent defective chart is the centerline. Percent defective charts are interpreted in the same manner as fraction defective charts.

SIX SIGMA TOOLS AT WORK

Making a Percent Defective Chart

Special Plastics Inc.'s Six Sigma team feels that a percent defective chart may be more understandable for their employees. Create a percent defective chart using the values given in Table 13.2. The centerline for a percent defective chart is

$$100\bar{p} = 100(0.031) = 3.1\%$$

where:

$$\bar{p} = \frac{312}{10,000}$$

The control limits for a percent defective chart are

$$UCL_{100p} = 100\left[0.031 + \frac{3\sqrt{0.031(1-0.031)}}{\sqrt{500}}\right] = 5.4\%$$

$$LCL_{100p} = 100\left[0.031 - \frac{3\sqrt{0.031(1-0.031)}}{\sqrt{500}}\right] = 0.8\%$$

Subgroup Number	n	np	p	100 p (%)
1	500	20	0.040	4.0
2	500	21	0.042	4.2
3	500	19	0.038	3.8
4	500	15	0.030	3.0
5	500	18	0.036	3.6
6	500	20	0.040	4.0
7	500	19	0.038	3.8
8	500	28	0.056	5.6
9	500	17	0.034	3.4
10	500	20	0.040	4.0
11	500	19	0.038	3.8
12	500	18	0.036	3.6
13	500	10	0.020	3.0
14	500	11	0.022	2.2
15	500	10	0.020	2.0
16	500	9	0.018	1.8
17	500	10	0.020	2.0
18	500	11	0.022	2.2
19	500	9	0.018	1.8
20	500	8	0.016	1.6
	10,000	312		

Table 13.2   Data Sheet: Special Plastics

Interpreting this chart (Figure 13.3), the process capability is 3.1 percent, the centerline of the control chart. Point 8 is above the upper control limit and should be investigated to determine if an assignable cause exists. A pattern exists on the chart: there is a significant decrease in the percent defective after point 13, reflecting the installation of a new machine.

Number Defective (np) Chart

A *number defective* (np) *chart* tracks the number of defective products or services produced by a process. A number defective chart eliminates the calculation of p, the fraction defective.

1. *Gather the data.* We must apply the same data gathering techniques we used in creating the p chart:

- Designate the specific characteristics or attributes for study
- Clearly define defective product
- Select the sample size n
- Determine the frequency of sampling
- Take random, representative samples

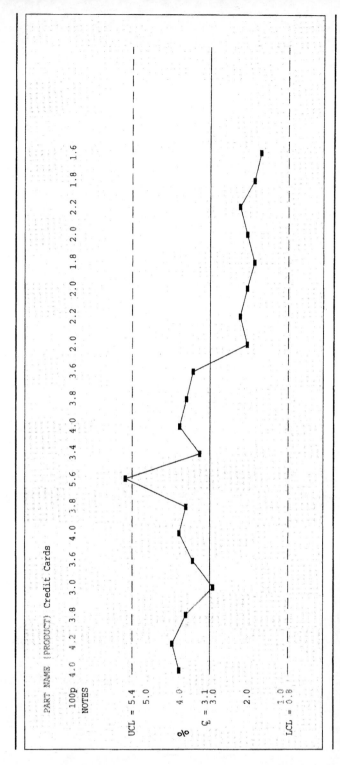

Figure 13.3 Percent Defective Chart

2. *Plot the number of defective units (np) on the control chart.* Once counted, the values of np for each subgroup are plotted on the chart. The scale for the np chart should reflect the magnitude of the data.

3. *Calculate the centerline and control limits.* The centerline of the control chart is the average of the total number defective. The number defective (np) values are added up and then divided by the total number of samples:

$$\text{Centerline } n\bar{p} = \frac{\sum_{i=1}^{n} np}{m}$$

The control limits for an np chart are found using the following formulas:

$$UCL_{np} = n\bar{p} + 3\sqrt{n\bar{p}(1 - \bar{p})}$$

$$LCL_{np} = n\bar{p} - 3\sqrt{n\bar{p}(1 - \bar{p})}$$

On occasion, the lower control limit of an np chart may have a negative value. When this occurs, the result of the LCL_{np} calculation should be rounded up to zero.

4. *Draw the centerline and control limits on the chart.* Using a solid line to denote the centerline and dashed lines for the control limits, draw the centerline and control limits on the chart.

5. *Interpret the chart.* Number defective (np) charts are interpreted in the same manner as are fraction defective charts. The process capability is $n\bar{p}$, the centerline of the control chart.

 SIX SIGMA TOOLS AT WORK

Making an np Chart

PCC Inc. receives shipments of circuit boards from its suppliers by the truckload. They keep track of the number of damaged, incomplete, or inoperative circuit boards found when the truck is unloaded. This information helps them make decisions about which suppliers to use in the future.

Step 1 Gather the Data. The inspectors have a clear understanding of what consti-tutes a defective circuit board by comparing the inspected circuit boards with stan-dards. The defective units are set aside to be counted. For the purposes of this example, each shipment contains the same number of circuit boards.

Circuit boards are randomly sampled from each truckload with a sample size of n = 50.

Step 2 Plot the Number of Defective Units (np) on the Control Chart. The results for the 20 most recent trucks are shown in Table 13.3. The values of np for each sub-group are plotted on the chart in Figure 13.4, which has been scaled to reflect the magnitude of the data.

Subgroup Number	n	np
1	50	4
2	50	6
3	50	5
4	50	2
5	50	3
6	50	5
7	50	4
8	50	7
9	50	2
10	50	3
11	50	1
12	50	4
13	50	3
14	50	5
15	50	2
16	50	5
17	50	6
18	50	3
19	50	1
20	50	2

Table 13.3   Data Sheet: PCC Inc.

Step 3 Calculate the Centerline and Control Limits. The average of the total number defective is found by adding up the number of defective values and dividing by the total number of samples. This is worked to two decimal places:

$$\text{Centerline } n\bar{p} = \frac{\sum_{i=1}^{n} np}{m} = \frac{73}{20} = 3.65$$

The control limits for an np chart are found using the following formulas:

$$\bar{p} = \frac{\sum_{i=1}^{n} np}{\sum_{i=1}^{n} n} = \frac{73}{1000} = 0.073$$

$$UCL_{np} = n\bar{p} + 3\sqrt{n\bar{p}(1 - \bar{p})}$$

$$= 3.65 + 3\sqrt{3.65(1 - 0.073)} = 9.17$$

$$LCL_{np} = n\bar{p} - 3\sqrt{n\bar{p}(1 - \bar{p})}$$

$$= 3.65 - 3\sqrt{3.65(1 - 0.073)} = -1.87 = 0$$

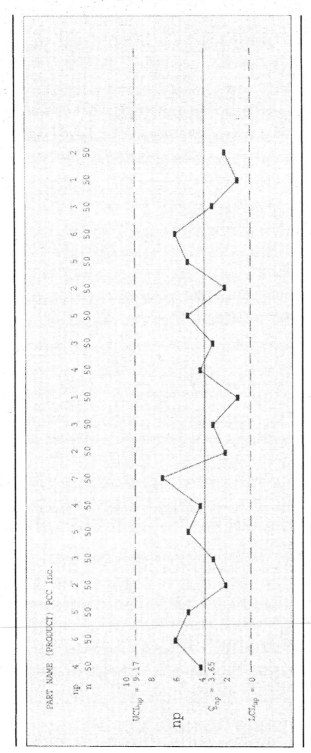

Figure 13.4 Number Defective (np) Chart

Step 4 Draw the Centerline and Control Limits on the Chart. Figure 13.4 uses a solid line to denote the centerline and dashed lines for the control limits.

Step 5 Interpret the Chart. A study of Figure 13.4 reveals that the chart is under control. The points flow smoothly back and forth across the centerline. The number of points on each side of the centerline are balanced, with the majority of the points near the centerline. There are no trends, runs, cycles, or sudden shifts in level apparent in the data. All of the points fall between the upper and lower control limits.

CHARTS FOR COUNTS OF DEFECTS

When the situation calls for tracking the count of defects, a number of defects (c) chart or a number of defects per unit (u) chart is appropriate. Charts for counts of defects monitor the number of defects found in a sample. Defects represent problems that exist with the product or service. Defects may or may not render the product or service unusable. Two types of charts recording defects may be used: a count of defects (c) chart or a count of defects per unit (u) chart.

Number of Defects (c) Chart

The **number of defects chart, or c chart,** *is used to track the count of defects observed in a single unit of product or single service experience,* n = 1. Charts counting defects are used when defects are scattered through a continuous flow of product such as bubbles in a sheet of glass, flaws in a bolt of fabric, discolorations in a ream of paper, or services such as mistakes on an insurance form or errors on a bill. Count-of-defects charts can combine the counts of a variety of defects, such as the number of mishandled, dented, missing, or unidentified suitcases to reach a particular airport carousel. A constant sample size must be used when creating a count of defects (c) chart.

1. *Gather the data.* Gathering the data requires that the area of opportunity of occurrence for each sample taken be equal, n = 1. The rate of occurrences of defects within a sample or area of opportunity (area of exposure) is plotted on the c chart. For this reason, the size of the piece of paper or fabric, the length of the steel, or the number of units must be equal for each sample taken. The number of defects will be determined by comparing the inspected product or service with a standard and counting the deviations from the standard. On a c chart, all defects have the same weight, regardless of the type of defect. The area of opportunity for these defects should be large, with a very small chance of a particular defect occurring at any one location.

2. *Count and plot c, the count of the number of defects, on the control chart.* As it is inspected, each item or subgroup will yield a count of the defects (c). It is this value that is plotted on the control chart. The scale for the c chart should reflect the number of defects discovered.

3. *Calculate the centerline and control limits.* The number of defects are added up and then divided by the total number of subgroups:

$$\text{Centerline } \bar{c} = \frac{\sum\limits_{i=1}^{n} c}{m}$$

The control limits for a c chart are found using the following formulas:

$$UCL_c = \bar{c} + 3\sqrt{\bar{c}}$$
$$LCL_c = \bar{c} - 3\sqrt{\bar{c}}$$

If the lower control limit of a c chart has a negative value, the LCL_c should be rounded up to zero.

4. *Draw the centerline and control limits on the chart.* Using a solid line to denote the centerline and dashed lines for the control limits, draw the centerline and control limits on the chart.

5. *Interpret the chart.* Charts for counts of defects are interpreted similarly to all control charts. The process capability is $\bar{c}$, the average count of defects in a sample and the centerline of the control chart.

 SIX SIGMA TOOLS AT WORK

Making a c Chart

Pure and White, a manufacturer of paper used in copy machines, monitors their production using a c chart. Paper is produced in large rolls, 12 ft long and with a 6 ft diameter. A sample is taken from each completed roll, n = 1, and checked in the lab for defects. Defects have been identified as discolorations, inconsistent paper thickness, flecks of dirt in the paper, moisture content, and ability to take ink. All of these defects have the same weight on the c chart. A sample may be taken from anywhere in the roll so the area of opportunity for these defects is large, while the overall quality of the paper creates only a very small chance of a particular defect occurring at any one location.

Step 1 Gather the Data (Table 13.4).

Step 2 Count and Plot c. As each roll is inspected, it yields a count of the defects (c) that is recorded in Table 13.4. This value is then plotted on the control chart shown in Figure 13.5.

Step 3 Calculate the Centerline and Control Limits. The centerline of the control chart is the average of the subgroup defects. The number of defects is added up and then divided by the total number of rolls of paper inspected:

$$\text{Centerline } \bar{c} = \frac{\sum\limits_{i=1}^{n} c}{m} = \frac{210}{20} = 10.5 \text{ rounded to } 11$$

Sample Number	c
1	10
2	11
3	12
4	10
5	9
6	22
7	8
8	10
9	11
10	9
11	12
12	7
13	10
14	11
15	10
16	12
17	9
18	10
19	8
20	9
	$\overline{210}$

Table 13.4   Data Sheet: Pure and White Paper

The control limits for a c chart are found using the following formulas:

$$UCL_c = \bar{c} + 3\sqrt{\bar{c}}$$
$$= 11 + 3\sqrt{11} = 21$$
$$LCL_c = \bar{c} - 3\sqrt{\bar{c}}$$
$$= 11 - 3\sqrt{11} = 1$$

Step 4 Draw the Centerline and Control Limits on the Chart. Using a solid line to denote the centerline and dashed lines for the control limits, draw the centerline and control limits on the chart (Figure 13.5).

Step 5 Interpret the Chart. Point 6 is out of control and should be investigated to determine the cause of so many defects. There are no other patterns present on the chart. Except for point 6, the chart is performing in a very steady manner.

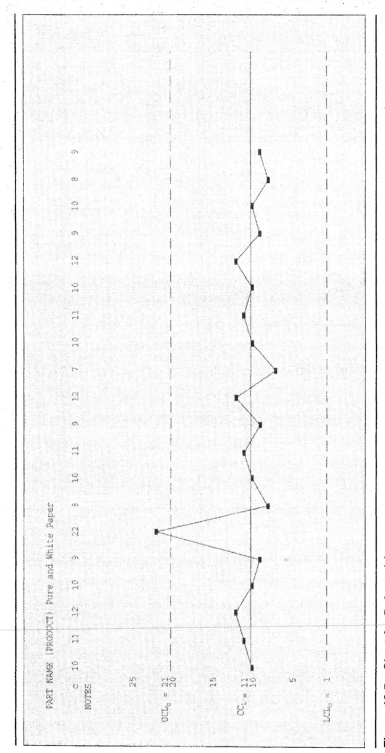

Figure 13.5 Chart for Defects (c)

273

Revising the c Chart

If improvements have been made to the process or the reasons behind special cause situations have been identified and corrected, c charts can be revised using the following formulas:

$$\text{Centerline } \bar{c}_{new} = \frac{\sum\limits_{i=1}^{n} c - c_d}{m - m_d}$$

$$\text{UCL}_{c_{new}} = \bar{c}_{new} + 3\sqrt{\bar{c}_{new}}$$

$$\text{LCL}_{c_{new}} = \bar{c}_{new} - 3\sqrt{\bar{c}_{new}}$$

 SIX SIGMA TOOLS AT WORK

Revising a c Chart

The Pure and White paper manufacturer investigated the out of control point on the c chart in Figure 13.5 and determined that a new operator had not added sufficient bleach to the pulp mixing tank. The operator was retrained in how to mix the correct combination of chemicals to make Pure and White paper. To revise the chart and determine the process capability, Pure and White followed this procedure:

$$\text{Centerline } \bar{c}_{new} = \frac{\sum\limits_{i=1}^{n} c - c_d}{m - m_d} = \frac{210 - 22}{20 - 1} = 10$$

$$\text{UCL}_{c_{new}} = \bar{c}_{new} + 3\sqrt{\bar{c}_{new}}$$

$$= 10 + 3\sqrt{10} = 20$$

$$\text{LCL}_{c_{new}} = \bar{c}_{new} - 3\sqrt{\bar{c}_{new}}$$

$$= 10 - 3\sqrt{10} = 0.5$$

Number of Defects per Unit (u) Charts: Constant Sample Size

A *number of defects per unit chart, or u chart, is a chart that studies the number of defects in a unit* ($n > 1$). The u chart is very similar to the c chart; however, unlike c charts, u charts can also be used with variable sample sizes. To create a number of defects per unit chart:

1. *Gather the data.*
2. *Calculate u, the number of defects per unit.* As it is inspected, each sample of size n will yield a count of defects (c). The number of defects per unit (u), used on

the u chart, is calculated using n, the number of inspected items, and c, the count of defects found:

$$u = \frac{c}{n}$$

3. *Calculate the centerline and control limits.* The centerline of the u chart is the average of the subgroup defects per unit. The number of defects are added up and then divided by the total number of samples:

$$\text{Centerline } \bar{u} = \frac{\sum\limits_{i=1}^{n} c}{\sum\limits_{i=1}^{n} n}$$

The control limits for the u chart are found using the following formulas:

$$UCL_u = \bar{u} + 3\frac{\sqrt{\bar{u}}}{\sqrt{n}}$$

$$LCL_u = \bar{u} - 3\frac{\sqrt{\bar{u}}}{\sqrt{n}}$$

If the lower control limit of a u chart has a negative value, the LCL_u should be rounded to zero.

4. *Draw the centerline and control limits on the chart.* Using a solid line to denote the centerline and dashed lines for the control limits, draw the centerline and control limits on the chart.

5. *Interpret the chart.* A u chart is interpreted in the same manner as is a p, np, or c chart. The chart should be studied for any nonrandom conditions such as runs, trends, cycles, or points out of control. The data points on a u chart should flow smoothly back and forth across the centerline. The number of points on each side of the centerline should be balanced, with the majority of the points near the centerline. Quality improvement efforts are reflected on a u chart when the count of defects per unit is reduced, as shown by a trend toward the lower control limit and therefore toward zero defects. The process capability is $\bar{u}$, the centerline of the control chart, the average number of defects per unit.

 SIX SIGMA TOOLS AT WORK

Making a u Chart

At Special Plastics, Inc., small plastic parts used to connect hoses are created on a separate production line from the credit card blanks. Special Plastics, Inc., uses u charts to collect data concerning the defects per unit in the process.

Step 1 Gather the Data. During inspection, a random sample of size 400 is taken once an hour. The hose connectors are visually inspected for a variety of defects, including flashing on inner diameters, burrs on the part exterior, incomplete threads, flashing on the ends of the connectors, incorrect plastic compound, and discolorations.

Step 2 Calculate u, the Number of Defects per Unit. Table 13.5 shows the number of defects (c) that each subgroup of sample size n = 400 yielded. The number of defects per unit (u) to be plotted on the chart is calculated by dividing c, the number of defects found, by n, the number of inspected items. Working the example to three decimal places, for the first sample,

$$u_i = \frac{c}{n} = \frac{10}{400} = 0.025$$

Step 3 Calculate the Centerline and Control Limits. The centerline of the u chart is the average of the subgroup defects per unit. The number of defects are added up and then divided by the total number of samples:

$$\text{Centerline } \bar{u} = \frac{\sum\limits_{i=1}^{n} c}{\sum\limits_{i=1}^{n} n} = \frac{210}{20(400)} = 0.026$$

Subgroup Number	n	c	u
1	400	12	0.030
2	400	7	0.018
3	400	10	0.025
4	400	11	0.028
5	400	10	0.025
6	400	12	0.030
7	400	9	0.023
8	400	10	0.025
9	400	8	0.020
10	400	9	0.023
11	400	10	0.025
12	400	11	0.028
13	400	12	0.030
14	400	10	0.025
15	400	9	0.023
16	400	22	0.055
17	400	8	0.020
18	400	10	0.025
19	400	11	0.028
20	400	9	0.023

Table 13.5   Data Sheet: Hose Connectors

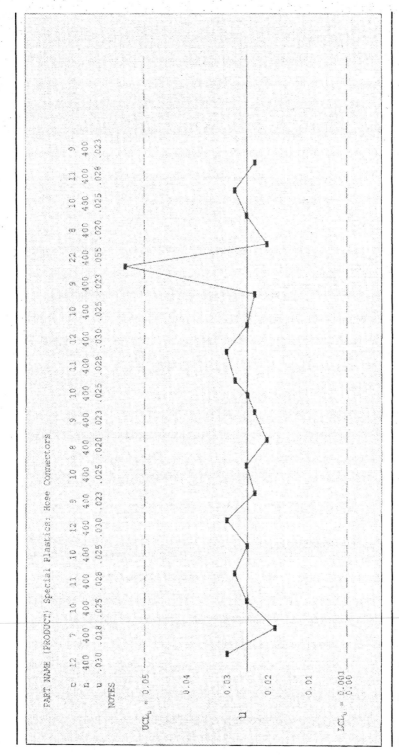

Figure 13.6 Chart for Defects per Unit (u)

277

Find the control limits for the u chart by using the following formulas:

$$UCL_u = \bar{u} + 3\frac{\sqrt{\bar{u}}}{\sqrt{n}}$$

$$= 0.026 + 3\frac{\sqrt{0.026}}{\sqrt{400}} = 0.05$$

$$LCL_u = \bar{u} - 3\frac{\sqrt{\bar{u}}}{\sqrt{n}}$$

$$= 0.026 - 3\frac{\sqrt{0.026}}{\sqrt{400}} = 0.001$$

Step 4 Create and Draw the Centerline and Control Limits on the Chart. Using a solid line to denote the centerline and dashed lines for the control limits, draw the centerline and control limits on the chart. Values for u are plotted on the control chart (Figure 13.6).

Step 5 Interpret the Chart. Except for point 16, the chart appears to be under statistical control. There are no runs or unusual patterns. Point 16 should be investigated to determine the cause of such a large number of defects per unit.

Revising the u Chart

The u chart is revised in the same fashion as are the other attribute charts. Once the assignable causes have been determined and the process modified to prevent their recurrence, the centerline and control limits can be recalculated using the following formula.

$$\text{Centerline } \bar{u} = \frac{\sum_{i=1}^{n} c - c_d}{\sum_{i=1}^{n} n - n_d}$$

The control limits for the u chart are found using the following formulas:

$$UCL_u = \bar{u}_{new} + 3\frac{\sqrt{\bar{u}_{new}}}{\sqrt{n}}$$

$$LCL_u = \bar{u}_{new} - 3\frac{\sqrt{\bar{u}_{new}}}{\sqrt{n}}$$

SUMMARY

With so many control charts, the choice of which chart to implement under what circumstances is actually less confusing than it first appears. To begin the selection process, care must be taken to identify the type of data to be gathered. What is the nature of the process under study? Are they variables data and therefore measurable? Or are they attribute data and therefore countable? Is there a sample size or is just one item being measured? Is there a sample size or are just the defects in an area of opportunity being counted? The flowchart in Figure 13.7 can assist you in choosing a chart.

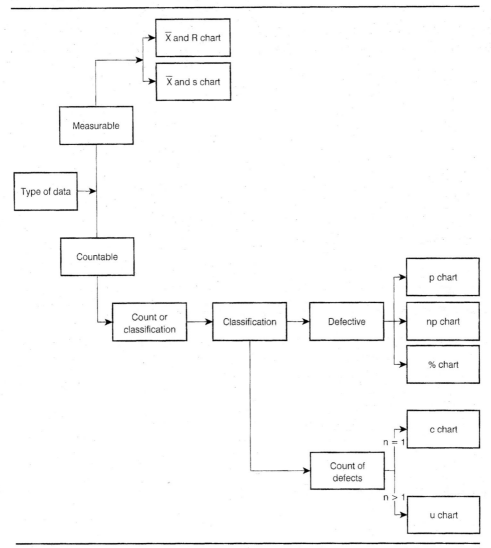

Figure 13.7 Control Chart Selection Flowchart

Choosing a Control Chart

1. Variables Data
   A. Use an $\overline{X}$ chart combined with an R or s chart
      1. The characteristic can be measured.
      2. The process is unable to hold tolerances.
      3. The process must be monitored for adjustments.
      4. Changes are being made to the process and those changes need to be monitored.

   5. Process stability and process capability must be monitored and demonstrated to a customer or regulating body.
   6. The process average and the process variation must be measured.
2. Attribute Data
   A. Use charts for defective units or fraction defective charts (p, np, 100p) when
      1. There is a need to monitor the portion of the lot that is defective.
      2. The characteristics under study in the process can be judged either defective or not.
      3. Process monitoring is desired but measurement data cannot be obtained because of the nature of the product or the expense.
   B. Use charts for defects (c, u) when
      1. There is a need to monitor the number of defects in a process (c charts for counts of defects, u charts for defects per unit).
      2. The characteristics under study in the process can be judged as having one or more defects.
      3. Process monitoring is desired but measurement data cannot be obtained because of the nature of the product or the expense.

σ ■ Take Away Tips

   1. For the fraction defective chart, the product or service being provided must be inspected and classed as either defective or not defective.
   2. Number defective (np) and percent defective charts may be easier to interpret than fraction defective (p) charts.
   3. Charts for counts of defects (c) and defects per unit (u) are used when the defects on the product or service being inspected can be counted. For c charts, n = 1; for u charts, n > 1.
   4. When interpreting p, np, c, or u charts, it is important to remember that values closer to zero are desirable. ■

σ ■ Formulas

Fraction Defective (p) Chart

$$p = \frac{np}{n}$$

$$\text{Centerline } \bar{p} = \frac{\sum\limits_{i=1}^{n} np}{\sum\limits_{i=1}^{n} n}$$

$$UCL_p = \bar{p} + 3\frac{\sqrt{\bar{p}(1 - \bar{p})}}{\sqrt{n}}$$

$$LCL_p = \bar{p} - 3\frac{\sqrt{\bar{p}(1 - \bar{p})}}{\sqrt{n}}$$

Revising:

$$\bar{p}_{new} = \frac{\sum_{i=1}^{n} np - np_d}{\sum_{i=1}^{n} n - n_d}$$

$$UCL_{p_{new}} = \bar{p}_{new} + 3\frac{\sqrt{\bar{p}_{new}(1 - \bar{p}_{new})}}{\sqrt{n}}$$

$$LCL_{p_{new}} = \bar{p}_{new} - 3\frac{\sqrt{\bar{p}_{new}(1 - \bar{p}_{new})}}{\sqrt{n}}$$

Number Defective (np) Chart

$$\text{Centerline } n\bar{p} = \frac{\sum_{i=1}^{n} np}{m}$$

$$UCL_{np} = n\bar{p} + 3\sqrt{n\bar{p}(1 - \bar{p})}$$

$$LCL_{np} = n\bar{p} - 3\sqrt{n\bar{p}(1 - \bar{p})}$$

Percent Defective (100p) Chart

The centerline for a percent defective chart is $100\bar{p}$

$$UCL_{100p} = 100\left[\bar{p} + \frac{3\sqrt{\bar{p}(1 - \bar{p})}}{\sqrt{n}}\right]$$

$$LCL_{100p} = 100\left[\bar{p} - \frac{3\sqrt{\bar{p}(1 - \bar{p})}}{\sqrt{n}}\right]$$

Count of Defects (c) Chart

$$n = 1$$

$$\text{Centerline } \bar{c} = \frac{\sum_{i=1}^{n} c}{m}$$

$$UCL_c = \bar{c} + 3\sqrt{\bar{c}}$$

$$LCL_c = \bar{c} - 3\sqrt{\bar{c}}$$

Revising:

$$\text{Centerline } \bar{c}_{new} = \frac{\sum\limits_{i=1}^{n} c - c_d}{m - m_d}$$

$$UCL_{c_{new}} = \bar{c}_{new} + 3\sqrt{\bar{c}_{new}}$$

$$LCL_{c_{new}} = \bar{c}_{new} - 3\sqrt{\bar{c}_{new}}$$

Defects per Unit (u) Chart

$$n > 1$$

$$u = \frac{c}{n}$$

$$\text{Centerline } \bar{u} = \frac{\sum\limits_{i=1}^{n} c}{\sum\limits_{i=1}^{n} n}$$

$$UCL_u = \bar{u} + 3\frac{\sqrt{\bar{u}}}{\sqrt{n}}$$

$$LCL_u = \bar{u} - 3\frac{\sqrt{\bar{u}}}{\sqrt{n}}$$

Chapter Questions

1. Given the following information about mistakes made on tax forms, make and interpret a fraction defective chart.

Sample Size	Defective	Sample Size	Defective	Sample Size	Defective
20	0	20	3	20	0
20	0	20	1	20	0
20	0	20	1	20	1
20	2	20	0	20	1
20	0	20	2	20	0
20	1	20	10	20	2
20	6	20	2	20	0
20	0	20	1	20	4
20	0	20	0	20	1
20	2	20	1	20	0

2. The following table gives the number of defective product found while inspecting a series of 12 consecutive lots of galvanized washers for finish

defects such as exposed steel, rough galvanizing, and discoloration. A sample size of n = 200 was used for each lot. Find the centerline and control limits for a fraction defective chart. If the manufacturer wishes to have a process capability of $\bar{p}$ = 0.005, is the process capable?

Sample Size	Defective	Sample Size	Defective
200	0	200	0
200	1	200	0
200	2	200	1
200	0	200	0
200	1	200	3
200	1	200	1

3. Thirst-Quench, Inc., has been in business for more than 50 years. Recently Thirst-Quench updated their machinery and processes, acknowledging their out-of-date style. They have decided to evaluate these changes. The engineer is to record data, evaluate those data, and implement strategy to keep quality at a maximum. The plant operates 8 hours a day, 5 days a week, and produces 25,000 bottles of Thirst-Quench each day. Problems that have arisen in the past include partially filled bottles, crooked labels, upsidedown labels, and no labels. Samples of size 150 are taken each hour. Create a p chart.

Subgroup Number	Number Inspected n	Number Defective np	Proportion Defective p
1	150	6	0.040
2	150	3	0.020
3	150	9	0.060
4	150	7	0.047
5	150	9	0.060
6	150	2	0.013
7	150	3	0.020
8	150	5	0.033
9	150	6	0.040
10	150	8	0.053
11	150	9	0.060
12	150	7	0.047
13	150	7	0.047
14	150	2	0.013
15	150	5	0.033
16	150	7	0.047
17	150	4	0.027

(continued)

18	150	3	0.020
19	150	9	0.060
20	150	8	0.053
21	150	8	0.053
22	150	6	0.040
23	150	2	0.013
24	150	9	0.060
25	150	7	0.047
26	150	3	0.020
27	150	4	0.027
28	150	6	0.040
29	150	5	0.033
30	150	4	0.027
Total	4500	173	

4. Nearly everyone who visits a doctor's office is covered by some form of insurance. For a doctor, the processing of forms in order to receive payment from an insurance company is a necessary part of doing business. If a form is filled out incorrectly, the form cannot be processed and is considered nonconforming (defective). Within each office, an individual is responsible for inspecting and correcting the forms before filing them with the appropriate insurance company. A local doctor's office is interested in determining whether or not errors on insurance forms are a major problem. Every week they take a sample of 20 forms to use in creating a p chart. Use the following information to create a p chart. How are they doing?

Defective

1	2	6	7	11	2	16	4	21	6
2	5	7	6	12	3	17	5	22	4
3	8	8	3	13	17	18	2	23	5
4	10	9	7	14	5	19	3	24	1
5	4	10	5	15	2	20	2	25	2

5. From a lot of 1,000 soup cans, a sample size 160 ($n = 160$) is taken. The following data show the results of 15 such subgroups. Use the data to create a number defective chart.

Lot	n	np	Lot	n	np	Lot	n	np
1	160	12	6	160	11	11	160	16
2	160	15	7	160	10	12	160	17
3	160	13	8	160	15	13	160	13
4	160	15	9	160	13	14	160	14
5	160	11	10	160	12	15	160	11

6. A manufacturer of lightbulbs is keeping track of the number of defective bulbs (the number that don't light). Create the centerline and control limits for a number defective chart. What is the capability of the process? Assume assignable causes and revise the chart.

	n	np		n	np		n	np		n	np
1	300	10	6	300	11	11	300	31	16	300	10
2	300	8	7	300	9	12	300	32	17	300	11
3	300	9	8	300	10	13	300	10	18	300	9
4	300	12	9	300	12	14	300	8	19	300	10
5	300	10	10	300	11	15	300	12	20	300	8

7. The Tri-State Foundry Company is a large volume producer of ball joints for various automotive producers. The ball joints are sampled four times daily. The sample size is a constant of 400 parts. The chart shows how many defective parts are found in a sample size. The 1.5 inch limit is a strict guideline because any parts that are larger will not work with the female coupling assembly. Create percent defective with the following data. Assume assignable causes and revise the chart.

Subgroup Number	Number Inspected n	Number Defective np	Subgroup Number	Number Inspected n	Number Defective np
1	400	3	11	400	5
2	400	4	12	400	0
3	400	1	13	400	2
4	400	7	14	400	2
5	400	6	15	400	4
6	400	3	16	400	8
7	400	11	17	400	5
8	400	13	18	400	3
9	400	4	19	400	1
10	400	10	20	400	12

8. A production line manufactures compact discs. Twice an hour, one CD is selected at random from those made during the hour. Each disc is inspected separately for imperfections (defects), such as scratches, nicks, discolorations, and dents. The resulting count of imperfections from each disc is recorded on a control chart. Use the following data to create a c chart. If the customer wants a process capability of 1, will this line be able to meet that requirement?

Hour	Imperfections	Hour	Imperfections	Hour	Imperfections
1	2	10	2	19	4
2	0	11	1	20	1
3	2	12	2	21	2
4	1	13	0	22	0
5	0	14	1	23	2
6	1	15	1	24	1
7	0	16	0	25	0
8	2	17	0		
9	0	18	2		

9. The Par Fore Golf Company is a producer of plastic divot fixers. They produce the fixers in bags of 30. They consider these bags a sample size of 1.
   The defects range from overall size to individual flaws in the production of
   the plastic tool. These tools are inspected four times daily. Create a chart
   with the following data. Assume assignable causes and revise the chart.

	Serial Number	Count of Defects	Comment
1	JG100	7	
2	JG101	3	
3	JG102	5	
4	JG103	4	
5	JG104	6	
6	JG105	6	
7	JG106	17	Wrong Mold Used
8	JG107	7	
9	JG108	2	
10	JG109	0	
11	JG110	3	
12	JG111	4	
13	JG112	2	
14	JG113	0	
15	JG114	21	Not Enough Time in Mold
16	JG115	3	
17	JG116	2	
18	JG117	7	
19	JG118	5	
20	JG119	9	
		113	

10. When printing full color glossy magazine advertising pages, editors do not like to see blemishes or pics (very small places where the color did not transfer to the paper). One person at the printer has the job of looking at samples of magazine pages ($n = 20$) and counting blemishes. Below are her results. The editors are interested in plotting the defects per unit on a u chart. Determine the centerline and control limits. Create a chart of this process. If the editors want only two defects per unit on average, how does this compare with the actual process average?

Subgroup Number	Count of Defects	Subgroup Number	Count of Defects
1	65	6	42
2	80	7	35
3	60	8	30
4	50	9	30
5	52	10	25

11. A manufacturer of holiday light strings tests 400 of the light strings each day. The light strings are plugged in and the number of unlit bulbs are counted and recorded. Unlit bulbs are considered defects, and they are replaced before the light strings are shipped to customers. These data are then used to aid process engineers in their problem-solving activities. Given the following information, create and graph the chart. How is their performance? What is the process capability?

Subgroup	Sample Size	Defects
1	400	50
2	400	23
3	400	27
4	400	32
5	400	26
6	400	38
7	400	57
8	400	31
9	400	48
10	400	34
11	400	37
12	400	44
13	400	34
14	400	32
15	400	50

(continued)

	16	400	49
	17	400	54
	18	400	38
	19	400	29
	20	400	47
		8,000	780

12. The Davis Plastic Company produces plastic Wiffle-ball bats for a major sporting goods company. These bats are inspected daily but are not inspected at a constant number each day. The control chart shows how many bats were inspected and how many defects were found per unit. Defects include wrong taper on bat, incomplete handle, bad knurl on grip, or deformed bat ends. Create a u chart with the following data. Assume assignable causes and revise the chart.

Date	Number Inspected n	Count of Defects c	Defects per Unit u
April			
17	126	149	1.18
18	84	91	1.08
19	96	89	0.93
20	101	97	0.96
21	100	140	1.40
24	112	112	1.00
25	79	89	1.13
26	93	119	1.28
27	88	128	1.46
28	105	117	1.11
May			
1	99	135	1.36
2	128	155	1.21
3	113	145	1.28
4	120	143	1.19
5	81	94	1.16
8	85	104	1.22
9	130	157	1.21
10	97	121	1.25
11	78	83	1.06
12	110	120	1.09
	2,025	2,388	

14

Reliability

Quality is a customer determination which is based on the customer's actual experience with the product or service.

Armand Feigenbaum

▨ Objectives:

1. To understand the importance of system reliability
2. To understand how performance during the life of a product, process, or system is affected by its design and configuration
3. To be able to compute the reliability of systems, including systems in series, parallel, and hybrid combinations
4. To know what to look for in a comprehensive reliability program ▨

Six Sigma organizations know that their customers are interested in quality over the long run. Reliability studies enable them to meet the long term needs and expectations of their customers. **Reliability**, *or quality over the long term, is the ability of a product to perform its intended function over a period of time and under prescribed environmental conditions.* The reliability of a system, subsystem, component, or part is dependent on many factors, including the quality of research performed at its conception, the original design and any subsequent design changes, the complexity of the design, the manufacturing processes, the handling received during shipping, the environment surrounding its use, the end user, and numerous other factors. The causes of unreliability are many. Improper design, less-than-specified construction materials, faulty manufacturing or assembly, inappropriate testing leading to unrealistic conclusions, and damage during shipment are all factors that may contribute to a lack of product reliability. Once the product reaches the user, improper start-ups, abuse, lack of maintenance, or misapplication can seriously affect the reliability of an item. Reliability studies are looking for the answers to such questions as: Will it work? How long will it last?

Recognizing that reliability, or quality over the long run, plays a key role in the consumer's perception of quality, Six Sigma companies understand the importance of having a sound reliability program. Reliability testing enables a company to better comprehend how their products will perform under normal usage as well as extreme or unexpected situations. Reliability programs provide information about product performance by systematically studying the product. To ensure product quality, reliability tests subject a product to a variety of conditions besides expected operational parameters. These conditions may include excessive use, vibration, damp, heat, cold, humidity, dust, corrosive materials, and other environmental or user stresses. By providing information about product performance, a sound reliability program can have a significant effect on a company's financial statements. Early product testing can prevent poorly designed products from reaching the marketplace. Later testing can improve upon products already in use.

RELIABILITY PROGRAMS

Six Sigma organizations have reliability programs that endeavor to incorporate reliability concepts into system design. Reliability issues surface in nearly every facet of system design, development, creation, use, and service. Their reliability programs include the areas of design, testing, manufacture, raw material and component purchases, production, packaging, shipping, marketing, field service, and maintenance. A sound reliability program developed and implemented to support an entire system will consider the following aspects:

1. The entire system. What composes the system? What goals does the system meet? What are the components of the system? How are they interrelated? How do the interrelationships influence system reliability? What are the system reliability requirements set by the customer?

Critical to ensuring system reliability is a complete understanding of purpose of the product. The consumer's reliability needs and expectations must be a part of product reliability. Also important is an understanding of the life of a product. How is it shipped? How is it transported and stored? What type of environment will it face during usage? Comprehensive knowledge of a product and its life is the foundation of a strong reliability program.

2. The humans in the system. What are their limitations? What are their capabilities? What knowledge do they have of the product? How will this knowledge affect their use of the product? How might they misuse the product?

Product reliability can be increased if greater emphasis is placed on proper training and education of the users of the product. Appropriate steps must also be taken to ensure that the sales department does not promise more than the product can deliver. Setting the expectations of the users is as important as showing them how to use a product.

3. Maintenance of the system. Can the components or subassemblies be maintained separately from the system? Are the system components accessible? Is the system designed for replacement components or subsystems? Are those components or subsystems available? Can those components or subsystems be misapplied or misused? Will maintenance be performed under difficult circumstances?

If and when a component or a system fails, those using the system or component will be interested in the length of time it takes to return the failed system, subsystem, or component to full operational status. Changes to product, process, or system design based on maintainability considerations are sure to include an investigation of factors such as ease of repair or replacement of components, costs, and time. Well designed policies, practices, and procedures for effective preventive maintenance before failures occur and timely corrective maintenance after a failure occurs increase overall system reliability.

4. Simplicity of design. Will a simple design be more effective than a complicated one? Will a reduction in the number of elements increase the system reliability? Will the addition of elements increase the system reliability?

Simple, straightforward designs will increase system reliability. Designs of this sort are less likely to break down and are more easily manufactured. In some instances, the effort to impress with the current technological wizardry decreases the product's reliability. The greater the number of components, the greater the complexity and the easier it is for some aspect of the product, process, or system to fail.

5. Redundant and fail-safe features. Can the addition of redundant components or fail-safe features prevent overall system failure? At what cost?

Incremental increases in reliability should be balanced against costs. Products can be overdesigned for their purposes. There is a diminishing return on investment for this approach to achieving a reliable product. Is it preferable to avoid specially designed parts and components for the sake of easy availability? Will interchangeability decrease maintenance complexity?

6. Manufacturing methods and purchasing requirements. Have the chosen manufacturing methods enhanced system quality and reliability? Have purchasing policies been designed to support quality and reliability?

Purchasing and manufacturing must be made aware of how critical it is to purchase and use the materials deemed appropriate for the life cycle of this product.

7. Maintenance of complete product or system performance records. Can this information be used to increase future system reliability?

System reliability information from tests or from actual experience with the product or system should be gathered in a manner that will be meaningful when used for decisions concerning product or system design changes, development of new products or systems, product or system manufacture, operation, maintenance, or support.

8. Communication. Have clear channels of communication been established among all those involved in the design, manufacture, shipment, maintenance, and use of the product or system?

While perhaps not a complete list, the above areas for consideration form the basis of a well structured reliability program. When the program provides answers to the questions, system reliability is enhanced.

 SIX SIGMA TOOLS AT WORK

Disasters That Could Have Been Averted

Sometimes it is difficult to comprehend that a complete reliability program improves overall system reliability. Consider some examples from real life events where the critical aspects we discussed above were ignored:

Aspect 1. The entire system

In 1989, United Airlines Flight 232 crashed in Sioux City, Iowa, despite heroic efforts on the part of the flight crew. The DC-10's tail engine exploded in flight and destroyed the plane's hydraulic lines. Although the plane could fly on its two wing-mounted engines, the loss of hydraulic power rendered the plane's main control systems (flaps and gear) inoperable. A study of the plane's design revealed that, although backup hydraulic systems existed, all three hydraulic lines, including backups, went through one channel, which rested on top of the third engine in the tail. When the engine failed, debris from the engine severed all the hydraulic lines at the same time. In his March 28, 1997, *USA Today* article, "Safety Hearings End Today on Cracks in Jet Engines," Robert Davis stated, "The nation's airlines could be forced to spend more time and money using new techniques for inspecting engines." Those familiar with reliability issues know that the problems are more complicated than an airline's maintenance practices.

Aspect 1. The entire system

During the summer of 1996, power outages plagued Western states, leaving offices, businesses, and homes without lights, air conditioning, elevators, computers, cash registers, faxes, electronic keys, ventilation, and a host of other services. Traffic chaos resulted when traffic signals failed to function. During one outage, 15 states were without power. This particular power failure occurred when circuit breakers at a transmission grid were tripped. The interrupted flow of power caused generators further down the line to overload. Automatic systems, activated in the event of an overload, cut power to millions of customers. Six weeks later, a second power grid failure resulted when sagging transmission lines triggered a domino effect similar to the previous outage. This outage affected 10 states and at least 5.6 million people for nearly 24 hours. When millions of people rely upon highly complex and integrated systems such as power transmission and satellites, these systems need careful consideration from a reliability point of view.

Not much has changed since 1996. Power outages continue to be prevalent. One massive power outage on August 14, 2003, left 50 million people in the U.S. and Canada without power for days. In the summer of 2004, Athens, Greece experienced a series of power outages that threatened to disrupt the Olympics. Studies of power outages reveal the shortcomings that contribute to these massive failures. Blackouts can be caused by unreliable or faulty equipment, voluntary reliability standards, overloaded transmission lines, untrained, unprepared, or overtaxed repair personal, and poor planning.

Aspect 2. The humans in the system

Often we think of reliability as an equipment based system, however, reliable systems are needed in other, more human oriented systems. As reported in the *Wall Street Journal* article "It's 9 P.M., Do You Know Where You Parked Your Car?" guest services managers at all major parking lots have systems in place designed to reunite patrons with their vehicles. While some guest services managers operate handheld computers running a license plate information location program which finds cars based on license plate information scanned from parked cars, most still rely on the guest's memory.

Aspect 3. Maintenance of the system

According to a 2004, Purdue University, study of 1300 aviation incidents and accidents, maintenance errors, such as incomplete or incorrect tasks, were the primary contributing factors in 14% of aviation incidents and 8% of accidents. These figures, compiled from 1984–2002 records, are for all types of planes, from propeller to jumbo jet. The leading cause: Failure to Follow Maintenance Procedures. Though weather, turbulence, and pilot error still contribute the largest share of accidents and incidents, these maintenance figures reveal a problem exists.

Aspect 4. Simplicity of design

The design of the rocket joints on the space shuttle Challenger was based on the highly successful Titan III rocket. The joints of the Titan contained a single O-ring. When adapting the design for the space shuttle, designers felt that adding a second O-ring would make the design even more reliable. Investigation of the design after the explosion revealed that the additional O-ring had contributed to the disaster. Designers have redesigned the rocket to include a *third* O-ring, but will it increase reliability?

Aspect 5. Redundant and fail-safe features

On December 20, 1997, air traffic over the central United States was disrupted by a multiple level power failure. Air traffic control systems maintain three backup systems. The combined reliability of such systems is considered to be greater than

99.5 percent. On December 20, however, one system was shut down for scheduled maintenance, the commercial power failed, and a technician mistakenly pulled a circuit card from the remaining power system. With no other backups, the air traffic control information system, including computers, software, and displays, was inoperable for about five hours. The unexpected failure of the redundant and backup systems needs to be carefully considered as part of overall reliability.

PRODUCT LIFE CYCLE CURVE

The life cycle of a product is commonly broken down into three phases: early failure, chance failure, and wear-out (Figure 14.1). The early failure, or infant mortality, phase is characterized by failures occurring very quickly after the product has been produced or put into use by the consumer. The curve during this phase is exponential, with the number of failures decreasing the longer the product is in use. Failures at this stage have a variety of causes. Some early failures are due to inappropriate or inadequate materials, marginal components, incorrect installation, or poor manufacturing techniques. Incomplete testing may not have revealed design weaknesses that become apparent only as the consumer uses the system. Inadequate quality checks could have allowed substandard products to leave the manufacturing area. The manufacturing processes or tooling may not have been capable of producing to the specifications needed by the designer. The consumer also plays a role in product reliability. Once the product reaches the consumer, steps must be taken to ensure that the consumer understands the appropriate environment for product use. Improper usage will affect the reliability of a product.

During the chance failure portion of a product's useful life, failures occur randomly. This may be due to inadequate or insufficient design margins. Manufacturing or material problems have the potential to cause intermittent failures. At this stage the consumer can also affect product reliability. Misapplication or misuse of the product by the consumer can lead to product failure. Overstressing the product is a common cause of random failures.

As the product ages, it approaches the final stage of its life cycle, the wear-out phase. During this phase, failures increase in number until few, if any, of the product are left. Wear-out failures are due to a variety of causes, some related to actual product function, some cosmetic. A system's reliability, useful operation, or desirability may decrease if it

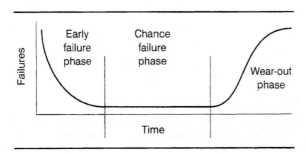

Figure 14.1   Life Cycle Curve

becomes scratched, dented, chipped, or otherwise damaged. Age and the associated wear, discolorations, and brittleness may lead to material failure. Normal wear could decrease reliability through misalignments, loose fittings, and interference between components. Combined stresses placed on the product (like the zipper or latches on a suitcase) during its lifetime of use are a source of decreased reliability. Neglect or inadequate preventive maintenance lessens product reliability and shortens product life.

 SIX SIGMA TOOLS AT WORK

Aircraft Landing Gear Life Cycle Management

Ever since Charles E. Taylor, the father of aviation maintenance, began working with the Wright Brothers to repair parts and components on such early models as the Wright B flier, aircraft maintenance programs have existed. Airlines recognize that the effectiveness of their organization depends on aircraft operational readiness, the overall reliability of their planes. The wisdom of participating in a preventive maintenance program is often justified by tracking reliability measures such as mean time to failure, mean time to repair, and availability rates.

Knowing that the reliability of landing gear components can materially affect aircraft operational readiness, CLP Corporation reviewed their two approaches to maintaining the reliability of their two separate fleets of aircraft. The objective of their review was to determine whether or not life cycle management of landing gear increased aircraft reliability and cost effectiveness.

In order to better manage maintenance, repair, and replacement costs, aircraft owners study their fleets, monitoring the reliability of key components. Aircraft landing gear reliability is often judged based on the number of takeoff-and-landing cycles completed. Planes, as well as their individual components, follow the life cycle curve presented in Figure 14.1. Fortunately, robust designs of key components and routine maintenance and repair often keep planes flying long after their predicted number of takeoff-and-landing cycles or flights has passed. In this example, the expected life of landing gear for both larger and smaller jets is eight thousand takeoff-and-landing cycles.

CLP's two jet fleets are managed as separate business entities. The smaller jets make short hops around the country, while the larger jets, with their greater fuel capacity, tend to be used for cross-country or cross-continent, longer duration flights. A study of the maintenance records revealed that CLP's smaller, 150-passenger jets experienced a greater number of landing gear reliability issues than the larger, 250-passenger jets. In short, the smaller jets are not as reliable as the larger jets.

At first glance, it may appear that the greater number of landing gear mishaps may be due to the smaller jets' greater number of landings and takeoffs. Further investigation uncovered that, as they aged, the smaller jets experienced lower landing gear reliability than the larger jets. Landing gear related mishaps accounted for nine percent of total aircraft mishaps from 1995 through 2004. Of 13 landing gear related mishaps, 11 occurred on smaller jets and two occurred on larger jets. True to the life cycle curve, as the jets have aged, failures have increased.

Although mishaps cannot always be prevented through maintenance, aircraft that had a program of landing gear maintenance experienced reduced mishap rates and had greater reliability. A fully defined life cycle management process for the larger jets' landing gear from the time of acquisition through production and deployment has been in place for several years. Because the smaller jets did not have this process in place, they were less reliable, needing maintenance, repair, and replacement at a greater rate and at higher costs than the larger jets.

The smaller jets have historically been maintained on an as-needed, on-location program rather than returning to a single maintenance facility. The larger jets, with their maintenance process, have all but emergency work taken care of at a single maintenance facility. One significant benefit of having repairs performed at a single location is the increase in worker knowledge of the aircraft of and its components. Another critical factor in reducing mean time to repair is that one location provides easy access to replacement parts. As the smaller jets aged, flight line maintenance becomes less effective, reliability levels decrease, and maintenance, repair, and replacement costs increase.

The larger jet management team maintained thorough records related to maintenance, repair, and replacement costs both before and after implementing the preventive maintenance program for the larger jets. In Table 14.1 these differences have been quantified using reliability concepts. The mean time between failure rates were calculated based on the number of failures observed by the maintenance staff and the number of landing and takeoff cycles the jets had completed. Aircraft availability calculations include the mean time to repair, that is, the average time it takes to return the jet to service after repairing a landing gear system component. The maintenance costs are the average total costs to repair or replace the failed landing gear.

The reliability calculations related to mean time between failure and availability show the significant difference between the costs associated with planned maintenance and unplanned maintenance, as well as the difference between availabilities

Table 14.1   Cost Analysis for Planned Maintenance Using Mean Time Between Failures

	MTBF with Planned Maintenance	Cost with Planned Maintenance	Aircraft Availability	MTBF w/o Planned Maintenance	Cost w/o Planned Maintenance	Aircraft Availability
Left Main Landing Gear*	8,300	$380,140	99%	3,917	$506,680	78%
Right Main Landing Gear*	8,186	$421,127	99%	3,043	$568,438	74%
Nose Landing Gear*	7,400	$407,392	98%	5,138	$473,413	68%

*Expected life: 8,000 takeoff-and-landing cycles.

of aircraft. Based on operational maintenance records, CLP Corporation recognized that reduced reliability related to landing gear, coupled with aging aircraft concerns, necessitated a change in its maintenance processes for its smaller jets. By comparison, the larger jets, with their maintenance process approach, have highly maintainable landing gear with an extended life and increased aircraft reliability. The landing gear maintenance process is only one of their many preventive maintenance programs. Overall, the larger jets' preventive maintenance program is projected to save the corporation over $100 million in a 10 year period.

Having a preventive maintenance process increases product reliability resulting in:

Increased effectiveness (availability for deployment)
Lower risk of failure
Increased component life
Reduced remote location maintenance workload
Greater maintenance knowledge at single facility
Increased ability to project life cycle costs associated with maintenance and
    component replacement
Lower risk of grounding an aircraft or an entire fleet
Fewer incidents needing crisis management
Increased morale

MEASURES OF RELIABILITY

Overall system reliability depends on the individual reliabilities associated with the parts, components, and subassemblies. Reliability tests exist to aid in determining if distinct patterns of failure exist during the product's or system's life cycle. Reliability tests determine what failed, how it failed, and the number of hours, cycles, actuations, or stresses it was able to bear before failure. Once these data are known, Six Sigma practioners can make decisions concerning product reliability expectations, corrective action steps, maintenance procedures, and costs of repair or replacement. Several different types of tests exist to judge the reliability of a product, including failure-terminated, time-terminated, and sequential tests. The name of each of these tests says a good deal about the type of the test. *Failure-terminated tests* are ended when a predetermined number of failures occur within the sample being tested. The decision concerning whether or not the product is acceptable is based on the number of products that have failed during the test. A *time-terminated test* is concluded when an established number of hours is reached. For this test, product is accepted on the basis of how many products failed before reaching the time limit. A *sequential test* relies on the accumulated results of the tests.

Failure Rate, Mean Life, And Availability

When system performance is time dependent, such as the length of time a system is expected to operate, then reliability is measured in terms of mean life, failure rates, availability, mean time between failures, and specific mission reliability. As a system is used, data concerning failures become available. This information can be utilized to estimate the mean life and failure rate of the system. Failure rate, λ, the probability of a failure during a stated period of time, cycle, or number of impacts, can be calculated as

$$\lambda_{estimated} = \frac{\text{number of failures observed}}{\text{sum of test times or cycles}}$$

From this, θ, the average life, can be calculated:

$$\theta_{estimated} = \frac{1}{\lambda}$$

or

$$\theta_{estimated} = \frac{\text{sum of test times or cycles}}{\text{number of failures observed}}$$

The average life θ is also known as the mean time between failure or the mean time to failure. Mean time between failure (MTBF), how much time has elapsed between failures, is used when speaking of repairable systems. Mean time to failure is used for nonrepairable systems.

 SIX SIGMA TOOLS AT WORK

Calculating Failure Rate and Average Life

Twenty windshield wiper motors are being tested using a time-terminated test. The test is concluded when a total of 200 hours of continuous operation have been completed. During this test, the number of windshield wipers that fail before reaching the time limit of 200 hours is counted. If three wipers failed after 125, 152, and 189 hours, calculate the failure rate λ and the average life θ:

$$\lambda_{estimated} = \frac{\text{number of failures observed}}{\text{sum of test times of cycles}}$$

$$= \frac{3}{125 + 152 + 189 + (17)200} = 0.0008$$

From this, θ, the average life, can be calculated:

$$\theta_{estimated} = \frac{1}{\lambda} = \frac{1}{0.0008} = 1250 \text{ hours}$$

or

$$\theta_{estimated} = \frac{\text{sum of test times or cycles}}{\text{number of failures observed}}$$

$$= \frac{125 + 152 + 189 + (17)200}{3} = 1289 \text{ hours}$$

The average life of the windshield wiper motor is 1289 hours.

Here, the difference between $\theta_{estimated}$ based on $1/\lambda$ and $\theta_{estimated}$ calculated directly is due to rounding.

Mean times between failures (MTBF) and mean times to failure (MTTF) describe reliability as a function of time. Here the amount of time that the system is actually operating is of great concern. For example, without their radar screen, air traffic controllers are sightless and therefore out of operation. To be considered reliable, the radar must be functional for a significant amount of the expected operating time. Since many systems need preventive or corrective maintenance, a system's reliability can be judged in terms of the amount of time it is available for use:

$$\text{Availability} = \frac{\text{mean time to failure (MTTF)}}{\text{MTTF} + \text{mean time to repair}}$$

MTBF values can be used in place of MTTF.

 SIX SIGMA TOOLS AT WORK

Determining Availability

Windshield wiper motors are readily available and easy to install. Calculate the availability of the windshield wipers on a bus driven eight hours a day, if the mean time between failure or average life θ is 1250 hours. When the windshield wiper motor must be replaced, the bus is out of service for a total of 24 hours.

$$\text{Availability} = \frac{\text{mean time between failure (MTBF)}}{\text{MTBF} + \text{mean time to repair}}$$

$$= \frac{1250}{1250 + 24} = 0.98$$

The bus is available 98 percent of the time.

Calculating System Reliability

When system performance is dependent on the number of cycles completed successfully, such as the number of times a coin operated washing machine accepts the coins and begins operation, then reliability is measured in terms of the probability of successful operation. **Reliability** is the probability that a product will not fail during a particular time period. Like probability, reliability takes on numerical values between 0.0 and 1.0. A reliability value of 0.78 is interpreted as 78 out of 100 parts will function as expected during a particular time period and 22 will not. If n is the total number of units being tested and s represents those units performing satisfactorily, then reliability R is given by

$$R = \frac{s}{n}$$

System reliability is determined by considering the reliability of the components and parts of the system.

Figure 14.2   System in Series

Reliability in Series

A system in series exists if proper system functioning depends on whether all the components in the system are functioning. Failure of any one component will cause system failure. Figure 14.2 portrays an example of a system in series. In the diagram, the system will function only if all four components are functioning. If one component fails, the entire system will cease functioning. The reliability of a system in series is dependent on the individual component reliabilities. To calculate series system reliability the individual independent component reliabilities are multiplied together:

$$R_s = r_1 \cdot r_2 \cdot r_3 \cdots \cdot r_n$$

where

$$R_s = \text{reliability of series system}$$
$$r_i = \text{reliability of component}$$
$$n = \text{number of components in system}$$

σ SIX SIGMA TOOLS AT WORK

Calculating Reliability in a Series System

The reliability values for the flashlight components pictured in Figure 14.3 are listed below. If the components work in series, what is the reliability of the system?

Battery	0.75	Screw cap	0.97
Lightbulb	0.85	Body	0.99
Switch	0.98	Lens	0.99
Spring	0.99		

$$R_s = r_1 \cdot r_2 \cdot r_3 \cdots \cdot r_n$$
$$= 0.75 \cdot 0.98 \cdot 0.85 \cdot 0.99 \cdot 0.97 \cdot 0.99 \cdot 0.99$$
$$= 0.59$$

This flashlight has a reliability of only 0.59. Perhaps the owner of this flashlight ought to keep two on hand!

The reliability of a system decreases as more components are added in series. This means that the series system reliability will never be greater than the reliability of the least reliable component. Sustained performance over the life of a product or process

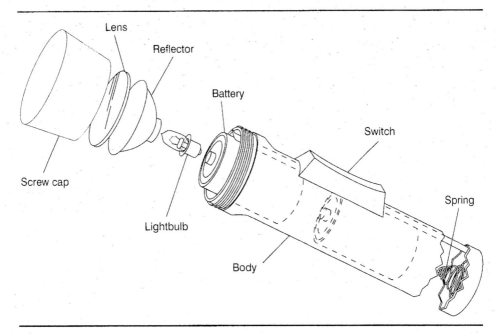

Figure 14.3   Flashlight

can be enhanced in several ways. Parallel systems and redundant or standby component configurations can be used to increase the overall system reliability.

Reliability in Parallel

A **parallel system** *is a system that is able to function if at least one of its components is functioning.* Figure 14.4 displays a system in parallel. The system will function provided at
least one component has not failed. In a parallel system, all of the components that
are in parallel with each other must fail in order to have a system failure. This is the
opposite of a series system in which, if one component fails, the entire system fails.
Since the duplicated or paralleled component takes over functioning for the failed
part, the reliability of this type of system is calculated on the basis of the sum of the
probabilities of the favorable outcomes: the probability that no components fail and

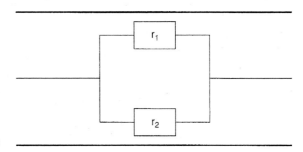

Figure 14.4   Parallel System

the combinations of the successful operation of one component but not the other(s). The reliability of a parallel system is given by

$$R_p = 1 - (1 - r_1)(1 - r_2)(1 - r_3) \cdots (1 - r_n)$$

where

$$R_p = \text{reliability of parallel system}$$
$$r_i = \text{reliability of component}$$
$$n = \text{number of components in system}$$

 SIX SIGMA TOOLS AT WORK

Determining Reliability in a Parallel System

On a twin engine aircraft, two alternators support a single electric system. If one were to fail, the other would allow the electrical system to continue to function. As shown in Figure 14.5 these alternators each have a reliability of 0.9200. Calculate their parallel reliability:

$$R_p = 1 - (1 - r_1)(1 - r_2)$$
$$= 1 - (1 - 0.9200)(1 - 0.9200) = 0.9936$$

Even though the alternators' reliability values individually are 0.9200, when combined they have a system reliability of 0.9936.

System reliability increases as components are added to a parallel system. Reliability in a parallel system will be no less than the reliability of the most reliable component. Parallel redundancy is often used to increase the reliability of a critical system; however, at some point there is a diminishing rate of return where the added costs outweigh the increased reliability. Parallel components are just one type of redundancy used to increase system reliability.

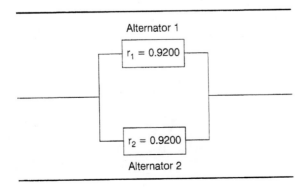

Alternator 1
$r_1 = 0.9200$

$r_2 = 0.9200$

Alternator 2

Figure 14.5   Systems in Parallel: Alternators

Reliability in Redundant Systems and Backup Components

Backup or spare components, used only if a primary component fails, increase overall system reliability. The likelihood of needing to access the spare or backup component in relation to the reliability of the primary component is shown mathematically as

$$R_b = r_1 + r_b(1 - r_1)$$

where

R_b = reliability of backup system
r_1 = reliability of primary component
r_b = reliability of backup component
r_1 = chance of having to use backup

 SIX SIGMA TOOLS AT WORK

Calculating Reliability in a Redundant System

A local hospital uses a generator to provide backup power in case of a complete electrical power failure. This generator is used to fuel the equipment in key areas of the hospital such as the operating rooms and intensive care units. In the past few years, the power supply system has been very reliable (0.9800). There has been only one incident where the hospital lost power. The generator is tested frequently to ensure that it is capable of operating at a moment's notice. It too is very reliable (0.9600). Calculate the reliability of this system:

$$R_b = r_1 + r_b(1 - r_1)$$
$$= 0.9800 + 0.9600(1 - 0.9800) = 0.9992$$

The overall reliability of this redundant system is 0.9992.

Reliability in Systems

Designers often use the advantages of parallel and redundant systems on critical components of an overall system. As the next Six Sigma Tools at Work feature shows, calculating the reliability of such a system involves breaking down the overall system into groups of series, parallel, and redundant components.

 SIX SIGMA TOOLS AT WORK

Calculating the Reliability of a Combination System

In an endeavor to discourage thievery, a local firm has installed the alarm system shown in Figure 14.6 This system contains series, parallel, and backup components. Calculate the reliability of the system.

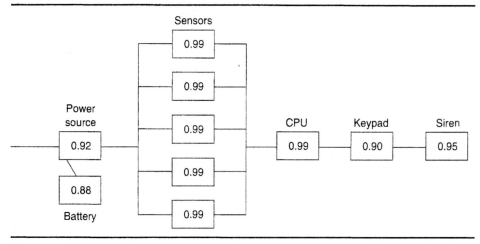

Figure 14.6   Reliability Diagram: Alarm System

To calculate the overall system reliability, begin by determining the overall reliability of the components in parallel. The combined reliability of the five sensors is

$$R_p = 1 - (1 - r_1)(1 - r_2)(1 - r_3) \cdots (1 - r_n)$$
$$= 1 - (1 - 0.99)(1 - 0.99)(1 - 0.99)(1 - 0.99)(1 - 0.99)$$
$$= 1.0$$

The combined reliability of the power source and battery is

$$R_b = r_1 + r_b(1 - r_1)$$
$$= 0.92 + 0.88(1 - 0.92)$$
$$= 0.99$$

The overall reliability of the system is

$$R_s = r_p \cdot r_{cpu} \cdot r_{keypad} \cdot r_{siren} \cdot r_b$$
$$= 1.0 \cdot 0.99 \cdot 0.90 \cdot 0.95 \cdot 0.99$$
$$= 0.84$$

The overall reliability of the system is 0.84.

SUMMARY

Six Sigma organizations study product or system reliability in order to predict its useful life. Reliability tests are conducted to determine if the predicted reliability has been achieved. Reliability programs are designed to improve product or system reliability through improved product design, manufacturing processes, maintenance, and servicing. Reliability engineers work to incorporate the aspects of reliability into products and services from their conception to useful life.

σ ■ Take Away Tips

1. Reliability refers to quality over the long term. The system's intended function, expected life, and environmental conditions all play a role in determining system reliability.
2. The three phases of a product's life cycle are early failure, chance failure, and wear-out.
3. Reliability tests aid in determining if distinct patterns of failure exist.
4. Failure rates can be determined by dividing the number of failures observed by the sum of their test times.
5. θ, or the average life, is the inverse of the failure rate.
6. A system's availability can be calculated by determining the mean time to failure and dividing that value by the total of the mean time to failure plus the mean time to repair.
7. Reliability is the probability that failure will not occur during a particular time period.
8. For a system in series, failure of any one component will cause system failure. The reliability of a series system will never be greater than that of its least reliable component.
9. For a system in parallel, all of the components in parallel must fail to have system failure. The reliability in a parallel system will be no less than the reliability of the most reliable component.
10. Overall system reliability can be increased through the use of parallel, backup, or redundant components.
11. Reliability programs are enacted to incorporate reliability concepts into system designs. A well thought out reliability program will include the eight considerations presented in this chapter. ■

σ ■ Formulas

$$\lambda_{estimated} = \frac{\text{number of failures observed}}{\text{sum of test times or cycles}}$$

$$\theta_{estimated} = \frac{1}{\lambda}$$

or

$$\theta_{estimated} = \frac{\text{sum of test times or cycles}}{\text{number of failures observed}}$$

$$\text{Availability} = \frac{\text{mean time to failure (MTTF)}}{\text{MTTF} + \text{mean time to repair}}$$

(MTBF values can be used in place of MTTF.)

$$R = \frac{s}{n}$$

$$R_s = r_1 \cdot r_2 \cdot r_3 \cdot \cdots \cdot r_n$$

$$R_p = 1 - (1 - r_1)(1 - r_2)(1 - r_3) \cdots (1 - r_n)$$

$$R_b = r_1 + r_b(1 - r_1)$$

Chapter Questions

1. Define reliability in your own words. Describe the key elements and why they are important.

2. Describe the three phases of the life history curve. Draw the curve and label it in detail (the axes, phases, type of product failure, etc.).

3. Determine the failure rate λ for the following: You have tested circuit boards for failures during a 500-hour continuous use test. Four of the 25 boards failed. The first board failed in 80 hours, the second failed in 150 hours, the third failed in 350 hours, the fourth in 465 hours. The other boards completed the 500-hour test satisfactorily. What is the mean life of the product?

4. Determine the failure rate for a 90-hour test of 12 items where 2 items fail at 45 and 72 hours, respectively. What is the mean life of the product?

5. A power station has installed ten new generators to provide electricity for a local metropolitan area. In the past year (8,776 hours), two of those generators have failed, one at 2,460 hours and one at 5,962 hours. It took five days, working 24 hours a day, to repair *each* generator. Using one year as the test period, what is the mean time between failure for these generators? Given the repair information, what is the availability of all ten generators?

6. Why is a parallel system more reliable than a system in series?

7. Given the system below, what is the system reliability?

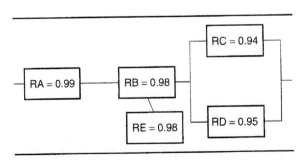

Question 7

8. Given the diagram of the system below, what is the system reliability?

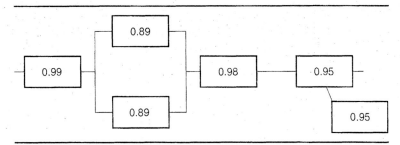

Question 8

9. What is the reliability of the system below?

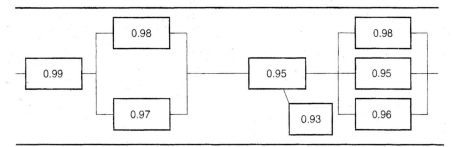

Question 9

10. Airbags are concealed in the center of the steering wheel and in dash-boards. When the front end of the vehicle strikes another object, the airbag inflates. The airbag will fully inflate upon impact in one-tenth of a second, providing a barrier to protect the driver. More advanced airbag systems have smart sensors which sense key elements related to the accident and determine the amount of force the detonator needs to emit. The diagram below shows the key elements that must operate in order for the airbag to inflate. Calculate the reliability of the system.

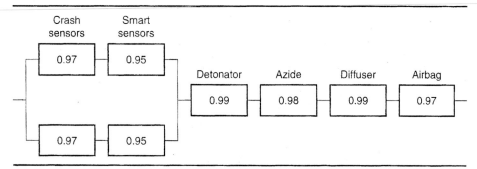

Question 10

11. Often we think of reliability as an equipment based system, however, reliable systems are needed in other, more human oriented systems. As reported in the *Wall Street Journal* article "It's 9 P.M., Do You Know Where You Parked Your Car?" guest services managers at all major parking lots have systems in place designed to reunite patrons with their vehicles. The reliability of these systems is dependent on the reliability of the components, the location finding aids. In many major parking lots, two methods are used at once: the guest's memory as well as a license plate information location computer program. First, though, guest services needs to recognize that a guest is lost. Find the reliability of the car locating system shown below.

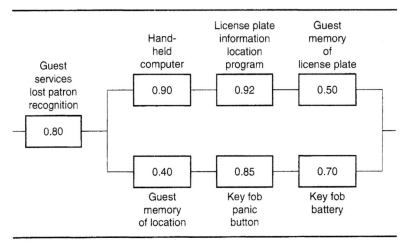

Question 11

15

Failure Modes and Effects Analysis

Will it fail?
What happens then?

■ **Objectives:**

1. To familiarize the reader with the concept of failure modes and effects analysis
2. To teach the reader to perform a failure modes and effects analysis ■

Six Sigma practitioners view failure modes and effects analysis (FMEA) as an effective failure prevention technique. FMEA is a systematic approach to identifying both the ways that a product, part, process, or service can fail and the effects of those failures. Once identified, these potential failure modes are rated by the severity of their effects and the probability the failure will occur. FMEAs generate a list of potential failures, rank the critical characteristics, and generate a list of actions that can be taken to eliminate the causes of failures or at least reduce their rate of occurrence. FMEAs are critical in the design of any system, process, service, or product, especially since they help identify potential failure modes that may adversely affect safety or government regulation compliance. Moreover, they identify these problems before the process or system is used or the product is put into production. Six Sigma organizations utilize FMEA to improve the quality and reliability of their products, services, and processes. Three types of FMEAs exist: system, process, and design.

SYSTEMS FMEA

Systems enable organizations to accomplish tasks on a grand scale. Insurance companies have systems that enable them to process a high volume of claims every day. Manufacturing systems allow users to track customer orders, inventory usage, and production rates. A systems FMEA focuses on the big picture in order to optimize system designs, whether for services or manufacturing industries, determining the possible ways the system can fail. System FMEAs study the functions of the system and reveal whether or not design deficiencies exist. System FMEAs also study the interactions of the system with other systems and how subsystems within the system support and interact with each other.

PROCESS FMEA

Process FMEAs assist in the design or redesign of manufacturing, assembly, or service processes. Process FMEAs identify the different ways that a process could fail and the effects of those failures. With this information, processes can be changed, controls can be developed, or detection methods can be put into place that will eliminate the possibility of process failure. Because they focus on potential process deficiencies, Six Sigma practitioners often use process FMEAs to identify and rank process improvement opportunities.

DESIGN FMEA

Design FMEAs focus on products. Used during the product development stage, design FMEAs seek to identify potential product failure modes and the likelihood of those failures occurring. Design FMEAs assist in evaluating product design requirements and alternatives. Because they identify design deficiencies, they alert manufacturers to potential safety concerns.

CREATING AN FMEA

Though the focus of the three types of FMEAs is different, their construction is similar. To conduct an FMEA, use a form similar to the one shown in Figure 15.1. The form should identify the FMEA, the system, process, or part under study, those responsible, important dates, and any other key data. Once the headings are complete, users brainstorm potential failure modes, causes, effects, and probabilities of occurrence.

FMEAs begin with the study of the system, process, or part. This information is listed by item and function (Figure 15.2). When studying the system, process, service, or part, ask these types of questions to help understand the system, process, service, or part:

> Where and how will this system (process, service, part) be used?
> In what conditions will this system (process, service, part) operate?
> What are the interactions with other systems (processes, services, parts)?
> What is the ultimate function of this system (process, service, part)?

Potential failure modes are the many different ways in which a system, process, service, or part may fail to perform its intended function (Figure 15.2). For each item, when determining potential failure modes, ask these types of questions:

> How can this system (process, service, part) fail to perform its intended function?
> How would it be recognized that it didn't perform its intended function?
> What could go wrong?
> How would it be recognized that something has gone wrong?

Potential failure causes are the different conditions that must be in place in order for the system, process, service, or part to fail (Figure 15.2). Be sure to find the proximate or true cause of the failure. For each item's potential failure mode, when determining potential failure causes, ask these types of questions:

> What might have triggered this reaction in the system (process, service, part)?
> What factors need to be in place to cause this failure to occur in the system (process, service, part)?
> What would cause this system (process, service, part) to fail in this manner?
> Under what circumstances would this system (process, service, part) fail to perform its intended function?

Failure Modes and Effects Analysis

System (Process, Part) _____

Date _____

Team _____

Item	Function	Potential Failure Modes	Potential Causes	Failure Effect	Existing Controls, Countermeasures, Detection Methods	Probability	Severity	Risk Priority Code	Recommended Action, Responsibility, Target Date

Figure 15.1 Failure Modes and Effects Analysis Format

Failure Modes and Effects Analysis

System (Process, Service, Part)   Vehicle Exterior Lighting System

Team SS 1   Date 2/14/06

Item	Function	Potential Failure Modes	Potential Causes	Failure Effect	Existing Controls, Counter-measures, Detection Methods	Probability	Severity	Risk Priority Code	Recommended Action, Responsibility, Target Date
Headlamp System	Provide lighting for vehicle traveling at night	Lightbulb fails to light	Burnt out Not receiving electric current	No light	Visual maintenance check				
		Electric current failure	Wire failure Detached Short	No light	Visual maintenance check				
		Actuation switch failure	Short Broken	No light	Visual maintenance check				
Turn indicator system	Provide turn signals information to nearby vehicles	Lightbulb fails to light	Burnt out No current	No signal lights	Visual maintenance check				
		Electric current failure							
		Actuation switch failure							

Figure 15.2   Vehicle Exterior Lighting System FMEA

What can cause this system (process, service, part) to fail to deliver its intended function?

The potential failure effect is the consequence(s) of a system, process, service, or part failing (Figure 15.2). For each item's potential failure mode, when determining potential failure effects, ask these types of questions:

If the system (process, service, part) fails, what will be the consequences on the operation, function, or status of the system (process, service, part)?
If the system (process, service, part) fails, what will be the consequences on the operation, function, or status of the related systems (processes, service, parts)?
If the system (process, service, part) fails, what will be the consequences for the customer?
If the system (process, service, part) fails, what will be the consequence on government regulations?

FMEAs capture the existing conditions or controls currently in place that work to prevent system, process, service, or part failure. These methods or controls are recorded on the FMEA for each failure mode. These existing countermeasures answer the questions:

How will this cause of failure be recognized?
How can this cause of failure be prevented?
How can this cause of failure be minimized?
How can this cause of failure be mitigated?

The severity of a failure refers to the seriousness of the effect of a potential failure mode. Having completed the sections of the FMEA dealing with failures, causes, and effects (modes), the severity of each effect must be assessed. Severity ratings can range from no effect to hazardous effect. How many severity ratings used in an FMEA is up to those creating it. Figure 15.3 provides examples of severity ratings.

FMEAs also estimate the probability of occurrence or the estimated frequency at which failure may occur during the life of the system, process, or part. In other words, what is the likelihood of this type of failure from this particular cause happening? The probability of occurrence can rank from impossible to almost certain. Figure 15.4 provides examples of occurrences ratings.

Using a risk priority code (RPC), FMEAs rank failures according to their severity and their chance of occurring. Risk priority codes identify and rank the potential design weaknesses so that users can focus their efforts and actions toward eliminating the most probable causes with the most severe results. As shown in Figure 15.5, a risk priority code is the product of the severity rating and the probability of occurrence. Items with RPCs of one are dealt with first.

Effect	Criteria
No Effect	No effect
Very Slight Effect	Very slight effect on performance, customer not annoyed. Non-vital component failure rarely noticed.
Slight Effect	Slight effect on performance. Customer slightly annoyed. Non-vital component failure noticed occasionally.
Minor Effect	Minor effect on performance. Customer will notice minor effect on system performance. Non-vital component failure always noticed.
Moderate Effect	Moderate effect on performance. Customer experiences some dissatisfaction. Non-vital component requires repair.
Significant Effect	Performance degraded, but operable and safe. Customer experiences discomfort. Non-vital component inoperable.
Major Effect	Performance severely affected but operable and safe. Customer dissatisfied. Subsystem inoperable.
Extreme Effect	Inoperable but safe. Customer very dissatisfied. System inoperable.
Serious Effect	Potentially hazardous effect. Compliance with government regulations in jeopardy.
Hazardous Effect	Hazardous effect. Safety-related. Sudden failure. Noncompliance with government regulations.

Figure 15.3   Severity Rating Examples

Occurrence	Criteria
Almost Impossible	Failure unlikely
Improbable	Rare number of failures likely
Remote	Very few failures likely
Possible	Few failures likely
Occasional	Occasional failures likely
Probable	Several failures likely
Moderately High	A moderate number of failures likely
Frequent	A high number of failures likely
Very High	A very high number of failures likely
Almost Certain	Failure almost certain to occur

Figure 15.4   Occurrence Ratings Examples

When FMEAs are complete, Six Sigma practitioners develop recommended actions designed to prevent or reduce the occurence of failure. Starting with items with an RPC equal to one, these actions are designed to reduce the chance of failure occurring as well as the consequences associated with failure. These recommendations will include responsibilities, target completion dates, and reporting requirements for the actions taken.

	Probability of Mishap					
Severity of Consequences	F Impossible	E Improbable	D Remote	C Occasional	B Probable	A Frequent
I Catastrophic			2		1	
II Critical				2		
III Marginal			3		2	2
IV Negligible						

Risk Zones		
Code		Action
1		Imperative to suppress
2		Operation requires written guidelines to operate
3		Operation permissible

Note: Personnel must not be exposed to hazards in Risk Zones 1 and 2.

Probability of Mishap		
Level	Descriptive Word	Definition
A	Frequent	Likely to occur repeatedly during life cycle of system
B	Probable	Likely to occur several times in life cycle of system
C	Occasional	Likely to occur some time in life cycle of system
D	Remote	Not likely to occur in life cycle of system, but possible
E	Improbable	Probability of occurrences cannot be distinguished from zero
F	Impossible	Physically impossible to occur

Figure 15.5   Risk Priority Codes

SIX SIGMA TOOLS AT WORK

Failure Modes and Effects Analysis

RQ Inc.'s management is concerned about overall air quality within the plant, particularly the plating department. Some of the materials used in this room can have an adverse effect on humans. For this reason, people in this room must wear personal protective devices. This area, located on an outside wall, is separated from the rest of the plant by floor-to-ceiling walls. Access to the area is limited to two doors. In order to verify the effectiveness of the proposed ventilation system upgrade, which consists of two exhaust fans with filters, RQ Inc.'s Six Sigma team conducted an FMEA (Figure 15.6).

Failure Modes and Effects Analysis

System (Process, Service, Part) Ventilation System

Team Jim, Norm, Peg   Date 4/15/06

Item	Function	Potential Failure Modes	Potential Causes	Failure Effect	Existing Controls, Counter-measures, Detection Methods	Probability	Severity	Risk Priority Code	Recommended Action, Responsibility, Target Date
Ventilation system exhaust fans	Maintain quality of air	Electrical: power short	Faulty wiring, crossed wiring, damaged insulation	Unacceptable level of toxins in air causing eye and skin irritation, lung and brain damage	Smoke detector	Occasional	Critical	2	Investigate design of exhaust electrical system
	Maintain quality of air circulation	Electrical: power failure	Power outage	Unacceptable level of toxins in air causing eye and skin irritation, lung and brain damage	None	Occasional	Critical	2	Investigate design of exhaust electrical system
		Broken fan blades	Faulty workmanship, damage by foreign object	Unacceptable level of toxins in air causing eye and skin irritation, lung and brain damage	Visual inspection	Improbable	Critical	3	

(continued)

Figure 15.6 Ventilation System FMEA

Function	Failure mode	Cause	Effect	Detection	Probability	Severity	Rating	Action
Maintain quality of air Maintain air circulation	Interference with fan blade rotation	Dirty, damaged during installation, poor design, damaged by foreign object	Fire, unacceptable level of toxins in air causing eye and skin irritation, lung and brain damage	Visual inspection, noise heard	Remote	Critical	3	
	Corrosion of motor works	Dirty, damaged during installation, poor design, damaged by foreign object	Unacceptable level of toxins in air causing eye and skin irritation, lung and brain damage	Visual inspection	Occasional	Critical	2	Establish preventive maintenance program for ventilation system
	Excessive dirt and grime on blades, unit unable to circulate air effectively	No routine maintenance	Unacceptable level of toxins in air causing eye and skin irritation, lung and brain damage	Visual inspection	Probable	Critical	1	Establish preventive maintenance program for ventilation system
	Power rating not correct or insufficient to circulate air	Not designed or selected correctly	Unacceptable level of toxins in air causing eye and skin irritation, lung and brain damage	Engineering design review	Remote	Critical	3	
Employees	Employees forget to turn on fans	No process in place for operation of fans	Unacceptable level of toxins in air causing eye and skin irritation, lung and brain damage	Visual inspection	Probable	Critical	1	Create procedures for ventilation system operation and enforce

Figure 15.6 (continued)

Item	Function	Failure mode	Cause	Effect	Detection	Occurrence	Severity	Rating	Recommended action
		Employees fail to notice if fans are on or not	No process in place for operation of fans	Unacceptable level of toxins in air causing eye and skin irritation, lung and brain damage	Visual inspection	Probable	Critical	1	Create procedures for ventilation system operation and enforce
		Employees don't know when to turn fans on	No process in place for operation of fans	Unacceptable level of toxins in air causing eye and skin irritation, lung and brain damage	None	Frequent	Critical	1	Create procedures for ventilation system operation and enforce
		Blockage of fan or air duct system	No routine maintenance	Unacceptable level of toxins in air causing eye and skin irritation, lung and brain damage	Visual inspection	Occasional	Critical	2	Establish preventive maintenance program for ventilation system
Power source	Provide electricity for fans	Loss of power	Loss of power from company	Unacceptable level of toxins in air causing eye and skin irritation, lung and brain damage	Visual	Occasional	Critical	2	Install emergency backup generators
			Internal failure	Unacceptable level of toxins in air causing eye and skin irritation, lung and brain damage	Visual	Occasional	Critical	2	Install emergency backup generators

Figure 15.6 (continued)

The Six Sigma team began their FMEA by listing the primary items and their functions in the ventilation system: exhaust fans, employees, and the power source. Their next step involved determining all of the potential failure modes for each of the primary items. Having established the list of potential failure modes, they identified potential causes for each potential failure. They also listed the effects of the failures. Existing controls, failure detection methods, and countermeasures were recorded next. Once a complete list of the potential failures and their causes and effects were identified, the team determined probabilities and severities in order to assign a risk priority code for each potential failure. Having completed the matrix, the team undertook the critical step of recommending specific actions, including target dates and responsibilities, in order to eliminate or reduce the probability or severity of a failure occurring.

Beginning with the RPCs with a value of one, the team first needs to investigate why no routine maintenance takes place. Their recommended action is to establish a preventive maintenance program for the ventilation system. A second set of RPCs with a value of one are all related to employee procedures. If the employees forget to turn on the ventilation system, fail to check if the fans are operational, or don't understand when to turn on the fans, the ventilation system cannot operate effectively. The Six Sigma teams recommends the creation and enforcement of procedures for ventilation system operation. They also recommend investigating the purchase of an air quality monitoring system designed to automatically activate the ventilation fans. Once the RPCs of one have been taken care of, the team can attack those with RPCs of two.

SUMMARY

Failure modes and effects analysis is an excellent method for capturing the relationship between the customer requirements and how a system, process, service, or part may fail to meet these requirements. It identifies the causes and effects of the failures within a system, process, service, or part by critically examining a system, process, service, or part. Once identified by the FMEA, weaknesses in the system, process, service, or part can be eliminated or strengthened.

σ *Take Away Tips*

1. FMEA is a method that seeks to identify failures and keep them from occurring.
2. FMEA divides the system, process, service, or part into manageable segments and records the ways the segment may fail.
3. FMEA uses the risk priority code to rate the degree of hazard associated with failure.
4. When complete, recommendations are made to eliminate the risk priority codes with a value of one. ■

Chapter Questions

1. Why do Six Sigma practitioners use failure modes and effects analysis?
2. Describe the three types of FMEAs discussed in this chapter.
3. Describe the steps involved in creating an FMEA.
4. Create and analyze an FMEA for a refrigerator.
5. Create and analyze an FMEA for a chain saw.
6. Create and analyze an FMEA for a prescription filling process.
7. Create and analyze an FMEA for the operation of a lathe, mill, or drill.
8. Create and analyze an FMEA for a hospital patient check-in procedure.
9. Create and analyze an FMEA for a food preparation area in a restaurant.
10. Create and analyze an FMEA for a product, service, or process that you are familiar with.

16

Design of Experiments

Analyzing historical data is a reactive approach to process improvement. In order to proactively study processes, Six Sigma practitioners use design of experiments to determine which process changes will work best.

■ Objectives:

1. To introduce the concept of design of experiments
2. To introduce the different styles of experiments
3. To introduce the terminology associated with design of experiments
4. To introduce the structure of a designed experiment ■

DESIGN OF EXPERIMENTS

Six Sigma organizations seek to optimize their processes, products, and services. A technique called design of experiments enables users to study the changes they plan to make to a process or product and determine whether or not these changes result in optimization. **Design of experiments (DOE)** *is a method of experimenting with the complex interactions among parameters in a process or product with the objective of optimizing the process or product.* To design an experiment means creating a situation in which an organized investigation into all the different factors that can affect process or product parameters occurs. The design of the experiment provides a layout of the different factors and the values at which those factors are to be tested.

A complete study of designing experiments is beyond the scope of this text. The following information is meant to serve as an introduction to design of experiments. The coverage of experiment design in this text is designed to provide the reader with a basic understanding of the terminology, concepts, and setups associated with experiment design. Readers interested in an in-depth study of experiment design should seek one of the many excellent texts in the area.

Trial and Error Experiments

A trial and error experiment involves making an educated guess about what should be done to effect change in a process or system. Trial and error experiments lack direction and focus. They are hindered by the effectiveness of the guesswork of those designing the experiments. In other words, a good solution to the problem may be found by using this method, but in all likelihood this hit or miss approach will yield nothing useful.

 SIX SIGMA TOOLS AT WORK

A Trial and Error Experiment

Researchers are studying the effects of tire pressure, vehicle speed, oil type, and gas type on gas mileage.

Speed	55 mph, 65 mph
Tire Pressure	28 psi, 35 psi
Oil	30 weight, 40 weight
Gas	Regular, Premium

As seen in Figure 16.1, many different permutations of the variables exist. As more variables are factored into an experiment, the complexity increases dramatically. If an experimenter were to randomly select speed, tire pressure, oil, and gas settings, he or she may have a difficult time determining which settings provide the best gas mileage. Since random selection is not an organized approach, it is not the best use of time and materials. Essentially, it is guesswork. Design of experiments is a method to arrive at the optimum settings more effectively.

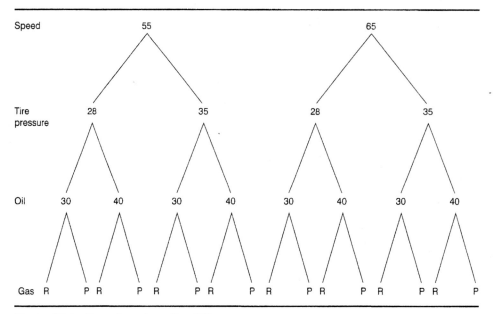

Speed

Tire pressure

Oil

Gas

Figure 16.1   Experiment on Gas Mileage

A properly designed experiment seeks to determine:

> which factors significantly affect the system under study
> how the magnitude of the factors affect the system
> the optimal level for each of the selected factors
> how to manipulate the factors to control the response

The experiment design must determine:

> the number of factors to include in the experiment
> the levels at which each factor will be tested
> the response variable
> the number of trials to be conducted at each level for each factor
> the conditions (settings) for each trial

Definitions

In order to better explain the concepts, an understanding of the vocabulary is very helpful. The following terms are commonly used in the design of experiments.

> Factor: A factor is the variable the experimenter will vary in order to determine its effect on a response variable. A factor is the variable that is set at different levels during an experiment, and results of those changes are observed. It may be time, temperature, an operator, or any other aspect of the system that can be controlled.
> Level: A level is the value chosen for the experiment and assigned to change the factor. For instance: Temperature; Level 1: 110° F; Level 2: 150° F.
> Controllable Factor: When a factor is controllable it is possible to establish and maintain the particular level throughout the experiment.

Effect: The effect is the result or outcome of the experiment. It is the value of the change in the response variable produced by a change in the factor level(s). The effect is the change exhibited by the response variable when the factor level is changed.

Response Variable: The variable(s) of interest used to describe the reaction of a process to variations in control variables (factors). It is the quality characteristic under study, the variable we want to have an effect on.

Degrees of Freedom: At its simplest level, the degrees of freedom in an experiment can be determined by examining the number of levels. For a factor with three levels, L_1 data can be compared with L_2 and L_3 data, but not with itself. Thus a factor with three levels has two degrees of freedom. Extending this to an experiment, the degrees of freedom can be calculated by multiplying the number of treatments by the number of repetitions of each trial and subtracting one ($f = n \times r - 1$).

Interaction: Two or more factors that together produce a result different than what the result of their separate effects would be. Well designed experiments allow two or more factor interactions to be tested, where other trial and error models only allow the factors to be independently evaluated.

Noise Factor: A noise factor is an uncontrollable, but measurable, source of variation in the functional characteristics of a product or process. This error term is used to evaluate the significance of changes in the factor levels.

Treatment: The specific combination of levels for each factor used for a particular run. The number of treatments is based on the number of factors and the levels associated with each factor. For example, if two factors (1, 2) exist and each can be at two levels (A, B), then four treatments are possible. The treatments are factor 1 at level A, factor 1 at level B, factor 2 at level A, factor 2 at level B. A treatment table will show all the levels of each factor for each run.

Run: A run is an experimental trial, the application of one treatment.

Replicate: When an experiment is replicated, it refers to a repeat of the treatment condition. The treatment is begun again from scratch.

Repetition: Repetitions are multiple runs of a particular treatment condition. Repeated measurements are taken from the same setup.

Significance: Significance is a statistical test used to indicate whether a factor or factor combination caused a significant change in the response variable. It shows the importance of a change in a factor in either a statistical sense or in a practical sense.

 SIX SIGMA TOOLS AT WORK

An Experiment Defined

A new product development team at MAR Manufacturing has been investigating the parameters surrounding their new part (Figure 16.2). The customer has specified that the part meet very tight tolerances for pierce height. A variety of factors are involved in

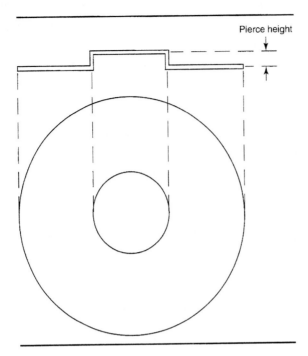

Figure 16.2 MAR Part

holding this tolerance. The team would like to determine which of three proposed material suppliers to use. Though all three meet MAR's specifications for material yield and tensile strength and for material thickness, there are minute differences in material properties. Because of the interactions with the material, the experiment will also need to determine which machine setting is optimal. For this 35 ton press, the experimenters would like to determine which setting—20, 25, or 30 tons—is appropriate. Several members of the team have worked together to design an appropriate experiment to test their assumptions. To better describe the experiment to other members of their group, they have created the following explanation based on DOE definitions.

Factor: Since factors are variables that are changed during an experiment, two factors in this experiment exist: material supplier and press tonnage. Team members believe that changes to these two factors will affect the response variable, pierce height.

Level: A level is the value assigned to change the factor. In this case, each factor has three levels: supplier (A, B, C) and press tonnage (20, 25, 30).

Supplier	Press Tonnage
A	20
B	25
C	30

Controllable Factor: When a factor is controllable it is possible to establish and maintain the particular level throughout the experiment. In this experiment, investigators are able to set the levels for both the material supplier and press tonnage factors.

Effect: The effect is the result or outcome of the experiment. Here the experimenters are interested in consistent pierce height, which is measured as shown in Figure 16.2.

Response Variable: The variable used to describe the reaction of a process to variations in the factors. In this example, the response variable is the pierce height.

Treatment: Since the number of treatments is based on the number of factors and the levels associated with each factor, and both factors have three levels, supplier (A, B, C) and press tonnage (20, 25, 30), the result is $3 \times 3 = 9$ treatments:

Supplier	Press Tonnage
A	20
A	25
A	30
B	20
B	25
B	30
C	20
C	25
C	30

Degrees of Freedom: The degree of freedom in an experiment is the total number of levels for all factors minus 1. Here we have three levels for each factor ($3 \times 3 = 9$) so our degrees of freedom is $9 - 1$ or 8.

Interaction: Since the two factors, supplier and press tonnage, will together produce a result different than what would result if only one or the other were changed, there is an interaction between the two that must be considered in the experiment.

Noise Factor: A noise factor is an uncontrollable but measurable source of variation. For this experiment, noise factors may be material thickness, material properties, and press operating temperatures.

Run: A run is an experimental trial, the application of one treatment to one experimental unit. The supplier A, press tonnage 25 combination is one run.

Replicate: When an experiment is replicated, it refers to a repeat of the treatment condition, a complete redo of the design.

Repetition: Repetitions are multiple results of a treatment condition; for example, the experimenters ran the supplier B, press tonnage 20 combination multiple times.

Significance: The determination of whether or not the changes to the factor levels had a significant effect on the response variable. In other words, did changing suppliers or press tonnage significantly affect pierce height?

Conducting an Experiment: Steps in Planned Experimentation

First and foremost, *plan your experiment!* Successful experiments depend on how well they are planned. Before creating the design of an experiment, those involved must gain a thorough understanding of the process being studied. Achieving a deep understanding of the process will allow those designing the experiment to identify the factors in the process or product that influence the outcome. While planning an experiment, answer the following questions:

What are you investigating?
What is the objective of your experiment?
What are you hoping to learn more about?
What are the critical factors?
Which of the factors can be controlled?
What resources will be used?

The following are typical steps in conducting an experiment:

1. *Establish the purpose by defining the problem.* Before beginning an experiment design, the experimenters should determine the purpose of the experiment. Knowing the objectives and goals of an experiment can help the experimenters select the most appropriate experiment design as well as analysis methods.

2. *Identify the components of the experiment.* When setting up your experiment, be sure to include the following critical information:

The number of factors the design will consider.
The number of levels (options) for each factor.
The settings for each level.
The response factor.
The number of trials to be conducted.

3. *Design the experiment.* Determine the appropriate structure of the experiment. Having determined the factors involved in your experiment, select a study template for your experiment. The types of templates will be covered later in this chapter.

4. *Perform the experiment.* Run your experiment and collect data about the results. Complete the runs as specified by the template at the levels and settings selected.

5. *Analyze the data.* Perform and analyze the resulting response variables in the experiment. Determine which factors were significant in determining the outcome of the response variables. At this point, rather than performing the calculations by hand, it is easier to enter the results into an analysis program, such as DOEpack from PQ Systems. Such software makes it easier to analyze your experiment. Using statistical tools to analyze your data will enable you to determine the optimal levels for each factor. Statistical analysis methods include: Analysis of Variance, Analysis of Means, Regression Analysis, Pairwise Comparison, Response Plots, and Effects Plots.

6. *Act on the results.* Once you have analyzed the information, apply the knowledge you gained from your experiment to the situation under study. Use the information determined about the significant factors to make changes to the process or product.

SIX SIGMA TOOLS AT WORK

Process Improvements Based on Design of Experiments

A process improvement team at KS Manufacturing studied an assembly process that welded two stamped steel parts together as the foundation of a component. The welds often failed in assembly. The goal of the team was to make the process more robust by eliminating weld failures. Team members consisted of representatives from manufacturing, engineering, setup, production, and quality.

The team turned to design of experiments when it became evident that studying the process using other quality tools and techniques hadn't provided the needed breakthrough to improve the process. An experiment based on the welds was designed and conducted. Careful analysis of the results of the runs is critical to gaining knowledge of the process. As they analyzed the results of the experiment, they realized that they were not capturing all of the main process variables. Something outside of the original design created a strong signal. Some unidentified factor that they didn't include in the original experiment was affecting the process.

This situation can sometimes occur with experimental design. Those closest to the process think they know the process inside and out and thus run the risk of overlooking something. Armed with this information, they conducted a second "screening" experiment. The structure of a screening experiment helps identify the true key variables in the process under study. The levels of these key variables can then be optimized in a follow-up experiment. Since they screen out key variables, screening experiments, which fully load the experiment design with variables, are usually the first type of experiment to be run. Is this case, the investigators would have been wiser to begin with such an experiment.

Analysis of the screening experiment enabled them to determine that some parts were cleaner than others. Here, cleaner means that some parts had less lubricant from the stamping process than others. This lubricant on the parts is what generated the noise, the unidentified signal, in the first experiment.

A third experiment was run in which the lubricant from the stamping operation was included as one of the variables. From this experiment, they were able to determine that the lubricant interfered with the ability of the weld to take hold. Excessive lubricant weakened the weld, resulting in the weld failures seen in assembly.

As a result of these experiments, the team decided to eliminate the lubricant variable altogether by changing to a lower viscosity water based lubricant. The end result is a welding process that is very consistent, eliminating the weld failures in assembly.

Experiment Designs

Characteristics of a Good Experiment Design

There are many characteristics associated with good experiment design. An experiment should be as simple as possible to set up and carry out. It should also be straightforward to analyze and interpret, as well as easy to communicate and explain to others. A good experiment design will include all the factors for which changes are possible. A well designed experiment should provide unbiased estimates of process variables and treatment effects (factors at different levels). This means that a well designed experiment will quickly screen out the factors that do not have a pronounced effect upon the response variable while also identifying the best levels for the factors that do have a pronounced effect upon the response variable. The experiment should plan for the analysis of the results, generating results that are free from ambiguity of interpretation. When analyzed, the experiment should provide the precision necessary to enable the experimenter to detect important differences between significant and insignificant variables. The analysis of the experiment must produce understandable results in a form which can be easily communicated to others interested in the information. The analysis should reliably be able to detect any signals that are present in the data. The experiment should point the experimenter in the direction of improvement.

Single Factor Experiments

A single factor experiment allows for the manipulation of only one factor during an experiment. Designers of these experiments select one factor and vary it while holding the other factors constant. The experiment is run for each variation of each factor, and the results are recorded. The objective in a single factor experiment is to isolate the changes in the response variable as they relate to a single factor. Single factor experiments are simple to analyze because only one thing changes at a time and the experimenter can see what effect that change has on the system or process. Unfortunately, single factor experiments are time consuming due to the need to change only one thing at a time, which results in dozens of repeated experiments. Another drawback of these types of experiments is that interactions between factors are not detectable. These experiments rarely arrive at an optimum setup because a change in one factor frequently requires adjustments to one or more of the other factors in order to achieve the best results. In life, single factor changes rarely occur that are not interrelated to other factors.

 SIX SIGMA TOOLS AT WORK

Single Factor Experiment Treatment Table

Researchers are studying the effects of tire pressure, gas type, oil type, and vehicle speed on gas mileage. Problem: What combination of factors provide the best gas mileage?

Factor	Level 1	Level 2
Tire Pressure	28 psi	35 psi
Speed	55 mph	65 mph
Oil	30 weight	40 weight
Gas	Regular	Premium

Response Variable: Gas mileage

Tire	Speed	Oil	Gas
28	55	30	R
35	55	30	R
28	65	30	R
28	55	40	R
28	55	30	P
35	65	40	P
28	65	40	P
35	55	40	P
35	65	30	P
35	65	40	P

In each of these treatments, only one factor is changing at a time. The others are reverting to their original settings (Level 1 or Level 2). Either the remaining three will all be at Level 1 or all at Level 2. Note the complexity this creates when trying to study all the different changes in levels. Realize also that this type of experimentation does not allow experimenters to study the interactions that occur when more than one factor is changed at a time within a treatment. In order to study all the interactions, a full factorial experiment must be conducted.

Full Factorial Experiments

A **full factorial design** *consists of all possible combinations of all selected levels of the factors to be investigated.* This type of experiment examines every possible combination of all factors at all levels. To determine the number of possible combinations or runs, multiply the number of levels for each factor by the number of factors. For example, in an experiment involving six factors at two levels, the total number of combinations will be $2 \times 2 \times 2 \times 2 \times 2 \times 2$, also represented in exponential notation as 2^6 or 64. If the experiment had four factors, two with two levels and two with three levels, a full factorial will have: 2 levels $\times$ 2 levels $\times$ 3 levels $\times$ 3 levels or 36 treatments. A full factorial design allows the most complete analysis because it can determine the:

> main effects of the factors manipulated on response variables
> effects of factor interactions on response variables

A full factorial design can estimate levels at which to set factors for the best results. This type of experiment design is used when adequate time and resources exist to complete all of the runs necessary. A full factorial experiment design is useful when it is important to study all the possible interactions that may exist. Unfortunately, a full factorial experiment design is time consuming and expensive due to the need for numerous runs.

SIX SIGMA TOOLS OF WORK

Full Factorial Experiment Treatment Table

Researchers are studying the effects of tire pressure, gas type, oil type, and vehicle speed on gas mileage. Problem: What combination of factors provide the best gas mileage?

Factor	Level 1	Level 2
Tire Pressure	28 psi	35 psi
Speed	55 mph	65 mph
Oil	30 weight	40 weight
Gas	Regular	Premium

Response variable: gas mileage

Tire	Speed	Oil	Gas
28	55	30	R
35	55	30	R
28	55	30	P
35	55	30	P
28	65	30	R
35	65	30	R
28	65	30	P
35	65	30	P
28	55	40	R
35	55	40	R
28	55	40	P
35	55	40	P
28	65	40	R
35	65	40	R
28	65	40	P
35	65	40	P

The complexity of this type of experimentation can be seen in Figure 16.1. Each path that is followed represents one treatment.

Fractional Factorial Experiments

To reduce the total number of experiments that have to be conducted to a practical level, a limited number of the possibilities shown by a full factorial experiment may be chosen. A fractional factorial experiment studies only a fraction or subset of all the possible combinations. A selected and controlled multiple number of factors are adjusted simultaneously. By using this method, the total number of experiments is reduced. Designed correctly, fractional factorial experiments still reveal the complex interactions between the factors, including which factors are more important than others. One must be careful when selecting the fractional or partial group of experiments to be run to ensure that the critical factors and their interactions are studied. Many different experiment designs

Factors / Treatment	A	B	C	D	E	F	G
1	−	−	−	−	−	−	−
2	−	−	−	+	+	+	+
3	−	+	+	+	+	−	−
4	−	+	+	−	−	+	+
5	+	+	−	−	+	+	−
6	+	+	−	+	−	−	+
7	+	−	+	+	−	+	−
8	+	−	+	−	+	−	+

Figure 16.3 The Basic Eight Run Plackett-Burman Design

exist, including Plackett-Burman Screening designs and Taguchi designs. When utilizing experiments in industry, reference texts and software "programs" can provide a wide variety of experiment designs from which an appropriate experiment design can be selected.

Plackett-Burman Screening Designs

Plackett-Burman screening designs are a subset of fractional factorial experiment designs. They provide an effective way to consider a large number of factors with a minimum number of runs. Users select the most appropriate design for their experiment needs. These screening designs are most effectively used when a large number of factors must be studied and time and resources are limited. Screening designs can be selected from pre-prepared tables from sources such as *Tables of Screening Designs* by Donald Wheeler. Figures 16.3 to 16.6 show several Plackett-Burman designs. The + and − signs show the levels of the factors [Level 1(−), Level 2(+)]. A, B, C, etc., represent the factors. Treatments are labeled 1 to 8.

Factors / Treatment	A	B	C	D	E	F	G	H	I	J	K
1	−	−	−	−	−	−	−	−	−	−	−
2	−	−	−	+	+	+	−	−	+	+	+
3	−	−	+	−	+	+	+	+	−	−	+
4	−	+	+	−	+	−	−	+	+	+	−
5	−	+	+	+	−	−	+	−	+	−	+
6	−	+	−	+	−	+	+	+	−	+	−
7	+	+	−	+	+	−	−	+	−	−	+
8	+	+	−	−	+	+	+	−	+	−	−
9	+	+	+	−	−	+	−	−	−	+	+
10	+	−	+	+	−	+	−	+	+	−	−
11	+	−	+	+	+	−	+	−	−	+	−
12	+	−	−	−	−	−	+	+	+	+	+

Figure 16.4 The Basic 12-Run Plackett-Burman Design

Factors / Treatment	A	B	C	D	E	F	G	H	I	J	K	L	M	N	O
1	−	−	−	−	−	−	−	−	−	−	−	−	−	−	−
2	−	−	−	−	−	−	−	+	+	+	+	+	+	+	+
3	−	−	−	+	+	+	+	+	+	+	+	−	−	−	−
4	−	−	−	+	+	+	+	−	−	−	−	+	+	+	+
5	−	+	+	+	+	−	−	−	−	+	+	+	+	−	−
6	−	+	+	+	+	−	−	+	+	−	−	−	−	+	+
7	−	+	+	−	−	+	+	+	+	−	−	+	+	−	−
8	−	+	+	−	−	+	+	−	−	+	+	−	−	+	+
9	+	+	−	−	+	+	−	−	+	+	−	−	+	+	−
10	+	+	−	−	+	+	−	+	+	−	−	+	+	−	−
11	+	+	−	+	−	−	+	+	−	−	+	−	+	+	−
12	+	+	−	+	−	−	+	−	+	+	−	+	−	−	+
13	+	−	+	+	−	+	−	−	+	−	+	+	−	+	−
14	+	−	+	+	−	+	−	+	−	+	−	−	+	−	+
15	+	−	+	−	+	−	+	+	−	+	−	+	−	+	−
16	+	−	+	−	+	−	+	−	+	−	+	−	+	−	+

Figure 16.5   The Basic 16-Run Plackett-Burman Design

Factors / Treatment	A	B	C	D
1	+	+	+	+
2	+	+	−	−
3	+	−	−	+
4	+	−	+	−
5	−	−	+	+
6	−	−	−	−
7	−	+	−	+
8	−	+	+	−

Figure 16.6   The Eight Run Reflected Plackett-Berman Design

 SIX SIGMA TOOLS AT WORK

Plackett-Burman Screening Designs Experiment Treatment Table

Researchers are studying the effects of tire pressure, gas type, oil type, and vehicle speed on gas mileage. Problem: What combination of factors provides the best gas mileage?

Factor	Level 1	Level 2
Tire Pressure	28 psi	35 psi
Speed	55 mph	65 mph
Oil	30 weight	40 weight
Gas	Regular	Premium

Response variable: gas mileage
Design: Plackett-Burman Eight Run Reflected (Figure 16.6)

Tire	Speed	Oil	Gas
35	65	40	P
35	65	30	R
35	55	30	P
35	55	40	R
28	55	40	P
28	55	30	R
28	65	30	P
28	65	40	R

Taguchi Designs

Taguchi designs use orthogonal arrays to determine the factors and their levels for the experiments to be conducted. Essentially, Taguchi uses orthogonal arrays that select only a few of the combinations found in a traditional factorial design. This method has the advantage of being very efficient; however, these experiments work best when there is minimal interaction among the factors. Taguchi designs are most effective when the experimenter already has a general feel for the interactions that may be present among the factors. A comparison of the total number of experiments needed using *factorial designs* versus *Taguchi designs* is shown in Table 16.1. Figure 16.7 shows the structure of a traditional factorial experiment and then the reduced Taguchi orthogonal array. The treatments chosen by Taguchi are labeled in the full factorial experiment as T-1, T-2, etc.

Table 16.1 Comparison of Factorial Design and Taguchi Design

		Total Number of Experiments	
Factors	*Level*	*Factorial Design*	*Taguchi*
2	2	4 (2^2)	4
3	2	8 (2^3)	4
4	2	16 (2^4)	8
7	2	128 (2^7)	8
4	3	81 (3^4)	9

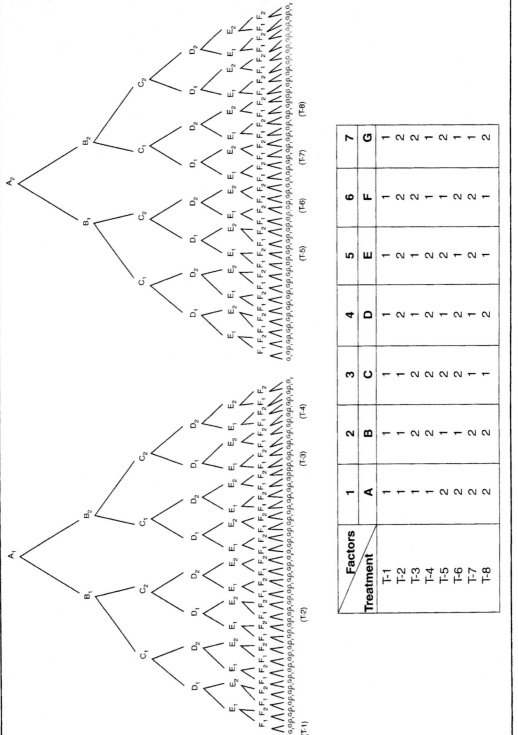

Factors	1	2	3	4	5	6	7
Treatment	A	B	C	D	E	F	G
T-1	1	1	1	1	1	1	1
T-2	1	1	1	2	2	2	2
T-3	1	2	2	1	1	2	2
T-4	1	2	2	2	2	1	1
T-5	2	1	2	1	2	1	2
T-6	2	1	2	2	1	2	1
T-7	2	2	1	1	2	2	1
T-8	2	2	1	2	1	1	2

Figure 16.7 Comparing a Full Factorial Experiment with a Taguchi Design

336

SIX SIGMA TOOLS AT WORK

Taguchi Design Experiment Treatment Table

Researchers are studying the effects of tire pressure, gas type, oil type, and vehicle speed on gas mileage. Problem: What combination of factors provides the best gas mileage?

Factor	Level 1	Level 2
Tire Pressure	28 psi	35 psi
Speed	55 mph	65 mph
Oil	30 weight	40 weight
Gas	Regular	Premium

Response variable: gas mileage
Design: $L_4(2^3)$ Taguchi array (Figure 16.8)

Tire	Speed	Oil	Gas
28	55	30	R
28	55	30	P
28	65	40	R
28	65	40	P
35	55	40	R
35	55	40	P
35	65	30	R
35	65	30	P

Note that a full factorial experiment would have required 16 treatments, while a Taguchi experiment required only 8.

Hypotheses and Experiment Errors

Experimenters approach each experiment with a hypothesis about how changes in various factors will affect the response variable. Often this hypothesis is expressed as:

H_0: the change in the factor will have no effect on the response variable.
H_1: the change in the factor will have an effect on the response variable.

Factor No.	1	2	3	4	5	6	7
1	1	1	1	1	1	1	1
2	1	1	1	2	2	2	2
3	1	2	2	1	1	2	2
4	1	2	2	2	2	1	1
5	2	1	2	1	2	1	2
6	2	1	2	2	1	2	1
7	2	2	1	1	2	2	1
8	2	2	1	2	1	1	2

Figure 16.8 $L_4(2^3)$ Orthogonal Array

SIX SIGMA TOOLS AT WORK

Hypotheses Testing

When a metal is selected for a part that will undergo a metal forming process such as stamping, often the metal is tested to determine its bending failure point. An experiment being conducted at MAR Inc. is testing the bending failure of a particular metal that has been provided by two different suppliers. In this experiment, a sample of the metal is bent back and forth until the metal separates at the fold. The experimenters are testing the following hypotheses:

H_0: there is no difference in the bending failure point (the response variable) with respect to the following factors: suppliers (A and B), or plating (none or plated).

H_1: there is a difference in the bending failure point with respect to supplier or plating.

Experiments are designed to test hypotheses, yet the experiments themselves are not infallible. This is why the significance of the factors affecting the response variables is studied. Experimenters are also cautious to determine if errors exist in the experiment. Errors exist in experiments for a variety of reasons, including a lack of uniformity of the material and inherent variability in the experimental technique. Two types of errors exist:

1. Type I Error: The hypothesis is *rejected* when it is *true*. For instance, a Type I error would occur if the experimenter drew the conclusion that a factor does not produce a significant effect on a response variable when, in fact, its effect is meaningful. A Type I error is designated with the symbol alpha (α).

2. Type II Error: The hypothesis is *accepted* when it is *false*. For instance, a Type II error would occur if the experimenter drew the conclusion that a factor produces a significant effect on a response variable when, in fact, its effect is negligible (a false alarm). A Type II error is designated with the symbol beta (β).

Table 16.2 shows the relationship of these types of errors.

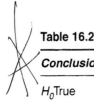

Table 16.2

Conclusion from Sample	H_0 True	H_0 False
H_0 True	Correct Conclusion	Type II Error β
H_0 False	Type I Error α	Correct Conclusion

Experimental Analysis Methods

An **analysis of means (ANOM)** *essentially compares subgroup averages and separates those that represent signals from those that do not.* An ANOM takes the form of a control chart that identifies subgroup averages that are detectably different from the grand average. In this chart, each treatment (experiment) is compared with the grand average. An ANOM is used whenever the experimenter wants to study the differences between the subgroup averages from different treatments of the factors in the experiment. To use an ANOM, you must have more than one observation per subgroup.

An **Analysis of Variance (ANOVA)** *is a measure of the confidence that can be placed on the results of the experiment.* This method is used to determine whether or not changes in factor levels have produced significant effects upon a response variable. An ANOVA analyzes the variability of the data. In this analysis, the variance of the controllable and noise factors is examined. By understanding the source and magnitude of the variance, the best operating conditions can be determined.

When conducting an ANOVA, the variance is estimated using two different methods. An ANOVA estimates the variance of the factors in the experiment by using information such as the degrees of freedom present, the sums of squares, and mean squares. If the estimates are similar, then detectable differences between the subgroup averages are unlikely. If the differences are large, then there is a difference between the subgroup averages that is not attributable to background noise alone. An ANOVA compares the ratio of the Between Subgroup Variance Estimate with that of the Within Subgroup Variance Estimate. The Between Subgroup Variation Estimate is sensitive to differences between the subgroup averages. The Within Subgroup Variation Estimate is not sensitive to this difference.

 SIX SIGMA TOOLS AT WORK

Optimizing Order Pick, Pack, and Ship Using Design of Experiments

Order picking, packing, and shipping from a warehouse can be quite complex. Orders are submitted by customers and consist of multiple product types in various quantities. The products on these orders must be picked from the correct storage locations, packaged for safe shipment, and labeled with the appropriate destination. This would be simple if the organization carried only a few items in inventory to be shipped to a few customers. The complexity increases exponentially as the number of items and customers increase.

Doing the job right at every step is critical, not only because the customer wants to receive the correct item, but because shipping costs are based on the cube of space the package uses up, whether in a truck or the cargo hold of a plane.

At CH Shipping, an automated distribution center, pickers, packers, and shippers handle orders that may contain as many as 50 unique products, numbering up to 5000 of each unique product. CH Shipping uses "wave" processing, also known as batch picking. This method consolidates orders from several customers into one optimal inventory picking cycle (Figure 16.9). Optimal picking cycles consolidate

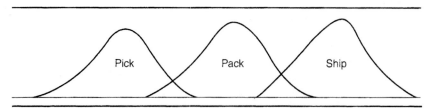

Figure 16.9   Department Workload Using Wave Order Processing

what has been ordered, the amount ordered, and where the items are stored in the warehouse. As shown in Figure 16.10, once the pick is complete, the wave continues to the packing department, where the orders are automatically sorted using barcodes by the individual customer order and packed. Once packed, the orders proceed to a shipping station to be labeled and staged for shipment via truck or plane. Buffer staging lanes exist between each area. Downtime in a particular area results if orders are not in the system or are held up at an upstream area.

Wave processing is different from "discrete" processing. Discrete processing involves picking one order at a time, packing it, and then readying it for shipment. To manage the wave, order characteristics that optimize flow include: how may times the picker visits a particular location in the warehouse, how many items are picked each time, and how much space is taken up by the items picked?

The key departments involved are: Pick, Pack, and Ship. Members of the workforce in these departments work together to ensure customers receive what they need, when they need it. In order to minimize costs, maximize flexibility, and enhance customer success, the Express Logistics Center Manager has asked the industrial engineers at CH Shipping to optimize order picking, packing, and shipping. In other words, they want to maximize the peaks and valleys in Figure 16.10 through the use of design of experiments. In order to do so, the team proposed the following experiment design:

Factors

>   *Quantity (Qty):* Total number of pieces picked within a given wave
>   *Lines:* The different items (products) on the order needing to be picked
>   *Cube:* The space needed for the quantity of lines for a particular order (largest outbound parcel box cube or tote cube; a tote is a box without a top)
>   *Weight:* The weight of the quantity of lines for a particular order

Level

Max Qty	Max Lines	Max Cube	Max Weight
5000 (+)	50 (+)	Parcel (+)	150 (+)
100 (−)	10 (−)	Tote (−)	25 (−)

Controllable Factors   When a factor is controllable it is possible to establish and maintain the particular level throughout the experiment. In this experiment, investigators are able to set the levels for the quantity, lines, cube, and weight.

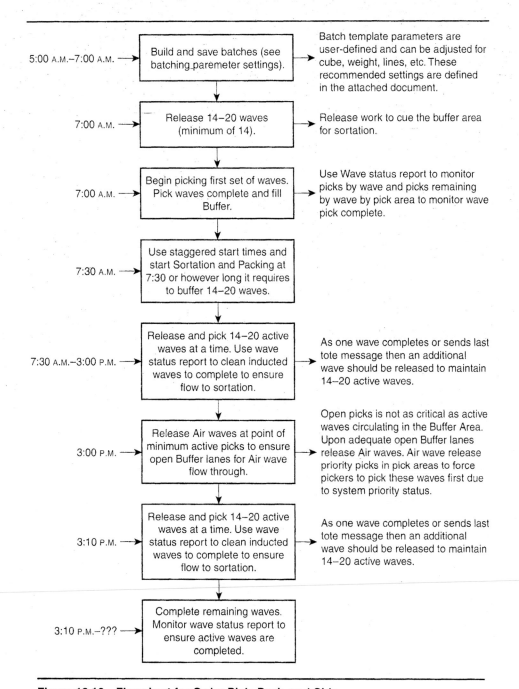

Figure 16.10   Flowchart for Order Pick, Pack, and Ship

Response Variables These variables are used to describe the reaction of a process to variations in the chosen factors. The response variable for this experiment is Order Per Hour.

Effect The effect is the result or outcome of the experiment. The investigators are interested in determining the optimal wave parameters. A wave is a batch of customer orders consolidated to optimize warehouse picking activities. Instead of picking one order at a time, many orders are picked.

Treatment The number of treatments is based on the number of factors and the levels associated with each factor. Based on the number of waves processed per day and the ease of wave building, a Full Factorial Design was chosen (Table 16.3).

Degrees of Freedom The degree of freedom in an experiment is the total number of levels for all factors minus 1. Here there are two levels for each factor ($4 \times 2 = 8$) so the degrees of freedom equals $8 - 1 = 7$

Interaction Since the four factors will work together to produce a result different from what would result if each were only used singly, interactions exist between the four that must be considered in the experiment.

Noise Factor A noise factor is an uncontrollable but measurable source of variation. For this experiment the noise factors are buffer downtime, pick downtime, and shipping downtime.

Run A run is an experimental trial, the application of one treatment to one experimental unit. A quantity of 100, with 10 lines, using a tote, and weighing 25 pounds is one run.

Table 16.3 Experiment Design for Optimizing Order Pick, Pack, and Ship

Test Wave	Max Qty	Max Lines	Max Cube	Max Weight
1	5000	50	Parcel	150
2	100	50	Parcel	150
3	5000	10	Parcel	150
4	100	10	Parcel	150
5	5000	50	Tote	150
6	100	50	Tote	150
7	5000	10	Tote	150
8	100	10	Tote	150
9	5000	50	Parcel	25
10	100	50	Parcel	25
11	5000	10	Parcel	25
12	100	10	Parcel	25
13	5000	50	Tote	25
14	100	50	Tote	25
15	5000	10	Tote	25
16	100	10	Tote	25

Replicate When an experiment is replicated, it refers to a repeat of the treatment condition, a complete rerunning of the design.

Repetition Repetitions are multiple results of a treatment condition.

Significance The determination of whether or not the changes to the factor levels had a significant effect on the response variable. In other words, did changing the quantity, lines, cube, or weight affect the result?

To conduct the experiment, the investigators set up controlled runs based on each of the 16 runs denoted by the Full Factorial Design (Table 16.3). These runs, from actual customer orders, took place on a Saturday, outside of the normal workweek.

Following the experiment, the investigators analyzed the results (Table 16.4) to identify the optimum wave settings to maximize flow through Pick, Pack, and Ship. They began their analysis with the most simple of methods: ANOG or Analysis of Good. This very simple but effective technique ranks the results of the experiment by the most desirable outcome: high orders per hour (Table 16.5). Run 9, with a quantity of 5000 and 50 lines allows 8.3 orders to be picked per hour.

Further statistical analysis using ANOVA and ANOM revealed that the factor having the most significant impact on Number of Orders Per Hour was Lines Per Wave, the number of products with a unique part number and their quantity. By comparison, the weight and cube size were insignificant. The experiment determined that the combination of unique part numbers that maximizes quantities results in the optimal picking sequence. Now, the company batches its orders based on the combination of unique part numbers that provides the greatest quantity. For instance, 25 unique part

Table 16.4   Experiment Results for Optimizing Pick, Pack, and Ship

Test Wave	Max Qty	Max Lines	Max Cube	Max Weight	Order/Hour
1	5000	50	Parcel	150	8.2
2	100	50	Parcel	150	8.1
3	5000	10	Parcel	150	6.1
4	100	10	Parcel	150	6.3
5	5000	50	Tote	150	7.9
6	100	50	Tote	150	8.2
7	5000	10	Tote	150	4.5
8	100	10	Tote	150	5.1
9	5000	50	Parcel	25	8.3
10	100	50	Parcel	25	8
11	5000	10	Parcel	25	5.9
12	100	10	Parcel	25	6.2
13	5000	50	Tote	25	7.8
14	100	50	Tote	25	8.1
15	5000	10	Tote	25	5.1
16	100	10	Tote	25	4.9

Table 16.5   Analysis of Good for Optimizing Order Pick, Pack, and Ship

ANOG Test Wave	Analysis of Good				
	Max Qty	Max Lines	Max Cube	Max Weight	Order/Hour
9	5000	50	Parcel	25	8.3
1	5000	50	Parcel	150	8.2
6	100	50	Tote	150	8.2
2	100	50	Parcel	150	8.1
14	100	50	Tote	25	8.1
10	100	50	Parcel	25	8
5	5000	50	Tote	150	7.9
13	5000	50	Tote	25	7.8
4	100	10	Parcel	150	6.3
12	100	10	Parcel	25	6.2
3	5000	10	Parcel	150	6.1
11	5000	10	Parcel	25	5.9
8	100	10	Tote	150	5.1
15	5000	10	Tote	25	5.1
16	100	10	Tote	25	4.9
7	5000	10	Tote	150	4.5

numbers whose order quantity totals to 4925 or 3 unique part numbers whose order quantity totals 4976 or 1 unique part number whose order quantity totals 5000. The goal is to have a high number of items in the pick.

SUMMARY

This chapter has provided only a basic introduction to the interesting and valuable techniques of quality function deployment and design of experiments. Both quality function deployment and design of experiments enable users to understand more about the products or processes they are studying. Both methods are assets to any problem solving adventure because they provide in-depth information about the complexities of the products and processes. Since both methods are complex and time consuming, they should be used judiciously.

σ ■ Take Away Tips

1. An experimental design is the plan or layout of an experiment. It shows the treatments to be included and the replication of the treatments.
2. Experimenters can study all the combinations of factors by utilizing a full factorial design.

3. Experimenters can study partial combinations of the factors by using fractional factorial experiment designs like Plackett-Burman or Taguchi.

4. Design of experiments seeks to investigate the interactions of factors and their effects on the response variable. ▇

Chapter Questions

1. When a metal is selected for a part that will undergo a metal forming process such as stamping, often the metal is tested to determine its bending failure point. An experiment being conducted at MAR Inc. is testing the bending failure of a particular metal. In this experiment, a sample of the metal is bent back and forth until the metal separates at the fold. Metal from two different suppliers is currently being studied. Plated metal from each supplier is being compared with non-plated metal. For each piece of metal from each supplier, the metal samples being tested are in two sizes, a 2 in. wide piece and a 3 in. wide piece. If all of the factors are to be tested at each of their levels, create a table showing the factors and their levels for the two sizes, two suppliers, and two surface finishes. Define the components of this experiment.

2. For the metal bending failure experiment, create a matrix showing all the different treatments a full factorial experiment would have run.

3. In plastic injection molding, temperature, time in mold, and injection pressure each play an important role in determining the strength of the part. At MAR Inc., experimenters are studying the effects on part strength when the temperature is set at either 250°, 275°, or 300°F; the time in mold is either 5, 7, or 9 seconds; and the injection pressure is either 200, 250, or 300 psi. Create a table showing the factors and their levels for this information.

4. For the information in the above plastic injection molding problem, define the components for this experiment.

5. For the above plastic injection molding problem, how many tests would be necessary to test every possible treatment (a full factorial experiment)? Create a tree similar to those shown in Figure 16.1 showing all possible treatments.

6. Researchers are studying the effects of tire pressure and vehicle speed on gas mileage. Create a hypothesis for the following information:

Factors	Levels
Tire Pressure	28 psi, 35 psi
Speed	55 mph, 65 mph

7. Describe the difference between the two types of errors that can occur with experiments.

8. A team is currently working to redesign a compressor assembly cell. The team has several design changes that they want to test using design of experiments. The ultimate objective of the experiment is to decrease the cell's assembly and packing throughput time. Currently, it takes 45 minutes to assemble and pack a compressor. The team is considering three changes:

   Reduce current 36 inch conveyor width to either 18 inch or 24 inch
   Install new parts presentation shelving, either flat surfaced or angled
   Line form: either straight or curved

   Create a table showing all the factors and their levels that will need to be tested. What is the response variable being investigated?

17

Lean Enterprises

On shop floors, the plane makers have also learned from car makers. At an Airbus factory in Wales, where it builds wings, production teams used to walk far to the stockroom for bags of bolts and rivets, and frequently left them scattered about—a wasteful and unsafe practice—because they lacked nearby storage. Using work-analysis methods developed by the auto industry, project teams studied which fasteners were needed where, and when, and then organized racks on the shop floor. Now carefully labeled bins contain tidy sets of supplies needed for specific tasks. The change has sped up work and saved over $100,000 in rivets and bolts at the Welsh factory alone.

Boeing, Airbus Look to Auto Companies for Production Tips,
The Wall Street Journal, April 1, 2005

▓ Objectives:

1. To familiarize the reader with the concept of lean manufacturing
2. To show the relationship between lean manufacturing and Six Sigma ▓

INTRODUCTION

Henry Ford said *"Time waste differs from material waste in that there can be no salvage."* With this in mind, he focused on ways to speed up the manufacturing process without sacrificing quality. He was the first to utilize a moving assembly line on a grand scale. On Ford Motor Company's final assembly line, car bodies slid down a ramp onto waiting chassis. This moving assembly line approach, so different from previous manufacturing methods, regularly broke daily production records.

In his books *The Machine that Changed the World* and *Lean Thinking*, Jim Womack presents the principles and practices related to lean manufacturing. A lean system provides what is needed, in the amount needed, when it is needed. The principal focus of lean thinking concentrates on value-added process flow. For a process to have value-added flow, there must be an uninterrupted adding of value to a product or service as it is being created. Interruptions or non–value-added activities found in the process, such as downtime, rework, waiting, and inspection, must be eliminated. In a lean process, the value-added time in the process equals more than 25% of the total lead time of that process.

Lean thinking is a mindset best described as a relentless war on waste. Some of the benefits of lean thinking include shorter lead times, less handling, lower costs for storage and subsequently floor space, and fewer customer service activities. Companies implementing lean thinking have reported significant reductions in cycle times, lead times, floor space usage, and inventory while at the same time they see a significant improvement in quality, inventory turns, profit margins, and customer responsiveness.

Lean enterprises realize that devising new methods to cut production costs, improve quality, speed assembly, and increase throughput are vital to staying competitive. The Six Sigma approach blends nicely with lean manufacturing techniques, enhancing the effectiveness of both. One of the critical aspects of these two approaches is the realization that working hard to keep things simple saves money. Six Sigma strengthens company performance by concentrating on reducing process variation. Lean thinking enhances company performance by focusing on the reduction of waste. Effective process improvement efforts involve both.

Lean thinking focuses on eliminating wasted time, effort, and material, particularly time, time wasted waiting for value to be added, or time wasted waiting in inventory for a customer or time wasted waiting for the next step in the process, etc. There are many sources of waste. Tadamitsu Tsurouka; a Honda process engineer, identified seven sources of waste:

Overproduction waste
Idle time waste (waiting time/queue time)
Delivery waste (transport/conveyance waste)
Waste in the work itself
Inventory waste
Wasted operator motion
Waste of rejected parts

Intellect can also be wasted. Lean thinking tackles the causes of these wastes. Lean projects focus on inadequate processes, inadequate tools/equipment, inefficient layouts, lack of training, inadequate suppliers, lack of standardization, poor management decisions, inadequate communication, mistakes by the operator, inadequate scheduling, etc.

LEAN THINKING

Lean thinking generates process improvement by following five key steps:

1. Study the process by directly observing the work activities, their connections, and flow.
2. Study the process to systematically eliminate wasteful activities, their connections, and flow.
3. Establish agreement among those affected by the process in terms of what the process needs to accomplish and how the process will accomplish it.
4. Attack and solve problems using a systematic method.
5. Integrate the above approach throughout the organization.

LEAN MEASURES

Like those of the Six Sigma methodology, three key performance measures related to lean thinking are: cycle time, value-creating time, and lead time. Cycle time represents how often a product is completed by a process or the time it takes an operator to complete all the steps in their work cycle before repeating them. Value creating time is the part of the cycle time during which the work activities actually transform the product in a way the customer is willing to pay for. Lead time is the time it takes for one piece to move all the way through a process from start to finish.

LEAN TOOLS

Lean thinking essentially takes a diverse set of tools, techniques, and practices and combines them into a system. Lean thinking tools include:

Kaizen
Value stream process mapping
5 Ss
Kanban (pull inventory management)
Error proofing (Poka-yoke, pronounced "poke-a-yoke")
Preventive and predictive maintenance
Setup time reduction (single minute exchange of dies; SMED)
Reduced lot sizes (single piece flow)
Line-balancing
Schedule leveling
Standardized work
Visual management

KAIZEN

Kaizen's guiding words are: combine, simplify, eliminate. Kaizen seeks to standardize processes while eliminating waste. Waste in a process or system can be removed by combining steps or activities, simplifying steps or activities, and eliminating any waste in a system or process. Kaizen practitioners go to the actual work area, work with the actual part or service, and learn the actual activities required in the work situation. Kaizen activities may take two forms: flow kaizen focusing on value stream improvement, and process kaizen focusing on the elimination of waste.

Kaizen activities are typically a concentrated improvement event that lasts for about a week. Teams meet on the first day for training and problem identification. From there they analyze the process by documenting activities, processes, and cycle times. This information enables them to discuss process improvement options. These improvement options are implemented and tested for their ability to solve the problem. This may involve rearranging existing equipment, creating mock-ups, or going through the motions of the newly designed process. The improvements are refined, tested again, and the results presented to management.

At Kaizen events, lean thinking and Six Sigma tools and techniques often blend together to enable participants to maximize the process, product, or service. As we have learned, Six Sigma tools and techniques emphasize root cause analysis through the use of a standardized problem-solving technique (DMAIC) in combination with statistical analysis and performance measures. Many of the examples used in this text are from Kaizen events. Lean thinking integrates lean tools into the Kaizen process.

 SIX SIGMA TOOLS AT WORK

Kaizen Event

At PLC, Inc. a Six Sigma kaizen team has been investigating the process of returning defective parts to suppliers. The original fourteen step process takes 175 hours, nearly four weeks, for a defective part to be returned to a supplier.

Recognizing that their kaizen team's purpose is to combine, simplify, and eliminate while creating a standardized defective part return process, the team looked for waste that could be removed by combining or simplifying steps and activities. The Six Sigma team went through the entire process to learn the actual activities required. During four meetings, the team developed a new process. The new process included nine steps and reduced the time from 175 hours to 69 hours.

When the team presented their proposed process changes to upper management, the managers asked the team to begin the exercise again, starting with a clean slate, keeping only what absolutely had to take place in order to get the job done. The team was given one hour to report their new process. The new process has four steps and takes one hour to complete. This process was achieved by focusing on what the customer absolutely had to have and eliminating all non–value-added activities.

Though they were able to develop a new, simplified process map for the defective part return process, while in their meeting, it dawned on the team members that, in the big scheme of things, why were they allowing defective parts at all?

The team members learned two things from this kaizen experience: it doesn't pay to spend time fixing a bad process and sometimes the reason for the process needs to be eliminated.

VALUE STREAM PROCESS MAPPING

Processes provide customers with goods and services and wherever there is a process, there is a value stream. Value streams, which include both value-added and non–value-added activities, are the actions required to create a product or service from raw material until it reaches the customer. Since lean thinking focuses on needs as perceived by the end customer, value stream maps should focus on what is important to meeting customer requirements. Value stream process mapping makes the current production situation clear by drawing the material and information flows related to the process. It provides a clearer understanding of the process by allowing users to visualize the process, recognize sources of waste, and eliminate non–value-added activities.

When doing value stream process mapping, accurately specify the value desired by the customer. Go to where the action is taking place and identify every step in the value stream. Collect current information by walking along the actual pathways of material and information flow. Really do the work required. This may require several walkthroughs, beginning with a quick walk along the entire value stream and continuing with subsequent visits to gather more detailed information. Process mapping is often easier if the process is worked backwards. Working backwards reduces the probability of missing an activity because it takes place more slowly, without jumps to the conclusion of "I know what is going to happen next." Process mapping is best done with pencil, paper, and stopwatch. Though many computer programs exist to help with process mapping, it is difficult to get them to where the action is taking place. After all, the point of creating the map is to understand the flow of information and material, not in creating a map. Once the map is complete, remove the waste. Based on the requirements of the customer, make value flow from the beginning to the end of the process.

Typical data gathered during the value stream mapping process includes cycle time and changeover time information, machine up-time, production batch sizes, number of operators, lead times, number of products and their variations, pack sizes, working time, scrap rates, rework rates, and others. Cycle time refers to the actual time it takes to complete a product, part, or service. It is the time it takes for an operator to go through their work activities one full cycle. Value creation time is rarely equal to cycle time. Value creation time is the time it takes to complete those work activities that actually transform the product into what the customer wants. Lead time is the time it takes to move one piece, part, product, or service all the way through the process. All of this information can be captured on the value stream map (Figure 17.1). When the value stream map is complete, it will show the areas that are in need of improvement. From this, create an improvement plan establishing what needs to be done and when, outlining measurable goals and objectives, complete with checkpoints, deadlines, and responsibilities laid out.

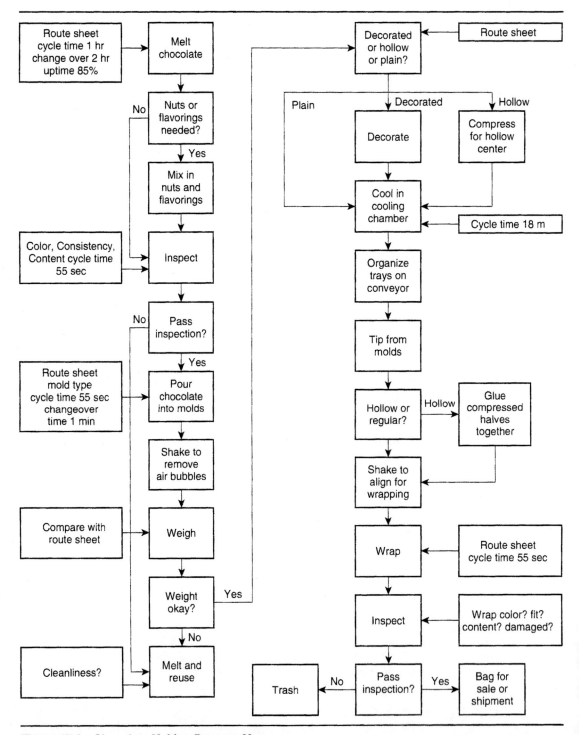

Figure 17.1   Chocolate Making Process Map

SIX SIGMA TOOLS AT WORK

Value-added Process Mapping

The chocolate candy manufacturing line at Yummy Chocolates is a fully automated line, requiring little human intervention. However, when a Six Sigma team reviewed cost of quality information related to production cost overruns, they found excessive scrap and rework rates, and high inspection and overtime costs. To tackle the cost overruns, they wanted to isolate and remove waste from the process, thus preventing defectives by removing the sources of variation. In order to enable them to better understand the production line activities, they mapped the process (Figure 17.1).

The process map revealed several non–value-added activities. Chocolate is melted and mixed until it reaches the right consistency, then it is poured into mold trays. As the chocolates leave the cooling chamber, two workers reorganize the chocolate mold trays on the conveyor belt. This prompted the Six Sigma team to ask: why are the trays bunching up on the conveyor in the first place? This non–value-added activity essentially wastes the time of two workers. It also could result in damaged chocolates if the trays were to flip over or off the conveyor.

Yummy Chocolates prides itself on quality product. To maintain high standards, before packaging, the process map reveals that four workers inspect nearly every piece of chocolate as it emerges from the wrapping machine. A full 25% of the chocolate production is thrown out in a large garbage can. Though this type of inspection prevents defective chocolates from reaching the customer, this is a very high internal failure cost of quality.

This huge waste of material, manpower, and production time prompted the Six Sigma team to ask: why are the chocolates being thrown away? The simple answer was that the chocolates didn't meet standards. They persevered and discovered that the rejected chocolates were improperly wrapped. Despite the large amount of chocolate being thrown away, no one had suggested that the wrapper machine should be repaired.

If the team hadn't studied the process carefully using value-added process mapping, these two enormous sources of waste and their associated costs would have gone unnoticed. Up until this study, Yummy Chocolates' employees considered these costs part of doing business. During a subsequent kaizen event, modifications made to the production flow through the cooling chamber and to the wrapping machine resulted in a manpower savings of five people (who were moved to other areas in the plant) and rejected chocolates went from 25% to 0.05%. Savings were evidenced in decreases in in-process inspection, scrap, rework, production cost overruns, overtime, inefficient and ineffective production, and employee lost time.

FIVE Ss

Lean thinking practitioners recognize that the five Ss are the foundation of a lean facility. The five Ss are activities that focus on creating orderliness in a facility, thus supporting error proofing, setup time reduction, single piece flow, line-balancing, visual management, and preventive maintenance. These five words serve as a reminder that process improvement lies in the basics.

Seiri	Separate
Seiton	Arrangement/orderliness
Seiso	Cleanliness
Seiketsu	Repeat seiri, seiton, and seiso at regular intervals
Shitsuki	Discipline

When work processes are arranged according to the five Ss, workers can expect to have everything they need to perform their work right at their fingertips. Whether it is a receptionist taking a phone message needing pen and paper or a computer program or a surgeon needed particular scalpels for an operation, their tools are right at hand, ready for use. Proper arrangement also includes having work surfaces and equipment designed for ease of use.

Seiri refers separating needed tools, parts, and instructions from unnecessary items. To define an unnecessary item, consider the 24 hour rule: If an item is not used or touched within 24 hours, it should be stored elsewhere.

Seiton, or orderliness, is quite simply "a place for everything and everything in its place." No work processes can be performed well if the work area is in disarray. Work centers utilizing five Ss often have taped or labeled locations for everything that is needed to perform the work. After each use, the operator returns the item to its convenient and marked location.

Seiso, cleanliness, focuses on the need to reduce the clutter. The only things kept at a work area should be those things that are needed to perform the work. Cleanliness also means that every day the work place should be straightened up, order restored, tools and equipment cleaned, and anything unnecessary disposed of properly.

Seiketsu reminds people to conduct seiri, seiton, and seiso at frequent intervals in order to maintain the workplace in pristine condition. It refers to regularly picking up, returning things to their proper location, and eliminating unneeded items.

Shitsuki, or discipline, is the self-control needed to continuously implement the other four Ss. When no one is looking, does disorder return? Does the work area get dirtier? Do unneeded items creep back in? The five Ss can fail if there is no effort to make a habit of the first four Ss. Management must be sure through audits and reward systems that the five Ss become ingrained in the organization's work practices.

Kanban (Pull Inventory Management)

Kanban improves process management by focusing on visual control of the process. Whether the kanban cards are physically present or digital on an Internet-based system, their purpose is to order the creation of a product or service on an as needed basis. Kanban cards follow the product through its stages of production. Information on the card includes the name of the part, the number of parts, instructions related to the part, the creation date of the card, the due date of the parts, and other pertinent information. Kanban cards keep track of inventory. To be genuinely called a pull inventory system, parts must not be produced or conveyed without a kanban. The number of parts must correspond with the number of parts needed as listed on the kanban.

 SIX SIGMA TOOLS AT WORK

Kanban

Through previous process improvements, QRC, Inc. reduced the amount of in-process inventory significantly. What little remained still needs to be managed. Controlling inventory means that it is easy to identify what has been made and when, as well as where it is and in what order it should be used. QRC, Inc. came up with a simple system. A small portion of their manufacturing floor was marked in bright yellow squares matching the size of the carts used to hold inventory awaiting processing. Each square had a corresponding label painted in it, A-1, B-1, C-1, A-2, B-2, etc. For each of these squares, small discs labeled with the square location were created.

When a cart needs to be parked, a disc is selected from the rack. The number on this disc represented the location in which to park the cart. After parking the cart, the disc is inserted into the top of the appropriate tube, each type of product being represented by a different tube. Since different tubes represent different types of inventory, the disc being placed in the tube matches the inventory on the cart. The more in-process inventory, the more discs in the tube, a visual representation of the in-process inventory for each type of product. This tube also serves to make sure that a first-in, first-out inventory control system is in place. When a cart is needed, the operator pulls a disc from the bottom of the tube. This tells the operator which cart needs to be taken next.

Error Proofing (Poka-yoke)

To eliminate waste at its source, lean thinking seeks to develop simple methods of preventing errors from occurring in a process. This concept of preventive action known as error proofing or poka-yoke follows five principles: elimination, replacement, facilitation, detection, and mitigation. Elimination refers to the need to design work and processes that eliminate the potential for error. Replacement means replacing a faulty process with another, more reliable process, that has less of a potential for error. When a process is facilitated, it is easer for the operator to perform without error. Detection encourages the use of methods that enable an error to be easily spotted, either at the original workstation or at the very next operation. This prevents errors from compounding as the work progresses. Mitigation, the final choice, refers to minimizing the effect of the error if it does occur.

Error proofing may be accomplished through the design and use of fail-safe devices, counts, redundancy, magnifying the senses, or special checking and control devices. Fail-safe devices may fool-proof an action by preventing the work from being done any other way. Mechanisms or work-holding devices may signal the operator when the work has been done correctly. Limiting mechanisms on tools may be used to prevent a tool from exceeding a certain position or amount of force. Counts or count-downs can help an operator keep track of where they are in a process. Redundancy can be effective when identifying parts, for instance, labeling a part both with color and a bar code. Double checks can be used to ascertain if the work has been completed correctly. Humans have five senses, seeing, hearing, feeling, tasting, and smelling. Tools that provide feedback in a variety of ways can alert an operator to whether or not their process is operating the right way. Lastly, special checking and control devices of varying levels of complexity may be designed to help an operator detect whether or not the work they are performing is correct.

 SIX SIGMA TOOLS AT WORK

Error Proofing

The quality specialist at RQM, Inc. received the following information concerning warranty claims.

Condition/Symptom   Customers have been requesting warranty service for inoperative and incorrectly reading fuel gages for recently purchased automobile models R and Q.

Probable Cause   Incorrect fuel gages or incorrect fuel pumps installed at the factory.

Immediate Corrective Action   Replace fuel units (pump, gages, tank) with correct parts depending on model.

Market Impact   To date there have been 39 warranty claims associated with fuel systems on models R and Q. Each claim costs $3,000 in parts and labor.

During a kaizen event, the quality specialist visited the Fuel System Creation workstation to study its layout (Figure 17.2). He created a process flow map (Figure 17.3). He was able to determine that the creation of the fuel system requires that the operator visually identify the handwritten designation for the fuel tank type and install the correct fuel system (pump and gage combination). Visiting the related workstations, he determined that the labeling of the tank is currently done by hand at the station where the part is unloaded from the paint rack. The part sequence, date, shift, and model type are written in a location visible to the person at the Fuel System Installation workstation, but not easily read by the operator at the Fuel System Creation workstation. The pumps and gages are not labeled, but arrive at the workstation on separate conveyors. The operator is responsible for designating the tank type and sequencing the tank into the correct production line for either model R or model Q. The unit then proceeds to the final assembly line.

Models R and Q are produced on the same final assembly line. Similar in size, they require fuel pumps, gages, and tanks which on the outside look remarkably similar. A variety of opportunities for error exist:

An R pump and gage combination my be installed on a model Q tank
A Q pump and gage combination may be installed in a model R tank

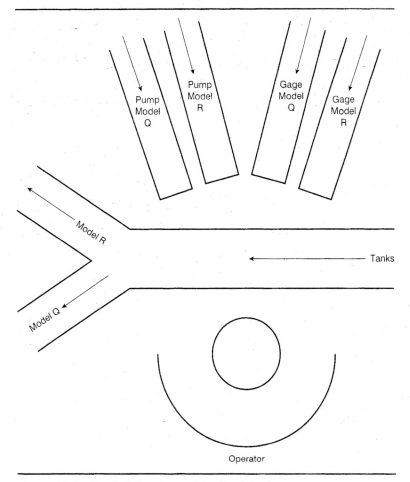

Figure 17.2 Workstation Layout for Fuel Systems

An R pump with a Q gage may be installed in a model Q tank
An R pump with a Q gage may be installed in a model R tank
A Q pump with an R gage may be installed in a model Q tank
A Q pump with a Q gage may be installed in a model R tank
The pump may be inoperable or substandard, repeating the same permutations above
The gage may be inoperable or substandard, repeating the same permutations above

With only 55 seconds in which to select and assemble a pump, a gage, and a tank, the possible errors are numerous. An operator might misread the handwritten identification on the fuel tank, select the wrong pump, select the wrong gage, or place the completed fuel system on the wrong assembly line.

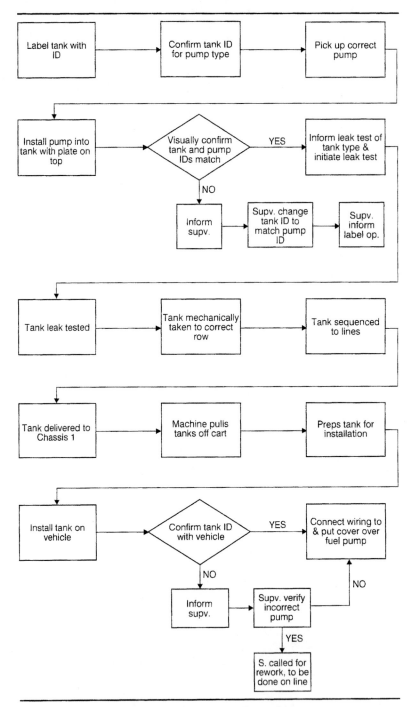

Figure 17.3   Process Flow Map for Fuel Systems

Countermeasures   In order to eliminate errors and foolproof the process, the following countermeasures were put into place:

Label all components with a barcode
Install barcode readers on the conveyors feeding the Fuel System Creation workstation
Install gates on all incoming and outgoing part conveyors
Utilize computer software that reads the type of tank and releases only the correct fuel pump and gage from material storage. This system also selects the appropriate conveyor line leaving the workstation.

This kaizen activity prevents future errors by more clearly identifying the incoming parts and limiting the choices the operator can make.

Preventive and Predictive Maintenance

Overall equipment effectiveness is a function of available time for value-added activities. Total available equipment time is reduced by planned downtimes and setup losses. Unfortunately, this is further reduced by unplanned downtimes, idling and minor stoppages for adjustments, speed losses, spoilage, and rework caused by faulty equipment. Unscheduled machine downtime, whether from parts shortages, setup time, absenteeism, reduced speeds, minor stoppages, or major machine breakdowns, represents wasted time and money. Preventive and predictive maintenance programs attack equipment failures as a source of waste. Preventive maintenance strives to maintain the equipment at the peak of its condition eliminating the waste of reduced speeds and minor stoppages. The benefits of practicing preventive and predictive maintenance include reduced costs, lower inventories, shorter lead-times, fewer breakdowns, jams, standbys, speed losses, and startup losses; shorter changeover times, improved productivity, increased flexibility, improved quality, etc.

Preventive maintenance requires that maintenance of equipment be planned, scheduled, and then executed to performance standards. These performance standards denote the plan for scheduled maintenance including the interval, how the downtime will be scheduled, and what type of work is to be done (basic check or major overhaul). This plan will also have procedures in place to make sure that appropriate parts/materials have been procured and labor scheduled. Because there is a distinct maintenance plan for each piece of equipment, there is also a budget in place to cover the costs. Also important are the maintenance records documenting what has taken place, machine performance, inspections, and lubrications.

Predictive maintenance monitors equipment performance. It seeks to measure, recognize, and use signals from the process to diagnose the condition of the equipment and determine when maintenance will be required. Many of the records kept for preventive maintenance are used in predictive maintenance.

Setup Time Reduction (Single Minute Exchange of Dies—SMED)

In the broad sense, setup time can be defined as the time between the production of the last good part in one series of parts and the production of the first good part in the next series of parts. Setup times encompass taking an existing setup apart, preparing for the next setup, installing the next setup, and determining whether or not the new setup can create good parts.

Lean thinking encourages the reduction of setup time. Though necessary, setup times do not add value and therefore are a source of waste. Tooling and equipment should be designed to allow easy changes from one tool to another. Setup processes should be studied for wasteful activities. Without quick changeovers, lead times remain long. Since the cost of changing over tooling is high, small batch sizes cannot be justified. Lengthy changeovers limit an organization's flexibility to respond quickly to customer needs.

 SIX SIGMA TOOLS AT WORK

Setup Time Reduction

QRC Corporation faces a dilemma. On the one hand, they are woefully short of the capacity required to take on a new, rather lucrative job from a customer. On the other hand, they are short of the funds needed to purchase a new stamping press vital to the new order. Management has approached the operators of the equipment to discuss their concerns. Together, they have decided to conduct a kaizen event focused on reducing the setup times on their existing machines. Nearly everyone, from engineers to operators, expressed concern that there was not any room for improvement at all.

On the first day, the first two hours of the morning is spent discussing the machines, how they operate, the importance of certain steps in the setup process, and the concerns of the operators and setup people. Following the meeting, the team returned to their workstations with one small change. Each operator and setup person was videotaped while performing their normal duties. After a few moments of discomfort, they forgot they were on camera.

On the morning of the second day, each of the four videos were watched by the team. Two things were immediately apparent to all who viewed the films. Operators often stopped their machines to make minor adjustments and during machine changeovers the setup people were always walking off in search of tools. When questioned, the response was "that's the way we've always done it."

Quickly changes were made. Setup personnel identified tools necessary for their jobs. Management invested in tool carts to contain the necessary tools. Setup personnel also identified minor machine and tooling modifications that could be made to greatly simplify their work. These changes, modest in scale, were rapidly implemented, especially when it was discovered that the improvements to setup would eliminate most, if not all, of the work stoppages for minor adjustments.

At the end of their kaizen event, the company was proudly able to report that the changes resulted in a capacity increase equal to one-third more production time.

This exceeded the capacity increase from a new machine by more than two times. The company accepted the new order, rewarded their employees monetarily for their help, and scheduled future kaizen events for other areas of the plant.

Reduced Batch Sizes (Single Piece Flow)

Reduced lot sizes result in shorter lead times, a shorter period of time between when a raw material arrives and is paid for and when a product or service reaches the customer and is paid for. Shorter lead times increase the number of inventory turns. Part of lean thinking's ultimate goal is to create continuous flow wherever possible. In a continuous flow environment, as each piece is created, it flows immediately to the next activity with no delays, storages, or work-in-process inventories. Kanban or pull systems work well with single piece flow because only what is needed is being made. Smaller lot sizes reveal problems quickly. The process of going from large batches to single piece flow requires much problem resolution.

In some situations, it won't be possible to meet single piece flow, however, as downtimes due to changeovers are reduced and smaller in-line equipment utilized, batch sizes will get smaller and smaller, providing many of the benefits of single piece flow. Single-piece flow does not work well when processes are too unreliable to be linked closely to other processes. It can also happen when raw materials or components have to travel a great distance. Also, some processes, such as injection molding, stamping, or forging, achieve better economies of scale by batch processing. Still, where continuous single piece flow is not possible, batches should be linked with the same pull system, making only what is needed. Safety stock or buffers should be temporary, not a crutch to avoid improvement. Kaizen efforts, using the five Ss and other lean tools, should focus on working toward SMED, single minute exchange of dies.

 SIX SIGMA TOOLS AT WORK

Single Piece Flow

In its article *Boeing, Airbus Look to Auto Companies for Production Tips*, The Wall Street Journal, April 1, 2005, reported that "Boeing, though, made one of the most dramatic production changes yet in 2001 when it began putting together planes on a huge moving line—a la Henry Ford and his Model T. The motion 'lent a sense of urgency to the process that we really didn't have when the planes were sitting still,' says Carolyn Corvi, the executive who oversaw the change. Ms. Corvi and other top Boeing executives made multiple visits to Toyota when they were first beginning to study how to convert the production process to a moving line. When many workers initially balked at the production line and unions filed complaints, Boeing took extra pains to win them over. The change paid off: Boeing halved the time it takes to assemble a single-aisle 737, and has started putting its other planes—including its oldest and largest product, the 747—on moving lines."

Line Balancing

When systems are in balance, the work is performed evenly over time with no peaks and valleys placing undue burdens on employees or machines. Each machine and each operator makes what is needed timed to match when it is needed. Unbalanced lines are evident when workstations make more than is needed or have to wait for production from the previous work center to reach them. Overproduction represents significant waste. Making more than the customer wants or more than can be sold means that valuable resources of time, material, and money have been spent to no benefit for the organization.

Schedule leveling and line balancing create a thread that links customer needs with production. Lean thinking focuses on getting processes to make only what is needed by their customer, either internal or external. All processes should be linked, from the raw material to the final customer. This smooth flow will provide the shortest lead time, highest quality, lowest cost, and least waste.

Value stream mapping and kanban systems will reveal where lines need to be balanced. Takt times, how often a single part should be produced, provide the starting point for line balancing.

$$\text{Takt time} = \frac{\text{Available working time per day}}{\text{Customer demand rate per day}}$$

Takt times are used to synchronize the pace of production to the demands of the customer. Because it is based on the customer requirements, this measure enables organizations to balance their lines. No operation should run faster than the takt time, just as no operation should produce more than what has been ordered by the customer.

Takt times do not leave a margin for error. To meet takt times, organizations have to remove sources of waste from their processes. The organization must be able to respond quickly to problems and eliminate possible causes of unplanned downtime.

 SIX SIGMA TOOLS AT WORK

Line Balancing

At QRC Inc., a Kaizen event studied the packaging of driver's side airbags. This three step process takes a completed driver's side airbag, folds it properly for instantaneous expansion, wraps it for insertion into the steering wheel, and inserts it into a metal bracket which will later hold the airbag to the interior of the steering column. The existing design resulted in an unbalanced line as evidenced by the percent load chart (also called a Yamhzumi chart) in Figure 17.4. Operators 1 and 2 are overburdened, and they are unable to keep Operator 3 busy.

Takt time calculations require that one driver's side airbag package must be created every minute. With this knowledge, the entire work area was redesigned to accommodate three operators for folding, two operators for wrapping, and one operator for insertion.

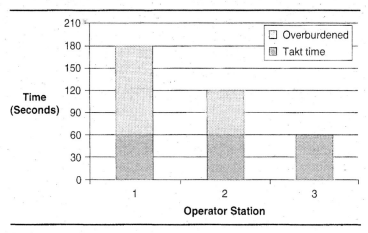

Figure 17.4   Percent Load Chart

Schedule Leveling

Much of the strength of a kanban system comes from level scheduling. Though level scheduling becomes more difficult the closer the work is to the customer's final product or service, being able to predict the amount of work to be performed in a day reduces the demands on the processes. Fluctuating customer demand can overwhelm the system's ability to respond appropriately. Uneven demand can result in waste associated with unpredictable downtime for setups or an excessive number of setups. Waste can also be found in the unpredictability in the mix and volume of customer demand.

Level scheduling enables an organization to link the customer schedule with the pace of manufacturing, thus it requires cooperation from the customer. The need to expedite disappears because the organization is neither ahead nor behind. The drawback is that responding to customer requirement changes becomes more complicated. To remain flexible, lean organizations develop the ability to make every part every day. Their processes are very flexible.

Standardized Work

In some organizations, standardized work is referred to as standard operating procedures. These standard operating procedures refer to the activities that must happen in order to complete a process. They mean that everyone doing that job does it exactly the same way each time. There would be no difference between the way operator A performs the work versus operator B. There would also be no difference between the fifth time they did the work or the 1000th time they performed the work. Kaizen improvement teams often create standard operating procedures as they make improvements to an area. In order to become a learning organization, when changes prove to be useful in one work area, these same countermeasures should be adopted for other similar areas.

SIX SIGMA TOOLS AT WORK

Standardized Work

XYZ Corporation asked a consultant to visit their plant to tackle noise related issues at workstation 18. While walking through the plant, the consultant noticed that other workstations contained equipment nearly identical to workstation 18. Sound pressure level comparisons between the other workstations and workstation 18 showed that workstation 18 had significantly higher noise levels. The consultant asked to see the other workstations and found that the equipment had been outfitted with three very effective sound dampening devices. She asked why these same countermeasures had not been adopted to workstation 18's equipment. The response: we never thought to do that, because that part of the plant is managed by a different supervisor. XYZ Corporation, since it didn't practice work standardization, failed to reap the benefits throughout their facility. Sharing success stories enables the entire organization to improve.

Visual Management

The lean thinking concept of visual management focuses on the need to organize work areas, storage areas, processes, and facilities in such a way as to be able to tell at a glance if something is misplaced or mismanaged. One common example of this approach are the lights that flash at a workstation if it is unable to meet its production quota or takt time. The flashing light draws attention to the area experiencing problems. Visual management can also been seen when kanban cards are used to keep track of inventory. Yet another example is lines on a workstation work surface or tool board marking locations for each tool used in the process. Visual management encourages a place for everything and everything in its place.

SUMMARY

Lean Thinking and Six Sigma Methodology, when used together, enable organizations to become more responsive to their customers. Lean principles and practices reduce process flow times and eliminate waste. Six Sigma principles and practices reduce process variation providing a more consistent product or service. Users of both Lean and Six Sigma recognize that lean methods are not designed to bring processes under statistical control and Six Sigma methods are not as effective at improving process speed. Successful organizations recognize that any and all helpful tools, techniques, and practices, when used together as a system, will lead to organizational improvement.

 ■ *Take Away Tips*

1. Six Sigma tools work to reduce variation and eliminate process defects while lean tools work to increase process speed.
2. Lean improvements often follow this cycle:
   a. Practice the five Ss.
   b. Develop a continuous flow that operates based on takt time.

    c. Establish a pull system to control production.

    d. Introduce line balancing and level scheduling.

    e. Practice kaizen to continually eliminate waste, reduce batch sizes, and create continuous flow.

3. Value stream mapping's biggest benefit is that it allows people to see and understand the entire flow of the process.

4. Each step in the process must be:

    Valuable (customer focused)

    Capable (Six Sigma tools and techniques)

    Available (total productive maintenance)

    Adequate (lean tools and techniques)

    Flexible (lean tools and techniques)

Chapter Questions

1. Describe the goals of lean manufacturing.

2. How does Six Sigma work together with lean manufacturing concepts?

3. Review the seven sources of waste provided in the chapter. Consider where you work, provide examples of each of these types of wastes in your organization.

4. Describe the five steps of lean process improvement in your own words.

5. Describe the Kaizen concept.

6. What is value stream process mapping? How does it go beyond traditional process mapping? Why is value stream process mapping such an important tool when trying to make organizational improvements?

7. Describe each of the five Ss. Go to an area in your organization or home and apply the five Ss. What changes did you make? What results did you see?

8. How do Kanban cards work?

9. Describe a process, system, or product that you have error proofed.

10. Why is preventive and predictive maintenance critical to overall system or process performance?

11. What tasks do you perform daily, either at home or at work? How would you go about reducing the setup times involved in these tasks? Select a task and make some changes to reduce the setup times. How much of a reduction did your changes provide?

12. What are the benefits of producing smaller batch sizes?

13. Describe what is meant by the term "line-balancing."

14. What is meant by the term "takt time"?

15. Describe a situation where you use visual management to monitor.

APPENDIX 1

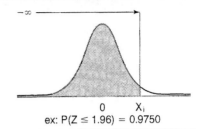

Normal Curve Areas P(Z ≤ Z$_0$)

ex: P(Z ≤ 1.96) = 0.9750

Z	0.09	0.08	0.07	0.06	0.05	0.04	0.03	0.02	0.01	0.00
−3.8	.0001	.0001	.0001	.0001	.0001	.0001	.0001	.0001	.0001	.0001
−3.7	.0001	.0001	.0001	.0001	.0001	.0001	.0001	.0001	.0001	.0001
−3.6	.0001	.0001	.0001	.0001	.0001	.0001	.0001	.0001	.0002	.0002
−3.5	.0002	.0002	.0002	.0002	.0002	.0002	.0002	.0002	.0002	.0002
−3.4	.0002	.0003	.0003	.0003	.0003	.0003	.0003	.0003	.0003	.0003
−3.3	.0003	.0004	.0004	.0004	.0004	.0004	.0004	.0005	.0005	.0005
−3.2	.0005	.0005	.0005	.0006	.0006	.0006	.0006	.0006	.0007	.0007
−3.1	.0007	.0007	.0008	.0008	.0008	.0008	.0009	.0009	.0009	.0010
−3.0	.0010	.0010	.0011	.0011	.0011	.0012	.0012	.0013	.0013	.0013
−2.9	.0014	.0014	.0015	.0015	.0016	.0016	.0017	.0018	.0018	.0019
−2.8	.0019	.0020	.0021	.0021	.0022	.0023	.0023	.0024	.0025	.0026
−2.7	.0026	.0027	.0028	.0029	.0030	.0031	.0032	.0033	.0034	.0035
−2.6	.0036	.0037	.0038	.0039	.0040	.0041	.0043	.0044	.0045	.0047
−2.5	.0048	.0049	.0051	.0052	.0054	.0055	.0057	.0059	.0060	.0062
−2.4	.0064	.0066	.0068	.0069	.0071	.0073	.0075	.0078	.0080	.0082
−2.3	.0084	.0087	.0089	.0091	.0094	.0096	.0099	.0102	.0104	.0107
−2.2	.0110	.0113	.0116	.0119	.0122	.0125	.0129	.0132	.0136	.0139
−2.1	.0143	.0146	.0150	.0154	.0158	.0162	.0166	.0170	.0174	.0179
−2.0	.0183	.0188	.0192	.0197	.0202	.0207	.0212	.0217	.0222	.0228
−1.9	.0233	.0239	.0244	.0250	.0256	.0262	.0268	.0274	.0281	.0287
−1.8	.0294	.0301	.0307	.0314	.0322	.0329	.0336	.0344	.0351	.0359
−1.7	.0367	.0375	.0384	.0392	.0401	.0409	.0418	.0427	.0436	.0446
−1.6	.0455	.0465	.0475	.0485	.0495	.0505	.0516	.0526	.0537	.0548
−1.5	.0559	.0571	.0582	.0594	.0606	.0618	.0630	.0643	.0655	.0668
−1.4	.0681	.0694	.0708	.0721	.0735	.0749	.0764	.0778	.0793	.0808
−1.3	.0823	.0838	.0853	.0869	.0885	.0901	.0918	.0934	.0951	.0968
−1.2	.0985	.1003	.1020	.1038	.1056	.1075	.1093	.1112	.1131	.1151
−1.1	.1170	.1190	.1210	.1230	.1251	.1271	.1292	.1314	.1335	.1357
−1.0	.1379	.1401	.1423	.1446	.1469	.1492	.1515	.1539	.1562	.1587
−0.9	.1611	.1635	.1660	.1685	.1711	.1736	.1762	.1788	.1814	.1841
−0.8	.1867	.1894	.1922	.1949	.1977	.2005	.2033	.2061	.2090	.2119
−0.7	.2148	.2177	.2206	.2236	.2266	.2296	.2327	.2358	.2389	.2420
−0.6	.2451	.2483	.2514	.2546	.2578	.2611	.2643	.2676	.2709	.2743
−0.5	.2776	.2810	.2843	.2877	.2912	.2946	.2981	.3015	.3050	.3085
−0.4	.3121	.3156	.3192	.3228	.3264	.3300	.3336	.3372	.3409	.3446
−0.3	.3483	.3520	.3557	.3594	.3632	.3669	.3707	.3745	.3783	.3821
−0.2	.3859	.3897	.3936	.3974	.4013	.4052	.4090	.4129	.4168	.4207
−0.1	.4247	.4286	.4325	.4364	.4404	.4443	.4483	.4522	.4562	.4602
−0.0	.4641	.4681	.4721	.4761	.4801	.4840	.4880	.4920	.4960	.5000

Z	0.00	0.01	0.02	0.03	0.04	0.05	0.06	0.07	0.08	0.09
+0.0	.5000	.5040	.5080	.5120	.5160	.5199	.5239	.5279	.5319	.5359
+0.1	.5398	.5438	.5478	.5517	.5557	.5596	.5636	.5675	.5714	.5753
+0.2	.5793	.5832	.5871	.5910	.5948	.5987	.6026	.6064	.6103	.6141
+0.3	.6179	.6217	.6255	.6293	.6331	.6368	.6406	.6443	.6480	.6517
+0.4	.6554	.6591	.6628	.6664	.6700	.6736	.6772	.6808	.6844	.6879
+0.5	.6915	.6950	.6985	.7019	.7054	.7088	.7123	.7157	.7190	.7224
+0.6	.7257	.7291	.7324	.7357	.7389	.7422	.7454	.7486	.7517	.7549
+0.7	.7580	.7611	.7642	.7673	.7704	.7734	.7764	.7794	.7823	.7852
+0.8	.7881	.7910	.7939	.7967	.7995	.8023	.8051	.8078	.8106	.8133
+0.9	.8159	.8186	.8212	.8238	.8264	.8289	.8315	.8340	.8365	.8389
+1.0	.8413	.8438	.8461	.8485	.8508	.8531	.8554	.8577	.8599	.8621
+1.1	.8643	.8665	.8686	.8708	.8729	.8749	.8770	.8790	.8810	.8830
+1.2	.8849	.8869	.8888	.8907	.8925	.8944	.8962	.8980	.8997	.9015
+1.3	.9032	.9049	.9066	.9082	.9099	.9115	.9131	.9147	.9162	.9177
+1.4	.9192	.9207	.9222	.9236	.9251	.9265	.9279	.9292	.9306	.9319
+1.5	.9332	.9345	.9357	.9370	.9382	.9394	.9406	.9418	.9429	.9441
+1.6	.9452	.9463	.9474	.9484	.9495	.9505	.9515	.9525	.9535	.9545
+1.7	.9554	.9564	.9573	.9582	.9591	.9599	.9608	.9616	.9625	.9633
+1.8	.9641	.9649	.9656	.9664	.9671	.9678	.9686	.9693	.9699	.9706
+1.9	.9713	.9719	.9726	.9732	.9738	.9744	.9750	.9756	.9761	.9767
+2.0	.9772	.9778	.9783	.9788	.9793	.9798	.9803	.9808	.9812	.9817
+2.1	.9821	.9826	.9830	.9834	.9838	.9842	.9846	.9850	.9854	.9857
+2.2	.9861	.9864	.9868	.9871	.9875	.9878	.9881	.9884	.9887	.9890
+2.3	.9893	.9896	.9898	.9901	.9904	.9906	.9909	.9911	.9913	.9916
+2.4	.9918	.9920	.9922	.9925	.9927	.9929	.9931	.9932	.9934	.9936
+2.5	.9938	.9940	.9941	.9943	.9945	.9946	.9948	.9949	.9951	.9952
+2.6	.9953	.9955	.9956	.9957	.9959	.9960	.9961	.9962	.9963	.9964
+2.7	.9965	.9966	.9967	.9968	.9969	.9970	.9971	.9972	.9973	.9974
+2.8	.9974	.9975	.9976	.9977	.9977	.9978	.9979	.9979	.9980	.9981
+2.9	.9981	.9982	.9982	.9983	.9984	.9984	.9985	.9985	.9986	.9986
+3.0	.9987	.9987	.9987	.9988	.9988	.9989	.9989	.9989	.9990	.9990
+3.1	.9990	.9991	.9991	.9991	.9992	.9992	.9992	.9992	.9993	.9993
+3.2	.9993	.9993	.9994	.9994	.9994	.9994	.9994	.9995	.9995	.9995
+3.3	.9995	.9995	.9995	.9996	.9996	.9996	.9996	.9996	.9996	.9997
+3.4	.9997	.9997	.9997	.9997	.9997	.9997	.9997	.9997	.9997	.9998
+3.5	.9998	.9998	.9998	.9998	.9998	.9998	.9998	.9998	.9998	.9998
+3.6	.9998	.9998	.9999	.9999	.9999	.9999	.9999	.9999	.9999	.9999
+3.7	.9999	.9999	.9999	.9999	.9999	.9999	.9999	.9999	.9999	.9999
+3.8	.9999	.9999	.9999	.9999	.9999	.9999	.9999	.9999	.9999	.9999

Factors for Computing Central Lines and 3s Control Limits for $\overline{X}$, s, and R Charts

Observations in Sample, n	Chart for Averages			Chart for Ranges							Chart for Standard Deviations				
	Factor for Central Line	Factors for Control Limits		Factor for Central Line	Factors for Control Limits					Factor for Central Line	Factors for Control Limits			
	A	A_2	A_3	d_2	d_1	D_1	D_2	D_3	D_4	c_4	B_3	B_4	B_5	B_6
2	2.121	1.880	2.659	1.128	0.853	0	3.686	0	3.267	0.7979	0	3.267	0	2.606
3	1.732	1.023	1.954	1.693	0.888	0	4.358	0	2.574	0.8862	0	2.568	0	2.276
4	1.500	0.729	1.628	2.059	0.880	0	4.698	0	2.282	0.9213	0	2.266	0	2.088
5	1.342	0.577	1.427	2.326	0.864	0	4.918	0	2.114	0.9400	0	2.089	0	1.964
6	1.225	0.483	1.287	2.534	0.848	0	5.078	0	2.004	0.9515	0.030	1.970	0.029	1.874
7	1.134	0.419	1.182	2.704	0.833	0.204	5.204	0.076	1.924	0.9594	0.118	1.882	0.113	1.806
8	1.061	0.373	1.099	2.847	0.820	0.388	5.306	0.136	1.864	0.9650	0.185	1.815	0.179	1.751
9	1.000	0.337	1.032	2.970	0.808	0.547	5.393	0.184	1.816	0.9693	0.239	1.761	0.232	1.707
10	0.949	0.308	0.975	3.078	0.797	0.687	5.469	0.223	1.777	0.9727	0.284	1.716	0.276	1.669
11	0.905	0.285	0.927	3.173	0.787	0.811	5.535	0.256	1.744	0.9754	0.321	1.679	0.313	1.637
12	0.866	0.266	0.886	3.258	0.778	0.922	5.594	0.283	1.717	0.9776	0.354	1.646	0.346	1.610
13	0.832	0.249	0.850	3.336	0.770	1.025	5.647	0.307	1.693	0.9794	0.382	1.618	0.374	1.585
14	0.802	0.235	0.817	3.407	0.763	1.118	5.696	0.328	1.672	0.9810	0.406	1.594	0.399	1.563
15	0.775	0.223	0.789	3.472	0.756	1.203	5.741	0.347	1.653	0.9823	0.428	1.572	0.421	1.544
16	0.750	0.212	0.763	3.532	0.750	1.282	5.782	0.363	1.637	0.9835	0.448	1.552	0.440	1.526
17	0.728	0.203	0.739	3.588	0.744	1.356	5.820	0.378	1.622	0.9845	0.466	1.534	0.458	1.511
18	0.707	0.194	0.718	3.640	0.739	1.424	5.856	0.391	1.608	0.9854	0.482	1.518	0.475	1.496
19	0.688	0.187	0.698	3.689	0.734	1.487	5.891	0.403	1.597	0.9862	0.497	1.503	0.490	1.483
20	0.671	0.180	0.680	3.735	0.729	1.549	5.921	0.415	1.585	0.9869	0.510	1.490	0.504	1.470

APPENDIX 3

Values of t Distribution

Values of t Distribution

df	$t_{0.10}$	$t_{0.05}$	$t_{0.025}$	$t_{0.01}$	$t_{0.005}$	df
1	3.078	6.314	12.706	31.821	63.656	1
2	1.886	2.920	4.303	6.965	9.925	2
3	1.638	2.353	3.182	4.541	5.841	3
4	1.533	2.132	2.776	3.747	4.604	4
5	1.476	2.015	2.571	3.365	4.032	5
6	1.440	1.943	2.447	3.143	3.707	6
7	1.415	1.895	2.365	2.998	3.499	7
8	1.397	1.860	2.306	2.896	3.355	8
9	1.383	1.833	2.262	2.821	3.250	9
10	1.372	1.812	2.228	2.764	3.169	10
11	1.363	1.796	2.201	2.718	3.106	11
12	1.356	1.782	2.179	2.681	3.055	12
13	1.350	1.771	2.160	2.650	3.012	13
14	1.345	1.761	2.145	2.624	2.977	14
15	1.341	1.753	2.131	2.602	2.947	15
16	1.337	1.746	2.120	2.583	2.921	16
17	1.333	1.740	2.110	2.567	2.898	17
18	1.330	1.734	2.101	2.552	2.878	18
19	1.328	1.729	2.093	2.539	2.861	19
20	1.325	1.725	2.086	2.528	2.845	20
21	1.323	1.721	2.080	2.518	2.831	21
22	1.321	1.717	2.074	2.508	2.819	22
23	1.319	1.714	2.069	2.500	2.807	23
24	1.318	1.711	2.064	2.492	2.797	24
25	1.316	1.708	2.060	2.485	2.787	25
26	1.315	1.706	2.056	2.479	2.779	26
27	1.314	1.703	2.052	2.473	2.771	27
28	1.313	1.701	2.048	2.467	2.763	28
29	1.311	1.699	2.045	2.462	2.756	29
30	1.310	1.697	2.042	2.457	2.750	30
31	1.309	1.696	2.040	2.453	2.744	31

(*continued*)

Values of t Distribution (*continued*)

df	$t_{0.10}$	$t_{0.05}$	$t_{0.025}$	$t_{0.01}$	$t_{0.005}$	df
32	1.309	1.694	2.037	2.449	2.738	32
33	1.308	1.692	2.035	2.445	2.733	33
34	1.307	1.691	2.032	2.441	2.728	34
35	1.306	1.690	2.030	2.438	2.724	35
40	1.303	1.684	2.021	2.423	2.704	40
45	1.301	1.679	2.014	2.412	2.690	45
50	1.299	1.676	2.009	2.403	2.678	50
55	1.297	1.673	2.004	2.396	2.668	55
60	1.296	1.671	2.000	2.390	2.660	60
70	1.294	1.667	1.994	2.381	2.648	70
80	1.292	1.664	1.990	2.374	2.639	80
90	1.291	1.662	1.987	2.368	2.632	90
100	1.290	1.660	1.984	2.364	2.626	100
200	1.286	1.653	1.972	2.345	2.601	200
400	1.284	1.649	1.966	2.336	2.588	400
600	1.283	1.647	1.964	2.333	2.584	600
800	1.283	1.647	1.963	2.331	2.582	800
999	1.282	1.646	1.962	2.330	2.581	999

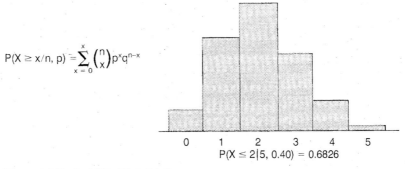

$$P(X \geq x/n, p) = \sum_{x=0}^{x} \binom{n}{x} p^x q^{n-x}$$

$$P(X \leq 2 | 5, 0.40) = 0.6826$$

Cumulative Binomial Probability Distribution

n = 5

d \ p	0.01	0.02	0.03	0.04	0.05	0.06	0.07	0.08	0.09	0.10
0	0.9510	0.9039	0.8587	0.8154	0.7738	0.7339	0.6957	0.6591	0.6240	0.5905
1	0.9990	0.9962	0.9915	0.9852	0.9774	0.9681	0.9575	0.9456	0.9326	0.9185
2	1.0000	0.9999	0.9997	0.9994	0.9998	0.9980	0.9969	0.9955	0.9937	0.9914
3	1.0000	1.0000	1.0000	1.0000	1.0000	0.9999	0.9999	0.9998	0.9997	0.9995
4	1.0000	1.0000	1.0000	1.0000	1.0000	1.0000	1.0000	1.0000	1.0000	1.0000

d \ p	0.11	0.12	0.13	0.14	0.15	0.16	0.17	0.18	0.19	0.20
0	0.5584	0.5277	0.4984	0.4704	0.4437	0.4182	0.3939	0.3707	0.3487	0.3277
1	0.9035	0.8875	0.8708	0.8533	0.8352	0.8165	0.7973	0.7776	0.7576	0.7373
2	0.9888	0.9857	0.9821	0.9780	0.9734	0.9682	0.9625	0.9563	0.9495	0.9421
3	0.9993	0.9991	0.9987	0.9983	0.9978	0.9971	0.9964	0.9955	0.9945	0.9933
4	1.0000	1.0000	1.0000	0.9999	0.9999	0.9999	0.9999	0.9998	0.9998	0.9997
5	1.0000	1.0000	1.0000	1.0000	1.0000	1.0000	1.0000	1.0000	1.0000	1.0000

d \ p	0.21	0.22	0.23	0.24	0.25	0.26	0.27	0.28	0.29	0.30
0	0.3077	0.2887	0.2707	0.2536	0.2373	0.2219	0.2073	0.1935	0.1804	0.1681
1	0.7167	0.6959	0.6749	0.6539	0.6328	0.6117	0.5907	0.5697	0.5489	0.5282
2	0.9341	0.9256	0.9164	0.9067	0.8965	0.8857	0.8743	0.8624	0.8499	0.8369
3	0.9919	0.9903	0.9886	0.9866	0.9844	0.9819	0.9792	0.9762	0.9728	0.9692
4	0.9996	0.9995	0.9994	0.9992	0.9990	0.9988	0.9986	0.9983	0.9979	0.9976
5	1.0000	1.0000	1.0000	1.0000	1.0000	1.0000	1.0000	1.0000	1.0000	1.0000

d \ p	0.31	0.32	0.33	0.34	0.35	0.36	0.37	0.38	0.39	0.40
0	0.1564	0.1454	0.1350	0.1252	0.1160	0.1074	0.0992	0.0916	0.0845	0.0778
1	0.5077	0.4875	0.4675	0.4478	0.4284	0.4094	0.3907	0.3724	0.3545	0.3370

(continued)

Cumulative Binomial Probability Distribution (*continued*)

n = 5

d \ p	0.31	0.32	0.33	0.34	0.35	0.36	0.37	0.38	0.39	0.40
2	0.8234	0.8095	0.7950	0.7801	0.7648	0.7491	0.7330	0.7165	0.6997	0.6826
3	0.9653	0.9610	0.9564	0.9514	0.9460	0.9402	0.9340	0.9274	0.9204	0.9130
4	0.9971	0.9966	0.9961	0.9955	0.9947	0.9940	0.9931	0.9921	0.9910	0.9898
5	1.0000	1.0000	1.0000	1.0000	1.0000	1.0000	1.0000	1.0000	1.0000	1.0000

d \ p	0.41	0.42	0.43	0.44	0.45	0.46	0.47	0.48	0.49	0.50
0	0.0715	0.0656	0.0602	0.0551	0.0503	0.0459	0.0418	0.0380	0.0345	0.0312
1	0.3199	0.3033	0.2871	0.2714	0.2562	0.2415	0.2272	0.2135	0.2002	0.1875
2	0.6651	0.6475	0.6295	0.6114	0.5931	0.5747	0.5561	0.5375	0.5187	0.5000
3	0.9051	0.8967	0.8879	0.8786	0.8688	0.8585	0.8478	0.8365	0.8247	0.8125
4	0.9884	0.9869	0.9853	0.9835	0.9815	0.9794	0.9771	0.9745	0.9718	0.9688
5	1.0000	1.0000	1.0000	1.0000	1.0000	1.0000	1.0000	1.0000	1.0000	1.0000

n = 6

d \ p	0.01	0.02	0.03	0.04	0.05	0.06	0.07	0.08	0.09	0.10
0	0.9415	0.8858	0.8330	0.7828	0.7351	0.6899	0.6470	0.6064	0.5679	0.5314
1	0.9985	0.9943	0.9875	0.9784	0.9672	0.9541	0.9392	0.9227	0.9048	0.8857
2	1.0000	0.9998	0.9995	0.9988	0.9978	0.9962	0.9942	0.9915	0.9882	0.9841
3	1.0000	1.0000	1.0000	1.0000	0.9999	0.9998	0.9997	0.9995	0.9992	0.9987
4	1.0000	1.0000	1.0000	1.0000	1.0000	1.0000	1.0000	1.0000	1.0000	0.9999
5	1.0000	1.0000	1.0000	1.0000	1.0000	1.0000	1.0000	1.0000	1.0000	1.0000

d \ p	0.11	0.12	0.13	0.14	0.15	0.16	0.17	0.18	0.19	0.20
0	0.4970	0.4644	0.4336	0.4046	0.3771	0.3513	0.3269	0.3040	0.2824	0.2621
1	0.8655	0.8444	0.8224	0.7997	0.7765	0.7528	0.7287	0.7044	0.6799	0.6554
2	0.9794	0.9739	0.9676	0.9605	0.9527	0.9440	0.9345	0.9241	0.9130	0.9011
3	0.9982	0.9975	0.9966	0.9955	0.9941	0.9925	0.9906	0.9884	0.9859	0.9830
4	0.9999	0.9999	0.9998	0.9997	0.9996	0.9995	0.9993	0.9990	0.9987	0.9984
5	1.0000	1.0000	1.0000	1.0000	1.0000	1.0000	1.0000	1.0000	1.0000	0.9999
6	1.0000	1.0000	1.0000	1.0000	1.0000	1.0000	1.0000	1.0000	1.0000	1.0000

d \ p	0.21	0.22	0.23	0.24	0.25	0.26	0.27	0.28	0.29	0.30
0	0.2431	0.2252	0.2084	0.1927	0.1780	0.1642	0.1513	0.1393	0.1281	0.1176
1	0.6308	0.6063	0.5820	0.5578	0.5339	0.5104	0.4872	0.4644	0.4420	0.4202
2	0.8885	0.8750	0.8609	0.8461	0.8306	0.8144	0.7977	0.7804	0.7626	0.7443
3	0.9798	0.9761	0.9720	0.9674	0.9624	0.9569	0.9508	0.9443	0.9372	0.9295
4	0.9980	0.9975	0.9969	0.9962	0.9954	0.9944	0.9933	0.9921	0.9907	0.9891
5	0.9999	0.9999	0.9999	0.9998	0.9998	0.9997	0.9996	0.9995	0.9994	0.9993
6	1.0000	1.0000	1.0000	1.0000	1.0000	1.0000	1.0000	1.0000	1.0000	1.0000

d \ p	0.31	0.32	0.33	0.34	0.35	0.36	0.37	0.38	0.39	0.40
0	0.1079	0.0989	0.0905	0.0827	0.0754	0.0687	0.0625	0.0568	0.0515	0.0467
1	0.3988	0.3780	0.3578	0.3381	0.3191	0.3006	0.2828	0.2657	0.2492	0.2333
2	0.7256	0.7064	0.6870	0.6672	0.6471	0.6268	0.6063	0.5857	0.5650	0.5443
3	0.9213	0.9125	0.9031	0.8931	0.8826	0.8714	0.8596	0.8473	0.8343	0.8208
4	0.9873	0.9852	0.9830	0.9805	0.9777	0.9746	0.9712	0.9675	0.9635	0.9590

Cumulative Binomial Probability Distribution (*continued*)

n = 6

d \ p	0.31	0.32	0.33	0.34	0.35	0.36	0.37	0.38	0.39	0.40
5	0.9991	0.9989	0.9987	0.9985	0.9982	0.9978	0.9974	0.9970	0.9965	0.9959
6	1.0000	1.0000	1.0000	1.0000	1.0000	1.0000	1.0000	1.0000	1.0000	1.0000

d \ p	0.41	0.42	0.43	0.44	0.45	0.46	0.47	0.48	0.49	0.50
0	0.0422	0.0381	0.0343	0.0308	0.0277	0.0248	0.0222	0.0198	0.0176	0.0156
1	0.2181	0.2035	0.1895	0.1762	0.1636	0.1515	0.1401	0.1293	0.1190	0.1094
2	0.5236	0.5029	0.4823	0.4618	0.4415	0.4214	0.4015	0.3820	0.3627	0.3437
3	0.8067	0.7920	0.7768	0.7610	0.7447	0.7280	0.7107	0.6930	0.6748	0.6562
4	0.9542	0.9490	0.9434	0.9373	0.9308	0.9238	0.9163	0.9083	0.8997	0.8906
5	0.9952	0.9945	0.9937	0.9927	0.9917	0.9905	0.9892	0.9878	0.9862	0.9844
6	1.0000	1.0000	1.0000	1.0000	1.0000	1.0000	1.0000	1.0000	1.0000	1.0000

n = 7

d \ p	0.01	0.02	0.03	0.04	0.05	0.06	0.07	0.08	0.09	0.10
0	0.9321	0.8681	0.8080	0.7514	0.6983	0.6485	0.6017	0.5578	0.5168	0.4783
1	0.9980	0.9921	0.9829	0.9706	0.9556	0.9382	0.9187	0.8974	0.8745	0.8503
2	1.0000	0.9997	0.9991	0.9980	0.9962	0.9937	0.9903	0.9860	0.9807	0.9743
3	1.0000	1.0000	1.0000	0.9999	0.9998	0.9996	0.9993	0.9998	0.9982	0.9973
4	1.0000	1.0000	1.0000	1.0000	1.0000	1.0000	1.0000	0.9999	0.9999	0.9998
5	1.0000	1.0000	1.0000	1.0000	1.0000	1.0000	1.0000	1.0000	1.0000	1.0000

d \ p	0.11	0.12	0.13	0.14	0.15	0.16	0.17	0.18	0.19	0.20
0	0.4423	0.4087	0.3773	0.3479	0.3206	0.2951	0.2714	0.2493	0.2288	0.2097
1	0.8250	0.7988	0.7719	0.7444	0.7166	0.6885	0.6604	0.6323	0.6044	0.5767
2	0.9669	0.9584	0.9487	0.9380	0.9262	0.9134	0.8995	0.8846	0.8687	0.8520
3	0.9961	0.9946	0.9928	0.9906	0.9879	0.9847	0.9811	0.9769	0.9721	0.9687
4	0.9997	0.9996	0.9994	0.9991	0.9988	0.9983	0.9978	0.9971	0.9963	0.9953
5	1.0000	1.0000	1.0000	1.0000	0.9999	0.9999	0.9999	0.9998	0.9997	0.9996
6	1.0000	1.0000	1.0000	1.0000	1.0000	1.0000	1.0000	1.0000	1.0000	1.0000

d \ p	0.21	0.22	0.23	0.24	0.25	0.26	0.27	0.28	0.29	0.30
0	0.1920	0.1757	0.1605	0.1465	0.1335	0.1215	0.1105	0.1003	0.0910	0.0824
1	0.5494	0.5225	0.4960	0.4702	0.4449	0.4204	0.3965	0.3734	0.3510	0.3294
2	0.8343	0.8159	0.7967	0.7769	0.7564	0.7354	0.7139	0.6919	0.6696	0.6471
3	0.9606	0.9539	0.9464	0.9383	0.9294	0.9198	0.9095	0.8984	0.8866	0.8740
4	0.9942	0.9928	0.9912	0.9893	0.9871	0.9847	0.9819	0.9787	0.9752	0.9712
5	0.9995	0.9994	0.9992	0.9989	0.9987	0.9983	0.9979	0.9974	0.9969	0.9962
6	1.0000	1.0000	1.0000	1.0000	0.9999	0.9999	0.9999	0.9999	0.9998	0.9998
7	1.0000	1.0000	1.0000	1.0000	1.0000	1.0000	1.0000	1.0000	1.0000	1.0000

d \ p	0.31	0.32	0.33	0.34	0.35	0.36	0.37	0.38	0.39	0.40
0	0.0745	0.0672	0.0606	0.0546	0.0490	0.0440	0.0394	0.0352	0.0314	0.0280
1	0.3086	0.2887	0.2696	0.2513	0.2338	0.2172	0.2013	0.1863	0.1721	0.1586
2	0.6243	0.6013	0.5783	0.5553	0.5323	0.5094	0.4868	0.4641	0.4419	0.4199
3	0.8606	0.8466	0.8318	0.8163	0.8002	0.7833	0.7659	0.7479	0.7293	0.7102

(*continued*)

Cumulative Binomial Probability Distribution (*continued*)

n = 7

d \ p	0.31	0.32	0.33	0.34	0.35	0.36	0.37	0.38	0.39	0.40
4	0.9668	0.9620	0.9566	0.9508	0.9444	0.9375	0.9299	0.9218	0.9131	0.9037
5	0.9954	0.9945	0.9935	0.9923	0.9910	0.9895	0.9877	0.9858	0.9836	0.9812
6	0.9997	0.9997	0.9996	0.9995	0.9994	0.9992	0.9991	0.9989	0.9986	0.9984
7	1.0000	1.0000	1.0000	1.0000	1.0000	1.0000	1.0000	1.0000	1.0000	1.0000

d \ p	0.41	0.42	0.43	0.44	0.45	0.46	0.47	0.48	0.49	0.50
0	0.0249	0.0221	0.0195	0.0173	0.0152	0.0134	0.0117	0.0103	0.0090	0.0078
1	0.1459	0.1340	0.1228	0.1123	0.1024	0.0932	0.0847	0.0767	0.0693	0.0625
2	0.3983	0.3771	0.3564	0.3362	0.3164	0.2973	0.2787	0.2607	0.2433	0.2266
3	0.6906	0.6706	0.6502	0.6294	0.6083	0.5869	0.5654	0.5437	0.5219	0.5000
4	0.8937	0.8831	0.8718	0.8598	0.8471	0.8337	0.8197	0.8049	0.7895	0.7734
5	0.9784	0.9754	0.9721	0.9684	0.9643	0.9598	0.9549	0.9496	0.9438	0.9375
6	0.9981	0.9977	0.9973	0.9968	0.9963	0.9956	0.9949	0.9941	0.9932	0.9922
7	1.0000	1.0000	1.0000	1.0000	1.0000	1.0000	1.0000	1.0000	1.0000	1.0000

n = 8

d \ p	0.01	0.02	0.03	0.04	0.05	0.06	0.07	0.08	0.09	0.10
0	0.9227	0.8508	0.7837	0.7214	0.6634	0.6096	0.5596	0.5132	0.4703	0.4305
1	0.9973	0.9897	0.9777	0.9619	0.9428	0.9208	0.8965	0.8702	0.8423	0.8131
2	0.9999	0.9996	0.9987	0.9969	0.9942	0.9904	0.9853	0.9789	0.9711	0.9619
3	1.0000	1.0000	0.9999	0.9998	0.9996	0.9993	0.9987	0.9978	0.9966	0.9950
4	1.0000	1.0000	1.0000	1.0000	1.0000	1.0000	0.9999	0.9999	0.9997	0.9996
5	1.0000	1.0000	1.0000	1.0000	1.0000	1.0000	1.0000	1.0000	1.0000	1.0000

d \ p	0.11	0.12	0.13	0.14	0.15	0.16	0.17	0.18	0.19	0.20
0	0.3937	0.3596	0.3282	0.2992	0.2725	0.2479	0.2252	0.2044	0.1853	0.1678
1	0.7829	0.7520	0.7206	0.6889	0.6572	0.6256	0.5943	0.5634	0.5330	0.5033
2	0.9513	0.9392	0.9257	0.9109	0.8948	0.8774	0.8588	0.8392	0.8185	0.7969
3	0.9929	0.9903	0.9871	0.9832	0.9786	0.9733	0.9672	0.9603	0.9524	0.9437
4	0.9993	0.9990	0.9985	0.9979	0.9971	0.9962	0.9950	0.9935	0.9917	0.9896
5	1.0000	0.9999	0.9999	0.9998	0.9998	0.9997	0.9995	0.9993	0.9991	0.9988
6	1.0000	1.0000	1.0000	1.0000	1.0000	1.0000	1.0000	1.0000	0.9999	0.9999
7	1.0000	1.0000	1.0000	1.0000	1.0000	1.0000	1.0000	1.0000	1.0000	1.0000

d \ p	0.21	0.22	0.23	0.24	0.25	0.26	0.27	0.28	0.29	0.30
0	0.1517	0.1370	0.1236	0.1113	0.1001	0.8990	0.0806	0.0722	0.0646	0.0576
1	0.4743	0.4462	0.4189	0.3925	0.3671	0.3427	0.3193	0.2969	0.2756	0.2553
2	0.7745	0.7514	0.7276	0.7033	0.6785	0.6535	0.6282	0.6027	0.5772	0.5518
3	0.9341	0.9235	0.9120	0.8996	0.8862	0.8719	0.8567	0.8406	0.8237	0.8059
4	0.9871	0.9842	0.9809	0.9770	0.9727	0.9678	0.9623	0.9562	0.9495	0.9420
5	0.9984	0.9979	0.9973	0.9966	0.9958	0.9948	0.9936	0.9922	0.9906	0.9887
6	0.9999	0.9998	0.9998	0.9997	0.9996	0.9995	0.9994	0.9992	0.9990	0.9987
7	1.0000	1.0000	1.0000	1.0000	1.0000	1.0000	1.0000	1.0000	0.9999	0.9999
8	1.0000	1.0000	1.0000	1.0000	1.0000	1.0000	1.0000	1.0000	1.0000	1.0000

Cumulative Binomial Probability Distribution (continued)

n = 8

d \ p	0.31	0.32	0.33	0.34	0.35	0.36	0.37	0.38	0.39	0.40
0	0.0514	0.0457	0.0406	0.0360	0.0319	0.0281	0.0248	0.0218	0.0192	0.0168
1	0.2360	0.2178	0.2006	0.1844	0.1691	0.1548	0.1414	0.1289	0.1172	0.1064
2	0.5264	0.5013	0.4764	0.4519	0.4278	0.4042	0.3811	0.3585	0.3366	0.3154
3	0.7874	0.7681	0.7481	0.7276	0.7064	0.6847	0.6626	0.6401	0.6172	0.5941
4	0.9339	0.9250	0.9154	0.9051	0.8939	0.8820	0.8693	0.8557	0.8414	0.8263
5	0.9866	0.9841	0.9813	0.9782	0.9747	0.9707	0.9664	0.9615	0.9561	0.9502
6	0.9984	0.9980	0.9976	0.9970	0.9964	0.9957	0.9949	0.9939	0.9928	0.9915
7	0.9999	0.9999	0.9999	0.9998	0.9998	0.9997	0.9996	0.9996	0.9995	0.9993
8	1.0000	1.0000	1.0000	1.0000	1.0000	1.0000	1.0000	1.0000	1.0000	1.0000

d \ p	0.41	0.42	0.43	0.44	0.45	0.46	0.47	0.48	0.49	0.50
0	0.0147	0.0128	0.0111	0.0097	0.0084	0.0072	0.0062	0.0053	0.0046	0.0039
1	0.0963	0.0870	0.0784	0.0705	0.0632	0.0565	0.0504	0.0448	0.0398	0.0352
2	0.2948	0.2750	0.2560	0.2376	0.2201	0.2034	0.1875	0.1724	0.1581	0.1445
3	0.5708	0.5473	0.5238	0.5004	0.4770	0.4537	0.4306	0.4078	0.3854	0.3633
4	0.8105	0.7938	0.7765	0.7584	0.7396	0.7202	0.7001	0.6795	0.6584	0.6367
5	0.9437	0.9366	0.9289	0.9206	0.9115	0.9018	0.8914	0.8802	0.8682	0.8555
6	0.9900	0.9883	0.9864	0.9843	0.9819	0.9792	0.9761	0.9728	0.9690	0.9648
7	0.9992	0.9990	0.9988	0.9986	0.9983	0.9980	0.9976	0.9972	0.9967	0.9961
8	1.0000	1.0000	1.0000	1.0000	1.0000	1.0000	1.0000	1.0000	1.0000	1.0000

n = 9

d \ p	0.01	0.02	0.03	0.04	0.05	0.06	0.07	0.08	0.09	0.10
0	0.9135	0.8337	0.7602	0.6925	0.6302	0.5730	0.5204	0.4722	0.4279	0.3874
1	0.9966	0.9869	0.9718	0.9522	0.9288	0.9022	0.8729	0.8417	0.8088	0.7748
2	0.9999	0.9994	0.9980	0.9955	0.9916	0.9862	0.9791	0.9702	0.9595	0.9470
3	1.0000	1.0000	0.9999	0.9997	0.9994	0.9987	0.9977	0.9963	0.9943	0.9917
4	1.0000	1.0000	1.0000	1.0000	1.0000	0.9999	0.9998	0.9997	0.9995	0.9991
5	1.0000	1.0000	1.0000	1.0000	1.0000	1.0000	1.0000	1.0000	1.0000	0.9999
6	1.0000	1.0000	1.0000	1.0000	1.0000	1.0000	1.0000	1.0000	1.0000	1.0000

d \ p	0.11	0.12	0.13	0.14	0.15	0.16	0.17	0.18	0.19	0.20
0	0.3504	0.3165	0.2855	0.2573	0.2316	0.2082	0.1869	0.1676	0.1501	0.1342
1	0.7401	0.7049	0.6696	0.6343	0.5995	0.5652	0.5315	0.4988	0.4670	0.4362
2	0.9327	0.9167	0.8991	0.8798	0.8591	0.8371	0.8139	0.7895	0.7643	0.7382
3	0.9883	0.9842	0.9791	0.9731	0.9661	0.9580	0.9488	0.9385	0.9270	0.9144
4	0.9986	0.9979	0.9970	0.9959	0.9944	0.9925	0.9902	0.9875	0.9842	0.9804
5	0.9999	0.9998	0.9997	0.9996	0.9994	0.9991	0.9987	0.9983	0.9977	0.9969
6	1.0000	1.0000	1.0000	1.0000	1.0000	0.9999	0.9999	0.9998	0.9998	0.9997
7	1.0000	1.0000	1.0000	1.0000	1.0000	1.0000	1.0000	1.0000	1.0000	1.0000

d \ p	0.21	0.22	0.23	0.24	0.25	0.26	0.27	0.28	0.29	0.30
0	0.1199	0.1069	0.0952	0.0846	0.0751	0.0665	0.0589	0.0520	0.0458	0.0404
1	0.4066	0.3782	0.3509	0.3250	0.3003	0.2770	0.2548	0.2340	0.2144	0.1960

(continued)

Cumulative Binomial Probability Distribution (*continued*)

n = 9

d \ p	0.21	0.22	0.23	0.24	0.25	0.26	0.27	0.28	0.29	0.30
2	0.7115	0.6842	0.6566	0.6287	0.6007	0.5727	0.5448	0.5171	0.4898	0.4628
3	0.9006	0.8856	0.8696	0.8525	0.8343	0.8151	0.7950	0.7740	0.7522	0.7297
4	0.9760	0.9709	0.9650	0.9584	0.9511	0.9429	0.9338	0.9238	0.9130	0.9012
5	0.9960	0.9949	0.9935	0.9919	0.9900	0.9878	0.9851	0.9821	0.9787	0.9747
6	0.9996	0.9994	0.9992	0.9990	0.9987	0.9983	0.9978	0.9972	0.9965	0.9957
7	1.0000	1.0000	0.9999	0.9999	0.9999	0.9999	0.9998	0.9997	0.9997	0.9996
8	1.0000	1.0000	1.0000	1.0000	1.0000	1.0000	1.0000	1.0000	1.0000	1.0000

d \ p	0.31	0.32	0.33	0.34	0.35	0.36	0.37	0.38	0.39	0.40
0	0.0355	1.0311	0.0272	0.0238	0.0207	0.0180	0.0156	0.0135	0.0117	0.0101
1	0.1788	0.1628	0.1478	0.1339	0.1211	0.1092	0.0983	0.0882	0.0790	0.0705
2	0.4364	0.4106	0.3854	0.3610	0.3373	0.3144	0.2924	0.2713	0.2511	0.2318
3	0.7065	0.6827	0.6585	0.6338	0.6089	0.5837	0.5584	0.5331	0.5078	0.4826
4	0.8885	0.8747	0.8602	0.8447	0.8283	0.8110	0.7928	0.7738	0.7540	0.7334
5	0.9702	0.9652	0.9596	0.9533	0.9464	0.9388	0.9304	0.9213	0.9114	0.9006
6	0.9947	0.9936	0.9922	0.9906	0.9888	0.9867	0.9843	0.9816	0.9785	0.9750
7	0.9994	0.9993	0.9991	0.9989	0.9986	0.9983	0.9979	0.9974	0.9969	0.9962
8	1.0000	1.0000	1.0000	0.9999	0.9999	0.9999	0.9999	0.9998	0.9998	0.9997
9	1.0000	1.0000	1.0000	1.0000	1.0000	1.0000	1.0000	1.0000	1.0000	1.0000

d \ p	0.41	0.42	0.43	0.44	0.45	0.46	0.47	0.48	0.49	0.50
0	0.0087	0.0074	0.0064	0.0054	0.0046	0.0039	0.0033	0.0028	0.0023	0.0020
1	0.0628	0.0558	0.0495	0.0437	0.0385	0.0338	0.0296	0.0259	0.0225	0.0195
2	0.2134	0.1961	0.1796	0.1641	0.1495	0.1358	0.1231	0.1111	0.1001	0.0898
3	0.4576	0.4330	0.4087	0.3848	0.3614	0.3386	0.3164	0.2948	0.2740	0.2539
4	0.7122	0.6903	0.6678	0.6449	0.6214	0.5976	0.5735	0.5491	0.5246	0.5000
5	0.8891	0.8767	0.8634	0.8492	0.8342	0.8183	0.8015	0.7839	0.7654	0.7461
6	0.9710	0.9666	0.9617	0.9563	0.9502	0.9436	0.9363	0.9283	0.9196	0.9102
7	0.9954	0.9945	0.9935	0.9923	0.9909	0.9893	0.9875	0.9855	0.9831	0.9805
8	0.9997	0.9996	0.9995	0.9994	0.9992	0.9991	0.9989	0.9986	0.9984	0.9980
9	1.0000	1.0000	1.0000	1.0000	1.0000	1.0000	1.0000	1.0000	1.0000	1.0000

n = 10

d \ p	0.01	0.02	0.03	0.04	0.05	0.06	0.07	0.08	0.09	0.10
0	0.9044	0.8171	0.7374	0.6648	0.5987	0.5386	0.4840	0.4344	0.3894	0.3487
1	0.9957	0.9838	0.9655	0.9418	0.9139	0.8824	0.8483	0.8121	0.7746	0.7361
2	0.9999	0.9991	0.9972	0.9938	0.9885	0.9812	0.9717	0.9599	0.9460	0.9298
3	1.0000	1.0000	0.9999	0.9996	0.9990	0.9980	0.9964	0.9942	0.9912	0.9872
4	1.0000	1.0000	1.0000	1.0000	0.9999	0.9998	0.9997	0.9994	0.9990	0.9984
5	1.0000	1.0000	1.0000	1.0000	1.0000	1.0000	1.0000	1.0000	0.9999	0.9999
6	1.0000	1.0000	1.0000	1.0000	1.0000	1.0000	1.0000	1.0000	1.0000	1.0000

d \ p	0.11	0.12	0.13	0.14	0.15	0.16	0.17	0.18	0.19	0.20
0	0.3118	0.2785	0.2484	0.2213	0.1969	0.1749	0.1552	0.1374	0.1216	0.1074
1	0.6972	0.6583	0.6196	0.5816	0.5443	0.5080	0.4730	0.4392	0.4068	0.3758
2	0.9116	0.8913	0.8692	0.8455	0.8202	0.7936	0.7659	0.7372	0.7078	0.6778

Cumulative Binomial Probability Distribution (*continued*)

n = 10

d \ p	0.11	0.12	0.13	0.14	0.15	0.16	0.17	0.18	0.19	0.20
3	0.9822	0.9761	0.9687	0.9600	0.9500	0.9386	0.9259	0.9117	0.8961	0.8791
4	0.9975	0.9963	0.9947	0.9927	0.9901	0.9870	0.9832	0.9787	0.9734	0.9672
5	0.9997	0.9996	0.9994	0.9990	0.9986	0.9980	0.9973	0.9963	0.9951	0.9936
6	1.0000	1.0000	0.9999	0.9999	0.9999	0.9998	0.9997	0.9996	0.9994	0.9991
7	1.0000	1.0000	1.0000	1.0000	1.0000	1.0000	1.0000	1.0000	0.9999	0.9999
8	1.0000	1.0000	1.0000	1.0000	1.0000	1.0000	1.0000	1.0000	1.0000	1.0000

d \ p	0.21	0.22	0.23	0.24	0.25	0.26	0.27	0.28	0.29	0.30
0	0.0947	0.0834	0.0733	0.0643	0.0563	0.0492	0.0430	0.0374	0.0326	0.0282
1	0.3464	0.3185	0.2921	0.2673	0.2440	0.2222	0.2019	0.1830	0.1655	0.1493
2	0.6474	0.6169	0.5863	0.5558	0.5256	0.4958	0.4665	0.4378	0.4099	0.3828
3	0.8609	0.8413	0.8206	0.7988	0.7759	0.7521	0.7274	0.7021	0.6761	0.6496
4	0.9601	0.9521	0.9431	0.9330	0.9219	0.9096	0.8963	0.8819	0.8663	0.8497
5	0.9918	0.9896	0.9870	0.9839	0.9803	0.9761	0.9713	0.9658	0.9596	0.9527
6	0.9988	0.9984	0.9979	0.9973	0.9965	0.9955	0.9944	0.9930	0.9913	0.9894
7	0.9999	0.9998	0.9998	0.9997	0.9996	0.9994	0.9993	0.9990	0.9988	0.9984
8	1.0000	1.0000	1.0000	1.0000	1.0000	1.0000	0.9999	0.9999	0.9999	0.9999
9	1.0000	1.0000	1.0000	1.0000	1.0000	1.0000	1.0000	1.0000	1.0000	1.0000

d \ p	0.31	0.32	0.33	0.34	0.35	0.36	0.37	0.38	0.39	0.40
0	0.0245	0.0211	0.0182	0.0157	0.0135	0.0115	0.0098	0.0084	0.0071	0.0060
1	0.1344	0.1206	0.1080	0.0965	0.0860	0.0764	0.0677	0.0598	0.0527	0.0464
2	0.3566	0.3313	0.3070	0.2838	0.2616	0.2405	0.2206	0.2017	0.1840	0.1673
3	0.6228	0.5956	0.5684	0.5411	0.5138	0.4868	0.4600	0.4336	0.4077	0.3823
4	0.8321	0.8133	0.7936	0.7730	0.7515	0.7292	0.7061	0.6823	0.6580	0.6331
5	0.9449	0.9363	0.9268	0.9164	0.9051	0.8928	0.8795	0.8652	0.8500	0.8338
6	0.9871	0.9845	0.9815	0.9780	0.9740	0.9695	0.9644	0.9587	0.9523	0.9452
7	0.9980	0.9975	0.9968	0.9961	0.9952	0.9941	0.9929	0.9914	0.9897	0.9877
8	0.9998	0.9997	0.9997	0.9996	0.9995	0.9993	0.9991	0.9989	0.9986	0.9983
9	1.0000	1.0000	1.0000	1.0000	1.0000	1.0000	1.0000	0.9999	0.9999	0.9999
10	1.0000	1.0000	1.0000	1.0000	1.0000	1.0000	1.0000	1.0000	1.0000	1.0000

d \ p	0.41	0.42	0.43	0.44	0.45	0.46	0.47	0.48	0.49	0.50
0	0.0051	0.0043	0.0036	0.0030	0.0025	0.0021	0.0017	0.0014	0.0012	0.0010
1	0.0406	0.0355	0.0309	0.0269	0.0233	0.0201	0.0173	0.0148	0.0126	0.0107
2	0.1517	0.1372	0.1236	0.1111	0.0996	0.0889	0.0791	0.0702	0.0621	0.0547
3	0.3575	0.3335	0.3102	0.2877	0.2660	0.2453	0.2255	0.2067	0.1888	0.1719
4	0.6078	0.5822	0.5564	0.5304	0.5044	0.4784	0.4526	0.4270	0.4018	0.3770
5	0.8166	0.7984	0.7793	0.7593	0.7384	0.7168	0.6943	0.6712	0.6474	0.6230
6	0.9374	0.9288	0.9194	0.9092	0.8980	0.8859	0.8729	0.8590	0.8440	0.8281
7	0.9854	0.9828	0.9798	0.9764	0.9726	0.9683	0.9634	0.9580	0.9520	0.9453
8	0.9979	0.9975	0.9969	0.9963	0.9955	0.9946	0.9935	0.9923	0.9909	0.9893
9	0.9999	0.9998	0.9998	0.9997	0.9997	0.9996	0.9995	0.9994	0.9992	0.9990
10	1.0000	1.0000	1.0000	1.0000	1.0000	1.0000	1.0000	1.0000	1.0000	1.0000

(*continued*)

Cumulative Binomial Probability Distribution (*continued*)

n = 11

d \ p	0.01	0.02	0.03	0.04	0.05	0.06	0.07	0.08	0.09	0.10
0	0.8953	0.8007	0.7153	0.6382	0.5688	0.5063	0.4501	0.3996	0.3544	0.3138
1	0.9948	0.9805	0.9587	0.9308	0.8981	0.8618	0.8228	0.7819	0.7399	0.6974
2	0.9998	0.9988	0.9963	0.9917	0.9848	0.9752	0.9630	0.9481	0.9305	0.9104
3	1.0000	1.0000	0.9998	0.9993	0.9984	0.9970	0.9947	0.9915	0.9871	0.9815
4	1.0000	1.0000	1.0000	1.0000	0.9999	0.9997	0.9995	0.9990	0.9983	0.9972
5	1.0000	1.0000	1.0000	1.0000	1.0000	1.0000	1.0000	0.9999	0.9998	0.9997
6	1.0000	1.0000	1.0000	1.0000	1.0000	1.0000	1.0000	1.0000	1.0000	1.0000

d \ p	0.11	0.12	0.13	0.14	0.15	0.16	0.17	0.18	0.19	0.20
0	0.2775	0.2451	0.2161	0.1903	0.1673	0.1469	0.1288	0.1127	0.0985	0.0859
1	0.6548	0.6127	0.5714	0.5311	0.4922	0.4547	0.4189	0.3849	0.3526	0.3221
2	0.8880	0.8634	0.8368	0.8085	0.7788	0.7479	0.7161	0.6836	0.6506	0.6174
3	0.9744	0.9659	0.9558	0.9440	0.9306	0.9514	0.8987	0.8803	0.8603	0.8389
4	0.9958	0.9939	0.9913	0.9881	0.9841	0.9793	0.9734	0.9666	0.9587	0.9496
5	0.9995	0.9992	0.9988	0.9982	0.9973	0.9963	0.9949	0.9932	0.9910	0.9883
6	1.0000	0.9999	0.9999	0.9998	0.9997	0.9995	0.9993	0.9990	0.9986	0.9980
7	1.0000	1.0000	1.0000	1.0000	1.0000	1.0000	0.9999	0.9999	0.9998	0.9998
8	1.0000	1.0000	1.0000	1.0000	1.0000	1.0000	1.0000	1.0000	1.0000	1.0000

d \ p	0.21	0.22	0.23	0.24	0.25	0.26	0.27	0.28	0.29	0.30
0	0.0748	0.0650	0.0564	0.0489	0.0422	0.0364	0.0314	0.0270	0.0231	0.0198
1	0.2935	0.2667	0.2418	0.2186	0.1971	0.1773	0.1590	0.1423	0.1270	0.1130
2	0.5842	0.5512	0.5186	0.4866	0.4552	0.4247	0.3951	0.3665	0.3390	0.3127
3	0.8160	0.7919	0.7667	0.7404	0.7133	0.6854	0.6570	0.6281	0.5889	0.5696
4	0.9393	0.9277	0.9149	0.9008	0.8554	0.8687	0.8507	0.8315	0.8112	0.7897
5	0.9852	0.9814	0.9769	0.9717	0.9657	0.9588	0.9510	0.9423	0.9326	0.9218
6	0.9973	0.9965	0.9954	0.9941	0.9924	0.9905	0.9881	0.9854	0.9821	0.9784
7	0.9997	0.9995	0.9993	0.9991	0.9988	0.9984	0.9979	0.9973	0.9966	0.9957
8	1.0000	1.0000	0.9999	0.9999	0.9999	0.9998	0.9998	0.9997	0.9996	0.9994
9	1.0000	1.0000	1.0000	1.0000	1.0000	1.0000	1.0000	1.0000	1.0000	1.0000

d \ p	0.31	0.32	0.33	0.34	0.35	0.36	0.37	0.38	0.39	0.40
0	0.0169	0.0144	0.0122	0.0104	0.0088	0.0074	0.0062	0.0052	0.0044	0.0036
1	0.1003	0.0888	0.0784	0.0690	0.0606	0.0530	0.0463	0.0403	0.0350	0.0302
2	0.2877	0.2639	0.2413	0.2201	0.2001	0.1814	0.1640	0.1478	0.1328	0.1189
3	0.5402	0.5110	0.4821	0.4536	0.4256	0.3981	0.3714	0.3455	0.3204	0.2963
4	0.7672	0.7437	0.7193	0.6941	0.6683	0.6419	0.6150	0.5878	0.5603	0.5328
5	0.9099	0.8969	0.8829	0.8676	0.8513	0.8339	0.8153	0.7957	0.7751	0.7535
6	0.9740	0.9691	0.9634	0.9570	0.9499	0.9419	0.9330	0.9232	0.9124	0.9006
7	0.9946	0.9933	0.9918	0.9899	0.9878	0.9852	0.9823	0.9790	0.9751	0.9707
8	0.9992	0.9990	0.9987	0.9984	0.9980	0.9974	0.9968	0.9961	0.9952	0.9941
9	0.9999	0.9999	0.9999	0.9998	0.9998	0.9997	0.9996	0.9995	0.9994	0.9993
10	1.0000	1.0000	1.0000	1.0000	1.0000	1.0000	1.0000	1.0000	1.0000	1.0000

d \ p	0.41	0.42	0.43	0.44	0.45	0.46	0.47	0.48	0.49	0.50
0	0.0030	0.0025	0.0021	0.0017	0.0014	0.0011	0.0009	0.0008	0.0006	0.0005
1	0.0261	0.0224	0.0192	0.0164	0.0139	0.0118	0.0100	0.0084	0.0070	0.0059

Cumulative Binomial Probability Distribution (continued)

n = 11

d \ p	0.41	0.42	0.43	0.44	0.45	0.46	0.47	0.48	0.49	0.50
2	0.1062	0.0945	0.0838	0.0740	0.0652	0.0572	0.0501	0.0436	0.0378	0.0327
3	0.2731	0.2510	0.2300	0.2100	0.1911	0.1734	0.1567	0.1412	0.1267	0.1133
4	0.5052	0.4777	0.4505	0.4236	0.3971	0.3712	0.3459	0.3213	0.2974	0.2744
5	0.7310	0.7076	0.6834	0.6586	0.6331	0.6071	0.5807	0.5540	0.5271	0.5000
6	0.8879	0.8740	0.8592	0.8432	0.8262	0.8081	0.7890	0.7688	0.7477	0.7256
7	0.9657	0.9601	0.9539	0.9468	0.9390	0.9304	0.9209	0.9105	0.8991	0.8867
8	0.9928	0.9913	0.9896	0.9875	0.9852	0.9825	0.9794	0.9759	0.9718	0.9673
9	0.9991	0.9988	0.9986	0.9982	0.9978	0.9973	0.9967	0.9960	0.9951	0.9941
10	0.9999	0.9999	0.9999	0.9999	0.9998	0.9998	0.9998	0.9997	0.9996	0.9995
11	1.0000	1.0000	1.0000	1.0000	1.0000	1.0000	1.0000	1.0000	1.0000	1.0000

n = 12

d \ p	0.01	0.02	0.03	0.04	0.05	0.06	0.07	0.08	0.09	0.10
0	0.8864	0.7847	0.6938	0.6127	0.5404	0.4759	0.4186	0.3677	0.3225	0.2824
1	0.9938	0.9769	0.9514	0.9191	0.8816	0.8405	0.7967	0.7513	0.7052	0.6590
2	0.9998	0.9985	0.9952	0.9893	0.9804	0.9684	0.9532	0.9348	0.9134	0.8891
3	1.0000	0.9999	0.9997	0.9990	0.9978	0.9957	0.9925	0.9880	0.9820	0.9744
4	1.0000	1.0000	1.0000	0.9999	0.9998	0.9996	0.9991	0.9984	0.9973	0.9957
5	1.0000	1.0000	1.0000	1.0000	1.0000	1.0000	0.9999	0.9998	0.9997	0.9996
6	1.0000	1.0000	1.0000	1.0000	1.0000	1.0000	1.0000	1.0000	1.0000	0.9999
7	1.0000	1.0000	1.0000	1.0000	1.0000	1.0000	1.0000	1.0000	1.0000	1.0000

d \ p	0.11	0.12	0.13	0.14	0.15	0.16	0.17	0.18	0.19	0.20
0	0.2470	0.2157	0.1880	0.1637	0.1422	0.1234	0.1069	0.0924	0.0798	0.0687
1	0.6133	0.5686	0.5252	0.4834	0.4435	0.4055	0.3696	0.3359	0.3043	0.2749
2	0.8623	0.8333	0.8023	0.7697	0.7358	0.7010	0.6656	0.6298	0.5940	0.5583
3	0.9649	0.9536	0.9403	0.9250	0.9078	0.8886	0.8676	0.8448	0.8205	0.7946
4	0.9935	0.9905	0.9867	0.9819	0.9761	0.9690	0.9607	0.9511	0.9400	0.9274
5	0.9991	0.9986	0.9978	0.9967	0.9954	0.9935	0.9912	0.9884	0.9849	0.9806
6	0.9999	0.9998	0.9997	0.9996	0.9993	0.9990	0.9985	0.9979	0.9971	0.9961
7	1.0000	1.0000	1.0000	1.0000	0.9999	0.9999	0.9998	0.9997	0.9996	0.9994
8	1.0000	1.0000	1.0000	1.0000	1.0000	1.0000	1.0000	1.0000	1.0000	0.9999
9	1.0000	1.0000	1.0000	1.0000	1.0000	1.0000	1.0000	1.0000	1.0000	1.0000

d \ p	0.21	0.22	0.23	0.24	0.25	0.26	0.27	0.28	0.29	0.30
0	0.0591	0.0507	0.0434	0.0371	0.0317	0.0270	0.0229	0.0194	0.0164	0.0138
1	0.2476	0.2224	0.1991	0.1778	0.1584	0.1406	0.1245	0.1100	0.0968	0.0850
2	0.5232	0.4886	0.4550	0.4222	0.3907	0.3603	0.3313	0.3037	0.2775	0.2528
3	0.7674	0.7390	0.7096	0.6795	0.6488	0.6176	0.5863	0.5548	0.5235	0.4925
4	0.9134	0.8979	0.8808	0.8623	0.8424	0.8210	0.7984	0.7746	0.7496	0.7237
5	0.9755	0.9696	0.9626	0.9547	0.9456	0.9354	0.9240	0.9113	0.8974	0.8822
6	0.9948	0.9932	0.9911	0.9887	0.9857	0.9822	0.9781	0.9733	0.9678	0.9614
7	0.9992	0.9989	0.9984	0.9979	0.9972	0.9964	0.9953	0.9940	0.9924	0.9905
8	0.9999	0.9999	0.9998	0.9997	0.9996	0.9995	0.9993	0.9990	0.9987	0.9983
9	1.0000	1.0000	1.0000	1.0000	1.0000	0.9999	0.9999	0.9999	0.9998	0.9998
10	1.0000	1.0000	1.0000	1.0000	1.0000	1.0000	1.0000	1.0000	1.0000	1.0000

(continued)

Cumulative Binomial Probability Distribution (*continued*)

n = 12

d \ p	0.31	0.32	0.33	0.34	0.35	0.36	0.37	0.38	0.39	0.40
0	0.0116	0.0098	0.0082	0.0068	0.0057	0.0047	0.0039	0.0032	0.0027	0.0022
1	0.0744	0.0650	0.0565	0.0491	0.0424	0.0366	0.0315	0.0270	0.0230	0.0196
2	0.2296	0.2078	0.1876	0.1687	0.1513	0.1352	0.1205	0.1069	0.0946	0.0834
3	0.4619	0.4319	0.4027	0.3742	0.3467	0.3201	0.2947	0.2704	0.2472	0.2253
4	0.6968	0.6692	0.6410	0.6124	0.5833	0.5541	0.5249	0.4957	0.4668	0.4382
5	0.8657	0.8479	0.8289	0.8087	0.7873	0.7648	0.7412	0.7167	0.6913	0.6652
6	0.9542	0.9460	0.9368	0.9266	0.9154	0.9030	0.8894	0.8747	0.8589	0.8418
7	0.9882	0.9856	0.9824	0.9787	0.9745	0.9696	0.9641	0.9578	0.9507	0.9427
8	0.9978	0.9972	0.9964	0.9955	0.9944	0.9930	0.9915	0.9896	0.9873	0.9847
9	0.9997	0.9996	0.9995	0.9993	0.9992	0.9989	0.9986	0.9982	0.9978	0.9972
10	1.0000	1.0000	1.0000	0.9999	0.9999	0.9999	0.9999	0.9998	0.9998	0.9997
11	1.0000	1.0000	1.0000	1.0000	1.0000	1.0000	1.0000	1.0000	1.0000	1.0000

d \ p	0.41	0.42	0.43	0.44	0.45	0.46	0.47	0.48	0.49	0.50
0	0.0018	0.0014	0.0012	0.0010	0.0008	0.0006	0.0005	0.0004	0.0003	0.0002
1	0.0166	0.0140	0.0118	0.0099	0.0083	0.0069	0.0057	0.0047	0.0039	0.0032
2	0.0733	0.0642	0.0560	0.0487	0.0421	0.0363	0.0312	0.0267	0.0227	0.0193
3	0.2047	0.1853	0.1671	0.1502	0.1345	0.1199	0.1066	0.0943	0.0832	0.0730
4	0.4101	0.3825	0.3557	0.3296	0.3044	0.2802	0.2570	0.2348	0.2138	0.1938
5	0.6384	0.6111	0.5833	0.5552	0.5269	0.4986	0.4703	0.4423	0.4145	0.3872
6	0.8235	0.8041	0.7836	0.7620	0.7393	0.7157	0.6911	0.6657	0.6396	0.6128
7	0.9338	0.9240	0.9131	0.9012	0.8883	0.8742	0.8589	0.8425	0.8249	0.8062
8	0.9817	0.9782	0.9742	0.9696	0.9644	0.9585	0.9519	0.9445	0.9362	0.9270
9	0.9965	0.9957	0.9947	0.9935	0.9921	0.9905	0.9886	0.9883	0.9837	0.9807
10	0.9996	0.9995	0.9993	0.9991	0.9989	0.9986	0.9983	0.9979	0.9974	0.9968
11	1.0000	1.0000	1.0000	0.9999	0.9999	0.9999	0.9999	0.9999	0.9998	0.9998
12	1.0000	1.0000	1.0000	1.0000	1.0000	1.0000	1.0000	1.0000	1.0000	1.0000

n = 13

d \ p	0.01	0.02	0.03	0.04	0.05	0.06	0.07	0.08	0.09	0.10
0	0.8775	0.7690	0.6730	0.5882	0.5133	0.4474	0.3893	0.3383	0.2935	0.2542
1	0.9928	0.9730	0.9436	0.9068	0.8646	0.8186	0.7702	0.7206	0.6707	0.6213
2	0.9997	0.9980	0.9938	0.9865	0.9755	0.9608	0.9422	0.9201	0.8946	0.8661
3	1.0000	0.9999	0.9995	0.9986	0.9969	0.9940	0.9897	0.9837	0.9758	0.9658
4	1.0000	1.0000	1.0000	0.9999	0.9997	0.9993	0.9987	0.9976	0.9959	0.9935
5	1.0000	1.0000	1.0000	1.0000	1.0000	0.9999	0.9999	0.9997	0.9995	0.9991
6	1.0000	1.0000	1.0000	1.0000	1.0000	1.0000	1.0000	1.0000	0.9999	0.9999
7	1.0000	1.0000	1.0000	1.0000	1.0000	1.0000	1.0000	1.0000	1.0000	1.0000

d \ p	0.11	0.12	0.13	0.14	0.15	0.16	0.17	0.18	0.19	0.20
0	0.2198	0.1898	0.1636	0.1408	0.1209	0.1037	0.0887	0.0758	0.0646	0.0550
1	0.5730	0.5262	0.4814	0.4386	0.3983	0.3604	0.3249	0.2920	0.2616	0.2336
2	0.8349	0.8015	0.7663	0.7296	0.6920	0.6537	0.6152	0.5769	0.5389	0.5017
3	0.9536	0.9391	0.9224	0.9033	0.8820	0.8586	0.8333	0.8061	0.7774	0.7473
4	0.9903	0.9861	0.9807	0.9740	0.9658	0.9562	0.9449	0.9319	0.9173	0.9009

Cumulative Binomial Probability Distribution (*continued*)

n = 13

d \ p	0.11	0.12	0.13	0.14	0.15	0.16	0.17	0.18	0.19	0.20
5	0.9985	0.9976	0.9964	0.9947	0.9925	0.9896	0.9861	0.9817	0.9763	0.9700
6	0.9998	0.9997	0.9995	0.9992	0.9987	0.9981	0.9973	0.9962	0.9948	0.9930
7	1.0000	1.0000	0.9999	0.9999	0.9998	0.9997	0.9996	0.9994	0.9991	0.9988
8	1.0000	1.0000	1.0000	1.0000	1.0000	1.0000	1.0000	0.9999	0.9999	0.9998
9	1.0000	1.0000	1.0000	1.0000	1.0000	1.0000	1.0000	1.0000	1.0000	1.0000

d \ p	0.21	0.22	0.23	0.24	0.25	0.26	0.27	0.28	0.29	0.30
0	0.0467	0.0396	0.0334	0.0282	0.0238	0.0200	0.0167	0.0140	0.0117	0.0097
1	0.2080	0.1846	0.1633	0.1441	0.1267	0.1111	0.0971	0.0846	0.0735	0.0637
2	0.4653	0.4301	0.3961	0.3636	0.3326	0.3032	0.2755	0.2495	0.2251	0.2025
3	0.7161	0.6839	0.6511	0.6178	0.5843	0.5507	0.5174	0.4845	0.4522	0.4206
4	0.8827	0.8629	0.8415	0.8184	0.7940	0.7681	0.7411	0.7130	0.6840	0.6543
5	0.9625	0.9538	0.9438	0.9325	0.9198	0.9056	0.8901	0.8730	0.8545	0.8346
6	0.9907	0.9880	0.9846	0.9805	0.9757	0.9701	0.9635	0.9560	0.9473	0.9376
7	0.9983	0.9976	0.9968	0.9957	0.9944	0.9927	0.9907	0.9882	0.9853	0.9818
8	0.9998	0.9996	0.9995	0.9993	0.9990	0.9987	0.9982	0.9976	0.9969	0.9960
9	1.0000	1.0000	0.9999	0.9999	0.9999	0.9998	0.9997	0.9996	0.9995	0.9993
10	1.0000	1.0000	1.0000	1.0000	1.0000	1.0000	1.0000	1.0000	0.9999	0.9999
11	1.0000	1.0000	1.0000	1.0000	1.0000	1.0000	1.0000	1.0000	1.0000	1.0000

d \ p	0.31	0.32	0.33	0.34	0.35	0.36	0.37	0.38	0.39	0.40
0	0.0080	0.0066	0.0055	0.0045	0.0037	0.0030	0.0025	0.0020	0.0016	0.0013
1	0.0550	0.0473	0.0406	0.0347	0.0296	0.0251	0.0213	0.0179	0.0151	0.0126
2	0.1815	0.1621	0.1443	0.1280	0.1132	0.0997	0.0875	0.0765	0.0667	0.0579
3	0.3899	0.3602	0.3317	0.3043	0.2783	0.2536	0.2302	0.2083	0.1877	0.1686
4	0.6240	0.5933	0.5624	0.5314	0.5005	0.4699	0.4397	0.4101	0.3812	0.3530
5	0.8133	0.7907	0.7669	0.7419	0.7159	0.6889	0.6612	0.6327	0.6038	0.5744
6	0.9267	0.9146	0.9012	0.8865	0.8705	0.8532	0.8346	0.8147	0.7935	0.7712
7	0.9777	0.9729	0.9674	0.9610	0.9538	0.9456	0.9365	0.9262	0.9149	0.9023
8	0.9948	0.9935	0.9918	0.9898	0.9874	0.9846	0.9813	0.9775	0.9730	0.9679
9	0.9991	0.9988	0.9985	0.9980	0.9975	0.9968	0.9960	0.9949	0.9937	0.9922
10	0.9999	0.9999	0.9998	0.9997	0.9997	0.9995	0.9994	0.9992	0.9990	0.9987
11	1.0000	1.0000	1.0000	1.0000	1.0000	1.0000	0.9999	0.9999	0.9999	0.9999
12	1.0000	1.0000	1.0000	1.0000	1.0000	1.0000	1.0000	1.0000	1.0000	1.0000

d \ p	0.41	0.42	0.43	0.44	0.45	0.46	0.47	0.48	0.49	0.50
0	0.0010	0.0008	0.0007	0.0005	0.0004	0.0003	0.0003	0.0002	0.0002	0.0001
1	0.0105	0.0088	0.0072	0.0060	0.0049	0.0040	0.0033	0.0026	0.0021	0.0017
2	0.0501	0.0431	0.0370	0.0316	0.0269	0.0228	0.0192	0.0162	0.0135	0.0112
3	0.1508	0.1344	0.1193	0.1055	0.0929	0.0815	0.0712	0.0619	0.0536	0.0461
4	0.3258	0.2997	0.2746	0.2507	0.2279	0.2065	0.1863	0.1674	0.1498	0.1334
5	0.5448	0.5151	0.4854	0.4559	0.4268	0.3981	0.3701	0.3427	0.3162	0.2905
6	0.7476	0.7230	0.6975	0.6710	0.6437	0.6158	0.5873	0.5585	0.5293	0.5000
7	0.8886	0.8736	0.8574	0.8400	0.8212	0.8012	0.7800	0.7576	0.7341	0.7095
8	0.9621	0.9554	0.9480	0.9395	0.9302	0.9197	0.9082	0.8955	0.8817	0.8666
9	0.9904	0.9883	0.9859	0.9830	0.9797	0.9758	0.9713	0.9662	0.9604	0.9539

(*continued*)

Cumulative Binomial Probability Distribution (*continued*)

n = 13

d \ p	0.41	0.42	0.43	0.44	0.45	0.46	0.47	0.48	0.49	0.50
10	0.9983	0.9979	0.9973	0.9967	0.9959	0.9949	0.9937	0.9923	0.9907	0.9888
11	0.9998	0.9998	0.9997	0.9996	0.9995	0.9993	0.9991	0.9989	0.9986	0.9983
12	1.0000	1.0000	1.0000	1.0000	1.0000	1.0000	0.9999	0.9999	0.9999	0.9999
13	1.0000	1.0000	1.0000	1.0000	1.0000	1.0000	1.0000	1.0000	1.0000	1.0000

n = 14

d \ p	0.01	0.02	0.03	0.04	0.05	0.06	0.07	0.08	0.09	0.10
0	0.8687	0.7536	0.6528	0.5647	0.4877	0.4205	0.3620	0.3112	0.2670	0.2288
1	0.9916	0.9690	0.9355	0.8941	0.8470	0.7963	0.7436	0.6900	0.6368	0.5846
2	0.9997	0.9975	0.9923	0.9833	0.9699	0.9522	0.9302	0.9042	0.8745	0.8416
3	1.0000	0.9999	0.9994	0.9981	0.9958	0.9920	0.9864	0.9786	0.9685	0.9559
4	1.0000	1.0000	1.0000	0.9998	0.9996	0.9990	0.9980	0.9965	0.9941	0.9908
5	1.0000	1.0000	1.0000	1.0000	1.0000	0.9999	0.9998	0.9996	0.9992	0.9985
6	1.0000	1.0000	1.0000	1.0000	1.0000	1.0000	1.0000	1.0000	0.9999	0.9998
7	1.0000	1.0000	1.0000	1.0000	1.0000	1.0000	1.0000	1.0000	1.0000	1.0000

d \ p	0.11	0.12	0.13	0.14	0.15	0.16	0.17	0.18	0.19	0.20
0	0.1956	0.1670	0.1423	0.1211	0.1028	0.0871	0.0736	0.0621	0.0523	0.0440
1	0.5342	0.4859	0.4401	0.3969	0.3567	0.3193	0.2848	0.2531	0.2242	0.1979
2	0.8061	0.7685	0.7292	0.6889	0.6479	0.6068	0.5659	0.5256	0.4862	0.4481
3	0.9406	0.9226	0.9021	0.8790	0.8535	0.8258	0.7962	0.7649	0.7321	0.6982
4	0.9863	0.9804	0.9731	0.9641	0.9533	0.9406	0.9259	0.9093	0.8907	0.8702
5	0.9976	0.9962	0.9943	0.9918	0.9885	0.9843	0.9791	0.9727	0.9651	0.9561
6	0.9997	0.9994	0.9991	0.9985	0.9978	0.9968	0.9954	0.9936	0.9913	0.9884
7	1.0000	0.9999	0.9999	0.9998	0.9997	0.9995	0.9992	0.9988	0.9983	0.9976
8	1.0000	1.0000	1.0000	1.0000	1.0000	0.9999	0.9999	0.9998	0.9997	0.9996
9	1.0000	1.0000	1.0000	1.0000	1.0000	1.0000	1.0000	1.0000	1.0000	1.0000

d \ p	0.21	0.22	0.23	0.24	0.25	0.26	0.27	0.28	0.29	0.30
0	0.0369	0.0309	0.0258	0.0214	0.0178	0.0148	0.0122	0.0101	0.0083	0.0068
1	0.1741	0.1527	0.1335	0.1163	0.1010	0.0874	0.0754	0.0648	0.0556	0.0475
2	0.4113	0.3761	0.3426	0.3109	0.2811	0.2533	0.2273	0.2033	0.1812	0.1608
3	0.6634	0.6281	0.5924	0.5568	0.5213	0.4864	0.4521	0.4187	0.3863	0.3552
4	0.8477	0.8235	0.7977	0.7703	0.7415	0.7116	0.6807	0.6490	0.6188	0.5842
5	0.9457	0.9338	0.9203	0.9051	0.8883	0.8699	0.8498	0.8282	0.8051	0.7805
6	0.9848	0.9804	0.9752	0.9890	0.9617	0.9533	0.9437	0.9327	0.9204	0.9067
7	0.9967	0.9955	0.9940	0.9921	0.9897	0.9868	0.9833	0.9792	0.9743	0.9685
8	0.9994	0.9992	0.9989	0.9984	0.9978	0.9971	0.9962	0.9950	0.9935	0.9917
9	0.9999	0.9999	0.9998	0.9998	0.9997	0.9995	0.9993	0.9991	0.9988	0.9983
10	1.0000	1.0000	1.0000	1.0000	1.0000	0.9999	0.9999	0.9999	0.9998	0.9998
11	1.0000	1.0000	1.0000	1.0000	1.0000	1.0000	1.0000	1.0000	1.0000	1.0000

d \ p	0.31	0.32	0.33	0.34	0.35	0.36	0.37	0.38	0.39	0.40
0	0.0055	0.0045	0.0037	0.0030	0.0024	0.0019	0.0016	0.0012	0.0010	0.0008
1	0.0404	0.0343	0.0290	0.0244	0.0205	0.0172	0.0143	0.0119	0.0098	0.0081

Cumulative Binomial Probability Distribution (*continued*)

n = 14

d \ p	0.31	0.32	0.33	0.34	0.35	0.36	0.37	0.38	0.39	0.40
2	0.1423	0.1254	0.1101	0.0963	0.0839	0.0729	0.0630	0.0543	0.0466	0.0398
3	0.3253	0.2968	0.2699	0.2444	0.2205	0.1982	0.1774	0.1582	0.1405	0.1243
4	0.5514	0.5187	0.4862	0.4542	0.4227	0.3920	0.3622	0.3334	0.3057	0.2793
5	0.7546	0.7276	0.6994	0.6703	0.6405	0.6101	0.5792	0.5481	0.5169	0.4859
6	0.8916	0.8750	0.8569	0.8374	0.8164	0.7941	0.7704	0.7455	0.7195	0.6925
7	0.9619	0.9542	0.9455	0.9357	0.9247	0.9124	0.8988	0.8838	0.8675	0.8499
8	0.9895	0.9869	0.9837	0.9800	0.9757	0.9706	0.9647	0.9580	0.9503	0.9417
9	0.9978	0.9971	0.9963	0.9952	0.9940	0.9924	0.9905	0.9883	0.9856	0.9825
10	0.9997	0.9995	0.9994	0.9992	0.9989	0.9986	0.9981	0.9976	0.9969	0.9961
11	1.0000	0.9999	0.9999	0.9999	0.9999	0.9998	0.9997	0.9997	0.9995	0.9994
12	1.0000	1.0000	1.0000	1.0000	1.0000	1.0000	1.0000	1.0000	1.0000	0.9999
13	1.0000	1.0000	1.0000	1.0000	1.0000	1.0000	1.0000	1.0000	1.0000	1.0000

d \ p	0.41	0.42	0.43	0.44	0.45	0.46	0.47	0.48	0.49	0.50
0	0.0006	0.0005	0.0004	0.0003	0.0002	0.0002	0.0001	0.0001	0.0001	0.0001
1	0.0066	0.0054	0.0044	0.0036	0.0029	0.0023	0.0019	0.0015	0.0012	0.0009
2	0.0339	0.0287	0.0242	0.0203	0.0170	0.0142	0.0117	0.0097	0.0079	0.0065
3	0.1095	0.0961	0.0839	0.0730	0.0632	0.0545	0.0468	0.0399	0.0339	0.0287
4	0.2541	0.2303	0.2078	0.1868	0.1672	0.1490	0.1322	0.1167	0.1026	0.0898
5	0.4550	0.4246	0.3948	0.3656	0.3373	0.3100	0.2837	0.2585	0.2346	0.2120
6	0.6645	0.6357	0.6063	0.5764	0.5461	0.5157	0.4852	0.4549	0.4249	0.3953
7	0.8308	0.8104	0.7887	0.7656	0.7414	0.7160	0.6895	0.6620	0.6337	0.6047
8	0.9320	0.9211	0.9090	0.8957	0.8811	0.8652	0.8480	0.8293	0.8094	0.7880
9	0.9788	0.9745	0.9696	0.9639	0.9574	0.9500	0.9417	0.9323	0.9218	0.9102
10	0.9551	0.9939	0.9924	0.9907	0.9886	0.9861	0.9832	0.9798	0.9759	0.9713
11	0.9992	0.9990	0.9987	0.9983	0.9978	0.9973	0.9966	0.9958	0.9947	0.9935
12	0.9999	0.9999	0.9999	0.9998	0.9997	0.9997	0.9996	0.9994	0.9993	0.9991
13	1.0000	1.0000	1.0000	1.0000	1.0000	1.0000	1.0000	1.0000	1.0000	0.9999
14	1.0000	1.0000	1.0000	1.0000	1.0000	1.0000	1.0000	1.0000	1.0000	1.0000

APPENDIX 5

The Poisson Distribution

$$P(c) = \frac{(np)^c}{c!}e^{-np} \text{ (Cumulative Values Are in Parentheses)}$$

c \ np_0	0.1		0.2		0.3		0.4		0.5	
0	0.905	(0.905)	0.819	(0.819)	0.741	(0.741)	0.670	(0.670)	0.607	(0.607)
1	0.091	(0.996)	0.164	(0.983)	0.222	(0.963)	0.268	(0.938)	0.303	(0.910)
2	0.004	(1.000)	0.016	(0.999)	0.033	(0.996)	0.054	(0.992)	0.076	(0.986)
3			0.010	(1.000)	0.004	(1.000)	0.007	(0.999)	0.013	(0.999)
4							0.001	(1.000)	0.001	(1.000)

c \ np_0	0.6		0.7		0.8		0.9		1.0	
0	0.549	(0.549)	0.497	(0.497)	0.449	(0.449)	0.406	(0.406)	0.368	(0.368)
1	0.329	(0.878)	0.349	(0.845)	0.359	(0.808)	0.366	(0.772)	0.368	(0.736)
2	0.099	(0.977)	0.122	(0.967)	0.144	(0.952)	0.166	(0.938)	0.184	(0.920)
3	0.020	(0.997)	0.028	(0.995)	0.039	(0.991)	0.049	(0.987)	0.061	(0.981)
4	0.003	(1.000)	0.005	(1.000)	0.008	(0.999)	0.011	(0.998)	0.016	(0.997)
5					0.001	(1.000)	0.002	(1.000)	0.003	(1.000)

c \ np_0	1.1		1.2		1.3		1.4		1.5	
0	0.333	(0.333)	0.301	(0.301)	0.273	(0.273)	0.247	(0.247)	0.223	(0.223)
1	0.366	(0.699)	0.361	(0.662)	0.354	(0.627)	0.345	(0.592)	0.335	(0.558)
2	0.201	(0.900)	0.217	(0.879)	0.230	(0.857)	0.242	(0.834)	0.251	(0.809)
3	0.074	(0.974)	0.087	(0.966)	0.100	(0.957)	0.113	(0.947)	0.126	(0.935)
4	0.021	(0.995)	0.026	(0.992)	0.032	(0.989)	0.039	(0.986)	0.047	(0.982)
5	0.004	(0.999)	0.007	(0.999)	0.009	(0.998)	0.011	(0.997)	0.014	(0.996)
6	0.001	(1.000)	0.001	(1.000)	0.002	(1.000)	0.003	(1.000)	0.004	(1.000)

c \ np_0	1.6		1.7		1.8		1.9		2.0	
0	0.202	(0.202)	0.183	(0.183)	0.165	(0.165)	0.150	(0.150)	0.135	(0.135)
1	0.323	(0.525)	0.311	(0.494)	0.298	(0.463)	0.284	(0.434)	0.271	(0.406)
2	0.258	(0.783)	0.264	(0.758)	0.268	(0.731)	0.270	(0.704)	0.271	(0.677)
3	0.138	(0.921)	0.149	(0.907)	0.161	(0.892)	0.171	(0.875)	0.180	(0.857)
4	0.055	(0.976)	0.064	(0.971)	0.072	(0.964)	0.081	(0.956)	0.090	(0.947)
5	0.018	(0.994)	0.022	(0.993)	0.026	(0.990)	0.031	(0.987)	0.036	(0.983)
6	0.005	(0.999)	0.006	(0.999)	0.008	(0.998)	0.010	(0.997)	0.012	(0.995)
7	0.001	(1.000)	0.001	(1.000)	0.002	(1.000)	0.003	(1.000)	0.004	(0.999)
8									0.001	(1.000)

c \ np_0	2.1		2.2		2.3		2.4		2.5	
0	0.123	(0.123)	0.111	(0.111)	0.100	(0.100)	0.091	(0.091)	0.082	(0.082)
1	0.257	(0.380)	0.244	(0.355)	0.231	(0.331)	0.218	(0.309)	0.205	(0.287)
2	0.270	(0.650)	0.268	(0.623)	0.265	(0.596)	0.261	(0.570)	0.256	(0.543)

The Poisson Distribution (continued)

c	2.1		2.2		2.3		2.4		2.5	
3	0.189	(0.839)	0.197	(0.820)	0.203	(0.799)	0.209	(0.779)	0.214	(0.757)
4	0.099	(0.938)	0.108	(0.928)	0.117	(0.916)	0.125	(0.904)	0.134	(0.891)
5	0.042	(0.980)	0.048	(0.976)	0.054	(0.970)	0.060	(0.964)	0.067	(0.958)
6	0.015	(0.995)	0.017	(0.993)	0.021	(0.991)	0.024	(0.988)	0.028	(0.986)
7	0.004	(0.999)	0.005	(0.998)	0.007	(0.998)	0.008	(0.996)	0.010	(0.996)
8	0.001	(1.000)	0.002	(1.000)	0.002	(1.000)	0.003	(0.999)	0.003	(0.999)
9							0.001	(1.000)	0.001	(1.000)

c	2.6		2.7		2.8		2.9		3.0	
0	0.074	(0.074)	0.067	(0.067)	0.061	(0.061)	0.055	(0.055)	0.050	(0.050)
1	0.193	(0.267)	0.182	(0.249)	0.170	(0.231)	0.160	(0.215)	0.149	(0.199)
2	0.251	(0.518)	0.245	(0.494)	0.238	(0.469)	0.231	(0.446)	0.224	(0.423)
3	0.218	(0.736)	0.221	(0.715)	0.223	(0.692)	0.224	(0.670)	0.224	(0.647)
4	0.141	(0.877)	0.149	(0.864)	0.156	(0.848)	0.162	(0.832)	0.168	(0.815)
5	0.074	(0.951)	0.080	(0.944)	0.087	(0.935)	0.094	(0.926)	0.101	(0.916)
6	0.032	(0.983)	0.036	(0.980)	0.041	(0.976)	0.045	(0.971)	0.050	(0.966)
7	0.012	(0.995)	0.014	(0.994)	0.016	(0.992)	0.019	(0.990)	0.022	(0.988)
8	0.004	(0.999)	0.005	(0.999)	0.006	(0.998)	0.007	(0.997)	0.008	(0.996)
9	0.001	(1.000)	0.001	(1.000)	0.002	(1.000)	0.002	(0.999)	0.003	(0.999)
10							0.001	(1.000)	0.001	(1.000)

c	3.1		3.2		3.3		3.4		3.5	
0	0.045	(0.045)	0.041	(0.041)	0.037	(0.037)	0.033	(0.033)	0.030	(0.030)
1	0.140	(0.185)	0.130	(0.171)	0.122	(0.159)	0.113	(0.146)	0.106	(0.136)
2	0.216	(0.401)	0.209	(0.380)	0.201	(0.360)	0.193	(0.339)	0.185	(0.321)
3	0.224	(0.625)	0.223	(0.603)	0.222	(0.582)	0.219	(0.558)	0.216	(0.537)
4	0.173	(0.798)	0.178	(0.781)	0.182	(0.764)	0.186	(0.744)	0.189	(0.726)
5	0.107	(0.905)	0.114	(0.895)	0.120	(0.884)	0.126	(0.870)	0.132	(0.858)
6	0.056	(0.961)	0.061	(0.956)	0.066	(0.950)	0.071	(0.941)	0.077	(0.935)
7	0.025	(0.986)	0.028	(0.984)	0.031	(0.981)	0.035	(0.976)	0.038	(0.973)
8	0.010	(0.996)	0.011	(0.995)	0.012	(0.993)	0.015	(0.991)	0.017	(0.990)
9	0.003	(0.999)	0.004	(0.999)	0.005	(0.998)	0.006	(0.997)	0.007	(0.997)
10	0.001	(1.000)	0.001	(1.000)	0.002	(1.000)	0.002	(0.999)	0.002	(0.999)
11							0.001	(1.000)	0.001	(1.000)

c	3.6		3.7		3.8		3.9		4.0	
0	0.027	(0.027)	0.025	(0.025)	0.022	(0.022)	0.020	(0.020)	0.018	(0.018)
1	0.098	(0.125)	0.091	(0.116)	0.085	(0.107)	0.079	(0.099)	0.073	(0.091)
2	0.177	(0.302)	0.169	(0.285)	0.161	(0.268)	0.154	(0.253)	0.147	(0.238)
3	0.213	(0.515)	0.209	(0.494)	0.205	(0.473)	0.200	(0.453)	0.195	(0.433)
4	0.191	(0.706)	0.193	(0.687)	0.194	(0.667)	0.195	(0.648)	0.195	(0.628)
5	0.138	(0.844)	0.143	(0.830)	0.148	(0.815)	0.152	(0.800)	0.157	(0.785)
6	0.083	(0.927)	0.088	(0.918)	0.094	(0.909)	0.099	(0.899)	0.104	(0.889)
7	0.042	(0.969)	0.047	(0.965)	0.051	(0.960)	0.055	(0.954)	0.060	(0.949)
8	0.019	(0.988)	0.022	(0.987)	0.024	(0.984)	0.027	(0.981)	0.030	(0.979)
9	0.008	(0.996)	0.009	(0.996)	0.010	(0.994)	0.012	(0.993)	0.013	(0.992)

(continued)

The Poisson Distribution (*continued*)

c \ np_0	3.6		3.7		3.8		3.9		4.0	
10	0.003	(0.999)	0.003	(0.999)	0.004	(0.998)	0.004	(0.997)	0.005	(0.997)
11	0.001	(1.000)	0.001	(1.000)	0.001	(0.999)	0.002	(0.999)	0.002	(0.999)
12					0.001	(1.000)	0.001	(1.000)	0.001	(1.000)

c \ np_0	4.1		4.2		4.3		4.4		4.5	
0	0.017	(0.017)	0.015	(0.015)	0.014	(0.014)	0.012	(0.012)	0.011	(0.011)
1	0.068	(0.085)	0.063	(0.078)	0.058	(0.072)	0.054	(0.066)	0.050	(0.061)
2	0.139	(0.224)	0.132	(0.210)	0.126	(0.198)	0.119	(0.185)	0.113	(0.174)
3	0.190	(0.414)	0.185	(0.395)	0.180	(0.378)	0.174	(0.359)	0.169	(0.343)
4	0.195	(0.609)	0.195	(0.590)	0.193	(0.571)	0.192	(0.551)	0.190	(0.533)
5	0.160	(0.769)	0.163	(0.753)	0.166	(0.737)	0.169	(0.720)	0.171	(0.704)
6	0.110	(0.879)	0.114	(0.867)	0.119	(0.856)	0.124	(0.844)	0.128	(0.832)
7	0.064	(0.943)	0.069	(0.936)	0.073	(0.929)	0.078	(0.922)	0.082	(0.914)
8	0.033	(0.976)	0.036	(0.972)	0.040	(0.969)	0.043	(0.965)	0.046	(0.960)
9	0.015	(0.991)	0.017	(0.989)	0.019	(0.988)	0.021	(0.986)	0.023	(0.983)
10	0.006	(0.997)	0.007	(0.996)	0.008	(0.996)	0.009	(0.995)	0.011	(0.994)
11	0.002	(0.999)	0.003	(0.999)	0.003	(0.999)	0.004	(0.999)	0.004	(0.998)
12	0.001	(1.000)	0.001	(1.000)	0.001	(1.000)	0.001	(1.000)	0.001	(0.999)
13									0.001	(1.000)

c \ np_0	4.6		4.7		4.8		4.9		5.0	
0	0.010	(0.010)	0.009	(0.009)	0.008	(0.008)	0.008	(0.008)	0.007	(0.007)
1	0.046	(0.056)	0.043	(0.052)	0.039	(0.047)	0.037	(0.045)	0.034	(0.041)
2	0.106	(0.162)	0.101	(0.153)	0.095	(0.142)	0.090	(0.135)	0.084	(0.125)
3	0.163	(0.325)	0.157	(0.310)	0.152	(0.294)	0.146	(0.281)	0.140	(0.265)
4	0.188	(0.513)	0.185	(0.495)	0.182	(0.476)	0.179	(0.460)	0.176	(0.441)
5	0.172	(0.685)	0.174	(0.669)	0.175	(0.651)	0.175	(0.635)	0.176	(0.617)
6	0.132	(0.817)	0.136	(0.805)	0.140	(0.791)	0.143	(0.778)	0.146	(0.763)
7	0.087	(0.904)	0.091	(0.896)	0.096	(0.887)	0.100	(0.878)	0.105	(0.868)
8	0.050	(0.954)	0.054	(0.950)	0.058	(0.945)	0.061	(0.939)	0.065	(0.933)
9	0.026	(0.980)	0.028	(0.978)	0.031	(0.976)	0.034	(0.973)	0.036	(0.969)
10	0.012	(0.992)	0.013	(0.991)	0.015	(0.991)	0.016	(0.989)	0.018	(0.987)
11	0.005	(0.997)	0.006	(0.997)	0.006	(0.997)	0.007	(0.996)	0.008	(0.995)
12	0.002	(0.999)	0.002	(0.999)	0.002	(0.999)	0.003	(0.999)	0.003	(0.998)
13	0.001	(1.000)	0.001	(1.000)	0.001	(1.000)	0.001	(1.000)	0.001	(0.999)
14									0.001	(1.000)

c \ np_0	6.0		7.0		8.0		9.0		10.0	
0	0.002	(0.002)	0.001	(0.001)	0.000	(0.000)	0.000	(0.000)	0.000	(0.000)
1	0.015	(0.017)	0.006	(0.007)	0.003	(0.003)	0.001	(0.001)	0.000	(0.000)
2	0.045	(0.062)	0.022	(0.029)	0.011	(0.014)	0.005	(0.006)	0.002	(0.002)
3	0.089	(0.151)	0.052	(0.081)	0.029	(0.043)	0.015	(0.021)	0.007	(0.009)
4	0.134	(0.285)	0.091	(0.172)	0.057	(0.100)	0.034	(0.055)	0.019	(0.028)
5	0.161	(0.446)	0.128	(0.300)	0.092	(0.192)	0.061	(0.116)	0.038	(0.066)
6	0.161	(0.607)	0.149	(0.449)	0.122	(0.314)	0.091	(0.091)	0.063	(0.129)
7	0.138	(0.745)	0.149	(0.598)	0.140	(0.454)	0.117	(0.324)	0.090	(0.219)
8	0.103	(0.848)	0.131	(0.729)	0.140	(0.594)	0.132	(0.456)	0.113	(0.332)
9	0.069	(0.917)	0.102	(0.831)	0.124	(0.718)	0.132	(0.588)	0.125	(0.457)

The Poisson Distribution (*continued*)

c / np_0	6.0		7.0		8.0		9.0		10.0	
10	0.041	(0.958)	0.071	(0.902)	0.099	(0.817)	0.119	(0.707)	0.125	(0.582)
11	0.023	(0.981)	0.045	(0.947)	0.072	(0.889)	0.097	(0.804)	0.114	(0.696)
12	0.011	(0.992)	0.026	(0.973)	0.048	(0.937)	0.073	(0.877)	0.095	(0.791)
13	0.005	(0.997)	0.014	(0.987)	0.030	(0.967)	0.050	(0.927)	0.073	(0.864)
14	0.002	(0.999)	0.007	(0.994)	0.017	(0.984)	0.032	(0.959)	0.052	(0.916)
15	0.001	(1.000)	0.003	(0.997)	0.009	(0.993)	0.019	(0.978)	0.035	(0.951)
16			0.002	(0.999)	0.004	(0.997)	0.011	(0.989)	0.022	(0.973)
17			0.001	(1.000)	0.002	(0.999)	0.006	(0.995)	0.013	(0.986)
18					0.001	(1.000)	0.003	(0.998)	0.007	(0.993)
19							0.001	(0.999)	0.004	(0.997)
20							0.001	(1.000)	0.002	(0.999)
21									0.001	(1.000)

c / np_0	11.0		12.0		13.0		14.0		15.0	
0	0.000	(0.000)	0.000	(0.000)	0.000	(0.000)	0.000	(0.000)	0.000	(0.000)
1	0.000	(0.000)	0.000	(0.000)	0.000	(0.000)	0.000	(0.000)	0.000	(0.000)
2	0.001	(0.001)	0.000	(0.000)	0.000	(0.000)	0.000	(0.000)	0.000	(0.000)
3	0.004	(0.005)	0.002	(0.002)	0.001	(0.001)	0.000	(0.000)	0.000	(0.000)
4	0.010	(0.015)	0.005	(0.007)	0.003	(0.004)	0.001	(0.001)	0.001	(0.001)
5	0.022	(0.037)	0.013	(0.020)	0.007	(0.011)	0.004	(0.005)	0.002	(0.003)
6	0.041	(0.078)	0.025	(0.045)	0.015	(0.026)	0.009	(0.014)	0.005	(0.008)
7	0.065	(0.143)	0.044	(0.089)	0.028	(0.054)	0.017	(0.031)	0.010	(0.018)
8	0.089	(0.232)	0.066	(0.155)	0.046	(0.100)	0.031	(0.062)	0.019	(0.037)
9	0.109	(0.341)	0.087	(0.242)	0.066	(0.166)	0.047	(0.109)	0.032	(0.069)
10	0.119	(0.460)	0.105	(0.347)	0.086	(0.252)	0.066	(0.175)	0.049	(0.118)
11	0.119	(0.579)	0.114	(0.461)	0.101	(0.353)	0.084	(0.259)	0.066	(0.184)
12	0.109	(0.688)	0.114	(0.575)	0.110	(0.463)	0.099	(0.358)	0.083	(0.267)
13	0.093	(0.781)	0.106	(0.681)	0.110	(0.573)	0.106	(0.464)	0.096	(0.363)
14	0.073	(0.854)	0.091	(0.772)	0.102	(0.675)	0.106	(0.570)	0.102	(0.465)
15	0.053	(0.907)	0.072	(0.844)	0.088	(0.763)	0.099	(0.669)	0.102	(0.567)
16	0.037	(0.944)	0.054	(0.898)	0.072	(0.835)	0.087	(0.756)	0.096	(0.663)
17	0.024	(0.968)	0.038	(0.936)	0.055	(0.890)	0.071	(0.827)	0.085	(0.748)
18	0.015	(0.983)	0.026	(0.962)	0.040	(0.930)	0.056	(0.883)	0.071	(0.819)
19	0.008	(0.991)	0.016	(0.978)	0.027	(0.957)	0.041	(0.924)	0.056	(0.875)
20	0.005	(0.996)	0.010	(0.988)	0.018	(0.975)	0.029	(0.953)	0.042	(0.917)
21	0.002	(0.998)	0.006	(0.994)	0.011	(0.986)	0.019	(0.972)	0.030	(0.947)
22	0.001	(0.999)	0.003	(0.997)	0.006	(0.992)	0.012	(0.984)	0.020	(0.967)
23	0.001	(1.000)	0.002	(0.999)	0.004	(0.996)	0.007	(0.991)	0.013	(0.980)
24			0.001	(1.000)	0.002	(0.998)	0.004	(0.995)	0.008	(0.988)
25					0.001	(0.999)	0.003	(0.998)	0.005	(0.993)
26					0.001	(1.000)	0.001	(0.999)	0.003	(0.996)
27							0.001	(1.000)	0.002	(0.998)
28									0.001	(0.999)
29									0.001	(1.000)

APPENDIX 6

Websites for Six Sigma and Quality

American Society for Quality: www.asq.org

American Society for Quality, Statistics Division: www.asq.org/about/divisions/stats

American Society for Quality, Quality Audit Division: www.asq.org/qad

American Society for Quality, Reliability Division: www.asq-rd.org

U.S. Commerce Department's National Institute of Standards: www.nist.gov

International Organization for Standardization (ISO 9000 & 14000): www.iso.org

Automotive Industry Action Group: www.aiag.org

Quality Information: www.itl.nist.gov/div898/handbook/pmc/pmc_d.htm

Six Sigma Information: www.sixsigma.com, www.isixsigma.com

Quality in Healthcare: www.jcaho.org

Information on Quality: www.qualitydigest.com, www.quality.org, www.qualityadvisor.com

Discussion Forum: www.insidequality.com

Juran: www.juran.com

Deming: http://deming.eng.clemson.edu/pub/den/deming_map/htm

European Foundation for Quality Management: www.efqm.org

Quality Standards: http://e-standards.asq.org/perl/catalog.cgi

American Productivity and Quality Center, Benchmarking Studies: www.apqc.org

Benchmarking Exchange: www.benchnet.com

Performance Measures: www.zigonperf.com

Lean Manufacturing: www.nwlean.net, www.lean.org

Quality Function Deployment Institute: www.nauticom.net/www.qfd

Statistical Abstract of the United States: www.census.gov/statab/www/

Chapter 9

9.10 Mean = 39
Mode = 34
Median = 38

9.11 Mean = 1.123
Mode = 1.122
Median = 1.123

9.13 Mean = 119.8
Mode = 119.8
Median = 119.8
Range = 0.8
Std. Dev = 0.4

9.14 Area = 0.8413

9.15 Area = 0.0047 or 0.47% of the parts are above 0.93 mm

9.16 Area = 0.9525

9.19 Mean = 0.0015
Mode = 0.0025, 0.0004
Median = 0.0014
σ = 0.0008
R = 0.0028
73.41% of the parts will meet spec.

Chapter 10

10.2 $\bar{\bar{X}}$ = 16, UCL_x = 20, LCL_x = 12,
$\bar{R}$ = 7, UCL_R = 15, LCL_R = 0

10.3 $\bar{\bar{X}}$ = 50.2, UCL_x = 50.7, LCL_x = 49.7,
$\bar{R}$ = 0.7, UCL_R = 1.6, LCL_R = 0

10.4 $\bar{\bar{X}}$ = 349, UCL_x = 357, LCL_x = 341,
$\bar{R}$ = 14, UCL_R = 30, LCL_R = 0

10.7 $\bar{\bar{X}}$ = 0.0627, UCL_x = 0.0629,
LCL_x = 0.0625, $\bar{R}$ = 0.0003,
UCL_R = 0.0006, LCL_R = 0

10.10 $\bar{\bar{X}}$ = 390, UCL_x = 488,
LCL_x = 292, $\bar{s}$ = 50,
UCL = 129, LCL = 0

Chapter 11

11.3 σ = 3, 6σ = 18, C_p = 0.44,
C_{pk} = 0.33

11.4 σ = 0.3, 6σ = 1.8, C_p = 0.6,
C_{pk} = 0.3

11.8 σ = 0.04, 6σ = 0.24, C_p = 0.42,
C_{pk} = 0.25

Chapter 12

12.1 0.50
P(orange and 5) = 1/24

12.2 P(orange) = 6/24
P(five) = 3/24

12.3 60

12.4 Combination = 3,003
Permutation = 360,360

12.5 P(performs) = 0.91

12.6 P(Fabric 1) = 0.285
P(Fabric 2/Style 1) = 0.19
P(Style 4) = 0.255
P(Style 3/Fabric 3) = 0.23

12.7 P(1) = 0.2

12.9 P(1) + P(0) = 0.262
P(1) = 0.238
P(0) = 0.024

12.10 P(1 or less) = 0.98

12.12 P(2) = 0.012

12.13 P(at least 1) = 0.59

12.14 P(3 in five min) = 0.13

12.15 P(more than 1 call) = 0.22

12.16 a. 2.71% of bikes will weigh
  below 8.3 kg
 b. Area between 8.0 kg and
   10.10 kg $= 0.9950 - 0.00375$
   $= 0.9913$

Chapter 13

13.1 $\bar{p} = 0.068$
  UCL $= 0.237$
  LCL $= 0$
13.2 $\bar{p} = 0.004$
  UCL $= 0.0174$
  LCL $= 0$
13.3 $\bar{p} = 0.038$
  UCL $= 0.085$
  LCL $= 0$
13.5 $\bar{p} = 0.0825$
  $n\bar{p} = 13$
  UCL $= 23$
  LCL $= 3$
13.6 $\bar{p} = 0.0405$
  $n\bar{p} = 12$
  UCL $= 22$
  LCL $= 2$
  process capability is $n\bar{p} = 12$

13.7 $\bar{p} = 0.013$
  $n\bar{p} = 5$
  UCL $= 12$
  LCL $= 0$
13.9 $\bar{c} = 6$
  UCL $= 13$
  LCL $= 0$
13.10 $\bar{u} = 2.345$
  UCL $= 3$
  LCL $= 1$
13.12 $\bar{u} = 1.18$
  $n_{ave} = 101$
  UCL $= 1.5$
  LCL $= 0.86$

Chapter 14

14.3 $\lambda = 0.00035$ $\theta = 2886.25$ hours
14.4 $\lambda = 0.00197$ $\theta = 508$ hours
14.7 Reliability of the system $= 0.9768$
14.8 Reliability of the system $= 0.9561$
14.9 Reliability of the system $= 0.9859$

BIBLIOGRAPHY

Abarca, D. "Making the Most of Internal Audits." *Quality Digest*, February 1999, pp. 26–28.

Adam, P., and R. VandeWater. "Benchmarking and the Bottom Line: Translating BPR into Bottom-Line Results." *Industrial Engineering*, February 1995, pp. 24–26.

Adcock, S. "FAA Orders Fix on Older 737s." *Newsday*, May 8, 1998.

Alsup, F., and R. Watson. *Practical Statistical Process Control*. New York: Van Nostrand Reinhold, 1993.

AMA Management Briefing. *World Class Quality*. New York: AMA Publications Division, 1990.

Amari, D., and James, D. "ISO 9001 Takes on a New Role—Crime Fighter." *Quality Progress*, May 2004, pp. 57–61.

American Society for Quality Control, P.O. Box 3005, Milwaukee, WI 53201-3005.

Azeredo, M., S. Silva, and K. Rekab. "Improve Molded Part Quality." *Quality Progress*, July 2003, pp. 72–76.

Bacus, H. "Liability: Trying Times." *Nation's Business*, February 1986, pp. 22–28.

Bamford, J. "Order in the Court." *Forbes*, January 27, 1986, pp. 46–47.

Bernowski, K., and B. Stratton. "How Do People Use the Baldrige Award Criteria?" *Quality Progress*, May 1995, pp. 43–47.

Berry, T. *Managing the Total Quality Transformation*. Milwaukee, WI: ASQC Quality Press, 1991.

Besterfield, D. *Quality Control*, 4th ed. Englewood Cliffs, NJ: Prentice Hall, 1994.

Biesada, A. "Strategic Benchmarking." *Financial World*, September 29, 1992, pp. 30–36.

Bishara, R., and M. Wyrick. "A Systematic Approach to Quality Assurance Auditing." *Quality Progress*, December 1994, pp. 67–69.

Block, M. "The White House Manages Green." *Quality Progress*, July 2003, pp. 90–91.

Bossert, J. "Lean and Six Sigma—Synergy Made in Heaven." *Quality Progress*, July 2003, pp. 31–32.

Bovet, S. F. "Use TQM, Benchmarking to Improve Productivity." *Public Relations Journal*, January 1994, p. 7.

Breyfogle, F., and B. Meadows. "Bottom-Line Success With Six Sigma." *Quality Progress*, May 2001, pp. 101–104.

Brocka, B., and M. Brocka. *Quality Management: Implementing the Best Ideas of the Masters*. Homewood, IL: Business One Irwin, 1992.

Bruder, K. "Public Benchmarking: A Practical Approach." *Public Press*, September 1994, pp. 9–14.

Brumm, E. "Managing Records for ISO 9000 Compliance." *Quality Progress*, January 1995, pp. 73–77.

Butz, H. "Strategic Planning: The Missing Link in TQM." *Quality Progress*, May 1995, pp. 105–108.

Byrnes, D. "Exploring the World of ISO 9000." *Quality*, October 1992, pp. 19–31.

Campanella, J., Ed. *Principles of Quality Costs*. Milwaukee, WI: ASQC Quality Press, 1990.

Camperi, J. A. "Vendor Approval and Audits in Total Quality Management." *Food Technology*, September 1994, pp. 160–162.

Carson, P. P. "Deming Versus Traditional Management Theorists on Goal Setting: Can Both Be Right?" *Business Horizons*, September 1993, pp. 79–84.

Chapman, C. D. "Clean House with Lean 55," *Quality Progress*, June 2005, pp. 27–32.

Cook, B. M. "Quality: The Pioneers Survey the Landscape." *Industry Week*, October 21, 1991, pp. 68–73.

Crosby, P. B. *The Eternally Successful Organization: The Art of Corporate Wellness*. New York: New American Library, 1988.

Crosby, P. B. *Quality Is Free*. New York: Penguin Books, 1979.

Crosby, P. B. *Quality Is Free: The Art of Making Quality Certain*. New York: McGraw-Hill, 1979.

Crosby, P. B. *Quality without Tears: The Art of Hassle-Free Management*. New York: McGraw-Hill, 1979.

Crownover, D. "Baldrige: It's Easy, Free, and It Works." *Quality Progress*, July 2003, pp. 37–41.

Crownover, D. *Take it to the Next Level*. Dallas: NextLevel Press, 1999.

Cullen, C. "Short Run SPC Re-emerges." *Quality*, April 1995, p. 44.

"Customer Satisfaction Hits Nine-Year High." *Quality Progress*, April 2004, p. 16.

Darden, W., W. Babin, M. Griffin, and R. Coulter. "Investigation of Products Liability Attitudes and Opinions: A Consumer Perspective," *Journal of Consumer Affairs*, June 22, 1994.

Davis, P. M. "New Emphasis on Product Warnings." *Design News*, August 6, 1990, p. 150.

Day, C. R. "Benchmarking's First Law: Know Thyself." *Industry Week*, February 17, 1992, p. 70.

Day, R. G. *Quality Function Deployment*. Milwaukee, WI: ASQ Quality Press, 1993.

Dean, M., and Tomovic, C. "Does Baldrige Make a Business Case for Quality?" *Quality Progress*, April 2004, pp. 40–45.

DeFoe, J. A. "The Tip of the Iceberg." *Quality Progress*, May 2001, pp. 29–37.

Deming, W. E. *The New Economics*. Cambridge, MA: MIT CAES, 1993.

Deming, W. E. *Out of the Crisis*. Cambridge, MA: MIT Press, 1986.

Dennis, P. *Lean Production Simplified: A Plain Language Guide to the World's Most Powerful Production System*. New York: Productivity Press, 2002.

DeToro, I. "The Ten Pitfalls of Benchmarking." *Quality Progress*, January 1995, pp. 61–63.

DeVor, R., T. Chang, and J. Sutherland. *Statistical Quality Design and Control*. New York: Macmillan, 1992.

Dobyns, L., and C. Crawford-Mason. *Quality or Else: The Revolution in World Business*. Boston: Houghton Mifflin, 1991.

Eaton, B. "Cessna's Approach to Internal Quality Audits." *IIE Solutions, Industrial Engineering*, June 1995, pp. 12–16.

Eureka, W. E., and N. E. Ryan. *The Customer Driven Company*. Dearborn, MI. ASI Press, 1988.

Farahmand, K., R. Becerra, and J. Greene. "ISO 9000 Certification: Johnson Controls' Inside Story." *Industrial Engineering*, September 1994, pp. 22–23.

Feigenbaum, A. V. "Changing Concepts and Management of Quality Worldwide." *Quality Progress*, December 1997, pp. 43–47.

Feigenbaum, A. V. *Total Quality Control*. New York: McGraw-Hill, 1983.

Feigenbaum, A. V. "The Future of Quality Management." *Quality Digest*, May 1998, pp. 24–30.

Feigenbaum, A. V. "How to Manage for Quality in Today's Economy." *Quality Progress*, May 2001, pp. 26–27.

Franco, V. R. "Adopting Six Sigma." *Quality Digest*, June 2001, pp. 28–32.

Frum, D. "Crash!" *Forbes*, November 8, 1993, p. 62.

Galpin, D., R. Dooley, J. Parker, and R. Bell. "Assess Remaining Component Life with Three Level Approach." *Power*, August 1990, pp. 69–72.

Gardner, R. A. "Resolving the Process Paradox." *Quality Progress*, March 2001, pp. 51–59.

Gerling, A. "How Jury Decided How Much the Coffee Spill Was Worth." *The Wall Street Journal*, September 4, 1994.

Gest, T. "Product Paranoia." *U.S. News & World Report*, February 24, 1992, pp. 67–69.

Geyelin, M. "Product Liability Suits Fare Worse Now." *The Wall Street Journal*, July 12, 1994.

Ghattas, R. G., and S. L. McKee. *Practical Project Management*. Upper Saddle River, NJ: Prentice Hall, 2001.

Gitlow, H. S. *Planning for Quality, Productivity, and Competitive Position*. Homewood, IL: Business One Irwin, 1990.

Gitlow, H. S., and S. J. Gitlow. *The Deming Guide to Quality and Competitive Position*. Englewood Cliffs, NJ: Prentice Hall, 1987.

Goetsch, D. L. *Effective Supervision*. Upper Saddle River, NJ: Prentice Hall, 2002.

Goetsch, D. L., and S. B. Davis. *ISO 14000 Environmental Management*. Upper Saddle River, NJ: Prentice Hall, 2001.

Goetsch, D. L., and S. B. Davis. *Understanding and Implementing ISO 9000 and ISO Standards*. Upper Saddle River, NJ: Prentice Hall, 1998.

Goodden, R. "How a Good Quality Management System Can Limit Lawsuits." *Quality Progress*, June 2001, pp. 55–59.

Goodden, R. L. *Product Liability Prevention: A Strategic Guide*. Milwaukee, WI: ASQ Quality Press, 2000.

Goodden, R. "Product Reliability Considerations Empower Quality Professionals." *Quality*, April 1995, p. 108.

Goodden, R. "Reduce the Impact of Product Liability on Your Organization." *Quality Progress*, January 1995, pp. 85–88.

Grahn, D. "The Five Drivers of Total Quality." *Quality Progress*, January 1995, pp. 65–70.

Grant, E., and T. Lang. "Why Product-Liability and Medical Malpractice Lawsuits Are So Numerous in the United States." *Quality Progress*, December 1994, pp. 63–65.

Grant, E., and R. Leavenworth. *Statistical Quality Control*. New York: McGraw-Hill, 1988.

Hare, L. "SPC: From Chaos to Wiping the Floor." *Quality Progress*, July 2003, pp. 58–63.

Hare, L., R. Hoerl, J. Hromi, and R. Snee. "The Role of Statistical Thinking in Management." *Quality Progress*, February 1995, pp. 53–59.

Harry, M., and R. Schroeder. *Six Sigma: The Breakthrough Management Strategy Revolutionizing the World's Top Corporations*. New York: Doubleday, 2000.

Himelstein, L. "Monkey See, Monkey Sue." *Business Week*, February 7, 1994, pp. 112–113.

Hockman, K., R. Grenville, and S. Jackson. "Road Map to ISO 9000 Registration." *Quality Progress*, May 1994, pp. 39–42.

Hoisington, S., and E. Menzer. "Learn to Talk Money." *Quality Progress*, May 2004, pp. 44–49.

Hoyer, R. W., and B. B. Hoyer. "What is Quality?" *Quality Progress*, July 2001, pp. 52–62.

Hutchins, G. "The State of Quality Auditing." *Quality Progress*, March 2001, pp. 25–29.

Hutchinson, E. E. "The Road to TL 9000: From the Bell Breakup to Today." *Quality Progress*, January 2001, pp. 33–37.

Hutton, D. W. *From Baldrige to the Bottom Line*. Milwaukee, WI: ASQ Quality Press, 2000.

Imai, M. *Gemba Kaizen: A Commonsense, Low Cost Approach to Management.* New York: McGraw-Hill, 1997.

Imai, M. *Kaizen: The Key to Japan's Competitive Success.* New York: McGraw-Hill/Irwin, 1986.

Ireson, W., and C. Coombs. *Handbook of Reliability Engineering and Management.* New York: McGraw-Hill, 1988.

"ISO Says 8 of 10 Cars to 'Run' on ISO 9001:2000." *Quality Progress,* July 2003, p. 12.

Ishikawa, K. *Guide to Quality Control,* rev. ed. White Plains, NY: Kraus International Publications, 1982.

Ishikawa, K. *What Is Total Quality Control? The Japanese Way.* Englewood Cliffs, NJ: Prentice Hall, 1985.

Jaffrey, S. "ISO 9001 Made Easy." *Quality Progress,* May 2004, p. 104.

Johnson, K. "Print Perfect." *Quality Progress,* July 2003, pp. 48–56.

Juran, J. "A Close Shave." *Quality Progress,* May 2004, pp. 41–43.

Juran, J. M. *Juran on Leadership for Quality: An Executive Handbook.* New York: Free Press, 1989.

Juran, J. M. *Juran on Planning for Quality.* New York: Free Press, 1988.

Juran, J. M. *Juran on Quality by Design: The New Steps for Planning Quality into Goods and Services.* New York: Free Press, 1992.

Juran, J. M. "The Quality Trilogy." *Quality Progress,* August 1986, pp. 19–24.

Juran, J. M., and F. M. Gryna. *Quality Planning and Analysis: From Product Development through Usage.* New York: McGraw-Hill, 1970.

Kackar, R. "Taguchi's Quality Philosophy: Analysis and Commentary." *Quality Progress,* December 1986, pp. 21–29.

Kanholm, J. "New and Improved ISO 9000:2000." *Quality Digest,* October 1999, pp. 28–32.

Kececioglu, D. *Reliability and Life Testing Handbook.* Englewood Cliffs, NJ: Prentice Hall, 1993.

Keller, C. "QOS—A Simple Method for Big or Small." *Quality Progress,* July 2003, pp. 28–31.

Ketola, J., and K. Roberts. *ISO 9001:2000 in a Nutshell,* 2d ed. Chico, CA: Paton Press, 2001.

Ketola, J., and K. Roberts. "Transition Planning for ISO 9001:2000." *Quality Digest,* March 2001, pp. 24–28.

Kolarik, W. J. *Creating Quality: Concepts, Systems, Strategies and Tools.* New York: McGraw-Hill, 1995.

Kubiak, T. "An Integrated Approach System." *Quality Progress,* July 2003, pp. 41–45.

Leibfried, K. H. *Benchmarking: A Tool for Continuous Improvement.* New York: Harper Business, 1992.

Levinson, W. A. "ISO 9000 at the Front Line." *Quality Progress,* March 2001, pp. 33–36.

Lunsford, J., and D. Michaels. "After Four Years in the Rear, Boeing Is Set to Jet Past Airbus." *The Wall Street Journal,* June 10, 2005.

Mader, D. "DFSS and Your Current Design Process." *Quality Progress,* July 2003, pp. 88–89.

Mason, R., and J. Young. "Multivariate Thinking." *Quality Progress,* April 2004, pp. 89–91.

May, M. "Lean Thinking for Knowledge Work." *Quality Progress,* June 2005, pp. 33–39.

McElroy, A., and I. Fruchtman. "Use Statistical Analysis to Predict Equipment Reliability." *Power,* October 1992, pp. 39–46.

Malcolm Baldrige National Quality Award, U.S. Department of Commerce, Technology Administration, National Institute of Standards and Technology, Gaithersburg, MD.

Marcus, A. "Limits on Personal-Injury Suits Urged." *The Wall Street Journal,* April 23, 1991.

Mathews, J. "The Cost of Quality." *Newsweek,* September 7, 1992, pp. 48–49.

Meier, B. "Court Rejects Coupon Settlement in Suit Over G.M. Pickup Trucks." *New York Times,* April 18, 1995.

Michaels, D., and I. Lunsford. "Boeing, Airbus Look to Auto Companies for Production Tips." *The Wall Street Journal*, April 1, 2005.

Milas, G. "How to Develop a Meaningful Employee Recognition Program." *Quality Progress*, May 1995, pp. 139–142.

Miller, I., and J. Freund. *Probability and Statistics for Engineers*. Englewood Cliffs, NJ: Prentice Hall, 1977.

Miller, J. R., and J. S. Morris. "Is Quality Free or Profitable?" *Quality Progress*, January 2000, pp. 50–53.

Moen, R., T. Nolan, and L. Provost. *Improving Quality through Planned Experimentation*. New York: McGraw-Hill, 1991.

Montgomery, D. *Introduction to Statistical Quality Control*. New York: John Wiley and Sons, Inc., 2001.

Moran, J. W., and P. C. La Londe. "ASQ Certification Program Gains Wider Recognition." *Quality Progress*, April 2000, pp. 29–41.

Mullenhour, P., and J. Flinchbaugh. "Bringing Lean Systems Thinking to Six Sigma." *Quality Digest*, March 2005, pp. 38–41.

Munoz, J., and C. Nielsen. "SPC: What Data Should I Collect? What Charts Should I Use?" *Quality Progress*, January 1991, pp. 50–52.

Munro, R. A. "Linking Six Sigma with QS-9000." *Quality Progress*, May 2000, pp. 47–53.

Nakhai, B., and J. Neves. "The Deming, Baldrige, and European Quality Awards." *Quality Progress*, April 1994, pp. 33–37.

Neave, H. *The Deming Dimension*. Knoxville, TN: SPC Press, 1990.

"Needed: A Backup for Ma Bell." *U.S. News & World Report*, September 30, 1991, p. 22.

Nelsen, D. "Your Gateway to Quality Knowledge." *Quality Progress*, April 2004, pp. 26–34.

Nesbitt, T. "Flowcharting Business Processes." *Quality*, March 1993, pp. 34–38.

Neuscheler-Fritsch, D., and R. Norris. "Capturing Financial Benefits From Six Sigma." *Quality Progress*, May 2001, pp. 39–44.

Ohno, T. *Toyota Production System: Beyond Large Scale Production*. New York: Productivity Press, 1988.

Okes, D. "Complexity Theory Simplifies Choices." *Quality Progress*, July 2003, pp. 35–37.

Orsini, J. "What's Up Down Under?" *Quality Progress*, January 1995, pp. 57–59.

Palmer, B. "Overcoming Resistance to Change." *Quality Progress*, April 2004, pp. 35–39.

Parsons, C. "The Big Spill: Hot Java and Life in the Fast Lane." *Gannett News Services*, October 25, 1994.

Pearson, T. A. "Measure for Six Sigma Success." *Quality Progress*, February 2001, pp. 35–40.

Phillips-Donaldson, D. "100 Years of Juran." *Quality Progress*, May 2004, pp. 25–39.

Pittle, D. "Product Safety: There's No Substitute for Safer Design." *Trial*, October 1991, pp. 110–114.

Pond, R. *Fundamentals of Statistical Quality Control*. New York: Merrill, 1994.

PQ Systems. *Applying Design of Experiments Using DOEpack*. Dayton, OH: PQ Systems, 2001.

Press, A., G. Carroll, and S. Waldman. "Are Lawyers Burning America?" *Newsweek*, March 20, 1995, pp. 30–35.

Prevette, S. "Systems Thinking—An Uncommon Answer." *Quality Progress*, July 2003, pp. 32–35.

Pritts, B. A. "Industry-wide Shakeout." *Quality Progress*, January 2001, pp. 61–64.

Ramberg, J. S. "Six Sigma: Fad or Fundamental." *Quality Digest*, May 2000, pp. 28–32.

Reid, R. D. "From Deming to ISO 9001:2000." *Quality Progress*, June 2001, pp. 66–70.

Reid, R. D. "Tips for Automotive Auditors." *Quality Progress*, May 2004, pp. 72–76.

Reid, R. D. "Why QS 9000 Was Developed and What's in Its Future?" *Quality Progress*, April 2000, pp. 115–117.

Rienzo, T. F. "Planning Deming Management for Service Organizations." *Business Horizons*, May 1993, pp. 19–29.

Rooney, S., and J. Rooney. "Lean Glossary." *Quality Progress*. June 2005, pp. 41–47.

Roy, R. *A Primer on the Taguchi Method*. New York: Van Norstrand Reinhold, 1990.

Roy, R. K. "Sixteen Steps to Improvement." *Quality Digest*, June 2001, pp. 24–27.

Russell, J. P. "Auditing ISO 9001:2000." *Quality Progress*, July 2001, pp. 147–148.

Russell, J. *Quality Management Benchmark Assessment*. Milwaukee, WI: ASQC Press, 1991.

Russell, J. "Quality Management Benchmark Assessment." *Quality Progress*, May 1995, pp. 57–61.

Savell, L. "Who's Liable When the Product Is Information?" *Editor and Publisher*, August 28, 1993, pp. 35–36.

Schonberger, R. "Make Cells Work for You." *Quality Progress*, April 2004, pp. 58–63.

Schwinn, D. R. "Six Sigma and More: On Not Losing Sight of the Big Picture." *Quality E-line*, May 2, 2001, www.pqsystems.com.

Scovronek, J. "Reliability Sample Testing, A Case History." *Quality Progress*, February 2001, pp. 43–45.

Shingo, S. *A Revolution in Manufacturing: The SMED System*. Nashville, TN: Productivity Press, 1985.

Shipley, D. "ISO 9000 Makes Integrated Systems User Friendly." *Quality Progress*, July 2003, pp. 25–28.

"Short-Run SPC Re-emerges." QEI Speaker Interview. *Quality*, April 1995, p. 44.

Smith, G. *Statistical Process Control and Quality Improvement*. New York: Merrill, 1991.

Smith, R. "The Benchmarking Boom." *Human Resources Focus*, April 1994, pp. 1–6.

Snee, R. D. "Dealing With the Achilles' Heel of Six Sigma Initiatives." *Quality Progress*, March 2001, pp. 66–72.

Spendolini, M. *The Benchmarking Book*. New York: Amcom, 1992.

Spigener, J. B., and P. A. Angelo. "What Would Deming Say?" *Quality Progress*, March 2001, pp. 61–64.

Srikanth, M., and S. Robertson. *Measurements for Effective Decision Making*. Wallingford, CT: Spectrum Publishing Co., 1995.

Stamatis, D. H. "Who Needs Six Sigma, Anyway?" *Quality Digest*, May 2000, pp. 33–38.

Stein, P. "By Their Measures Shall Ye Know Them." *Quality Progress*, May 2001, pp. 72–74.

Stevens, T. "Dr. Deming: Management Today Does Not Know What Its Job Is." *Industry Week*, January 17, 1994, pp. 20–28.

Surak, J. G. "Quality in Commercial Food Processing." *Quality Progress*, February 1999, pp. 25–29.

Taguchi, G. *Introduction to Quality Engineering*. Dearborn, MI: ASI Press, 1986.

Tobias, R. *Applied Reliability*. New York: Van Nostrand Reinhold, 1986.

Torok, J. "The Where and Why: A 1-2-3 Model for Project Success." *Quality Progress*, April 2004, pp. 46–50.

Toyoda, E. Toyota: Fifty Years in Motion. Kodansha International, 1987.

Travalini, M. "The Evolution of a Quality Culture." *Quality Progress*, May 2001, pp. 105–108.

Traver, R. "Nine-Step Process Solves Product Variability Problems." *Quality*, April 1995, p. 94.

"U.S. FAA: FAA Orders Immediate Inspection for High-time Boeing 737s, Extends Inspection Order." *M2 Press Wire*, May 11, 1998.

Vardeman, S. *Statistics for Engineering Problem Solving*. Boston: PWS Publishing, 1994.

Vardeman, S., and J. Jobe. *Statistical Quality Assurance Methods for Engineers*. New York: John Wiley and Sons, Inc., 1999.

Vermani, S. "Capability Analysis of Complex Parts." *Quality Progress*, July 2003, pp. 65–71.

Verseput, R. "Digging into DOE." *Quality Digest*, June 2001, pp. 33–36.

Voelkel, J. "What is 3.4 per Million?" *Quality Progress*, May 2004, pp. 63–65.

Voelkel, J., and C. Chapman. "Value Stream Mapping." *Quality Progress*, May 2003, pp. 65–69.

Walpole, R., and R. Myers. *Probability and Statistics for Engineers and Scientists*. New York: Macmillan, 1989.

Walters, J. "The Benchmarking Craze." *Governing*, April 1994, pp. 33–37.

Walton, M. *Deming Management at Work*. New York: Pedigree Books, 1991.

Walton, M. *The Deming Management Method*. New York: Putnam, 1986.

Watson, G. "Digital Hammers and Electronic Nails—Tools of the Next Generation." *Quality Progress*, July 1998, pp. 21–26.

Watson, R. "Modified Pre-control." *Quality*, October 1992, p. 61.

Watson, G. "The Legacy of Ishikawa." *Quality Progress*, April 2004, pp. 54–57.

Weiler, G. "What Do CEOs Think About Quality?" *Quality Progress*, May 2004, pp. 52–56.

Weimer, G. A. "Benchmarking Maps the Route to Quality." *Industry Week*, July 20, 1992, pp. 54–55.

West, J. E. "Implementing ISO 9001:2000, Early Feedback Indicates Six Areas of Challenge." *Quality Progress*, May 2001, pp. 65–70.

Wheeler, D. *Advanced Topics in Statistical Process Control*. Knoxville, TN: SPC Press, 1995.

Wheeler, D. *Short Run SPC*. Knoxville, TN: SPC Press, 1991.

Wheeler, D. *Understanding Industrial Experimentation*. Knoxville, TN: SPC Press, Inc., 1990.

Wheeler, D. *Understanding Variation: The Key to Managing Chaos*. Knoxville, TN: SPC Press, 1993.

Wheeler, D., and D. Chambers. *Understanding Statistical Process Control*. Knoxville, TN: SPC Press, 1992.

Wiesendanger, B. "Benchmarking for Beginners." *Sales and Marketing Management*, November 1992, pp. 59–64.

Wilson, L. *Eight-step Process to Successful ISO 9000 Implementation*. Milwaukee, WI: ASQC Press, 1996.

Winslow, R. "Hospitals' Weak Systems Hurt Patients, Study Says." *The Wall Street Journal*, July 5, 1995.

Womack, J., D. Jones, and D. Roos. *The Machine That Changed the World, The Story of Lean Production*. New York: Harper Perennial, 1991.

Womack, J., and D. Jones. *Lean Thinking: Banish Waste and Create Wealth in Your Corporation*. New York: Simon and Schuster, 1996.

Zaciewski, R. "Attribute Charts Are Alive and Kicking." *Quality*, March 1992, pp. 8–10.

Index